GEORGE IV
PRINCE OF WALES

D0097817

A _Car Car View_ BOOK

CHRISTOPHER HIBBERT

GEORGE IV

PRINCE OF WALES

1762-1811

1817

HARPER & ROW, PUBLISHERS
New York, Evanston, San Francisco, London

B
George IV

FIRST U.S. EDITION

Library of Congress Cataloging in Publication Data
Hibbert, Christopher, 1924–
  George IV: Prince of Wales 1762–1811.
  Includes bibliographical references.
  1. George IV, King of Great Britain, 1762–1830.
DA538.A1H5   1974   942.07'4'0924 [B]   72–9122
ISBN 0-06-011884-9

FOR BILL AND PAM WYNNE WILLSON

Contents

Contents

PART TWO, 1794–1811

List of Illustrations

These photographs, grouped in a separate section,
will be found following page 114.

List of Illustrations

Illustration Acknowledgements

The author and publishers are grateful to the following for permission to reproduce photographs: The Trustees of the Wallace Collection for Nos 7, 36, 39; Fishmongers' Company for No 23; Radio Times Hulton Picture Library for Nos 10, 11, 13, 18, 19; Walker Art Gallery for No 40; Trustees of the Chatsworth Settlement, Devonshire Collection, Chatsworth for No 8; The Bearsted Collection, Upton House (property of the National Trust) for No 24; Courtauld Institute of Art for Nos 14, 28; Brighton Art Gallery and Museum for No 12; The Earl of Jersey for No 35; National Portrait Gallery for Nos 15, 30; BPC Library/California Palace of the Legion of Honor for No 9. Nos 1–6, 16, 17, 20, 21, 22, 25, 26, 27, 29, 31 are reproduced by gracious permission of Her Majesty The Queen; Nos 33, 34 are from W. H. Pyne *Royal Residences* and Nos 37, 38 are from John Nash *Views of the Royal Pavilion at Brighton*.

Author's Note

This biography of King George IV is based largely upon his papers in the Royal Archives at Windsor Castle, and I have to thank Her Majesty the Queen for graciously permitting me to make full use of them. Most of the King's correspondence is now generally available in the eleven volumes comprehensively and meticulously edited by Professor Aspinall to whom all students of the period will be indebted. In addition to this correspondence, I have been granted access to those papers which could not be released at the time Professor Aspinall was compiling his edition, or which concern topics (such as accounts and Princess Caroline's affairs) outside its scope. I would also like to thank Mr Robert Mackworth-Young, Her Majesty's Librarian, and Miss Jane Langton, Registrar of the Archives, and her staff, for their generous help and advice when I was working in the Castle.

Although the Royal Archives provide by far the most vital and abundant sources for the King's life, there are numerous important manuscript sources elsewhere, and I am most grateful to the Duke of Devonshire for access to the Devonshire Collections; to the Marquess of Hertford for access to the Ragley Manuscripts; to the Earl of Halifax for use of the Hickleton Papers; to the Earl of Crawford and Balcarres for use of the Crawford Muniments; to the Earl of Harrowby for use of the Harrowby Manuscripts; to Earl Fitzwilliam and the Trustees of the Wentworth Woodhouse Estate for allowing me to quote from the Wentworth Woodhouse Muniments; to the Earl of Denbigh for permission to quote from the Denbigh Manuscripts; to the Duke of Wellington for use of the Wellington Papers; to the Trustees of Chequers for permission to consult manuscripts in the library at Chequers; to the Bishop and Dean of Worcester for allowing me to see the Hurd Manuscripts at Hartlebury Castle; to the Director of the Royal Pavilion, Brighton, for permission to study and quote from various letters in his care; to Mrs Hervé Coatalen for letting me see the correspondence of Sir Walter Farquhar and the Hook Manuscripts; to Lieutenant-Colonel H. E. Scott for use of some material from the King's papers which are in his possession; and to the

Chairman and Secretary of Brooks's for allowing me to consult the records of the Club.

For helping me find the relevant papers I want to thank Mr T. S. Wragg, the Duke of Devonshire's Librarian; Mr M. W. Farr, the Warwickshire County Archivist, and his staff who have charge of the Ragley Papers; Major T. L. Ingram, Lord Halifax's archivist; Miss Rosamund Campbell, the Earl of Harrowby's archivist; Mr A. R. C. Grant, the Duke of Wellington's librarian; Mr C. F. Penruddock, Secretary to the Chequers Trust; Mr L. W. Greenwood, librarian at Hartlebury Castle; Mr Derek Rogers of the Royal Pavilion; and Mr John Bebbington who, as Sheffield City Librarian, has charge of the Wentworth Woodhouse Muniments.

I have also made use of the Fremantle Collection and the Goderich Papers at Aylesbury; the Finch Manuscripts at the Bodleian, Oxford; the Pretyman Papers at Ipswich; the Waller of Woodcote Manuscripts at Warwick; the Earl Grey Papers at Durham; the Fitzwilliam Manuscripts, the Brooke Records and Lord Dover's papers and diaries at Delapre Abbey; the Markham Papers at York; the Capell Manuscripts at Hertford; and the Brougham Manuscripts in the Library of University College, London. I would, accordingly, like to express my thanks for their help to Mr E. J. Davis, the County of Buckingham Archivist; Mrs Mary Clapinson of the Department of Western Manuscripts, Bodleian Library, Oxford; Mr W. R. Serjeant of the Ipswich and East Suffolk Record Office; Mr J. E. Fagg and Dr J. M. Fewster of the Department of Palaeography and Diplomatic in the University of Durham; Mr P. I. King, Chief Archivist to the Northampton and Huntingdonshire Archives Committee; Mrs N. K. M. Gurney, Archivist at the Borthwick Institute of Historical Research in the University of York; Mr Peter Walne, the Hertfordshire County Archivist; and Mr Joseph W. Scott, Librarian, University College, London.

I have also to acknowledge the generous help of Dr F. Taylor, Librarian of the John Rylands Library, Manchester; Mr J. N. Allen and his staff at Brighton Reference Library; Miss G. M. A. Beck of the Borough of Guildford Muniment Room; Miss A. Green, the Royal County of Berkshire Archivist; the staffs of the Oxfordshire County Record Office, and of the Public Record Office of Northern Ireland; and Mrs Patricia Gill, the West Sussex County Archivist, who kindly answered various questions concerning the Petworth House Archives which are in her care at Chichester.

Author's Note

Mr Michael Brock, Vice-President of Wolfson College, Oxford, has been kind enough to read the book in proof and has made several valuable suggestions for its improvement. I am most grateful also to Mrs Joan St George Saunders for working for me in the British Museum and the Public Record Office, to Mrs Stewart Ryan for reading newspapers for me in the Newspaper Library at Colindale, to Miss Barbara Mason for transcribing some of the Wentworth Woodhouse Muniments at Sheffield, to Miss Mary Cosh, author of *Inverary and the Argylls*, for some information concerning Lady Augusta Campbell, to Mrs Frances Hawes, Lord Brougham's biographer, for taking extracts from the diaries and letters of Lady Anne Barnard at Balcarres, and to my son, Tom, and my daughter, Kate, for transcribing various other manuscripts. Mrs Barbro Steele has kindly helped me to translate some of the more obscure letters which Princess Caroline wrote to her husband in her idiosyncratic French.

For their generous and expert help in a variety of other ways I want also to thank Sir Owen Morshead, Mr Oliver Millar, Mr Geoffrey de Bellaigue, Lord Adam Gordon, Mr David Higham, Mr. Cuthbert Fitzherbert, Mr. D. A. Hartley Russell, Mrs Eve Weiss, Mr Edward Miller, Dr Clifford Musgrave, Mr Roger Mortimer, Mrs Alan Glendining, Mrs John Rae, Miss Clare Pollen, Mrs Elisabeth Webb, Mr Anthony Berry and Mr J. R. Rudd of Messrs Berry Brothers & Rudd of St James's Street, Mr Brian Hill, Mr Roger Fulford, Dr A. J. Salmon and Mrs George Onslow.

Finally I want to say how grateful I am to Mr George Walker and Mr Hamish Francis for having read the proofs and to my wife for having compiled the index.

C.H.

Quotations from manuscript sources have been given with the original spelling preserved. For the sake of easy reading the punctuation has occasionally been altered, capitalization modified and abbreviations have been written out in full.

PART ONE
1762-1794

I

Childhood and Education
1762-1778
*

'An extremely promising pupil'

At St James's Palace, during the late afternoon of 12 August 1762, Lord Cantelupe, Vice-Chamberlain to Queen Charlotte, was told that her Majesty was in labour; he was instructed to hold himself ready to notify the King immediately the baby was born. Towards six o'clock the Queen's pains increased, and it was clear that the birth was imminent. This was her first pregnancy, and it was a severe labour; but the hopeful, earnest little mother was a healthy girl of eighteen, and the midwife expected no complications. She 'scarce cried out at all,' the Duchess of Northumberland, a Lady of the Bedchamber, later recorded, 'and at twenty-four minutes past seven she was delivered'.[1]

Forestalling Lord Cantelupe, the Earl of Huntingdon – the incompetent and soon to be dismissed Groom of the Stole – officiously hastened to the King's apartment to inform him that he was the father of a baby girl. Protesting that he was 'but little anxious as to the sex of the child', so long as the Queen was safe, the King immediately went to his wife's bedchamber where, soon after his arrival, he was shown as 'strong, large and pretty boy . . . as ever was seen'.[2]

Within a fortnight this large and pretty boy, created Prince of Wales and Earl of Chester and, by right of birth, Duke of Cornwall, Duke of Rothesay, Earl of Carrick and Baron of Renfrew, was placed on display at St James's Palace where, on the afternoons of Drawing-Room days, between one o'clock and three, visitors were admitted to the precincts of his cradle which were separated from the rest of the room by a Chinese lattice screen.[3] As they awaited their turn to inspect him, they were regaled in an ante-room – as the custom of his mother's family dictated – with cake and caudle, a warm gruel spiced and sweetened and mixed with wine, a beverage much favoured in both Germany and England as a tonic for women in childbed. Drawn more perhaps by the refreshments than by the Prince, so 'vast a tumult' of people came to the Palace that £500 worth of cake was given away, and about eight gallons of caudle consumed every day that his Royal Highness was on display.[4]

Soon after the last of these daily receptions was concluded the little Prince was christened in the Queen's drawing-room by the Archbishop of Canterbury. The Queen, dressed in a white and silver gown with a richly jewelled stomacher, lay on her bed of state, the crimson velvet hangings of which were trimmed with gold, lined with satin, and adorned with gilded carving and plumes of white feathers. At the foot of her bed, on a table, was a large gilt baptismal bowl. The child was brought into the room on a white satin pillow, conducted by a procession of attendants under the leadership of the Lord Chamberlain, the Duke of Devonshire. His sponsors were his formidable grandmother, Augusta, the Princess Dowager of Wales, his maternal uncle, Adolphus Frederick IV, Duke of Mecklenburg-Strelitz, and his great-uncle, the Duke of Cumberland, whom he afterwards claimed dimly to remember – though the Duke died soon after his godson's third birthday – as an old man 'dressed in a snuff-coloured suit of clothes down to his knees'. 'He took me in his arms,' the Prince recalled, 'and placed me on his knee, where he held me a long time. The enormity of his bulk excited my wonder.'[5]

The names chosen were George Augustus Frederick; and as these were bestowed upon the child – who cried 'most lustily' throughout the ceremony – his father, then aged twenty-four, was seen to be deeply moved, and to behave with the 'most affecting piety'.[6]

Already the Prince had been provided with a considerable establishment, including a wet-nurse, a necessary woman, a sempstress and two rockers of the cradle who were all under the authority of the royal governess, Lady Charlotte Finch, daughter of the Earl of Pomfret, 'a woman of remarkable sense and philosophy'.[7] Lady Charlotte's chief deputy was Mrs Henrietta Coultworth; the dry-nurse was Mrs Chapman, 'a fine active woman', affectionate and capable.[8]

In the care of these kindly and efficient women George Augustus Frederick, Prince of Wales, grew and prospered. As he was taken out to enjoy the fresh air of Hyde Park, the crowds that followed him, so Lord Bath told a friend, called out to each other, 'God bless him, he is a lusty, jolly, young dog truly!'[9] His mother had him painted in her arms by Francis Cotes and commissioned a model of him in wax which, side by side with numerous other portraits of her first-born baby in miniature, enamel and marble, she kept in her room on a velvet cushion under a bell-glass.

By the age of two and a half the Prince had progressed so well that he was able to pronounce a formal answer, 'with great propriety and suitableness of action', to the representatives of a charitable institution to whom he handed a donation of £100.[10] When he was four and obliged to stay in bed with the curtains drawn after a smallpox inoculation, he answered an inquiry from his mother's Keeper of the Robes, Mrs Schwellenberg, as to whether he found the restriction unpleasantly tedious by observing with an impressively precocious gravity, 'Not at all, I lie and make reflections.'[11] By the age of five he had been taught to write in a neat, round hand by Mr Bulley, the royal writing master; he had also been taught the rudiments of English grammar by the 'quiet, patient, plodding, persevering' Miss Frederica Planta;[12] and at the age of six he was reported to be making good progress with all his other lessons which began after breakfast at seven and continued till he sat down to dinner at three. It was, indeed, generally supposed that he was a highly promising child, healthy and intelligent, a little hot-tempered, perhaps, and somewhat lacking in determination – having suffered a few falls in trying to learn how to skate, he could not be induced to try again.[13] But it was hoped that any flaws of character, or defects of physique, which might manifest themselves, would soon be eradicated by the moral and physical training to be enjoyed or endured at the Queen's House in London, and at Richmond Lodge and Kew.

In these two royal country residences the Prince spent his earliest years. They had been chosen by his father as the most suitable background for the kind of quiet, regular, domestic, country family life which he and his wife, though both so young, preferred to the glitter of St James's. The King, indeed, had little choice. Richmond Palace, which had been used as a nursery by King James II, had fallen into decay; so had Windsor Castle, neglected since the death of Queen Anne and now partially occupied by families with real or pretended claims upon royal favour. Hampton Court was in relatively good order, having been a favourite palace of the King's grandfather King George II; but, as it brought him unwelcome memories of an unhappy childhood, the King did not like it and declined to live in it.

So, there being no other country retreats convenient to London and available to him, the King was obliged to use Richmond Lodge, formerly the Keeper's Lodge in the large park to the north of Richmond Palace, which had been allotted to Queen Charlotte as part of her marriage settlement. But it was a small house, and as the Queen gave birth to new babies with seasonal regularity it became so excessively overcrowded that a larger one became essential. In 1771, the family's problems were solved by the death of the King's mother: the White House at Kew, where she had lived since the death of her husband, then became vacant and the King and Queen moved in.

By then, although she was not yet twenty-eight, the Queen already had eight children, five boys and three girls. Frederick, later Duke of York, the Prince of Wales's eldest brother, had been born in 1763; Prince William in 1765; Princess Charlotte in 1766; Prince Edward in 1767; Princess Augusta in 1768; Princess Elizabeth in 1770 and Prince Ernest in 1771.* Since the White House, commodious as it was, was not extensive enough for all these children and their various attendants, the two eldest sons, the Prince of Wales, aged eleven, and Prince Frederick, aged ten, were placed under tutors at the Dutch House nearby.

The Dutch House – now known as Kew Palace, since the White House, apart from the Kitchen Wing, was demolished in 1802 – had been built in 1631 by a rich London merchant of Dutch descent. A substantial red-brick gabled house of three storeys, with attics and a basement, it was one of a number of houses at Kew which were leased or owned by the royal

---

* There were seven further children yet to come, Prince Augustus in 1773, Prince Adolphus in 1774, Princess Mary in 1776, Princess Sophia in 1777, Octavius and Alfred in 1779 and 1780, and Amelia in 1783. Alfred died when he was a baby in 1782 and, to his father's great distress, Octavius also died the next year. 'There will be no heaven for me,' the King declared miserably, 'if Octavius is not there.'

4

family, or by various members of the Court whose numerous liveried servants could be seen on summer evenings strolling about amidst the cattle grazing on the Green.

At the Dutch House a more rigorous stage of the Prince of Wales's education began under the direction of Robert D'Arcy, fourth Earl of Holdernesse, his Governor. Holdernesse was, in Horace Walpole's opinion, a 'formal piece of dullness' who had proved himself, when in office in various administrations, 'an unthinking and unparliamentary minister'.[14] His duties as Lord Warden of the Cinque Ports and Lord Lieutenant of the North Riding of Yorkshire, combined with increasing ill health which drove him to live abroad in 1774, did not allow him time to give much personal attention to the problems of his charges. He was obliged to leave most of the details of their education to the Princes' Sub-Governor, Leonard Smelt, and their Preceptor, Dr William Markham, Bishop of Chester.

Smelt was a talented and versatile officer in the Royal Engineers, experienced in the art of military sketching and plan drawing, yet having at the same time a deep love and knowledge of literature and art. He had served at the battles of Dettingen and Fontenoy, had been sent out to survey and report on the defences of Newfoundland, and had returned to become the friend not only of George III but of Joshua Reynolds, Fanny Burney, and several other members of Dr Johnson's circle.

William Markham was also a remarkable man. Of humble parentage, he had gained a place at Westminster School and a studentship at Christ Church, Oxford. At the age of thirty-four he had been appointed Headmaster of Westminster School; in 1767 he had been nominated Dean of Christ Church; and in 1771, two months before he became – on the recommendation of Lord Mansfield – the Prince's Preceptor, he had been consecrated Bishop of Chester. A tall and portly man, inclined to be both pompous and short-tempered, though not unkindly, he combined an 'almost martial bearing' with a deep fund of learning. Jeremy Bentham, who was a pupil at Westminster when he was headmaster, said that 'his business was rather in courting the great than in attending to the school. He had a great deal of pomp, especially when he lifted his hand, waved it, and repeated Latin verses . . . We stood prodigiously in awe of him.'[15] He had a very rich wife, the daughter of an English merchant of Rotterdam, who provided him with thirteen children. Destined one day to become Archbishop of York, at the time of his appointment as director of the

5

'religious and learned part of the young Prince's education', he was fifty-two years old, the same age as Leonard Smelt.

Under their watchful care, the Prince and his brother, Frederick, were kept hard at work, or at some form of supervised recreation from early in the morning until eight o'clock at night, in accordance with the strict commands of the King, who strongly believed that no change for the better could be expected in the 'unprincipled days' in which they lived except by 'an early attention to the education of the rising generation'.[16] They were instructed in the classics, of course, learned French, German and Italian; and the Prince of Wales, at least, acquired a fair grasp of all these languages, though he became fluent only in French. His handwriting, trained by laborious transcription of the wise words of Pliny and Bacon in his copy-book, was neat and legible;[17] he found 'great facility' in getting Greek epigrams by heart;[18] and if his spelling was – and always remained – highly idiosyncratic, it was a good deal less eccentric than that of the Earl of Holdernesse, his Governor. Shortly after his tenth birthday, his great-aunt Amelia had cause to thank him for a 'very fine wrote letter'. 'It is far beyond what I could have expected of a prince of your age,' she told him. 'I cannot say enough, Sir, how charmed I am at seeing you so forward in every proper qualification for your rank. I hope you will not dislike a little ball about Christmas when the young gentlemen that have the honour to be liked by you have holy days.'[19]

The Prince received constant moral guidance. His father warned him, 'little dependence can be placed on any thing in this world and the best method of continually pursuing your duty is the continually placing before your eyes that the Supreme Being has put you in an exalted station; and that you are therefore accountable to Him for your conduct.' Nothing must distract the Prince from the path of dutiful conduct nor from the way of truth.[20]

The Earl of Holdernesse, who was, despite Horace Walpole's unfavourable opinion, conscientious and sensible, also urged the Prince of Wales always to be truthful: 'Truth is the first quality of a man; the higher the rank the more to be adhered to.'[21] Lord Holdernesse further advised him to be moderate in his diet and to beware of those who poured that species of poison in the ear which was 'the more dangerous as it is pleasing in the first sensation, tho' followed by ruin and destruction';[22] for the Prince, at the age of twelve, was already threatening to become excessively fond of both food and flattery.

His mother, though she seemed more concerned that his bodily constitution should remain unimpaired, also urged him to 'disdain all flattery' and 'abhor all vice', to 'fear God', to do 'justice unto everybody and avoid partiality', above all to display 'the highest love, affection and duty towards the King'.[23]

This last injunction, the Prince of Wales found it increasingly difficult to obey. His father had seemed to love him when he was a baby – as, indeed, the King obviously loved all his children when they were babies – but the older the Prince grew the further he felt removed from his affection. It was as though his father had wanted him to remain a baby for ever and resented, even recoiled from, his progress towards puberty. He was made to wear babies' cambric frocks with hemstitched tucks and hems and Valenciennes lace cuffs long after other children of his age had been given more suitable clothes; it was said of him that he caught hold of his frilled collar one day and exclaimed in exasperation to a servant, '*See how I am treated!*'[24]

Apart from that of his brother Frederick, he was denied the close companionship of any other children, just as he was constantly and carefully sheltered from any adult who might fill his mind with thoughts about the wonders and excitements of the outside world. That world must be veiled from him, his father repeatedly insisted, by those who 'cirrounded' him.[25] He must be taught the virtues of rigorous simplicity, hard work, punctuality and regularity, and, at the first sign of laziness, laxness or untruthfulness, he must be beaten. And beaten he was. One of his sisters later recalled how she had seen him and Prince Frederick, 'held by their tutors to be flogged like dogs with a long whip'.[26]

Occasionally the Prince went to a concert or an opera; sometimes there were fireworks displays and country dances on family birthdays; on Thursdays, when the royal gardens were open to the public, carriages came into the drives, and boats with musicians aboard were rowed up the Thames to the little islands opposite the Dutch House; in the evenings when the Queen gave commerce parties, the Prince was allowed into her drawing-room up till ten o'clock; once or twice an artist, Zoffany or Gainsborough, came to paint his portrait. But these were rare breaks in the tedium of his days, rare glimpses of the world beyond the garden walls of Kew and of his mother's house in London.

*

In May 1776, when the Prince was thirteen, Lord Holdernesse resigned in consequence of a 'nursery revolution' which also led to the dismissal of the Sub-preceptor, Cyril Jackson, whom the Governor blamed for the Princes' increasingly contemptuous treatment of him since his return from the Continent.[27] Holdernesse's place was at first taken by Lord Bruce, 'a formal, dull man, totally ignorant of and unversed in the world';[28] then by Bruce's eldest brother, the Duke of Montagu, 'one of the weakest and most ignorant men living',[29] who possessed, however, a 'formal coldness of character' that was said to make him 'uncommonly well fitted' for the post.[30] At the same time Dr Markham, having supported the Sub-Preceptor in his quarrel with the Governor,[31] was replaced by Dr Richard Hurd, Bishop of Lichfield and Coventry, who was expected by the King to impose upon his eldest sons an even more exacting regime than they had already grown accustomed to.* Hurd was 'a stiff and cold, but correct gentleman', with a courtly, decorous manner which 'endeared him highly to devout old ladies', and which, in combination with a high, though questionable, reputation as a literary critic and philosopher, had recommended him to the King.[32] The Bishop's chaplain, the Rev William Arnold, replaced Jackson as Sub-Preceptor, and Lieutenant-Colonel George Hotham became Sub-Governor in place of Smelt. At the same time, to complete the 'nursery revolution', all the Prince's servants were replaced by men of sterner mettle.[33]

Soon after his appointment, Hurd drew up his rigorous *Plans of Study for the Princes*, a programme of education covering the widespread fields of religion, morals, government and laws, mathematics and natural philosophy, history ('sacred', 'profane' and 'modern') and 'polite literature' (this being devoted mainly to Greek and Latin writers, the only three English writers considered worthy of detailed study being Shakespeare, Milton and Pope).[34]

---

* The Prince of Wales, who liked Markham and considered him 'one of his best friends', had asked that he might be allowed to remain their Preceptor after Lord Holdernesse's resignation, but the King had refused the request on the grounds that the Prince 'would secretly feel a kind of victory if the Bishop remained'. After his schooldays he continued on good terms with his former Preceptor, addressing him in 1800 as 'my dear much loved friend', and signing himself 'your old and *most gratefully attached* pupil' (Markham MSS, York). He quite often dined with him when, as Archbishop of York, Markham was staying in London at his house in Bloomsbury Square and, on a visit to Yorkshire in 1806, he called upon him at Bishopthorpe where he dutifully fell to his knees to receive his blessing (*Markham Memoir*, 42, 76–7). The Prince was less sorry to part from Cyril Jackson 'who used to have a silver pencil-case in his hand while we were at our lessons,' Prince Frederick recalled, 'and he has frequently given us such knocks with it on our foreheads that the blood followed them'. (*Rogers Table-Talk*, 116).

Strong emphasis still lay upon the classics, as it would have done, with far greater force, had the Prince attended a public school. Even on Sunday mornings his classical training was not abated, for the Greek Testament had 'to be constantly read'.[35]

The Prince thought that Hurd was not such a good teacher as Markham who was 'a much greater, wiser, and more learned man'. When he was instructed to translate Homer and hesitated over a word, Markham had taken the trouble to explain it to him; but Hurd, as though he were not quite sure of the meaning himself, merely referred his pupil to the dictionary.[36]

The education supervised by Hurd, however, was by no means a narrow one. The Prince was taught to play the 'cello by John Crosdill, and to sing pleasantly as well as to construe Latin; he was helped to cultivate a taste for the fine arts as well as to understand Euclid. He was taught to fence and to box by Henry Angelo and to draw by Alexander Cozens. In his own garden at Kew he was instructed in the elements of agriculture, sowed and harvested his own crops and even baked his own bread.

He was infinitely more knowledgeable and versatile at sixteen than his father had been at that age, for George III had been appallingly ill-educated under the direction of a Governor who was alleged to have been 'perfectly satisfied that he had done his duty so long as he was unremitting in his exhortations to his royal pupil to turn out his toes'.[37]

At sixteen, in fact, the Prince of Wales was both accomplished and attractive. 'His countenance was of a sweetness and intelligence quite irresistible,' recalled one of the Queen's German attendants, Charlotte Albert. 'He had an elegant person, engaging and distinguished manners, added to an affectionate disposition and the cheerfulness of youth.' He was rather given to practical jokes, she added, instancing the occasion on which the oboist, Johann Christian Fischer, a greedy and nervous man, was invited to a meal by the Prince after a concert. Fischer was told that something especially delicious had been prepared for him. He sat down eagerly; the cover was lifted, and out jumped a live rabbit. But despite these thoughtless pranks, the Prince was a very likeable boy, Fräulein Albert thought, and very gifted.[38] Miss Planta thought so, too. 'He is a fine boy,' she said, 'has an open countenance, a manly air . . . he possesses the most obliging politeness, such as can only spring from goodness of heart, and by the accounts I hear he is most amiable . . .'[39]

His tutors agreed. Bishop Hurd assured a friend that he was 'an extremely promising pupil',[40] confirming the earlier verdict of Lord Holdernesse who, when living in Switzerland, received reports of the Prince's 'accomplishments from many quarters', 'pleasing reports' which were confirmed by 'the most competant judges', his tutors.[41]

The Prince's appearance at this time was also pleasing. It was fairly accurately described by himself in a letter to one of his sisters' attendants:

'[He] is now approaching the bloom of youth, he is rather above the common size, his limbs well-proportioned, and upon the whole well made, though rather too great a penchant to grow fat. The features of his countenance carry with them too much of an air of hauteur, his forehead well shaped, his eyes though none of the best, and though grey are yet passable, tolerable good eyebrows and eyelashes, un petit nez retroussé cependant assez aimé, a good mouth though rather large, with fine teeth, a tolerable good chin, but the whole of the countenance is too round. I forgot to add my uggly ears. As hair is generally looked upon as a beauty, he has more hair than usually falls to everyone's share . . .'[42]

It was beautiful hair, recorded Lady Anne Lindsay a few years later, 'waved in profusion with all the glossy lustre of youth on it'. 'His eyes,' she added, 'were of a clear blue, lively full of play and intelligence . . . They saw everyone, neglected no one . . . His nose was a companionable one, not the haughty one of his brother, Frederick, the Duke of York . . . He smiled often . . .'[43]

In the letter describing his appearance which he wrote to his sister's attendant the Prince went on to describe what he liked to consider a generally rather pleasant personality.

'His sentiments and thoughts are open and generous,' he wrote, 'above doing anything that is mean (too susceptible, even to believing people his friends, and placing too much confidence in them, from not yet having a sufficient knowledge of the world or if its practices), grateful and friendly to excess where he finds *a real friend*. His heart is good and tender if it is allowed to show its notions. . . . He has a *strict notion of honour*, rather too familiar to his inferiors but will not suffer himself to be browbeaten or treated with haughtiness by his superiors. Now for his vices, or rather let us call them weaknesses – too subject to give loose or vent to his passions of every kind, too subject to be in a passion, but he never bears malice or rancour in his heart . . . he is rather too fond of wine and women . . .'[44]

To this modest list of weaknesses his father would have added many others, including vanity and a capricious waywardness. For accomplished as his son was admitted to be, charming as were his manners and entertaining his conversation, in the eyes of George III, his eldest son's gifts were not such as to compensate for the manifold faults to be found in him. Five years before, when he was twelve, the King had complained to Holdernesse of his 'duplicity', his 'bad habit . . . of not speaking the truth'.[45] Now that he was approaching manhood and 'some new arrangements' concerning him would soon have to be made, the King wrote to the Prince himself to warn him about his faulty character and misdemeanours: he had not made that progress in his studies which, 'from the ability and assiduity' of those placed about him for that purpose, his father had reason to expect; his proficiency in German, in particular, was 'very moderate', yet in Germany he would one day have possessions that would place him 'in one of the superior stations in that great Empire'; moreover, his reading of history had been very cursory and, although he had 'acquired a general view of the principal facts in ancient and modern history', he had 'no insight into the springs which caused them, or any comprehensive knowledge of the Constitution, laws, finances, commerce, etc., . . . of the other European states'.

The Prince's attitude towards his religious duties, his father went on, had regrettably shown that he was deficient in gratitude to 'the Great Creator', and evidently unwilling 'implicitly to obey His will as conveighed to us in the Scriptures'. Above all, his 'love of dissipation' had for months, even at his present age, been 'trumpeted in the public papers'. It was high time that he realized that 'the good or bad example set by those in the higher stations must have some effect on the general conduct of those in inferior ones'. He could certainly be of the greatest assistance to his father, but only if he would connect himself 'with those young men who seem to be of worthy characters and to wish to make themselves of utility and ornament to their country'. His chosen companions of the present did not fall into that category.[46]

The King's strictures on this need were certainly well justified, so Fräulein Albert said. For some time the Prince had been contriving to mix with characters whom his father had due cause to consider most unworthy. 'Some of those about [him],' she wrote, 'swerved from principle, and introduced improper company' when their Majesties believed him to be in bed.[47] There was, for instance, the tall and pretty wife of one of the grooms about the Court. She was 'a great slattern, and more low and vulgar than that class of people usually are', but the Prince took a strong fancy to her, so it was arranged that her husband, 'a dressed-up horror, impertinent and disgusting', should be brought up from the stables and given a place about the person of the Prince which would enable his wife to appear in the royal apartments without undue comment.[48]

Two of the worst influences on the Prince, in the King's opinion, were his uncles, the Dukes of Gloucester and Cumberland. The Duke of Gloucester was the King's eldest brother; he had given great offence by his secret marriage in 1766 at her house in Pall Mall to the Dowager Countess Waldegrave who was not only the widow of the King's detested Governor, Lord Waldegrave – a 'depraved, worthless man', in his charge's opinion – but was also an illegitimate daughter of Sir Edward Walpole, a well-known Whig. When the marriage came to light, the Duke was banished from Court. During the Prince of Wales's childhood, he had spent much of his time abroad, mostly in Italy; but on his visits to England he provided the newspapers with a great deal of salacious gossip about his amours with various young women of the town.

The sexual adventures of Gloucester's younger brother, the Duke of Cumberland, whose uncle, the Prince's sponsor, had died in 1765, were even more offensive to the rigid morality of the King. When Cumberland was twenty-five his brothers had had to find £10,000 to compensate the Earl of Grosvenor whose wife had committed adultery with him. He had had a subsequent affair with a woman named Olive Wilmot whose daughter, insisting that her mother had been married to him, called herself Princess Olive of Cumberland.[49] And in 1771 he had further outraged the King by marrying a widow, Mrs Anne Horton, daughter of Lord Irnham, afterwards Earl of Carhampton, a beautiful, intelligent and amusing woman, but 'vulgar, noisy, indelicate' and much given to jokes and banter of unparalleled coarseness.

To prevent such shameful marriages in future the King had instigated the Royal Marriage Act which provided that no member of the royal family could marry without the sovereign's consent, though if that consent were refused to someone over twenty-five a year's notice could be given to the Privy Council and then the marriage could take place despite the sovereign's refusal. This Act was passed in 1772; but it was not for another eight years that the King was reconciled to either of the brothers – whose choice of wives had prompted it – and permitted them to return to

Court. Even then relations between them remained strained, particularly between the King and the Duke of Cumberland who was not only a reprobate, who not only ran a faro table at his house in Pall Mall, but was also a 'great Whig'. As for his blasphemous and extravagant Duchess, the King could never reconcile himself to her, since he believed, with some justice, that she lent herself to 'facilitate or gratify the Prince of Wales's inclinations'.[50]

2

Mrs Robinson
and Mme von Hardenburg
1778-1782

*

'A certain sort of ladies'

When he was sixteen the Prince – having already seduced, so it was supposed, a maid of honour to the Queen – fell in love with Mary Hamilton, the third Duke of Hamilton's twenty-three-year-old great-granddaughter, one of his sister's attendants. For weeks he wrote to her almost every day – seventy-five of his letters to her survive – assuring her of his everlasting devotion. He had first conceived his passion for her in the early spring of 1779 when he confided in her one evening that he was desperately in love without telling her who was the object of the 'most secret thoughts' of his soul. The next day he declared in a letter that his 'fair incognita' was her 'dear, dear, dear self'. 'Your manners, your sentiments, the tender feelings of your heart,' he wrote, 'so totally coincide with my ideas, not to mention the many advantages you have in person over many other ladies, that I not only highly esteem you, but even love you more than words or ideas can express.'[1]

In subsequent letters, at once passionate and stilted, he protested that if he had been placed in a different station in life he would have had the happiness of calling her his very own. 'For after the impetuous ardor of youth, and the violent impulse of passion is passed,' he assured her, 'then it is that one wishes to find in a companion for life such sentiments and such feelings as you possess and which I have known very few women enjoy to so superior a degree as yourself.' He loved her with 'enthusiastic fondness', he doted upon her and adored her 'beyond the idea of everything that is human'; he could not help lamenting that his rank prevented, 'at least for the present', his being united with her whom alone he could love; 'impetuosity, ardor', no word was too strong for his 'present sentiments'.

He sent her a lock of his abundant light brown hair and asked for some of hers which would be dearer to him than life itself; on the back of the locket containing it she was not to have her dear name inscribed, just the date of her birth, an event 'ever so dear' to him, and on the front was to be the motto, 'Toujours aimée'. He would give her in exchange a bracelet which would be inscribed with the date of *his* birth, and the motto, 'Gravé à jamais dans mon coeur'.[2]

Miss Hamilton replied to his incessant messages with caution. She could, without injuring her honour, accept his 'friendship', but she could not offer him more; her virtue was more precious to her than her life. She begged him not to offend her delicacy by sending her presents. 'My God,' she replied to one particularly impassioned letter, 'what will become of you if you suffer yourself to be led away with such impetuosity.' She could never act 'so base a part as to encourage such warm declarations'.

So the Prince reluctantly agreed to address her no longer 'with the impetuous passion of a lover urging his suit', but with the endearing names of 'friend and sister'. As a brother he wrote to her asking for her frank criticisms of his conduct; and she, taking him at his word, condemned his taste for low companions and for the 'indelicate, ungentlemanlike and wicked practice' he had 'thought proper to adopt of swearing'. He acknowledged the faults, excusing himself on the grounds that he had picked up the habit of swearing from hearing 'people in the Army do so', and he had thought it necessary to show that he had now become a man by giving in 'too much to this infamous practice'. He also sought Miss Hamilton's advice about his clothes in which he already took an inordinate interest, sending her patterns and pieces of cloth and pearl-coloured silk from his tailor and asking her to put pins in the ones she liked best.[3]

At the beginning of December 1779 the correspondence was abruptly terminated, for the Prince had fallen violently in love with someone else less virtuous, a girl of astonishing beauty and notoriously exhibitionist habits, Mary Robinson.

*

Mary Robinson was born in Bristol of Irish descent, the daughter of the captain of a whaler who had himself been born in America. Her father abandoned his family when she was a child to establish a whale fishery manned by Esquimaux on the coast of Labrador; and Mary was sent to school in London where her dancing-master, who was also ballet-master at Drury Lane, gained for her an introduction to David Garrick. Garrick offered her the part of Cordelia in *King Lear*; but her marriage at the age of fifteen to an articled clerk named Thomas Robinson, who was wrongly supposed by her mother to be a man of property, led to her temporarily abandoning the idea of becoming an actress. Instead, she and her husband took to leading an extravagant life which ended with their both being imprisoned for debt, together with their baby daughter. On her release she sought out Garrick who arranged her *dèbut* as Juliet at Drury Lane in 1776. Thereafter she appeared in numerous successful productions, becoming one of the most celebrated young actresses of her day, and undoubtedly the most eccentric. She was to be seen every day, before the theatre opened, riding in her carriage on the doors of which was a device in the shape of a basket, or, as some from a distance were led to suppose, a coronet. Accompanied by her husband and by several other men who hoped to become her lovers, she dressed herself in a variety of outlandish but fetching costumes that showed her lovely face and body to best advantage.[4]

On 3 December 1779 *The Winter's Tale* was produced at Drury Lane by royal command. Mary Robinson appeared as Perdita; and William Smith, who was also in the cast as Leontes, prophesied that she would captivate the Prince of Wales, so lovely did she look in the part. The Prince was indeed captivated. Throughout her performance he stared at her fixedly and during one scene overwhelmed her with confusion, so she confessed, by making flattering remarks about her as she stood on the stage beneath his box. At the end of the performance he stood up and bowed to her, and 'just as the curtain was falling', she later recorded, 'my eyes met [his]; and with a look that I *never shall forget*, he gently inclined his head a second time; I felt the compliment, and blushed my gratitude'.[5]

A few days later one of his friends, Lord Malden, called at her house in Covent Garden and, with evident embarrassment, took a letter out of his pocket and handed it to her. It was addressed to 'Perdita' and signed 'Florizel'. She supposed at first that it had been written by Malden himself, but he assured her that it came from the Prince of Wales. The next day Lord Malden called again with a second letter and a request that she should go to the oratorio on a certain evening when the Prince and the Royal Family were also to be present.

As at the Drury Lane Theatre, so at the oratorio, the Prince stared at her, bowed to her, and smiled at her with such marked insistence that 'many of the audience observed it'. He asked one of the gentlemen in attendance to fetch him a glass of water which, gazing at her earnestly, he raised towards her before drinking. 'Several persons in the pit' immediately turned round towards the balcony box in which Mrs Robinson was sitting.

During the next few weeks the Prince wrote to her almost every day, sent Lord Malden to her with fond messages, gave her a lock of his hair in an envelope on which he wrote, 'To be redeemed', and presented her with a miniature of himself by Jeremiah Meyer accompanied by two mottoes written on either side of a piece of paper cut into the shape of a heart: '*Je ne change qu'en mourant*', and 'Unalterable to my Perdita through life'.[6] To Mary Hamilton, to whom he had recently expressed the same sentiments, her 'very affectionate Brother' bade farewell: '*Adieu, Adieu, Adieu, toujours chère*. Oh! Mrs Robinson.'[7]*

Up till now the Prince had not succeeded in meeting Mrs Robinson who seems to have been reluctant to risk incurring the wrath of his parents. He begged her, through Lord Malden, to come to his apartments in Buckingham House disguised as a boy, but 'the indelicacy of such a step, as well as the dangers of detection' made her shrink from the proposal. At length, however, provoked by the repeated infidelities of her husband whom she found one day on returning from a rehearsal in her

---

* Miss Hamilton, having discovered some particulars about Mrs Robinson's way of life, urgently and repeatedly warned the Prince that a female in her line had 'too much trick and art not to be a very dangerous object'. 'For the love of Heaven, stop, O stop my friend and do not thus headlong plunge yourself into vice', she ended her final appeal. 'I conjure you to strive to conquer this unhappy infatuation . . . you are preparing wretchedness for yourself . . . you will repent – but it will then be too late . . . I want to raise your virtues; for you have virtues . . .' The letter was never answered. The Prince and Mary Hamilton – who married John Dickenson in 1785 – remained on friendly terms, however, and often met in later years. At a ball at Carlton House in 1784 she had 'two long conversations with him . . . in the old friendly stile', and a few months later, when she saw him from the window of her coach walking down Curzon Street, 'he smiled, kissed his hand several times, made [her] a graceful bow – the carriage proceeded and he walked on – presently he returned . . . and came to the coach door'. There ensued a pleasant conversation during which he held Miss Hamilton's hand 'the whole time which greatly distressed [her] as there were many bye'. The Prince always spoke of her with affection and respect, and she, when criticisms of his behaviour were voiced in her presence, 'took his part' as often as she could (*Hamilton Letters*, 190, 260).

bed with one of her maids, Mrs Robinson succumbed to the Prince's entreaties and agreed to meet him for a few minutes at Kew in the company of his brother, Frederick.

It was agreed that she would dine with Lord Malden at the inn on the island between Kew and Brentford. They were to watch for the signal of a handkerchief being waved from the opposite shore, then they were to take a boat for the landing place by the iron gates of the Palace. They arrived there safely and the Prince, with Frederick at his side, ran down the avenue to meet them. But there was only time for the exchange of a few words when, as the moon rose, the noise of people approaching from the Palace disturbed them and she and Lord Malden had to run back to the boat.

Other meetings soon followed, however; further love letters were exchanged; the Prince fell deeper and deeper in love; and 'Perdita', so she afterwards recorded, would never forget how charming he was to her, how graceful, how 'irresistibly sweet' was his smile, how tender his 'melodious voice'.[8] He promised – and in writing repeated the promise – that he would give her a for ine of £20,000 immediately he came of age. On the strength of this assurance, she gave up her career on the stage to become his mistress. She was twenty-one then; he was seventeen.

He took no trouble to disguise the connexion and soon it was the common talk of London. Cartoons of 'Perdita' and 'Florizel' appeared in shop windows, and Mrs Robinson was 'overwhelmed by the gazing of the multitude' whenever she appeared in public. She was 'frequently obliged to quit Ranelagh, owing to the crowd which staring curiosity had assembled' around her box; and she could scarcely venture 'to enter a shop without experiencing the greatest inconvenience'.[9]

But the Prince's passion for 'Perdita' was soon spent. Within a few months he was said to be tired of her and to be casting longing looks in the direction of Mrs Grace Dalrymple Elliott, the divorced wife of a rich physician. And one day, after Mrs Robinson had offended him by being rude in public to a friend of his, he wrote to tell her curtly that they must 'meet no more'. Declining to accept so abrupt a dismissal, she prevailed upon him to agree to meet her once more, and the subsequent discussion appears to have been pleasant enough. 'We passed some hours in the most friendly and delightful conversation,' she informed a friend, 'and I began to flatter myself that all our differences were adjusted. But no words can express my surprise and chagrin, when, on meeting his Royal Highness *the very next day* in Hyde Park, he turned his head to avoid seeing me, and even affected *not to know me*!'[10]

Mrs Robinson made further efforts to see him, but he declined to receive her and did not even answer the indignant, resentful letters in which she complained that he had destroyed her career and that all she now had to show for having given way to his entreaties and believed his false promises was thousands of pounds' worth of debts. The once happy intrigue had degenerated into what he described to Prince Frederick as the 'old infernal cause Robinson'.[11]

Lord Malden, acting for Mrs Robinson, and Colonel Hotham, representing the Prince, found it extremely difficult to arrange a satisfactory settlement. When she was offered £5,000 for the return of the compromising letters which he had written to her, she angrily refused the 'insulting proposal'. She protested that she would 'quit England instantly', that 'no earthly power' would ever induce her to receive the 'smallest support' from him or to part with her valuable papers, that she hoped he would feel 'every degree of satisfaction' when reflecting upon the disgraceful way in which he had treated her.[12] Later, when a financial settlement seemed to be all that she could hope for, she insisted that £5,000 was totally inadequate; her present debts alone amounted to £5,600. Moreover, she must have some undertaking that the Prince would give her substantially more when it was in his power to do so.[13] But the Prince was adamant: he could not possibly bind himself for the future without the King's consent; he did not want 'anything more to do with the business'. Well then, Mrs Robinson retorted, the Prince's behaviour was 'so ungenerous and illiberal' that she felt herself justified 'in any step' that her necessities might urge her to make.[14]

Eventually it was agreed that, in addition to the capital sum of £5,000, she should have an annuity of £500, half of which her daughter would continue to receive after her death.[15]*

*

* Her great inducement in agreeing to this sordid settlement, she informed Colonel Hotham, was 'to restore His Royal Highness's peace of mind'. She was so 'shocked' by the implication that she was returning the letters for money that she felt compelled to demand in writing an acknowledgement of the fact that she had not *sold* papers so dear to her, papers which she had ever valued as dearly as her very 'existance' (Capell Manuscripts FH/IX/8 M275, FH/IX/23 M295). Having collected the money, she went to live in Paris where she resisted, so she claimed, the ardent and persistent overtures of the Duke of Orleans. On her return to England in straitened circumstances she made for Brighton and, on arrival at the Ship Hotel, she wrote to

The King, who had had to approach Lord North, the Prime Minister, for the money to pay Mrs Robinson, was more dismayed by his son than ever. His own sexual urges were very strong but he had never given way to them; he had been in love with Lady Sarah Lennox when he had married, but he had never been unfaithful to the Queen. And now their son, whose duty it was to set a good example to the nation, had landed himself in this 'shameful scrape'.

The King was now more determined than ever to keep the Prince on a tight rein. Soon after his eighteenth birthday on 12 August 1780 the Prince had been granted his own establishment, but he was still required to live with his parents at Buckingham House or in the apartments along the east front of the castle at Windsor which had now been made for him; and he was also still required to remain under the care of Bishop Hurd who was not allowed to give up the Preceptorship, of which he had felt the 'full weight', until December.[16]

In a long letter informing him what arrangements had been made for him in 'this middle state between manhood and childhood', the King informed the Prince about the limitations to be imposed upon his future conduct:

'. . . As you may at times be desirous of dining with some of your attendants, I shall consent when I am in town that you may have a dinner in your apartment on Sundays and Thursdays, but I cannot afford it oftener. . . . You may very naturally chuse to go oftener to plays and operas than I may. I shall not object to it when I am in town, provided you give me previous notice that we may not expect you in the evening, but then you must go in your box attended by your regular attendants, as all Princes of Wales have heretofore done. Whenever you are desirous of dancing, on an intimation to the Queen or me, we shall very

inform the Prince of her sad situation. He replied that the 'scene of distress' which she so pathetically painted quite overcame him and he promised that, should it be within the compass of his means to serve her, he would certainly do so (MS letter, Chequers Library). Soon afterwards the Prince was relieved of further responsibility for her by Colonel Banastre Tarleton, Member of Parliament for Liverpool, whose mistress she remained for about sixteen years. Towards the end of her life, having become paralysed from the waist down, she devoted herself to literature, producing numerous poems and several plays. In these years the Prince, by then quite forgiven for his past treatment of her, was a regular visitor at her house in St James's Place where she received her guests elegantly reclining upon a sofa in her small drawing-room. Suffering from 'acute rheumatic disorders . . . aggravated by pecuniary distress', she died at the age of forty in 1800 and was buried in the churchyard at Old Windsor (Wraxall, v, 368-9). A last request, so it was reported, was that a lock of her hair should be sent to the Prince as 'a mark of her regard' (Huish, i, 68). Her daughter, Miss Maria Elizabeth Robinson, continued to receive half her pension as had been agreed (RA Geo. IV. Box 7; RA 29859-68).

readily forward it, and shall have no other wish on such occasions but to make the Ball agreeable to you; but I shall not permit the going to balls or assemblies at private houses, which never has been the custom for Princes of Wales. As to masquerades, you already know my disapprobation of them in this country, and I cannot by any means agree to any of my children ever going to them.

Of course you will come every Sunday to church and to the Drawing Room at St James's when I appear there, as also at the Thursday Drawing Room.

When I ride out of a morning I shall ever expect you to accompany me. On other days I shall not object to your doing it also, provided it is for exercise, not lounging about Hyde Park. Whenever you ride out or go in a carriage, one of your attendants must accompany you. . . . Be but open with me and you will ever find me desirous of making you as happy as I can, but I must not forget, nor must you, that in the exalted station you are placed in, every step is of consequence, and that your future character will greatly depend in the world on the propriety of your conduct at the present period. . . . I can reason more coolly on paper than in conversation, but should you at any time wish to talk on any subject, you will never find me unwilling to enter into it. Indeed, I wish more and more to have you as a friend and in that light to guide you, rather than with the authority of a parent . . .'[17]

A few days after this letter was written, the Prince lost the company of his beloved brother, Frederick, who, seventeen years old and a colonel, was sent out to Hanover to improve his German and to complete his military education. So distressed was he at parting from him, 'so much affected with the misfortune of being deprived for so long a period of the sole companion of his youth', that the Prince 'stood in a state of entire insensibility, totally unable to speak . . .'[18]

Three weeks later he was forced to say good-bye to his 'best friend', Lieutenant-Colonel Gerard Lake, a man eighteen years older than himself who had recently been appointed his First Equerry and was now going out to fight in America. A talented, popular, 'sensible, worthy and gentlemanlike' man, one day to become Commander-in-Chief in India, Lake was a 'pleasing exception' to the list of 'unsuitable' companions with whom the Prince chose to spend much of his time.[19] 'Our parting, as you may suppose,' the Prince told Frederick, 'was a very severe trial to us both, especially as we had received so great a shock in our late separation from you. You know how much I love him, and therefore will easily conceive what a loss he is to me at the present moment, more especially as I have not you, my dear brother, with me, from whom I could always meet with disinterested advice.'[20]

Well aware of how much he was in need of their advice, both Lake and Frederick continued to offer it from their respective posts. Lake ventured to hope that the Prince's good sense ('of which no one had a greater share') would prevent his becoming the dupe of any political party, and strongly urged him 'not to write any more letters to a certain sort of ladies', adding that the trouble he had already got himself into on that account ought to be a 'sufficient warning'. Above all, Lake advised him not to allow himself, as he was inclined to do through his good nature, to be imposed upon by people who had 'not the smallest pretensions' to his 'civility or attentions' and who presumed upon that good nature to become troublesome to him. 'Believe me,' Lake assured him, offering pertinent and much-needed counsel, 'a knowledge of the world and of man is very necessary, and the most difficult to be acquired. Allow me to say it is more so for you, as the retired and private education unavoidably chalked out for a Prince has prevented you from knowing so much of them as young men who have reaped the benefit of a publick school in general do at your age; besides, your situation is such as to make people very anxious to be upon the best footing with you, and I am sorry to say that too many there are in this world who, to gain your favour, will acquiesce and encourage you in doing things that they themselves perhaps would be the first to condemn, and when they find the world disapproving your conduct, will lay the blame entirely upon yourself.'[21]

Prince Frederick was not so well suited as Lake to offer his brother advice about 'a certain sort of ladies' since he was already deeply involved with Letitia Smith, an adventuress who was believed to have also been the mistress of the highwayman John Rann, better known as 'Sixteen-String Jack' from the sixteen silk tassels that he always wore tied to his breeches' knees. In the first letter that he wrote to his brother in Hanover, the Prince of Wales told him that he had met Mrs Smith at one of those masquerades at the Pantheon which his father had so expressly forbidden him to attend. He had beckoned to her; she had recognized him and followed him up to the gallery where their conversation was totally about Prince Frederick. She said that she could not live without him, that she had been excessively ill, and that she was resolved to set out for Hanover to be with him. 'In short,' the Prince of Wales concluded, 'I believe no woman ever loved a man more passionately than she does you. She cried very much.'[22] Soon afterwards, she married Sir John Lade.

If Prince Frederick was not well qualified to advise his brother about women, he did think he could and should advise him to try to get on better terms with his parents. In letters asking for a variety of articles to be sent out to Hanover, from 'Huzza breeches' and dancing pumps to sabres, indian ink and books of country dances, Prince Frederick besought him

'to be upon as good a footing as possible with the King, for really it is of so much consequence to yourself that it appears to me quite ridiculous that you do not at least attempt [it]. . . . For God's sake do everything which you can to keep well with him, at least upon decent terms; consider he is vexed enough in publick affairs. It is therefore your business not to make that still worse . . . You know, my dearest brother, I hate *preaching* full as much as you do, and constraint if possible more, but still for both your sakes I entreat you to keep as well together as possible. I know you will. Excuse what I write to you because it comes from the heart.'[23]

But the Prince of Wales could not bring himself to follow his brother's advice to keep on good terms with his parents. It was as though their dull, domestic way of living and their constant criticism of his extravagance, incited him to further dissipation and expenditure. Certainly the Prince never tired of complaining that he was exasperated by his father's attitude towards him. He was always so 'excessively cross, ill-tempered and uncommonly grumpy', as well as being 'so stingy' that he would 'hardly allow himself three coats in a year';[24] while the Queen was really quite as bad, accusing her son of 'various high crimes and misdemeanours'. The 'unkind behaviour' of both of them was 'hardly bearable'.[25] He answered his mother back, he confessed, and 'in the vulgar English phraze gave her as good as she brought' until she fell into silence. She said that she criticized his conduct upon her own initiative, without the King's knowledge; but the Prince felt sure, from 'the language she used and the style she spoke in' that the King was behind it all.[26]

As month followed month in 1781, there were almost daily reports of the Prince of Wales's wild behaviour, of his riding 'like a madman' in Hyde Park, of drunken brawls in the gardens at Vauxhall and Ranelagh. And there was talk of his successful conquest of the easily conquered Grace Dalrymple Elliott whose illegitimate daughter, Georgiana Augusta Frederica Seymour, may have been his, as the mother liked to suppose, though she may equally well have been fathered by one of Mrs Elliott's other lovers, George Selwyn, Charles William Windham or Lord Cholmondeley. The King asked Prince Frederick, his favourite son, who

23

was working hard and getting on well in Hanover, to write to his brother to remonstrate with him as forcibly as he could. Frederick did so, entreating him for God's sake to take care of his health: 'You cannot stand this kind of life.'[27]

The Prince paid no attention. In vain his father complained that it was 'allmost certain that some unpleasant mention of him' was now to be found in the newspapers each morning. 'Draw your conclusion,' the King wrote, 'whether you must not give me many an uneasy moment. I wish to live with you as a friend, but then by your behaviour you must deserve it. If I did not state these things I should not fulfil my duty either to my God or to my country. . . . When you read this carefully over, you will find an affectionate father trying to save his son from perdition.'[28]

The King had hoped that the payment of £5,000 on his behalf to enable him to rid himself of Mrs Robinson might have persuaded him to 'act in a manner worthy of approbation'.[29] Yet his conduct had in no way improved since then; he drank as hard as ever; he had found another unsuitable mistress; he mixed with increasingly profligate company. The King made it abundantly clear that he strongly disapproved of his going to dine with Lord Chesterfield, a man of highly questionable principles, and of his close friendship with Colonel Anthony St Leger and Charles William Windham, two young rakes whom 'all good men' despised.[30] But the Prince continued to consort with them and was reported to have got so drunk in their company at Lord Chesterfield's house at Blackheath that he was obliged to lie down on a bed.[31] After another drunken evening at Chesterfield's, during which a ferocious dog had savaged a footman and the host had fallen down the stairs, he had been rendered totally incapable of driving home and had had to leave the reins of his phaeton to his uncle, the Duke of Cumberland.[32]

As he had been warned by Prince Frederick, he could not stand this kind of life. He fell seriously ill and for two days his physician, Sir Richard Jebb, felt much alarmed for him, while he himself thought that he might die.[33] He was compelled to remain in his bedchamber for a fortnight, his face covered with red, eruptive blotches and 'dreadful to behold', without ever tasting anything but barley water 'or some damned wishy washy stuff of that sort'.[34]

As soon as he had recovered, however, the Prince was away again on his indecorous adventures. It was rumoured that, having tired of Mrs Elliott, he had brief affairs with numerous other women, nearly all of whom were older than himself. The best known of these supposed mistresses were Lady Augusta Campbell, the beautiful, wayward daughter of the fifth Duke of Argyll, who was later unhappily married to 'that most indifferent *sposo*', Colonel Clavering; Lady Melbourne, a tall, lively, handsome woman whose fourth child, George Lamb, brother of the future Prime Minister, was said to be the Prince's; the pretty, chubby singer, Elizabeth Billington, formerly the mistress, it was supposed, of the Duke of Rutland and wife of James Billington, a double-bass player in the Drury Lane orchestra; and Maria Amelia, Countess of Salisbury, a devoted foxhunter, twelve years the Prince's senior.

The Prince was also said to have made advances to the two beautiful daughters of the first Earl Spencer, Henrietta, Countess of Bessborough, and Georgiana, the extravagant, intelligent wife of the fifth Duke of Devonshire.* No one seemed certain whether or not he had succeeded in making love to either of them. Perhaps he had not, for he was known to have become very sulky when they did take lovers, when Henrietta succumbed to the charms of Lord Granville Leveson Gower, and Georgiana became the mistress of the proud and handsome Charles Grey whom the Prince ever afterwards disliked.[35]

*

It was certain, however, that the Prince did manage to make love to the brash and scheming Countess von Hardenburg, wife of Count Karl August von Hardenburg who had come to London in hopes of being appointed Hanoverian envoy to the Court of St James's. The Prince had been introduced to the Countess in the spring of 1781 at a concert in the

---

* The Duchess drew a candid portrait of the Prince as he appeared to her in September 1782, soon after his twentieth birthday: 'The Prince of Wales is rather tall and has a figure which though striking is not perfect. He is inclined to be too fat and looks too much like a woman in men's cloaths, but the gracefulness of his manner and his height certainly make him a pleasing figure. His face is very handsome and he is fond of dress even to a tawdry degree. . . . He is goodnatured and rather extravagant. From the usual turn of his character and some shabby traits to his mistresses one should imagine he was more inclined to extravagance than generosity, though at the same time two or three very generous things to his friends in distress do him the highest honour. . . . He certainly does not want for understanding, and his jokes have the appearance of wit. He appears to have an inclination to meddle in politics, he loves being of consequence, and whether it is in intrigue of state or gallantry, he often thinks more is intended than really is. He has a great deal of quickness, and like the King has a wonderful knack at knowing all that is going forward' (Chatsworth MSS, *Georgiana*, Appendix ii, 289). 'He has his father's passion,' Betsy Sheridan confirmed, 'for knowing who and what every one is' (Sheridan, *Journal*, 168).

Queen's apartment. Formerly the Countess Reventlow, she was an attractive, provocative woman, by turns flirtatious and aloof, who, soon after Prince Frederick's arrival in Hanover, had attempted to seduce him at a dance. At their first meeting, the Prince of Wales took little notice of her; she was, he decided, 'a very devilish, agreeable, pleasant little woman, but devilish severe'.[36] Some time later, however, when he met her again at one of the Queen's card parties at Windsor, he thought her 'devinely pretty'.[37] It was clear that she was bored. The Prince afterwards discovered that she disliked all card games – as he did himself – unless they were games of chance and played merely for gambling. One of his sisters tried to teach her how to play, placing the cards on the table for her; but she paid little attention to the rules, repeatedly glancing up to catch the Prince's eye. From that moment, he confessed to Prince Frederick, he fell madly in love with her. 'O did you but know how I adore her,' he exclaimed, 'how I love her, how I would sacrifice every earthly thing to her; by Heavens I shall go distracted: my brain will split.'[38]

She remained at Windsor a fortnight during which the Prince showed her every possible attention. One day he said to her that after seeing so much of her in the country it was a pity that he could not see her as frequently in London. Could he not see her some morning after eleven o'clock when her husband was out? She affected great indignation at this improper suggestion; but when the Prince apologized with his usual grace and charm, protesting that he had not intended to give her the slightest offence, she forgave him. He seemed no nearer making love to her, however, and in his feverish anxiety to do so, he fell ill again. He became 'much emaciated', he said; he contracted a violent cough; he spat blood; Sir Richard Jebb had to be called in once again. His illness, real, imagined or contrived, had the desired effect: one morning when he called upon the Countess at her house in Old Windsor while her husband was out he complained piteously of her cruelty to him, and she replied, 'I certainly am very much attached to you, I do love you most sincerely, and it affords me great delight to think that you are attached to me, but I must tell you that I was once very much attached to another person, and did think that a woman never could love but once very sincerely during her life. If, after such a declaration, you can attach yourself to me, it will be an additional proof of your love, but should you not, for God's sake let us drop all thoughts of love and part very good friends.'[39]

The Prince assured her that he loved her more than ever after this avowal; but two or three more days elapsed before 'she would consent to any idea of completing [his] happiness'. At last, however, she did consent; and 'O my beloved brother,' he wrote as though still 'in ecstasy', to Prince Frederick, 'I enjoyed ... the pleasures of Elyssium ... thus did our connexion go forward in the most delightful manner that you can form any idea to yourself of.'[40]

No one knew anything about the affair except his Equerry, Lieutenant-Colonel Samuel Hulse, until there appeared in the *Morning Herald* a piece of gossip to the effect that the Prince of Wales's carriage was every day to be seen outside the house of a certain German baroness in Cork Street. The story was untrue – the journalist had been misled by the Duke of Gloucester's carriage being frequently seen outside the house of a Polish countess – but when Count von Hardenburg heard about it, he demanded that his wife write to the Prince and terminate the affair immediately. Von Hardenburg himself also wrote to the Prince who 'almost fell into fits' when he received the packet and thought he 'should have run distracted' when he opened it. He replied that he was certainly very strongly attached to Madame von Hardenburg, but that she had always treated him with the 'utmost coolness'; he was the only person to blame in the whole affair. He then wrote a most passionate letter to the Countess, and, thinking everything was at an end, sent an express to Lord Southampton, the Groom of the Stole and head of his Establishment, desiring him to go to the King to ask for permission for him to go abroad as 'an unfortunate affair had of late happened' which made him 'excessively miserable'.[41] The King replied that he could not possibly consider his going abroad for any reason whatever.[42]

Soon after the receipt of this letter, the Prince was handed one from the Countess, professing her attachment to him, reminding him of all his vows, and proposing that they run away together that night. Torn between fear of the appalling scandal that an elopement would cause, and the desire to possess her, the Prince as he admitted lost his senses entirely. At first he agreed to go away with her, then he shrank from the step, excusing himself on the grounds that, although she was the object of all his tenderness and all his love, he could not expose her to the possibility of her perishing for want; his father's 'severe disposition' would hardly soften sufficiently for him to condone and support such a relationship.

Not knowing to whom else he could turn, he threw himself, in his own phrase, at his mother's feet. He confessed the whole truth to her, and

27

having done so, he fainted. She 'cried excessively', and, moved by his distress, was deeply sympathetic.[43] It was decided that Colonel Hulse should be sent to the Countess to tell her that an accident prevented the Prince going with her, and that the King must be informed of his son's latest imbroglio. The King acted promptly; he sent for von Hardenburg who was immediately packed off to the Continent with his wife.

On her arrival back in Hanover, the Countess quarrelled with Prince Frederick who decided that he hated her almost as much as he did the devil, and congratulated his brother on having got off so lightly. The Prince of Wales could scarcely believe that his angel could behave in the way that his brother now described. He found it impossible to think of her without the 'strongest love and regard'; but he had to admit that he had entertained some doubts about her while their connexion lasted. She 'appeared to be very capricious and very singular in some things'; 'in short it was a very miserable, and unhappy affair altogether', and no doubt it was all for the best that it was ended.[44]

3

Carlton House and Brooks's
1782-1784

*

'A shameful squandering of public money'

To disentangle the Prince from the arms of designing mistresses had not proved unduly difficult, but the King was far less successful in separating his son from undesirable male companions. Protest and threaten as he would about Anthony St Leger, for example, the King could not induce the Prince to forego the company of so racy and entertaining a friend. In the spring of 1782, shortly before his twentieth birthday, the Prince went so far as to absent himself without permission from one of his Majesty's levees to dash up to Northamptonshire to hunt with St Leger. The King wrote sternly to insist on 'the like not being done again'; if his son's conduct did not amend, he would take steps that certainly would be 'disagreable'.[1] The Prince replied that, although his conduct in the world was 'in great measure different from the limited plan' drawn up for him, which in his youth and inexperience he had 'inconsiderately acquiesed in', he flattered himself that his behaviour, far from deserving censure, 'merited the strictest approbation'.[2] And he carried on misbehaving and enjoying himself as before.

But although he complained about his son's misconduct with St Leger, the King's concern over this friendship was trivial compared with his anxiety about the increasing intimacy between the Prince and that abominable Whig politician, Charles James Fox.

Fox, a Member of Parliament from the age of nineteen, had come into prominence during the American war, the mismanagement of which under the Tory administration of Lord North he roundly condemned in speeches of marvellous eloquence. To the dismay of the King, Lord

29

North was forced to resign in March 1782, and Fox, now thirty-three, accepted office as one of the secretaries of state in the new government headed by the Whig, Lord Rockingham. The following year he became Foreign Secretary in a coalition government of which the Duke of Portland was the nominal leader; and when he went to kiss hands with the King on his appointment, it was noticed that his Majesty put back his ears like a horse bent on throwing its rider.[3]

It was not only that Fox was politically unacceptable to the King, he was morally unacceptable too. The son of an enormously rich father who had vastly increased his fortune during eight years of office as Paymaster-General of the Forces, Charles had been sent to Eton and Oxford and on the Grand Tour, and had early developed that insatiable passion for gambling which was to lead to his being almost constantly in debt throughout the whole of his life. Walpole said that in his mid-twenties he would arrive to speak in the House of Commons after playing hazard at Almack's for more than twenty-four hours at a stretch. For the whole of the night before a debate on the Thirty-nine Articles he sat up gambling, and by five o'clock the next afternoon, a Wednesday, he had lost £11,000. 'On the Thursday he spoke in this debate; went to dinner at past eleven at night; from thence to White's, where he drank until seven the next morning; thence to Almack's where he won £6,000; and between three and four in the afternoon' he set out for the races at Newmarket.[4]

Walpole went on to say that in three nights he and his brother lost £32,000 between them, and added, 'There being a report that Charles was going to be married, it was told to his father . . . who replied: "I am glad of it, for then he will go to bed at least one night." '[5]

When he did get married his choice of a wife was as shocking as his gambling and his drinking. For a time he became the lover of 'Perdita' Robinson after she had been discarded by the Prince of Wales. Then, having grown tired of her almost as quickly as the Prince had done, he took up with Mrs Elizabeth Bridget Armistead, a delightful woman of unknown provenance, but strong Cockney pronunciation, who had also had a brief affair with the Prince of Wales. He grew deeply attached to her and eventually, having lived with her for several years, he married her in 1795, keeping the marriage secret, however, until they made a trip abroad together in 1802.[6]

No one could feel in the least surprised that the friendship between such a man as Fox and the Prince was deeply distressing to the King. It was well known that Fox's followers 'were strangely licentious in their conversation about the King'; that at Brooks's Club, where his disciples met, bets were taken on the duration of the present reign; and it was equally well known that the Prince frequently went to Brooks's and to Fox's lodgings in St James's Street where his friend, still in his 'foul linen night-gown', unwashed and unshaved, with his bushy hair dishevelled and 'his shagged breast quite open', received his morning visitors to discuss with them the topics of the day.[7]

But nor could anyone who knew Fox feel surprised that the young Prince admired him so. A hard-drinking gambler who had taken over two of the Prince's former mistresses, paunchy, untidy, graceless, with a swarthy skin, a double chin and black, shaggy eyebrows, he was at the same time a man of extraordinary charm and good-nature. His smile, like the Prince's, was delightful, his intellect brilliant, his expression animated, his conversation entrancing. His friendship with the Prince, thirteen years younger than himself, was not merely politically useful, it was genuinely felt. The Prince's regard for him was near to idolatry.

As the Prince's twenty-first birthday approached, it became necessary to consider the matter of his personal income and it naturally fell to Fox, as a leading member of the Cabinet and as an intimate friend, to play a crucial part in the negotiations.

A previous administration had led the Prince to believe that on being granted a separate establishment, he would receive the splendid income of £100,000 a year. But when the new administration, avowedly more friendly to the Prince and unwilling to appear less generous, suggested this figure to the King, his Majesty was horrified. He drafted a letter to Colonel George Hotham, the Treasurer of the Prince's Household, to tell him that although he wished to have his son settled with comfort, £100,000 a year was the sum granted to his grandfather, who had had a wife and nine children to support, and that the weight of taxes which the people of the country laboured under made it wholly unreasonable. In a revised version of this letter sent to Hotham on 21 June, the King asked him to tell the Prince that he did not think it advisable to apply to Parliament for any further assistance than such as would enable the Prince to have £50,000, 'with the revenues of Cornwal'. This would make the Prince's income about £27,000 more than he himself had received in a similar situation. The letter ended with a sadly familiar complaint: 'The

Prince of Wales on the smallest reflection must feel that I have little reason to approve of any part of his conduct for the last three years; that his neglect of every religious duty is notorious; his want of common civility to the Queen and me, not less so; besides his total disobedience of every injunction I had given and which he, in presence of his brother and the gentlemen then about them both, declared himself contented with. I must hope he will now think it behoves him to take up a fresh line of conduct more worthy of his station.'[8]

To the Duke of Portland, the King subsequently complained of the outrageous idea of granting an income of £100,000, so long as the Prince remained unmarried. It was 'a shameful squandering of public money, besides an encouragement of extravagance'.[9] It was impossible for the King 'to find words expressive enough' of his 'utter indignation and astonishment'. He had at least hoped that when the Duke of Portland came into office he would have thought himself obliged to have the King's interest and 'that of the Public at heart, and not have neglected both to gratify the passions of an ill-advised young man'. He deemed £50,000, in addition to the revenues of the Duchy of Cornwall, which amounted to about £12,000 a year, perfectly adequate.[10]

As the letters flew backwards and forwards between Downing Street and Windsor, and no hope of a compromise appeared, Fox began to fear that the dispute would bring down the government. 'There is great reason to think our administration will not outlive tomorrow,' he wrote on 17 June, 'or that at least it will be at an end in a very few days.'[11]

Just at this fateful moment the King suddenly relented. He sent for Portland and in 'an agony of tears' confessed that he had 'gone too far', and begged the Duke to rescue him.[12] The Duke called in Fox who persuaded the Prince to keep the peace within the royal family and to save the government by accepting £50,000 and the Duchy of Cornwall revenues on the understanding that a capital sum would also be provided. This capital sum was fixed at £60,000. It was to be provided by Parliament – the £50,000 a year allowance was to come from the Civil List – and half of it was to be allocated to the liquidation of the Prince's debts. By 19 June the storm was for the moment dissipated. The Prince, Fox decided, had 'behaved in the handsomest manner'.[13]

But the storm clouds were still there. The Secretary for War felt that the government could never now gain the King's favour. There might be a wary politeness; but there would be 'no peerages, no marks of *real* support'.[14] As for the King, every morning when he woke up he wished, so he said, that he were eighty, or ninety, or dead.[15]

As part of the settlement it had been agreed that the Prince should have his own house. There was no country house available, as the King informed George Hotham, although the apartments the Prince occupied at Windsor would 'always be kept ready to receive him'; but as for a London residence, his Majesty was willing to grant him the use of the house the Prince's grandmother, the Princess Dowager of Wales, had inhabited in Pall Mall, provided he did not give any of the ground away and took upon himself 'all repairs, taxes and the keeping of the garden'.[16]

This house was Carlton House, adjoining the Duke of Cumberland's mansion, on the southern side of Pall Mall; and the King's condition that the Prince should be responsible for the upkeep of the garden was well-advised. For, though the house, which had been built at the beginning of the eighteenth century, was unremarkable, the gardens were both extensive and beautiful. They had been laid out by William Kent, one of the Earl of Burlington's protégés, who had been an influential leader in the revolt against the formal gardening of the seventeenth century. They stretched down Pall Mall as far as Marlborough House, the elegant mansion built by Sir Christopher Wren for the tiresome first Duchess who had lived there until her death in 1744. As informal and natural as any town gardens could be expected to be, they were noted for some splendid elms, charming bowers and grottoes, and a number of irregularly placed statues.

Carlton House itself had never been a small house and had been considerably enlarged by the Princess Dowager of Wales who had added to it the house next door, bought from George Bubb Dodington; but it was still not large enough for the Prince who, now that he had a place of his own at last, determined that it should be as grandly imposing as possible. He instructed Henry Holland to make it so.

The son of a Fulham master builder, Holland had become the partner of the landscape gardener Lancelot ('Capability') Brown whose architectural practice he took over and whose daughter he married. Like many other eighteenth-century architects, he had turned to speculative building; and on land in Chelsea (leased from Lord Cadogan), he had built Cadogan Place, Hans Place and Sloane Street – the two last named in honour of Sir Hans Sloane, the physician and collector whose daughter, Jane, was Cadogan's wife. It was, however, Holland's work in 1776–78 as

architect of Brooks's Club – a commission which brought him into contact with the Whig aristocracy for whom all his most important works
were executed[17] – that gained for him the admiration of the Prince of
Wales. The subscription room in Brooks's – an interior that still sur-
vives – was a room with which the Prince was well acquainted and could
not but have predisposed him in the architect's favour. The French influence, particularly the influence of Louis XVI's Paris which was so
marked a feature of Holland's style and was reflected in the French sympathies of the Whig circle, was soon to be evident in the remodelled
interior of Carlton House.[18]

Holland began work on the old-fashioned and in parts dilapidated
house in the early autumn of 1783, and by the beginning of November
the Prince was already living there as the work went on around him. Improvements were to continue intermittently for almost thirty years, at a
cost which the Prince himself was to admit was 'enormous'; but within a
few months of his moving into the house it had already become magnificent.

A splendid hall, decorated with Ionic columns of brown Siena marble,
led to an octagon and a graceful double staircase. Above were the state
apartments, the Prince's exotic bow-windowed bedroom – where his
friends visited him of a morning as he lay 'in his bed, rolling about from
side to side in a state approaching to nudity'[19] – his dressing-room and
bathroom. Beyond the music room there was a drawing-room decorated
in the Chinese taste, a taste which had had many cultivated admirers in
England since the 1750s, and which Sir William Chambers, one of the
leading architects of his time, had encouraged by the temples and pagodas
he had built at Kew for the Prince's grandmother. An agent was sent to
China to buy furniture for this room, for which the mercer's bill alone
amounted to £6,817,[20] and for which £441 was spent on lanterns.[21] All the
rooms at Carlton House were as beautifully and expensively furnished,
mostly with pieces chosen by the Prince himself, often after consultation
with the Duchess of Devonshire who was not likely to have urged economy.
Below were a whole new range of servants' quarters, pantries, larders,
sculleries, kitchens and cellars. Outside in the garden more statues were
erected, a waterfall was constructed, a temple with an Italian marble floor
was built; there was even an observatory.

Relentlessly, without regard to cost and in defiance of the King's
known wishes, more and more splendours were gradually added to Carlton
House. Adjoining houses were bought and demolished to make way for

new wings. Craftsmen, decorators, cabinet-makers, metal-workers and wood-carvers were brought over from France and set to work in the house until it was considered finer than any other in England; worthy, in the opinion of the novelist Robert Plumer Ward, to stand comparison with Versailles;[22] and, in that of Count Münster, with the Palace of St Petersburg which was, however, not its equal 'in elegance or richness'.[23] To many visitors, indeed, it became altogether too rich, almost vulgar in its opulence. This was emphatically the opinion of Robert Smirke, the rather staid architect of numerous public buildings in London, who in later years observed that the apartments were 'overdone with finery'.[24] Yet the Prince, undeterred by criticisms of either his taste or his expenditure, continued to lavish money upon it, making it more majestic than ever, buying numerous fine English and Dutch pictures, notably some beautiful van Dycks, with which to decorate its walls, building on a whole suite of new rooms, some Corinthian, others Gothic – including a magnificent fan-vaulted Gothic conservatory designed in the manner of a small cathedral – until it was quite dazzling in its magnificence.[25]

It was furnished throughout with the most exquisite pieces, many of them from France. It was highly appropriate that a full-length portrait of the Prince's friend, the Duke of Orleans, Louis XVI's cousin, should have hung in a prominent position in one of the principal rooms – until peremptorily removed when the Duke became Philippe Egalité, supporter of the Jacobins.[26] For, both now and later, whenever the exigencies of the Revolution and the subsequent wars allowed, his friends and agents went to France to buy furniture and *objets d'art*, pictures, girandoles, clocks, looking-glasses, bronzes, Sèvres china, Gobelin tapestries and countless other treasures on his behalf. The sale rooms and dealers' shops of London were similarly scoured for the most comprehensive collection of French works of art ever assembled by an English monarch. Cabinets, chests and tables by Riesener, Weisweiler, Jacob and Carlin, marble busts by Coysevox, bronzes by Keller, candelabra by Thomire, pictures by Pater, Vernet, Greuze, Le Main and Claude were bought for the Prince week after week, year after year, and carefully arranged in the various rooms at Carlton House under his discerning eye.[27]

Although its interior was rather too ornate for some tastes, the classical dignity of the façade, with its fine Corinthian portico, added by Henry Holland, was almost universally admired. Its 'august simplicity', in Horace Walpole's view, made Robert Adam's 'gingerbread and sippets of em-

35

broidery' seem decidedly meretricious. When it was finished it would certainly be 'the most perfect' palace in Europe, though Walpole could not conceive whence the money was to come. 'All the tin mines in Cornwall would not pay a quarter.'[28]

In March 1784, when the first stages of the alteration were more or less complete, the Prince gave a splendid, celebratory ball in his new palace; and in May nine huge marquees were put up in the gardens for an even more magnificent fête during which the guests were entertained on the newly mown grass by four bands playing triumphant airs. This second reception was held to celebrate an event that had given the Prince as much pleasure as the King distress.

*

On 11 November the year before, the opening day of the new session of Parliament, the Prince, exquisitely dressed in black velvet lined with pink satin and embroidered in gold, wearing shoes with pink heels, his hair frizzed and curled, had taken his seat in the House of Lords. Afterwards in the House of Commons he had approvingly listened to Fox's lively speech on the treaties recently concluded with France, Spain and the United States – a speech, which 'was allowed by all those who heard it', the *Morning Chronicle* reported the next day, 'to be one of the ablest, and at the same time one of the most fair and honest ever delivered from the mouth of a Minister at the opening of a session of Parliament'.[29]

But Fox's days of power were almost at an end. A week after the opening of the new session he introduced a Bill for reforming the government of India. The need for such reform had long been recognized; yet Fox's opponents had little difficulty in representing it not only as an attack upon the rights of the East India Company, and thus a threat to all charter companies, but also as a means of obtaining a controlling interest in Indian affairs for the Whig majority in the House of Commons. Fox was alleged to be attempting to crown himself King of Bengal; and in a celebrated caricature, which the victim thought did more than anything else to raise public opinion against his Bill, James Sayers depicted him in the opulent clothes of an Indian potentate, black-bearded and enormously fat, riding an elephant through the streets of the city – 'Carlo Khan's Triumphant Entry into Leadenhall Street'. The King, firmly persuaded that Fox was using the Bill to undermine his royal prerogative, made it known that whoever voted for it was not his friend. The warning had the required effect: the

Bill passed the Commons, though many Members stayed away rather than vote for it, but it was defeated in the Lords by nineteen votes.

The next day, shortly before midnight, Fox was informed by a special messenger that the King had no further use for his services; and the following morning, 19 December 1783, it was announced in the House of Commons that William Pitt, the twenty-four-year-old second son of the Earl of Chatham, who had vehemently opposed Fox's India Bill in the Commons, had accepted office as First Lord of the Treasury and Chancellor of the Exchequer.

Yet although he had succeeded in clearing Fox out of the government, the King could not keep him out of parliament. In the elections that followed the fall of the administration of which he had been so prominent a member, Fox was returned for Westminster. One of his most influential canvassers was the Duchess of Devonshire who tirelessly drove about the streets in her carriage, a fox's brush stuck in her hat, with her sister and other attractive young ladies. They knocked on the 'most blackguard houses in Long Acre' at eight o'clock in the morning, talking, persuading, arguing, buying votes with kisses. In the triumphal procession that escorted the candidate through London in a laurel-decked chair after his victory, the Duchess's carriage was prominent. So too was that of the Prince of Wales who – 'with Mr Fox's full concurrence'[30] – had prudently not attended the House of Lords on the day that Fox's India Bill had been defeated, but was happy now to be seen wearing his friend's colours of buff and blue, the colours of Washington's volunteers. As the procession passed Devonshire House the Prince stood on the garden wall, the Duchess of Devonshire on one side of him, the Duchess of Portland on the other, to cheer it on its way.

He gave a breakfast for Fox the next day at Carlton House from which the guests did not depart until after six o'clock in the evening, 'the weather being uncommonly fine'.[31] Their host then went on to a dinner party at the house of Mrs Crewe, wife of the Member for the County of Chester, where he proposed the apt toast 'Buff and Blue and Mrs Crewe!' to which his hostess brightly replied, 'Buff and Blue and All of You!'[32]

Some days later the Prince held a second fête 'of the most expensive, magnificent and varied description, prolonged in defiance of usage, and almost of human nature, from the noon of one day to the following morning'. At the splendid banquet the ladies were waited upon by the

Prince himself. 'It must be owned', Sir Nathaniel Wraxall grudgingly allowed, 'that on these occasions, for which he seemed particularly formed, he appeared to great advantage. Louis XIV himself could scarcely have eclipsed the son of George III in a ballroom, or when doing the honours of his palace surrounded by the pomp and attributes of luxury and royal state.'[33]

At yet another party held in celebration of Fox's victory, however, the Prince's behaviour was less admired. Indeed, according to Thomas Orde, Member for Aylesbury and a former Secretary of the Treasury, so many bumpers of wine did he drink that he fell flat on his face in the middle of a quadrille and, on being raised from the floor, was violently sick.[34]

*

Sometimes, after several days of heavy drinking and excitement, the Prince was obliged to take to his bed with a high fever. As a cure, he did not hesitate to open up a vein with a lancet himself whenever his doctors decided that he had been bled enough already. Prince Frederick wrote once again to caution him about the ill effects his way of life would have upon his constitution; so, too, more than once, did his uncle the Duke of Gloucester. 'I need not ask you if you amuse yourself well,' Gloucester wrote; 'the publick papers inform us of that very largely. I only hope your health may keep pace with your spirits. . . . If I was not afraid that you would call me an old gentleman, I would add that I had heard that you was not attentive enough to your health.'[35]

But the Prince disregarded all warnings and, as soon as he had recovered, went on drinking as hard and eating as much and living as recklessly as ever.

Those who dismissed him as a gormandizing, irresponsible, extravagant drunkard and whoremonger were, his friends insisted, being unjust to him. Certainly there were occasions enough when he behaved outrageously; certainly he squandered money as though he had not the least conception of its value and was consequently cheated by dishonest tradesmen.* It was true that he drank to excess, being proud to declare that he never flinched at a bumper and was 'not even upon indifferent occasions a *shirker*'.[36] And it was true that he had many friends unsuitable for a

---

* Lord Charlemont gave Dr Alexander Haliday an example of this: 'The Prince who was, as he ought to have been, fond of encouraging manufacturers, visited a carpet maker who had lately discovered a new and beautiful fabric in that line. Pleased with the beauty and ingenuity of the discovery, he bespoke a carpet and was charged for it ten times as much as an ordinary gentleman might have purchased it for' (HMCR, Charlemont MSS, ii, 261).

Prince of Wales, particularly amongst those who frequented the green-rooms of the theatres, or who, like his crony the Hon George Hanger, a beautifully powdered dandy who always wore a rose in his buttonhole, were constantly hiding from their creditors.

He spent much of his time with Sarah Siddons's brother, John Philip Kemble, who swallowed wine by 'pailfuls', and with Richard Cosway, who was said to have turned his house into a brothel. He was frequently drunk in the company of Richard Brinsley Sheridan. But then Kemble was a great actor who, after four years' training for the priesthood at the English College at Douai, could declaim as easily in Latin as in French; Cosway was a miniaturist of genius; and Sheridan, having achieved enduring fame with *The Rivals*, *The School for Scandal* and *The Critic* had entered Parliament with the help of the Duchess of Devonshire and, as a supporter of Fox, had become Secretary of the Treasury in the Duke of Portland's administration. Moreover, the Prince had many staider friends who found his company delightful. His conversation, full of amusing anecdote and aided by an excellent memory, was nearly always entertaining when he was not drunk; and his talent for mimicry was truly remarkable. John Wilson Croker never saw 'his equal for a combination of personal imitation with the power of exhibiting the mental character'.[37] The Duke of Wellington said that 'he had a most extraordinary talent for imitating the manner, gestures, and even the voice of other people, so much so that he could give you the exact idea of anyone however unlike they were to himself'.[38] While George Brummell thought that his 'powers of mimicry were so extraordinary that if his lot had fallen that way, he would have been the best comic actor in Europe'.[39]

When in more serious mood his conversation was somewhat marred by a habit of introducing classical quotations from a severely limited repertoire. Indeed, those who heard him talk often, so Lord Erskine said, discovered that he only used two, one from Homer and one from Virgil, 'which he never failed to sport when there was any opportunity of introducing them'.[40] Yet even so intelligent and discriminating a man as Henry Brougham described his conversation as that of 'a very clever person'.[41] He was often genuinely witty and could hold his own almost as well with the 'sprightly wits' of the Sublime Society of Beefsteaks, to whose select membership he was elected in April 1784, as with the fashionable denizens of Ranelagh, Vauxhall and the Pantheon. Lord Charlemont believed that if he could be persuaded to drink less, he might well live to be a 'blessing' to the country.[42] And Edmund Burke went so far as to suggest that should he ever resolve to quit a course of life in which he found 'little more than disgust', he might even 'become a great king'.[43]

His grace of manner was extraordinary: the cutler who taught him to shave, contrasting his deftness with the awkwardness of his father, said that he performed 'the operation with a facility and grace not to be described in words'.[44] And his charm, when he chose to exercise it, most men found fascinating and women scarcely resistible. The extremely rich dilettante, William Beckford, decided after one memorable party that the 'Prince, brighter than sunshine, cast a brilliant gleam wherever he moved'; lively, kindly and 'insinuating', he was 'graciousness personified'.[45] The young William Lamb, later to become a frequent guest at Carlton House, found him vastly entertaining, a brilliant mimic of his father's Ministers.[46] George Canning, meeting him for the first time was 'charmed beyond measure' and 'far beyond' his expectation with 'the elegance of his address and the gentlemanliness of his manner'. So was Charles Bannister, the good-natured actor and singer, who said that the Prince was 'always most gracious'; he would ask for a song, with inimitable politeness' and then compliment the performer with a 'taste peculiar to himself'.[48]

A more fastidious observer, the mordant gossip and poet Samuel Rogers, found him 'very agreeable'.[49] And even the Prince's ancient great-aunt Amelia, whose guttural German accents he imitated only too faithfully and whose guests were usually limited to 'Methusalems' like herself playing commerce and cribbage, welcomed him to her table.[50] Charles Burney, the musical historian – and a man, it must be admitted, naturally predisposed in favour of royalty – was deeply impressed by him: 'I was astonished to find him amidst such constant dissipation possessed of so much learning, wit, knowledge of books in general, discrimination of character as well as original humour,' he told his daughter. 'H.R.H. took me aside and talked exclusively about music near half an hour, and as long concerning Greek literature to your brother [the classical scholar in conversation with whom he managed to introduce his quotation from Homer*] . . . He may with truth be said to have as much wit as Charles II with much more learning. As to music he is an excellent critic.'[51] After a subsequent conversation, Burney decided that there was no one with

---

* While no great scholar, the Prince's interest in the classics was not feigned. In 1800, there having been discovered a library of papyri in the recently unearthed city of Herculaneum,

whom he enjoyed talking about music more than 'this most captivating Prince'.[52]

Charles Bannister agreed with Burney that the Prince was an excellent judge of music.[53] At the age of four he had attended a performance specially given for him at Covent Garden of the children's operetta, *The Fairy Favour*, with music by Johann Christian Bach, and ever since then music had been one taste at least that he shared with his father. He became a regular patron of operas and subscription concerts, and was himself a performer of more than average ability. He had a pleasant tenor voice, which had been trained by Sir William Parsons, the Master and Conductor of the King's Band, and he still played the 'cello with creditable skill for an amateur, 'quite tolerably' in the expert opinion of Joseph Haydn with whom he once played in a concert.[54]

It was, however, his taste and judgement as a connoisseur of the visual arts that was more widely admired. Already he was a munificent patron; and since he enjoyed contemplating likenesses of himself and his friends and was generous with them as presents, portraitists were continuously at work on his behalf.* His mother was constantly receiving pictures of him to add to her collection; one day a miniature would come, the next a 'fine print, most generally esteemed by those who [had] seen it', which it was hoped she might consider 'not entirely unworthy' of a place in her boudoir at Frogmore, her country house in the grounds of Windsor Park.[55] Prince Frederick was similarly favoured, once with a wax model of his brother which the Prince of Wales reckoned as being 'remarkably like, except its being too fat, especially about the chin';[56] and on a later occasion with a half-length portrait painted by Gainsborough who was commissioned to do a similar one for Gerard Lake.[57] Gainsborough was soon afterwards asked to paint other portraits of the Prince, of Anthony St Leger, and, for one of the rooms at Carlton House, portraits of three of the Prince's sisters.

---

the Prince undertook to pay for their unrolling and copying. Since the Cambridge scholar who was chosen to supervise the work proved utterly incompetent, the Prince's scheme, as he admitted, met with only 'partial success'. However, ninety-four of the papyri were copied, and the Prince was able to present the facsimiles to Oxford University which in 1810 rewarded him with the honorary degree of Doctor of Civil Law. (Hayter, *Herculanean Manuscripts*; MS. Gr Class, c 10, Bodleian, Oxford: Richardson *(George IV)*, 100–3).

* He was always delighted to sit for a portrait. When, for instance, Lord Charlemont expressed his 'anxiety to have his portrait painted by the first of painters', the Prince could not disguise his pleasure. He immediately offered to go to Sir Joshua Reynold's house 'whenever he was prepared to receive him' (HMCR, Charlemont MSS, ii, 116).

The Prince also asked Nathaniel Dance to paint his portrait, sat for Joshua Reynolds, and commissioned no less than thirty pictures from Richard Cosway. Nor were the Prince's commissions only for portraits; Gainsborough, for instance, was asked for two landscapes at a time when his work in this *genre* was not widely esteemed.[58] The names of other artists, who then or within a year or so regularly appeared in the Prince's accounts, were W. H. Craft, Richard Collins, John Hoppner – who provided portraits of Haydn, Nelson and the Duke of Bedford – George Garrard, George Romney and George Stubbs.[59]*

One of the earliest portraits of the Prince shows him as depicted by Stubbs trotting through a meadow with two little dogs by his horse's hooves. The Prince enjoyed riding at this time and was known to have ridden all the way from London to Brighton and back on the same day, covering a distance of 108 miles in ten hours.[60] He often went out fox-hunting and stag-hunting, too, riding as hard and long as his father, who encouraged his taste for the sport in the hope that it might distract him from more harmful pleasures. He also enjoyed shooting and considered himself 'an exceeding good shot',[61] though he once had the misfortune to wound Lord Clermont in several places with small shot during a shooting party in Norfolk.[62] Above all, he prided himself on his skill at four-in-hand driving, once in a phaeton-and-four covering twenty-two miles in two hours at a trot which, as he boasted to Prince Frederick, was reckoned 'pretty good driving'.[63]

If only, his father admonished him, he would spend more of his time in these healthy open-air pursuits instead of living so debauched a life in London, his character would be less open to censure. As it was, the King felt obliged to write frequent letters to his son, 'reprobating in each of them', observed a confidant to whom the Prince showed them, 'his extravagance and dissipated manner of living. They were void of every expression of parental kindness or affection'.[64] It was never suggested to him that he might occupy himself in some capacity that might fit him for his future office. As though he were jealous of his heir, indeed as though he hated him *as* his heir – a common sin of rulers – the King did all he could to keep his son well clear of positions of power and influence. As the

---

* Gainsborough died in 1788, and £1,262 was still owing to his widow in 1795 when considerable sums were also outstanding to all the painters mentioned above and to several others less well known. Cosway was owed £1,631. Stubbs £1,076. All were eventually paid (RA Geo. IV, Box 7).

Bishop of Llandaff put it to the Duke of Queensberry, 'he was a man occupied in trifles, because he had no opportunity of displaying his talents in the conduct of great concerns'.[65]

For want of anything more pressing to do, he spent hour after hour in the company of tailors and shoemakers, hosiers and mercers. John Rossi, the sculptor, was once kept waiting for three hours – the previous day for five hours – while the Prince tried on 'at least forty pair of boots' and conducted 'many trials of patterns and cuttings'.[66] To one of his father's angry reproaches about his trivial life and late rising, he was alleged to have bitterly replied that he always found the day was 'long enough for doing nothing'.[67]

4

The Secret Marriage
1784-1786

*

'Mrs Fitzherbert is arrived in London for the Season'

By the time of Fox's success in the Westminster election of 1784 relations between the Prince and his father had deteriorated so far that they seemed incapable of improvement. The King, he told Prince Frederick, was 'so excessively unkind' to him that there were moments when he felt he could 'hardly ever put up with it . . . sometimes not speaking to me when he sees me for three weeks together, and hardly ever at Court, speaking to people on each side of me and then missing me, and then when he does honour me with a word, 'tis merely " 'tis very hot or very cold" . . . and then sometimes when I go to his house never taking any notice of me at all, as if I was not there.'[1] The Queen, on the contrary, was much kinder to him now than she had been in the recent past; he could not say enough of what he felt for her; they were as close to each other as they had been when he was a child; her goodness to him was such that he would 'bear anything to save her a moment's uneasiness'.[2] But though he esteemed his father and used him with 'all possible duty, deference, and respect', he remained unalterably estranged from him.[3] Really, he concluded on a later occasion, 'he hates me; he always did, from seven years old. . . . He wants to see me at variance with my brother. . . . He will never be reconciled to me.'[4]

The King did not agree that he was used by his son with all possible respect. Indeed, in August 1784, when the Prince wrote to him to say that 'the very embarrassed situation' of his affairs made it necessary for him to ask permission to go abroad immediately,[5] the King in his reply described

44

his conduct as 'reprehensible'. Moreover, it had 'grown worse every year, and in a more glaring manner since his removal to Carlton House',[6] upon which well over £1,000 a month had been spent upon furnishings alone since he had taken possession.[7]

Although the Prince had told his father that he 'proposed only painting' the house and 'putting handsome furniture where necessary', in a 'very few weeks this was forgot'. 'Large additional buildings erected,' the King continued, increasingly indignant and ungrammatical, 'and, lest these should not waste enough money, the most expensive fêtes given, and at this hour considerable additional are again begun; yet the Prince of Wales chooses to term his difficulties as occasioned by necessary expenses. . . . If he has deranged his affairs he ought to take a manly resolution to diminish his expenses and thus establish a sinking fund to clear those debts, which would in some measure palliate with the public for an extravagance which everyone but his flatterers have universally blamed; the Prince of Wales ought to know that every step he takes is of consequence, that if he once loses the good opinion of this nation it is not to be regained.

'I have found myself under the disagreeable necessity of showing the Prince of Wales's letter to the Queen, who is as much hurt as me, and coincides in the opinion that if his improper plan [of going abroad] was put into execution his character would be for ever blasted in this country, and also in all Europe. I therefore insist on his giving up a measure that would be a public breach with me.'[8]

In defiance of this strongly worded warning, the following week the Prince repeated his intention of going abroad: he saw no 'fresh reason for altering his resolution of travelling' which his 'embarrassing difficulties' made absolutely necessary. He had 'an idea of residing for some time at Brunswick', an expedient that he hoped would meet with his Majesty's approbation, since he would be 'truly hurt' at a public breach. It was quite out of the question for him to make sufficient 'retrenchments out of [his] annual expence' to extricate himself from his difficulties. 'It would be merely a drop of water in the sea!'[9]

The King's reply to this was a short, firm injunction to the Prince from 'his father and his Sovereign strictly to charge and command him . . . not to leave the realm without having obtained particular leave'.[10] The King was, however, prepared to see what he could do to help the Prince out of his financial difficulties, and he asked Lord Southampton, as head of his Royal Highness's Household, to ascertain the exact amount of his debts.[11]

Reluctant to leave the country against the King's orders, though still protesting his intention of so doing at any moment, the Prince asked Southampton to get George Hotham, his Treasurer, to make out as accurate a statement of his debts as he could.[12]

Hotham was horrified by the figures which he accordingly unearthed, even though many items were not brought to his notice. He discovered 'with equal grief and vexation', as he told the Prince in a letter dated 27 October 1784, that he was totally in the hands and at the mercy of his builder, his upholsterer, his jeweller and his tailor, the two former of whom were carrying out works 'to an enormous amount, without a single care or enquiry from whence money was to arise for their discharge'. He had borrowed sums totalling £25,000, the particulars of most of which he had 'not yet been pleased to divulge'. Then there was the 'amazing expense' of the stables, which alone were costing no less than £31,000 a year, although the Prince's income was no more than £12,500 a quarter in all, excluding the 'precarious supply' from the Duchy of Cornwall. Yet far from finding that any economies were intended, Hotham discovered to his 'great mortification' that the cost of keeping race horses was to go up 'beyond all kind of calculation whatever'. It was clear that the Prince's 'torrents of expense' had run up the total amount of his debts to an immense figure, and that it would take months to arrive at an accurate estimate of them.[13]

In the meantime, it was scarcely surprising that the Prince felt wholly incapable of living on his present income and continued to express to his father his wish to live abroad to 'practice a system of economy'.[14] This, however, was not the real reason for his wanting to leave England. He had another, more urgent, secret reason which he was anxious that his father should not discover.

*

In a letter informing Prince Frederick of his resolve to live abroad, the Prince had referred to this secret; but since he knew that his packets were often opened in the post, he thought it 'safest to preserve it in petto' till he had the happiness of seeing his brother again. It was a secret which, combined with bouts of excessive drinking, had brought on a 'violent and nasty fever'. He had lost so much weight that he thought his brother 'cd. not possibly know' him.[15] The trouble was that he was once more in love and this time with a lady who composedly spurned his passionate advances.

This lady was Mrs Maria Fitzherbert, a widow six years older than himself, who had recently come to live in London after the death of her second husband at Nice. The Prince had seen her for the first time in Lady Anne Lindsay's box at the Opera; he had taken Lady Anne aside after the performance to ask her what angel it was that had sat beside her in a white hood.[16]

Mrs Fitzherbert was the eldest of six children of Walter Smythe, and the granddaughter of Sir John Smythe, a baronet of an old Roman Catholic family from the north of England. Little is known of her childhood, except that she was educated at an English convent kept by Conceptionist nuns in Paris and that on one of her holidays she was taken to see Louis XV dine in public at Versailles. Here she was so amused to see him pull a chicken to pieces with his fingers that she broke the customary silence by bursting into laughter, a breach of etiquette which was nevertheless rewarded by the present of a box of sugar-plums handed to her, on the King's instructions, by the Duc de Soubise.

At the age of seventeen she was married to a middle-aged landowner, Edward Weld, who died within a year, after falling from his horse. Three years later she married her second husband, Thomas Fitzherbert, who also died soon afterwards, leaving her a substantial income on which she was able to live comfortably, first at Nice and then in Paris before returning to England.

On her return she rented Marble Hill at Twickenham, a lovely house of the English Palladian School built by George II for his mistress Henrietta Howard. She also had a house in London, at the Oxford Street end of Park Street, the lease of which had been left to her by her husband. She lived quietly at first, rarely going out and seeing few people beyond the circles of her own family and of those other Roman Catholic families to which her marriages had related her. Then, in March 1784, the *Morning Herald* announced, 'Mrs Fitzherbert is arrived in London for the season'.

The appearance of this charming, graceful woman in society was an immediate success. She was not particularly good-looking; her chin was too big, her nose too long, her mouth ill-shaped; but she had a pleasantly rounded figure, a fine bosom and lovely dark brown eyes, while her clear skin and golden hair were as perfect as they had been at the time of her first marriage. She had a 'very mild, benignant' expression 'without much animation', and was 'rather heavy than brilliant in conversation', though a good, encouraging listener.[17] Everyone who knew her liked her, though those who knew her well had cause to complain of a certain haughtiness in her manner and a rather quick temper. Soon after seeing her for the first time the Prince was 'really mad for love'. In a letter Lord Wentworth received from his sister on 10 March, he was reported to be making 'fierce love to the widow Fitzherbert', and it was expected that he would succeed.[18]

In her turn, she was attracted by him, flattered by his attentions and obvious desire for her. But there could be no question of her becoming his mistress; she was devoutly Roman Catholic, irreproachably respectable. Yet if she could not live with him outside marriage for moral reasons, neither could she marry him for legal ones: the Royal Marriage Act stood in the way.[19] The more firmly she resisted the Prince's advances, the more passionate, the more feverishly excitable he became. Swearing that he could not live without her, breaking into tears, throwing himself upon his bed and threatening to kill himself, he wore his friends and attendants out by his recurrent outbursts of emotion. She meant far more to him, he protested, than any other woman, any other person in the world, had ever done; he would give up anything for her, he would forfeit all rights to the throne for her. And this he would undoubtedly have to do if he married her, for the Act of Settlement provided that anyone who married a Roman Catholic could never become monarch of England. Nevertheless, since she so firmly declined to become his mistress, he was determined to marry her, despite all the provisions of the Act of Settlement and the Royal Marriage Act. The year before, he had assured Prince Frederick, who had recommended the daughter of the Hereditary Prince of Hesse-Cassel as a suitable wife, that he did not intend to marry until he was 'near the area of thirty'.[20] But now at twenty-two – Mrs Fitzherbert was twenty-eight – he was determined to marry immediately. Less sure herself that she wanted to marry him or should marry him, and warned of his inconstancy, Mrs Fitzherbert decided to go abroad. On hearing of her intention, the Prince became more frenzied than ever; and one day in November he attempted in desperation to prevent her.

Four members of his Household arrived at her house in the 'utmost consternation' to tell her what he had done. They were Lord Southampton, Lord Onslow, the Hon Edward Bouverie, and Thomas Keate, the Prince's surgeon. They told her that 'the life of the Prince was in imminent danger – that he had stabbed himself – and that only *her* immediate presence would save him'. At first she refused to go, 'saying that nothing would induce her to enter Carlton House', fearing that once she went there her reputation would be irrevocably lost. They pleaded with her; she remained adamant; she would not go. At length she was persuaded to change her mind, provided that another lady went with her. The Duchess of Devonshire was selected as a suitable chaperone; and so, having called for the Duchess at Devonshire House on the way, the four men returned to Carlton House with Mrs Fitzherbert.[21]

The Prince was lying in a downstairs room overlooking St James's Park; he was covered in blood and very pale; a glass of brandy was by his side. What exactly had happened was somewhat obscure. The Prince said that he had stabbed himself with a sword; other reports had it that he had used a dagger, or that he had tried to shoot himself, had missed, and had then seized a table knife. A later rumour was to the effect that he had not stabbed himself at all, but had torn off the bandages which Keate had placed over his side when he had been blooded to relieve his feverish tension, had thereby opened up the wound and had smeared the gushing blood all over his chest and shirt. Whatever the cause of the bleeding, Mrs Fitzherbert was so overcome by the sight of it that she almost fainted; and when the Prince assured her that 'nothing would induce him to live unless she promised to become his wife, and permitted him to put a ring round her finger', she weakly assented. The Duchess of Devonshire removed a ring from her finger, and it was placed upon her own.[22]

As soon as she had arrived home and recovered her composure, Mrs Fitzherbert regretted what she had done. She did not afterwards blame the Prince, and always denied any suggestion that he had not been in earnest. To her relative, Lord Stourton, who said that he thought 'some trick had been practised', she upheld that this was certainly not so: she had 'frequently seen the scar'.[23] But Mrs Fitzherbert did blame the Prince's attendants for conspiring to take advantage of her shock to make her go through the ceremony of promising to marry him. She wrote a sharp note to Lord Southampton protesting against his conduct; and in a deposition written by the Duchess of Devonshire and signed by both of them she contended that 'promises obtain'd in such a manner are entirely void'.[24] The next day, accompanied by her friend, Lady Anne Lindsay, she sailed for France and made for Aix-la-Chapelle. From there she went on to Holland, and, after visits to Antwerp, Paris and Switzerland – where she saw a great deal of the Duke of Gloucester who found her 'a most aimiable and esteemable lady' and did all he could to 'make her long exil as bareable' as possible[25] – she settled at Plombières.

The Prince, quickly recovered from his wound, longed to follow her; and, according to Lord Holland, 'he did not conceal his passion, nor his despair at her leaving England for the Continent'.[26] Thus began the correspondence with the King in which he requested, and was refused, permission to live abroad on account of his mounting expenses and debts.

Although all reference to Mrs Fitzherbert was studiously avoided in this correspondence, it cannot have been long before his father heard of the affair which had become the subject of conversation and speculation in every drawing-room in London, and realized that his son wanted to leave the country for love and not for money. The fear that the Prince would get married to the woman in some foreign Catholic church must surely have appalled him.

Prevented by his father from following Mrs Fitzherbert as he had wanted to do, the Prince, having despatched agents after her to discover where she had gone, bombarded her with a series of fiercely passionate letters, beginning with one that scrawled its way over eighteen pages and ending with one that stretched to forty-two. He protested that ever since that day when she had promised to marry him at Carlton House, he had 'look'd upon [himself] as married'; he could not live without her; he would kill himself unless they were re-united; he had broken off connections with all other women. He called her his *dearest and only belov'd Maria*, his 'adored wife', his *dearest wife*, his *beloved wife*. He besought her never to marry anyone else but him, and in one letter (thirty-seven pages long) made the extraordinary promise that the King would 'connive' at their union. He pleaded with her to believe that he had not a single desire in life that did not 'center' on her.[27] 'Save me, save me,' he begged, 'save me on my knees I conjure you from myself.'[28]

'Come then, Oh! come, dearest of wives, best and most adored of women, come and for ever crown with bliss him who will through life endeavour to convince you by his love and attention of his wishes to be the best of husbands and who will ever remain until the latest moments of his existence, *unalterably thine*.' He inscribed himself *'her lover and her husband*, titles [he] would not exchange for the possessions of the whole universe'.[29] So many letters did he write and so many couriers were needed to carry them that the ceaseless activity aroused the suspicion of the French government, and three of the couriers were at different times arrested and thrown into prison.[30]

When he was not writing letters 'he cried by the hour', so Mrs Armistead told Lord Holland, and 'testified the sincerity and violence of his passion and his despair by the most extravagant expressions and actions, rolling on the floor, striking his forehead, tearing his hair, falling into hystericks, and swearing that he would abandon the country, forego the Crown, sell his jewels and plate, and scrape together a competence to fly with the object of his affections to America'.[31]

In his agitated state, the Prince began to drink more heavily than ever. Mary Noel was told that he had appeared at the opera soon after Christmas hopelessly drunk with three or four companions all in the same state. If he went on like this he would kill himself, she thought; for he had already been very ill.[32] A few months later she was further shocked to learn of his behaviour while staying at Lord Radnor's for Salisbury races. He was there with Lady Bamfylde, wife of Sir Charles Bamfylde, with whom he was seeking consolation in Mrs Fitzherbert's absence. 'He came to the ball on Wednesday last and made the town mad. He has got his present déesse, Lady Bamfylde, with him at Lady Radnor's which causes many speculations as Lady Radnor and still more my Lord was not thought to be inclined to that sort of politesse. Lady Bamfylde is the only woman in the house and the Prince opened the ball with her at Salisbury and drove her all the time the next day on the course in Mr Bouverie's phaeton. She is grown fat, old and ugly but his Royal Highness is not noted for his taste in females.'[33]

*

For over a year Mrs Fitzherbert remained on the Continent wondering what to do, 'irresolute and inconsequent' in Lady Anne Lindsay's words, changing her mind from day to day, once writing a letter to the Abbess of the English convent at Liège to ask if 'a couple of English ladies could have apartments in their house', but then deciding not to send the letter after all. Lady Anne seems to have found her rather trying and irritable. She quarrelled with her French maid who accused her of treating her servants *'comme des chiens'*; and sometimes she quarrelled with Lady Anne.[34] In November, tired of her self-imposed exile, she decided to return to England. 'I have told him I will be his,' she wrote to Lady Anne who had returned to England before her. 'I know I injure him and perhaps destroy for ever my own tranquility.'[35]

*

As soon as Charles James Fox heard of her return, he wrote to the Prince in an attempt to dissuade him from taking the 'very desperate step' he supposed must now be imminent. He was naturally anxious that the Prince, who had proved himself a staunch friend of his party, should do nothing to endanger his future succession to the throne; and so, in a long and concerned letter, he warned him of all the dangers and disadvantages that would attend his secret marriage, particularly in view of the nation's 'old prejudices against Catholicks' and in view also of the Duke of York being 'professedly' the King's favourite son, 'and likely to be married agreeably to [his] wishes'. In any case, the marriage could not be a real one because of the Royal Marriage Act; any children there might be would not be legitimate. If he were Mrs Fitzherbert's father or brother, Fox contended, he 'would advise her not by any means to agree to [a marriage], and to prefer any other species of connection . . . to one leading to so much misery and mischief'.[36]

The Prince, however, could not be dissuaded from his purpose. Lady Anne Lindsay hoped that he could be induced to marry Princess Louisa of Orange, a match which had been 'much pressed on him by his family'. She was 'grieved that affections so generous and tender as his seemed to be' should be lavished on the 'lovely, but inconsequent and violent woman' that she now considered Mrs Fitzherbert to be. She had painted a miniature of Princess Louisa, a 'pretty, pleasing and good girl', while she had been in Holland; but the Prince, refusing to consider anyone other than Mrs Fitzherbert, replied that he admired the artist more than the subject.[37] Before her flight abroad he had tried and failed to persuade Mrs Fitzherbert to become his mistress. He had therefore made up his mind to marry her, and marry her he would. But first he had to reassure Fox that he did not intend to do so. 'My dear Charles,' he wrote to him. 'Your letter of last night afforded me more satisfaction than I can find words to express; as it is an additional proof to me (which, I assure you, I did not want) of your having that true regard and affection for me which is not only the wish but the ambition of my life to merit. Make yourself easy, my dear friend. Believe me, the world will soon be convinced that there not only is, but never was, any ground for these reports, which of late have been so malevolently circulated.'[38]

Having thus by implication denied his intention of getting married, he continued the search he had already begun for a clergyman to perform the ceremony. A clergyman of the Church of England was required, as, before the second Relief Act of 1791, marriages, even between people who were both Roman Catholics, were not legally binding if they had been solemnized only by a Roman Catholic priest. Moreover, if the details of the marriage should ever become public knowledge, the fact that it had been performed according to the rites of the Church of Rome would be regarded as an added, unforgivable offence by the more earnestly Protestant people of the country. To find an Anglican parson willing to officiate was not easy, however, since the Royal Marriage Act provided that both the witnesses and the clergyman present at a marriage that contravened it were guilty of felony. His secretary unsuccessfully approached the Rev Philip Rosenhagen, a shady military chaplain, and he himself interviewed the Rev S. Johnes Knight, Rector of Welwyn in Hertfordshire, a sporting parson, fond of good food and drink, who, as a close friend of Lord North, had known the Prince since he was a child. The Prince, wearing a dressing-gown and apparently having just got out of bed, spoke to Johnes Knight in his dressing-room at Carlton House, stressing his great love for Mrs Fitzherbert, lifting up his shirt to show the scar on his side where he had fallen on his sword, and speaking of his determination to repeal the Royal Marriage Act the instant he came to the throne. 'If you refuse to marry me,' he said vehemently at length, 'I must find out another clergyman who will.'

'This vehemence of his made me apprehensive that the Prince might get some clergyman to marry him for the chance of Church preferment, and then that this same divine for a larger bribe would betray the Prince's secret to Mr Pitt, who was then Prime Minister,' Johnes Knight, who lived to be nearly a hundred, confessed to his daughter after the Prince's death. 'This made me unable to resist the Prince's importunity, and I could not bear to see him so miserable . . . Dearest Louisa, do not blame me for this weakness; bear in mind I was young, and could not help being flattered by the attentions of a Prince, who was one of the best arguers, in his own cause, I have ever known. . . . Whoever he wished to gain he talked to so frankly, and on subjects most interesting to his hearer, and his tact was so nice that he never failed in the most minute circumstance which he supposed might captivate those with whom he, for the present hour, chose to accociate.'[39]

Having agreed that he would be walking in the street outside Mrs Fitzherbert's house on a certain day between seven and eight o'clock in the evening, Johnes Knight left Carlton House 'after thanks in abundance' had been 'showered' on him. But no sooner had he got out into the street than the Rector lost his nerve and changed his mind. Pleading as an excuse a conversation he had had with Colonel Gerard Lake, recently returned from America, in the Mount Coffee House the evening before, when he had concurred with Lake's belief that no clergyman would be found to perform the threatened ceremony, Johnes Knight wrote to the Prince to be excused from his promise.

The Prince sent him 'a very kind answer' releasing him from his engagement, and renewed his search.[40] At length a suitably rash and ambitious clergyman was found. This was the Rev John Burt, a young curate, who was incarcerated in the Fleet Prison for debt. On the strength of a promise that he would be made one of the Prince's chaplains, that he would be created a bishop when the Prince became King, and that he would receive £500 with which to liquidate his debts, Burt agreed to undertake the service.*

At dusk on the evening of 15 December 1785 the Prince arrived at Mrs Fitzherbert's house and walked into the drawing-room, the doors of which were locked behind him. John Burt was already there; so also was Mrs Fitzherbert's uncle, Henry Errington, who had been guardian to his niece ever since her father, his brother-in-law, had become too ill to care for her himself. Errington had at first advised against the marriage, but recognizing that it would probably take place with or without his agreement, he had consented to give his niece away. The only other person in the room, other than Mrs Fitzherbert herself, was her younger brother, John Smythe.

The ceremony was conducted without interruption – it was afterwards said that Orlando Bridgeman, a mutual friend of the Prince and the Smythe family, stood guard outside the door – and when it was concluded the Prince wrote out a certificate of marriage which he, Mrs Fitzherbert, Errington and Smythe all signed. The certificate was given to Mrs Fitzherbert for her to keep in a safe place.[41] Immediately after the ceremony the Prince and Mrs Fitzherbert left for a short honeymoon at

---

* The Prince fulfilled his promise to Burt by appointing him a chaplain; but, before the larger promise of a bishopric could be fulfilled, Burt died at the age of thirty, having confessed his celebration of the marriage (*Abbot Diary* i, 68). Shortly before his death, while Vicar of Twickenham, he made application to be considered for the appointment of Dean of Peterborough, Rector of St George's, Bloomsbury, and Prebend of Rochester. The Prince supported the application which might have been successful had not the Lord Chancellor mislaid the papers (RA 5021-2, 38633-4: Asp/P, ii, 143, 212).

Ormeley Lodge on Ham Common near Richmond. The roads were deep in snow, and their carriage broke down at Hammersmith where they had supper at an inn before continuing their journey. The honeymoon was of no more than a week's duration; before Christmas they had returned to London where they already were the subject of constant inquiry and heated debate.

Apart from the witnesses, there were several people who knew for a fact that the wedding had taken place. These included the Duke and Duchess of Cumberland, Sir James Harris, British Minister at the Hague who on a recent leave in England had acted for the government in the still-continuing negotiations over the Prince's debts and had thereby gained his friendship and confidence, and one or two members of his Household. There were several others, like the Duke of Dorset[42] and Pitt,[43] who did not know for sure that the marriage had taken place, but who strongly suspected it; and there were many more who, having picked up hints from friends and acquaintances, spread rumours and reports which, so Horace Walpole said, reached 'even from London to Rome'. There was no other talk in the streets than the 'hubbub' about the marriage.[44] 'Surely there cannot be any truth in the reports of the Prince's being married to a Catholic widow?' the Earl of Denbigh asked Major Bulkeley. 'Is it believed or not? If true the consequences yet may be dreadful to our posterity'.[45]

Lady Palmerston said the general belief was that Mrs Fitzherbert was to move into Carlton House, if she was not in fact already there; that she had been married to the Prince by a Roman Catholic priest, and that she was to be granted £6,000 a year and made a Duchess.[46] The Duke of Rutland was informed by Robert Hobart on 27 December that the town buzzed with talk of the Prince's marriage: 'He has taken a box for Mrs Fitzherbert at the Opera, and constantly passes the greater part of the night with her. I do not hear of Prince Carnaby [Sir Carnaby Haggerston, husband of Mrs Fitzherbert's sister, Frances] being yet arrived in town. Walt Smith [Walter Smythe, her eldest brother] appears already much elated with the honour that is intended, or rather the dishonour which has already attended his family.'[47]

Another correspondent of the Duke of Rutland, Thomas Orde, was not at all certain that the Prince and Mrs Fitzherbert were married; the reports were 'full of contradictions'; many of the people said to be present were certainly not there, and the Rev S. Johnes Knight who was alleged to have performed the ceremony had assured Orde that he had certainly not done so.[48] But the Marquess of Lothian told the Duke a different story: 'You ask me my opinion respecting the Prince's marriage. I think it has all the appearance of being true. I believe, when he has been spoken to about it, he has been violent, but I cannot find out he has denied it peremptorily. Most people believe it, and I confess I am one of the number. Though I dined alone with him, and you know the general topic of his conversation about women, he never mentioned *her* to me amongst others. I am very sorry for it, for it does him infinite mischief, particularly amongst the trading and lower sort of people, and if true must ruin him in every light.'[49]

The Roman Catholic Lady Jerningham told her daughter Charlotte who was at an Ursuline Convent in Paris, 'Mrs Fitzherbert has, I believe, been married to the Prince. But it is a very hazardous undertaking, as there are two Acts of Parliament against the validity of such an alliance. . . . God knows how it will turn out – it may be the glory of our belief, or it may be to the great dismay and destruction of it! She had taken a box to herself at the opera, a thing which no lady but the Duchess of Cumberland ever did – a hundred guineas a year! The Prince is very assiduous in attending her in all publick places, but she lives at her own house, and he at his. Do you remember seeing her when she was the Widow Weld? She came to see me one morning in Charles Street and you found her face *too fat.*'[50]

It was quite true, as Lady Jerningham said, that the Prince and Mrs Fitzherbert lived in separate houses, though she moved from Park Street to a mansion in St James's Square which she rented from Lord Uxbridge so as to be nearer Carlton House. When they were seen out together at the opera or a private party, he behaved with the utmost deference to her, never forgetting to go through the form of saying to her 'with the most respectful bow, "Madam, may I be allowed the honour of seeing you home in my carriage?" '[51]

In these early months of their marriage, they were virtually inseparable: he let it be known that where he went, she was to be asked also; if she were not asked, he would not go. Moreover, the usual rules of precedence had to be suspended: she was always to be placed at the same table as himself.

Despite the ambiguity of her position, she was welcomed almost everywhere. The families of her first two husbands behaved rather coolly towards her; so at first did the Duchess of Portland and the celebrated hostess, Lady Sefton, whose husband's family was connected with the Erringtons. But these were rare exceptions. The rest of her family remained on good terms with her, as did the Duchess of Devonshire whose friendly reception of her after her return to England from the Continent encouraged other leading Whig ladies to treat her in the same way. Both she and the Prince were often to be seen dining with Lord and Lady Clermont at their splendid house in Berkeley Square where the Prince had the privilege 'of commanding a dinner and naming the persons to be invited of both sexes.'[52] Even the old-fashioned Tory, the Marchioness of Salisbury, received her at her house as she had done in the past.

But although Mrs Fitzherbert was welcomed back into society, although her gracious, unpretentious, quiet manner was universally commended, there were naturally those who felt that the exact nature of her status would have to be clarified. The caricatures of James Gillray, the finest draughtsman among London's political satirists, whose fame was by now rivalling that of James Sayers, were being sold in large numbers and were being perused and discussed in every coffee-house. One of them, which appeared in March 1786 and was 'designed by Carlo Khan', depicted the Prince and Mrs Fitzherbert being married in a French church. The officiating priest, wearing a cassock and an immense biretta, is Edmund Burke, well known for his advocacy of political concessions for Roman Catholics; the two witnesses are the Prince's disreputable friend the Hon George Hanger, and Sheridan, who stands with a napkin under his arm and a bottle of wine in each of his coat pockets, prepared to serve the wedding breakfast. The bride is being given away by Fox, who, as the Prince's intimate friend, was wrongly supposed to have connived at the match and was accused by the Prince's first biographer of having actually attended the ceremony which was alleged to have taken place at his house in Grafton Street.[53] The bridegroom is shown holding a ring in his right hand, with his bride's hand in his left, and looking upon her magnificent bosom with evident pleasure. A sequel to this caricature, entitled 'The Morning after Marriage', portrays Mrs Fitzherbert sitting on a bed and putting on one of her stockings as the Prince, resting on a table with garter hanging down towards slippered foot, stretches and scratches his head.

If the reports to which such caricatures gave rise were not true, the Marquess of Lothian thought it was high time they were 'publicly contradicted'. He was 'amazed that some member of Parliament has not mentioned it in the house'.[54] No one did mention it in the House, however, until the Prince's continuing financial difficulties induced him to provoke discussion of it himself.

*

Happy as the Prince was with Mrs Fitzherbert, the 'most unpleasant business' of his mounting debts was a constant source of distress. The King was prepared to help him, but, as he often assured him, there were certain points which 'must be cleared up first' if the matter was to be discussed any further. 'I can as yet form no judgment of what steps can be taken,' the King complained, 'as I neither know the amount to which his debts have now arisen, nor what security there will be that his future expenses shall be confined within his income.'[55]

In his reply the Prince confessed that his 'load of debts' had increased to nearly double what they had been two years before. In fact, when Colonel Hotham had finished doing his complicated sums a month later it appeared that the total amounted to no less a sum than £269,878 6s. 7¼d.[56] Faced with this fearsome figure the King held it 'impossible to enter on the consideration of any means to relieve him until' he had received 'a sufficient explanation of his past expenses' and saw 'a prospect of reasonable security against a continuance of his extravagance'. It 'would be necessary to have as clear an explanation as the nature of the thing will admit, of his past expenditure, and above all to ascertain that it will be confined within proper limits in future'.[57]

The Prince, deeming it impossible to give either the explanation or the undertaking demanded, answered loftily that his father would receive no further disturbance from him, as he was now convinced that he had 'no reason to expect either at present or in future the smallest assistance from [his] Majesty'.[58] If the Prince chose to interpret what had passed in this way, the King briefly replied, that was his own affair and the consequences of his doing so could be 'imputed only to his own determination'.[59]

It was hinted to the Prince that his father would prove more amenable if the Prince would marry some suitable foreign princess. But when this matter was mentioned to him, the Prince burst out vehemently, 'I will never marry. My resolution is taken on that subject. I have settled it with Frederick. No, I will never marry. . . . Frederick will marry, and the crown will descend to his children . . .'[60]

It was also suggested that the King might prove less intractable if the

Prince were to abandon his open support of the Whig opposition. This, however, was equally impossible. He would never 'abandon Charles' and his other friends.[61]

So the Prince decided to make a dramatic gesture: he would shut up Carlton House, sell his carriages and his horses, and dismiss his Household with the exceptions of Hotham, Lake, Samuel Hulse, one of his equerries, and Henry Lyte, his Master of the Robes and Keeper of the Privy Purse, who were now all to be known as his Inspectors of Accounts.[62] He took a 'firm determination not to appear again in public' till he could do so 'with that dignity and splendour' to which his rank in life entitled him.[63]

Except for the King, who felt that the Prince was flaunting his poverty before the world merely to draw attention to his father's meanness, and for Prince Frederick, recently created Duke of York, who was 'sincerely sorry that things [had] gone so far' and that his brother had thought it necessary to take 'so very publick a step',[64] most people commended the Prince and sympathized with his decision. The Duke of Cumberland had the 'happyness of assuring' him from Spa that his 'manly conduct' was 'universally approved'.[65] His brother, Prince William, who was himself in acute financial embarrassment due to 'the old gentleman' keeping him 'under like a slave', wrote from his naval station at Dominique to commend him 'extreamly'.[66] Fox cordially congratulated him on his 'manly and judicious step' which had 'united the universal opinion of all descriptions of men in his favour'. But Fox also thought it advisable to suggest that £35,000 to £40,000 a year of his allowances from the King should be assigned to trustees for the express purpose of paying it to his creditors by instalments, as otherwise the Prince's enemies would say that he was merely saving up the money to spend later upon himself.[67]

Well-wishers, with or without hopes of future gain, offered him various sums of money. John Lethbridge, a rich Somerset landowner who was created a baronet in 1804, offered 'some few thousands' for the Prince's present use.[68] Sir Charles Barrow, Member of Parliament for Gloucester and a leading supporter of Fox, asked him to 'condescend to accept' £2,000.[69] Wisely, the Prince declined the money. He had determined upon total renunciation until provided with what he considered a proper allowance. It was supposed that he might leave the country until this was done, and go to live in Hanover. Instead he left for Sussex, 'an *outside passenger on the Brighton Dilly*',[70] leaving Mrs Fitzherbert to follow him later.

5

Brighton and Westminster
1786-1787
*

'A subject of the greatest delicacy'

Only a few years before, Brighthelmstone, as it was then generally called, had been no more than a small fishing town whose cramped, squat houses were constantly threatened by the encroaching sea. In two fearful storms at the beginning of the century, much of the town had been swept away; and by the 1720s it was feared, so a visitor recorded, that the sea 'would eat up the whole town, above one hundred houses having been devoured by the water in a few years past'.[1]

The fortunes of Brighthelmstone began slightly to improve in the next decade when it became a port of embarkation for the Continent and a packet-boat sailed weekly for Dieppe; but by 1740 there were probably no more than a thousand inhabitants living *'almost underground'*. It was not a place that attracted many visitors, though within the next few years there appeared one or two bathing-machines on the beach and, on occasions, a man or woman could be seen floundering in the sea – the women in long flannel gowns attended by Amazonian 'dippers', the naked men accompanied by 'bathers' whose duty it was to ensure that their charges were thoroughly immersed.[2]

Then, in 1753, a doctor from Lewes built himself a house on the sea-front. This was Dr Richard Russell whose advocacy of bathing in sea-water – and even drinking sea-water – as a sovereign cure for various ailments had long been celebrated and whose medical treatise, *A Dissertation Concerning the Use of Sea Water in Diseases of the Glands,* originally written in Latin, had appeared in an English translation the year before. For some time Dr Russell, much impressed by the sparkling sea and invigorating air of Brighthelmstone – or Brighton as it soon came to be called – had been sending his patients there for a cure which involved bathing in the sea, drinking its water – combined with a macabre variety of preparations, from crab's eyes and burnt sponge to snails, tar, lice and viper's flesh – and, inevitably, blood-letting. The success of this cure, followed by Dr Russell's own arrival in the town and the subsequent discovery nearby at Hove of a spring of chalybeate waters, whose beneficial properties rivalled those of Tunbridge Wells, ensured the future of Brighton as a popular seaside spa.

By the time Mr and Mrs Henry Thrale had become regular visitors to Brighton in the late 1760s – and occasional hosts there to Dr Johnson – the two principal inns, the Castle Tavern and the Old Ship, had been considerably enlarged. Both of them were provided with elegant Assembly Rooms, the Castle's being designed by Robert Adam's disciple, John Crunden, the architect of Boodle's Club in St James's, the Old Ship's by Robert Golden, who also designed a 'set of baths' for one of Dr Russell's successors, Dr John Awsiter. Soon the hot and cold sea-water baths near the Steine (the broad thoroughfare where the roads from London and Lewes meet) were famous all over England.

The Duke of Gloucester had visited the town in 1765, and some years later the Duke of Cumberland had spent the first of several seasons there, renting first Dr Russell's house on the front, and then Grove House, the Hon George Windham's large, red-brick, bow-fronted mansion on the Steine. It was to Grove House that the Prince of Wales had come on a visit to his uncle and aunt, the Cumberlands, in September 1783.

It had been a Sunday, and the bells of the town had been rung in greeting. The guns of the battery had fired a royal salute; and in the evening the streets had been illuminated and a display of fireworks had been given outside Grove House. The Prince had stayed for eleven days, going for walks, riding out with the stag hounds, attending a performance at the North Street Theatre and a ball at the Assembly Rooms at the Castle Inn, 'the most splendid ever known at that place'.[3]

It was clear that he had liked Brighton very much and had found the company of his raffish uncle far more congenial than that of his censorious father. It had been exhilarating to be able to escape from the restrictions of his parents' staid Court, and the 'usual circle of old tabbies', to the lubricious delights of Grove House.[4]

The next summer the Prince had returned, apparently on the advice of his physicians who had advocated sea-bathing as a cure for the swollen glands in his throat, an unsightly affliction which distressed him deeply and which, it was said, led to his wearing those extremely high, starched neckcloths that became so fashionable.

On his second visit to Brighton, the Prince had stayed once more at Grove House, and had enjoyed himself even more than on his previous visit. He had been able to go to Brighton Races which he had just missed the year before; he had bathed in the sea; and on a groin on the beach one day he had met a pretty, well-shaped girl, though 'one of the most illiterate and ignorant of human beings', Charlotte Fortescue.[5] Struck again by a *coup de foudre*, the Prince had besieged her with protestations of his love, imploring her to abandon herself to his passion. Like Mme von Hardenburg, she had contrived to hold him off while provoking and increasing his desire; but the desire had soon been quenched when he found out that Miss Fortescue, while seeming so fresh and innocent in her nervous, appealing rebuffs of his advances, had been displaying an unseemly enthusiasm for the rakish charms of the Hon George Hanger. The Prince had evidently found other, more complaisant girls, however, for as the *Morning Post* informed its readers, 'The visit of a certain gay, illustrious character at Brighton, has frightened away a number of old maids, who used constantly to frequent that place. The history of [his] gallantries ... has something in it so voluminous, and tremendous to boot, that the old tabbies shake in their boots when his R— H— is mentioned.'[6]

Either on this visit to Brighton or on the next in the summer of 1785, the Prince had decided that he would like to have a house there of his own, and had asked Louis Weltje to find him one.

Weltje was far more to the Prince than his Comptroller and Clerk of the Kitchen and Cellars as those who recognized his untidy figure and porcine features in Gillray's cartoons well knew. He was admittedly an expert cook, despite an unpromising training as a baker of Westphalian gingerbread; but it was his keen financial sense and his adroitness as a negotiator that particularly recommended him to the Prince as a valued servant. Self-important, not to say arrogant, he had for some years worked in the Duke of Brunswick's kitchen before coming over to England, where he opened a club in St James's Street. He became a naturalized British subject in 1786; but he never learned to speak English properly, giving his orders in the kitchen and conducting his negotiations in a 'barbarous

Anglo-Westphalian jargon'.[7] This, however, had not prevented his acquiring a handsome fortune from his property speculations.

The house he chose for the Prince at Brighton was on the east side of the Steine, 'a respectable farmhouse' with a pleasant view of the seafront. It was leased from Thomas Kemp, Member of Parliament for Lewes, whose son, an indefatigable builder, was later to give his name to that part of Brighton known as Kemp Town. Although the arrangements for its lease had not yet been concluded, it was presumably to this house that the Prince, intent upon economy, retired from London in July 1786, establishing Mrs Fitzherbert in a small villa nearby.

Here on the Steine at Brighton, the Prince spent the summer and early autumn of 1786, living quietly, walking about the town and along the front, bowing and smiling to the passers-by who greeted him with friendly respect, passing the days – though he was still only twenty-four – as any retired gentleman on holiday might have done. He gambled a little, though he was not now, as he said himself, really 'a gaming-man'. He drank far less than usual and entertained but a few of his London friends other than Sheridan, who was almost his only contact with the gay London world of Devonshire House and the Pantheon, of green-rooms and Brooks's, which he appeared to have utterly rejected. He seemed quite content to walk and drive and talk with Mrs Fitzherbert who was said to be pregnant.[8]*

*

* Mrs Fitzherbert never denied having had children. Her relative, Lord Stourton, wrote to Lord Albemarle in 1833 to suggest that she might write on the back of the marriage certificate, 'No issue from this marriage.' To this, so Lord Stourton said, 'she smilingly objected on the score of delicacy'. The year before her death, however, she wrote a paper which ended with the words. 'I Maria Fitzherbert moreover testify that my union with George, Prince of Wales, was without issue.' But although she indicated a space where the document was to be signed, she never did sign it.

Sir Shane Leslie investigated the story that a son of the marriage, known as James Ord, was taken to America and educated by Jesuits at Georgetown College with funds provided by the British Embassy. He found little evidence to support the story. He did, however, believe that it was less easy to dispose of the story that Mrs Fitzherbert's adopted niece, Mary Anne Smythe, was in reality her daughter by the Prince. She was supposed to have been the illegitimate daughter of Mrs Fitzherbert's brother, John Smythe, who, according to family information, had no children. She married the Hon Edward Stafford-Jerningham, brother of Lord Stafford. Her grandson, the late Lord Stafford, thought that there was 'strong circumstantial evidence' to support the family tradition that his great-grandparents were Mrs Fitzherbert and the Prince of Wales.

There was also talk of a boy born in 1793 at Lille where Mrs Fitzherbert, who was then

The summer passed and the autumn, and the Prince moved from Brighton to various borrowed houses, to the Duke of Gloucester's house at Bagshot, to Lord North's mansion, Bushey Park. For six months he persevered in his determination to economize; but he found it very hard. Mrs Fitzherbert believed that the King would eventually relent and come to his help. The Prince, however, entertained no such illusion and knew that he would have to make approaches elsewhere. For a time he was tempted to borrow in France, as he was urged to do by the Duke of Orleans, but Sheridan succeeded in dissuading him from taking so compromising a step. If he could not turn to France, then, the Prince insisted, he must turn to Parliament.

Few of his Whig supporters encouraged such a move: to bring up the matter of the Prince's finances in Parliament would almost certainly lead to questions being asked about Mrs Fitzherbert whose 'Reported Marriage to the Prince of Wales' was the title of a recent, widely read ironical pamphlet by the politician and former clergyman, John Horne Tooke. In this pamphlet, it was argued that 'a most amiable and justly valued female character' was '*legally*, really, worthily, and *happily for this country*, her Royal Highness the Princess of Wales'.[9] In view of the strength of Protestant feeling in the country, it would be disastrous for the Opposition if they were shown to be supporting the claims of a man who was married to a Roman Catholic. It was the Duke of Portland's firmly held opinion that the less said about the Prince of Wales in Parliament the better. *Quieta non movere* was his motto for the day.

The Prince, however, was not prepared to let sleeping dogs lie much longer. He must raise more money. His recent conduct could not have failed to win him a good measure of public support. If the Whigs would not raise the subject on his behalf in Parliament, an independent Member must be found who would. Such a Member presented himself in the form of Alderman Nathaniel Newnham, a rich and independent merchant, who sat for the City of London.

---

thirty-seven, was alleged to have gone after a quarrel with the Prince, and of another boy, brought up by Sir James Harris and given his name. Her adopted daughter, Mary Seymour, intimated in later years that Mrs Fitzherbert had had more than one child by the Prince. But although she certainly loved children and told Lady Jerningham that she would have liked to have had 'a dozen of her own', it seems unlikely that the birth of babies could so successfully have been concealed from their parents' contemporaries who were constantly expecting them. No references to any children that there may have been of the marriage survived the later destruction of most of her papers; nor are there any references to children of hers in the Royal Archives.

On 20 April 1787 Alderman Newnham rose in the House to ask 'whether it was the design of Ministers to bring forward any proposition to rescue the Prince of Wales from his present very embarrassed situation. For though his conduct during his difficulties had reflected greater honour and glory on his character than the most splendid diadem of Europe had upon the wearer of it, yet it must be very disagreeable to His Royal Highness to be deprived of those comforts and enjoyments which so properly belonged to his rank.' To this, Pitt replied that it was not the government's duty to bring forward such a subject except at the command of the King and they 'had not been honoured with such a command'. Undeterred by this, Newnham gave notice that he would bring forward a motion on 4 May.[10]

Anxious to forestall the embarrassing disclosures that might ensue, Pitt, 'perceiving that the House was so full', took the opportunity on 24 April 'of alluding to a subject of the highest importance' and 'the greatest delicacy'. He wished to know 'the scope and tendency of the motion coming on next week'. After a pause, Newnham cautiously repeated that its object was 'to rescue His Royal Highness from his present embarrassed situation';[11] and three days later, regretting that the government had taken no steps to rescue the Prince themselves, he moved that 'an humble address be presented to His Majesty, praying him to take into his royal consideration the present embarrassed state of affairs of His Royal Highness, the Prince of Wales, and to grant him such relief as his royal wisdom should think fit'.

At this point, there rose a sturdy figure on the Tory benches, a bluff, down-to-earth Church of England squire from Devon, John Rolle, who commented in the full, thick dialect of his county that the question had extremely grave implications because it was 'a question which went immediately to affect our constitution in Church and State'. Now, as one Member put it, 'the fat was in the fire'. There could be no other question involving Church and State than that concerning the alleged marriage of the Prince to Mrs Fitzherbert.

Fox was not in the House that day and it was left to Sheridan to uphold the Prince's cause. At first he affected not to comprehend Rolle's meaning. Then, when Pitt stood up to threaten that, if Newnham persevered in his motion, he might be driven, 'though with infinite reluctance, to the disclosure of circumstances which he should otherwise think it his duty to conceal', Sheridan countered by bravely suggesting that the insinuations which had been thrown out made it quite impossible for the friends of the Prince of Wales to withdraw their motion. Fearing that he had gone too far, Pitt later that day withdrew the ineffectual threat he had made earlier: the particulars to which he had alluded, he now claimed, related 'only to the pecuniary embarrassments of the Prince of Wales' and had nothing to do with 'any extraneous circumstances'.[12]

Sheridan had played his part in the game of bluff and counterbluff with considerable skill; but the game was not yet ended, and when he went that night to make his report at Carlton House, part of which had now been opened up again, the Prince was much agitated.[13] They both well knew that John Rolle and his supporters would not let the matter rest in the unresolved state in which the debate had left it. It was all very well for the Prince to reply haughtily that he 'never received verbal messages except from the King' when Pitt, through Lord Southampton, made some sort of apology for the indiscreet words he had let slip in the House. But some positive action would have to be taken the next time the matter was raised. The Prince recognized by now what this action would have to be; and Sheridan, who was on good terms with Mrs Fitzherbert, was sent to call upon her to warn her that some explanation would have to be made. Without mentioning outright the possibility that the marriage might have to be denied, Sheridan urged her to consider how extremely dangerous the Prince's position was, and how the least hint from her that there was a secret hidden in their relationship might ruin them both. Mrs Fitzherbert had no intention of saying anything; her loyalty to the Prince was absolute and unshakeable. She was also aware of her own danger. She was 'like a dog with a log tied round its neck,' she said to Sheridan. They 'must protect' her.[14]

Sheridan certainly felt concerned to protect her. But his affection for her was not shared by Fox. Mrs Fitzherbert had made it clear to Fox that she disapproved of him. She had never forgiven him for suggesting that the Prince should make her his mistress. Consequently Fox's friendship with the Prince, though outwardly as cordial as ever, had not been the same since his young friend had fallen under her influence.

Fox was well aware of the dangerous ground on which he would be treading, but he would derive much satisfaction from formally denying the marriage in the House. He would thus floor Pitt and Rolle and the rest of his and the Prince's Tory adversaries, remove objections to an open discussion of the Prince's finances, and clear himself of the charges implicit in newspaper columns and caricatures that he had been present at a wedding which he had, in fact, strongly opposed and which, so far as he had been led to believe, had not even taken place.

He had the Prince's letter assuring him that 'there never was any grounds for these reports . . . so malevolently circulated'. He had also, apparently, since then referred in the Prince's presence to the continuing and persistent rumour of his marriage but the Prince had 'contradicted the supposition at once, with *"pooh"*, "nonsense", "ridiculous", etc.'[15] To the end of his life, whenever occasion demanded, the Prince continued to deny that he had ever been married to Mrs Fitzherbert. It was as though he had actually succeeded in persuading himself that the ceremony had never taken place; or, if it had taken place, that it was illegal and therefore not a real marriage at all, and consequently one that could be denied with impunity.

In any case, Fox was prepared to deny it; and on 30 April, in a crowded and expectant House, he did deny it in unequivocal terms, referring with passionate indignation to the 'miserable calumny', the 'monstrous report of a fact which had not the smallest degree of foundation'. It was a 'low malicious falsehood', a 'tale in every particular unfounded' for which there was not 'the shadow of anything like reality'. He denied 'the calumny in question . . . *in toto*, in point of fact as well as law. The fact not only never could have happened legally, but never did happen in any way whatsoever.' He had His Royal Highness's 'direct authority' for this declaration.[16]

Although John Rolle remained unconvinced, observing that 'the House would judge for themselves of the propriety of the answer' which had been given to him, Fox was satisfied when he left the House that his conduct had been just and proper. Some time later, however, at Brooks's he met Orlando Bridgeman who came up to him and said, 'Mr Fox, I hear that you have denied in the House the Prince's marriage to Mrs Fitzherbert. You have been misinformed. I was at the marriage.'[17]

Fox now understood that he had landed himself in a most dangerous position. Even though the deception was the Prince's and not his, he had been the means of conveying the lie to the House. Yet, if he recanted, it would mean the ruin of the Prince's reputation together with his own political hopes, for he felt sure that the Whigs would never regain power without the Prince's support. He prudently decided to say nothing more on the matter. For a year he contrived to avoid meeting the Prince, who nevertheless continued in correspondence to address him as 'my dear friend' and proposed himself as a guest at a country house where he knew Fox would be staying in the unfulfilled hopes of meeting him there.[18]

Mrs Fitzherbert's dislike and distrust of Fox were naturally deeper than ever now that he had as much as declared that she was the Prince's mistress, the position to which he had long before hoped to consign her. When the Prince visited her on the morning of 1 May, he took hold of her hand and caressed her and, according to one report, said to her, ' "Only conceive, Maria, what Fox did yesterday. He went down to the House and denied that you and I were man and wife! Did you ever hear of such a thing?!" Mrs Fitzherbert made no reply, but changed countenance and turned pale.'[19]

According to his own account, given years afterwards, the Prince found Mrs Fitzherbert already 'in an agony of tears' when he arrived. She was 'deeply afflicted and furious against Fox'.[20] Lady Anne Lindsay confirmed that she 'burst into tears, said that she had indeed been shamefully used, that the Prince had been "LIKE A MAD THING" at the liberty Fox had taken in exceeding his commission, but that as to herself she did not care three straws about the matter'.[21] But later she angrily complained to Sir Philip Francis that Fox had 'rolled her in the kennel like a street walker; that he knew every word was a lie, and so on, in a torrent of virulence'. Francis, feeling himself incapable of damming the torrent, gave up trying to do so and made his retreat 'as well and as fast' as he could.[22]

Clearly something would have to be done to pacify her, the Prince decided. She was so angry that her character and religion had been thus compromised that she threatened to break off all connection with him, and for a time she refused to see him.

The Prince had felt 'more comfortable' on the night after Fox's denial had been made in the House,[23] but he was far from comfortable now. He sent for Charles Grey, one of Fox's friends, who found him very agitated, 'pacing in a hurried manner about the room'. Somehow Fox's denial must be modified in such a way that Mrs Fitzherbert would be pacified, and would return to him. 'Charles certainly went too far last night,' he complained. 'You, my dear Grey, shall explain it.' Then he admitted 'with prodigious agitation' that a ceremony had taken place.

Grey declined to smooth the matter over, since to do so would be to 'question Mr Fox's veracity'. His Royal Highness must speak to Fox himself. 'This answer chagrined, disappointed and agitated the Prince exceedingly; and after some exclamations of annoyance he threw himself on a sofa, muttering, "Well, then, Sheridan must say something." '[24]

Sheridan was more amenable than Grey. He immediately agreed to do what the Prince required of him, though to salvage Mrs Fitzherbert's name while implying at the same time that no marriage had taken place was no enviable task. He rose to attempt it in a speech to the Commons on 4 May.

The House settled down to listen to him in a mood of indulgence. Within the past two or three days agreement had been reached over the matter of the Prince's finances, and Alderman Newnham had been 'extremely happy' to announce that he now declined bringing his motion forward. John Rolle had caused a few moments' tension by observing 'that if it should hereafter appear that any concession had been made humilitating to the country, or dishonourable in itself, he would be the first man to stand up and stigmatize it as it deserved'. But most Members were prepared to express their satisfaction with William Drake, a Member notorious for the loudness of his speeches, who provoked a 'universal roar of laughter' when he said that he would like to declare his 'unfeigned joy in what had occurred' by joining in the general expressions of contentment with his own 'feeble voice'.

Sheridan's speech was long, conciliatory and equivocal, combining flattering remarks about the Prince of Wales's honourable behaviour in the embarrassing affair now so happily concluded with the requisite references to *'another person . . .* on whose conduct truth could fix no just reproach, and whose character claimed, and was entitled to, the truest and most general respect'.[25]

Sheridan acquitted himself as well as any Member could have expected him to do. The House murmured its approval; but it could not be supposed that Members were convinced either of the Prince's honourable conduct or of the irreproachable situation of the other person. Indeed, Daniel Pulteney, an independent Member, said that when they heard Sheridan emphasizing how 'truly respectable' was Mrs Fitzherbert's situation so soon after Fox had dragged it through the gutter, 'everyone smiled'.[26]

Mrs Fitzherbert herself was only partially mollified. Gillray portrayed her holding a crucifix and sitting abandoned on a rock, while, in a boat named *Honour*, the Prince and Fox sail unconcernedly away, the Prince protesting, 'I never saw her in my life', and Fox supporting the denial, 'No, never in his life, damme'.

She still refused to see the Prince, who worked himself up into one of his familiar violent fevers for which he was severely bled. To offset the debilitating effects of the bleeding he drank great quantities of wine, and when wine failed to produce the desired result he tried liqueurs of 'every description'.[27] At a ball at Lady Hopetoun's he arrived so 'stupified' that he could do nothing but sit down and gaze about him, 'pale as ashes, with glazed eyes set in his head'. Supper and an accompanying bottle and a half of champagne were, however, only too restorative. He 'posted himself in the doorway, to the terror of everybody that went by, flung his arms round the Duchess of Ancaster's neck and kissed her with a great *smack*, threatened to pull Lord Galloway's wig off and knock out his false teeth, and played all the pranks of a drunken man upon the stage, till some of his companions called for his carriage, and almost forced him away'.[28]

A few weeks after this ball the Prince was reported to be 'in great danger';[29] and, as he had done in the days when he had first fallen in love with Mrs Fitzherbert, threatened to kill himself.

Although she could not but feel that the Prince had thrown over her reputation for the sake of an increased allowance, Mrs Fitzherbert began to relax in her hard attitude towards him. She was encouraged to do so by the sympathy with which she was received and the respect with which she was treated in London society. As the Archbishop of Canterbury noticed, it was all 'very odd'; she was 'more received than ever' she had been before and stood 'more forward'.[30] 'I do not know what rules the ladies govern themselves by', Edmund Malone wrote to Lord Charlemont. 'She is courted and queens it as much as ever.'[31] The Duchesses of Cumberland and Devonshire remained unwavering in their support; the Duchess of Portland warmed to her; Lord and Lady Sefton, who had been far less friendly of late, welcomed her back to their house; even the Tory Duchess of Gordon, who was on good terms with the Queen, announced her belief that Fox had lied, and invited both Mrs Fitzherbert and the Prince, now partially recovered from his illness, to a ball. They both accepted, and were seen dancing together.[32]

So all was forgiven at last. The Prince and Mrs Fitzherbert were reconciled once more, and it was hinted that Fox had exceeded his instructions. The Prince, whose birthday that year had not been noticed at Court, was once again welcomed at Windsor. The Queen greeted him affectionately. The King spoke to him for three hours, and the Prince assured his father that he did 'most sincerely mean never to incur any future debts, which must indoubtedly be as disagreeable to the King as painful to himself'.[33]

6

The King's Illness
1787-1788
*

'An agitation of spirits nearly bordering on delirium'

The final settlement was that the Prince would receive another £10,000 a year from the King out of the Civil List, and from Parliament £161,000 with which to pay his debts, together with £60,000 towards the completion of Carlton House. His finances in order at last, he returned to Brighton on 6 July 1787 with Mrs Fitzherbert in a more contented frame of mind than he had enjoyed for many months.

The 'pretty picturesque cottage' on the Steine which Weltje had taken for him had by now disappeared and had been replaced by a far more imposing structure on which one hundred and fifty craftsmen and labourers, under the direction of Henry Holland, had been hard at work for several weeks.[1]*

This first version of the Prince's Marine Pavilion was a long, low Graeco-Roman house faced with cream-coloured tiles, the centrepiece of which was a domed rotunda encircled by six Ionic columns bearing classical statues. The handsome, bow-fronted wings which flanked the rotunda to north and south were provided with those decorative ironwork balconies which were soon to become so distinctive a feature of the town.

The brightly-coloured interior, like the interior of Carlton House,

* The financial arrangements were that Weltje should lease the house at a rent of £150 with an option to purchase it, and that he should pay for its enlargement and improvement, letting it to the Prince at an agreed rent compatible with its improved condition. Weltje's total outlay, including £5,850 for the freehold of the house and grounds, and all the builders' costs, was £22,338; the rent was fixed at £1,000 a year, rising in 1799 to £1,155. The Prince eventually bought the property for £22,000; and Weltje was glad to be rid of it, for he experienced great difficulty in collecting the money due to him (RA 31467).

owed much to French influences, as befitted a fashionable supporter of the Whigs. The corridors were painted 'French blue'; the library was 'fitted up in the French style' with yellow-papered walls; the dining-room was painted yellow and maroon with a pale blue ceiling. The Prince's bedroom, over the breakfast room in the southern wing, was hung with quilted chintz; and as he lay in his bed, which was curtained like a tent and draped in green and white chequered silk, he could enjoy, by means of judiciously placed looking-glasses, 'an extensive view of the sea and Steine'.[2]

The Prince and Mrs Fitzherbert spent most of the rest of that year in Brighton. The Prince, a journalist reported, had never been seen 'in better health or more buoyant spirits'.[3] He walked every evening in obvious contentment on the Steine; he played cricket in a white beaver hat in the Pavilion grounds; he regularly attended the performances at the theatre in North Street; each morning, if the weather was fine, he went down to bathe in the sea, attended by Brighton's famous 'bather', the tough old sailor 'Smoker' Miles. Indeed, he did not like to miss his bathe even when the sea was rough; and on one occasion he came down on to the beach and walked purposefully towards his machine as the waves crashed upon the shingle with the utmost violence.

'I shall bathe this morning, "Smoker",' he said to Miles.

'No, no, Your Royal Highness, it's too dangerous.'

'But I will.'

'Come, come, this won't do,' protested 'Smoker', standing in front of the Prince with his fists raised and clenched like a boxer. 'I'll be damned if you shall bathe. What do you think your royal father would think of me if you were drowned? He would say, "This is all owing to you, 'Smoker'. If you had taken proper care of him, poor George would still be alive." '[4]

The Prince gave way with good humour and walked back to the Marine Pavilion. His good humour this year was, in fact, proverbial, as all who knew him then agreed. His servants were devoted to him, finding him at once a generous and understanding master, who never dismissed any of them unjustly or failed to provide them on retirement with a satisfactory pension.[5]* To the tradesmen of the town, to which his patronage was

---

* The Prince's annual bill for pensions paid to former servants, servants' dependants, old friends, superannuated mistresses and their relations increased each year, until by the time of his death it amounted to £20,252. Among the pensioners listed in the Royal Archives are Charles James Fox's widow in receipt of £500 a year, Louis Weltje's widow, £90, four illegiti-

bringing such prosperity, the Prince was a very paragon, even though his bills were not always paid with the most exact promptitude. A characteristic story was told amongst them of one of their number, overwhelmed with business worries, who had tried to commit suicide. Hearing of the man's distress, the Prince – though he usually chose to give away money personally, deriving an obvious pleasure from the gratitude evoked – had immediately despatched a page to the unhappy tradesman with the contents of his pocket-book. 'Bid him make use of these,' he had instructed the page. 'I may perhaps owe him something, and under the circumstances the routine of payment must appear odious.' The pocket-book was found to contain bank-notes to the amount of over £700.[6] The Prince was quite as spontaneously generous, though rather more discriminating in the amounts of his largesse, towards the various charities of the town.*

Even the most censorious could find little to complain of now in his general conduct. On 9 August the usually condemnatory *Morning Post* informed its readers that he was gaining 'many hearts by his affability and good humour'. He was also 'certainly more sober'; and his company was 'much better than it used to be'.

At the time of the Lewes races that year his company included the stately Duchess of Rutland, the Princesse de Lamballe, Lord and Lady Abergavenny and Lord Clermont, a perfectly respectable party. To be sure, the Duke and Duchess of Cumberland and the wicked little Duke of Queensberry were also members of it, but there were no stories of wild or

---

mate sons of his brother, Prince William, £200 each, and numerous retired servants granted sums ranging from £200 for a housekeeper to £30 for 'the late page Hownam's children' (RA Geo. IV. Box 7; RA 30269–30270).

The Prince's generosity is also evident in his annual bill for contributions to charities. He gave £1,000 each year to the 'poor of London' and a great number of lesser sums to all manner of worthy causes and needy individuals. £10. 10s, for example, went to the 'Committee appointed for bettering or abolishing the present disgraceful Trade by Chimney Sweepers' (RA 30066). £6. 6s went to one Sarah West who wrote to him, 'I am one of the unfortunate women that have lived with officers – you know there is no provision for them (it would be Encouraging Vice) – I resided with Lieut Hill of the 64th Regiment in the American War – and was the mother of four children' (RA 30306).

* He did not always remember to fulfil his promises, however. Sir John Macpherson told Sir Nathaniel Wraxall that when the Prince heard that Flora Macdonald, the Jacobite heroine, was still alive and living in reduced circumstances, he displayed much concern and asked Macpherson to pay her a pension of £50 on his behalf. 'She died at the end of two years,' Macpherson added, 'but his Royal Highness entirely forgot to reimburse me, and the annuity came out of my own pocket' (Wraxall, v, 356–7).

indecent behaviour. For this Mrs Fitzherbert was given much of the credit.

Now that Fox was keeping out of the Prince's way, her influence over him was said to be complete, while his behaviour towards her was more attentive and courteous than ever. Present after present arrived for her at her house in Brighton until he had spent well over £50,000 on jewellery, silver and furniture for her.[7] In London he took and furnished a splendid house for her near Carlton House in Pall Mall, where she lived as though she were indeed Princess of Wales. Here homage was paid to her by her numerous friends and those who wished to profit – though few ever did profit – from her intimacy with the Prince, and here she entertained in truly regal style. Her old friend Mary Frampton was invited to one of her assemblies and found that, although her own manners remained 'quiet, civil and unpretending' and no one ever accused her of using her great influence improperly, she was surrounded with all the magnificent trappings of a princess. She was attended by a respectable lady of impeccable antecedents, Miss Isabella Pigot; male attendants in green and gold 'besides the usual livery servants, were stationed in the rooms and up the staircase to announce the company, and carry about refreshments, etc. The house was new and beautifully furnished – one room was hung with puckered blue satin. . . . A whole length portrait of the Prince of Wales was conspicuous in one of the drawing-rooms and his bust and that of the Duke of York, ornamented the dining-room.'[8]

The Duke, after an absence of over six years, had at last been permitted to come home and the Prince, in high excitement, had driven all through the night to Windsor to greet him. In the early years of his stay in Hanover, the Duke had been much annoyed that his brother, who was a very lazy correspondent, did not write to him more often. On several occasions he had been driven to scold him for his 'excessive long silence', to complain that he had been quite forgotten, that it was a 'little hard' not to receive a single line for ten months at a stretch. Eventually he 'lost all patience'.[9] But now this irritation was entirely forgotten in the excitement and pleasure of reunion. They hugged each other warmly after gazing silently into each other's eyes, and the Prince was moved to tears. He invited his brother down to Brighton and gave a splendid party there to celebrate his return. He proudly introduced him to Mrs Fitzherbert, who grew very fond of him – as most people did – and then took him off to London for further celebrations. It seemed, indeed, as though the Prince had merely been waiting for the excuse of his brother's homecoming to relapse into the dissolute life from which Mrs Fitzherbert appeared to have saved him.

The Duke's friend and the head of his Household, Major-General Richard Grenville, a 'silent, reserved' man[10] who had accompanied him to Hanover and had now returned with him, complained that they were 'totally guided' by the Prince of Wales and 'thoroughly initiated into all the extravagances and debaucheries of this most *virtuous* metropolis'.[11] General James Grant, who sat in the Commons for Sutherlandshire and was notorious for his own gormandizing, confirmed that the Prince had taught his brother to '*drink* in the most liberal and copious way, and the Duke in return has been equally successful in teaching his brother to lose his money at all sorts of play – quinze, hazard, etc., to the amount, as we are told, of very large sums'.[12] Within a few months, however, the Prince's behaviour was to provoke far stronger condemnation than this.

*

Early one morning in October 1788 the King sent an urgent message to his physician, Sir George Baker, asking him to come to see him 'as soon as convenient' and to bring with him 'one of the opium pills in case the pain should not have entirely subsided'.[13]

The pain of which the King complained was 'a very acute' one 'in the pit of the stomach shooting to the back and sides, and making respiration difficult'. It had seized him so violently in the middle of the night that he had been rendered speechless for several minutes. He had suffered something of the sort in 1765 and in the summer of 1787 when he had been forced to lie down on his bed as the only tolerable posture he could find; but that painful attack had passed within a few days and he had regained his strength at Cheltenham, although his behaviour there had struck some observers as being more than a little eccentric. This new attack was considerably more severe and was attended by other unpleasant symptoms: he complained of cramp in the legs and of severe rheumatism which afflicted all his limbs and made him lame; his arms displayed the remains of a rash which he had shown the week before to his daughter, Princess Elizabeth, who had remarked how 'very red' it looked, 'and in great weals, as if it had been scourged with cords'.[14]

Sir George gave it as his opinion that the illness was caused by the King's 'having walked on the grass several hours, and, without having changed his stockings, which were very wet, went to St James's; and that at night he ate four large pears for supper'.[15] Castor oil and senna were prescribed; but these resulted in further 'excruciating pain' in the stomach which necessitated a dose of laudanum. The laudanum counteracting the purgatives, these were repeated which necessitated a second dose of the anodyne. 'Within twenty-four hours,' the Queen's Lady of the Bedchamber, Lady Harcourt recorded, 'he took three doses of each.'[16]

By the end of this period he was feverish; the whites of his eyes had turned yellow and his urine brown. The next day both his feet were swollen and painful; and by 20 October his stomach was again so agonizing that he could not attempt 'an erect posture'. With characteristic conscientiousness, he tried to attend to business by writing a letter to Pitt, and by commenting on the despatches he had received from him; but he found he could not concentrate. He made mistakes; he repeated himself; he wandered off the point; his handwriting grew big and shaky until he was forced to conclude, 'I am afraid Mr Pitt will perceive I am not quite in a situation to write at present.'[17]

Two days later his mental distress had increased to such an extent that when Sir George Baker called upon him he found his patient 'in a most furious passion of anger'. For three hours he railed against Sir George, castigating him and his accursed remedies, threatening to forbid the importation of senna into the country, ordering that it must never be given to any member of the Royal Family, repeating himself frequently, displaying 'an agitation of spirits nearly bordering on delirium'.[18]

In spite of his deplorable condition the King insisted, after spending a quieter night than usual, in appearing at the levee at St James's on 24 October to prove there was no cause for alarm, to 'stop further lies and any fall of the stocks'. His appearance was scarcely likely, however, to dispel worry; for his dress was disordered, his legs were wrapped in flannel, and his speech was slurred and hurried. On his return to Windsor it was clear that the effort had considerably worsened his condition.

No one was at all sure what exactly this condition was. Sir Gilbert Elliot recognized that the King was 'certainly in a bad state of health', but he did not think that the complaint was anything too serious.[19] The *Morning Post* assured its readers that it was a sort of dropsical disorder, 'by no means of the alarming kind';[20] while the *Gentleman's Magazine* announced that it was no more than 'a regular fit of the gout'.[21]

At Windsor, though, it was obvious to all who came into contact with his Majesty that his illness was something far worse than gout or dropsy. Fanny Burney, Queen Charlotte's Keeper of the Robes, who encountered him unexpectedly on the evening of the day after the levee, found that he spoke in 'a manner so uncommon that a high fever alone could account for it; a rapidity, a hoarseness of voice, a volubility, an earnestness – a vehemence, rather – it startled me inexpressibly'. 'He is all agitation, all emotion,' Miss Burney continued in her journal the next day, 'yet all benevolence and goodness, even to a degree that makes it touching to hear him speak. He assures everybody of his health.'[22]

He admitted, though, that he could not sleep any more; and once in the Queen's dressing-room, Miss Burney heard him tell his wife 'at least a hundred times' not to speak to him when he got to his own room next door for he was greatly in need of rest. He lost weight and began to look very frail. To Lady Effingham, one of the Queen's Ladies of the Bedchamber, he said pathetically, showing her the walking stick without which he could not get about any more, 'My dear Effy, you see me all at once an old man.'[23]

The Queen grew 'more and more uneasy' on his behalf, and although she tried to appear calm the effort was sometimes beyond her, and alone in her room she burst into tears.[24] She again sent for Sir George Baker, who on arrival at Windsor on Monday 27 October found the King attending a concert throughout which he talked continually, 'making frequent and sudden transitions from one subject to another . . . and was continually sitting and rising'.[25] The previous day in chapel he had stood up suddenly in the middle of the sermon, and throwing his arms round the Queen and the Princesses, had exclaimed loudly, 'You know what it is to be nervous. But was you ever as bad as this?'[26]

He realized, before Baker did, that he was in danger of losing his reason. 'They would make me believe I have the gout,' he complained, kicking one foot against the other, 'but if it was gout, how could I kick the part without any pain?' He knew only too well that he was becoming excessively loquacious, but once he had started talking he found it almost impossible to stop. He told his attendants to keep him quiet by reading aloud to him, but he kept on talking just the same.

Music lost its power to soothe him, and he began to experience difficulty in hearing it.[27] He also began to find it difficult to read; 'his vision was confused . . . a mist floated before his eyes'. He 'likewise mentioned to me, as a cause of great distress,' Baker recorded in his diary, 'that having in the morning selected a certain prayer, he has found himself repeating a prayer which he had not proposed to make use of'.[28] Then one day, apparently, he burst into tears on the Duke of York's shoulder and cried out in anguish, 'I wish to God I may die, for I am going to be mad.'[29]

Both the Duke and the Prince of Wales had been most attentive to their father so far. The Prince came up from Carlton House to visit the King on 30 October, and the Duke, who was at Windsor the next day, assured his brother that their father had spoken of him 'with tears in his eyes and with the greatest affection', saying how happy he had made him by coming to see him. The Prince himself, so the King said, also wept to see his father so ill.[30] Thereafter the Duke sent regular reports upon their father's health to his brother who himself returned to his apartments in the Castle on the morning of 5 November.[31]

That day, however, as Fanny Burney recorded in her diary, proved to be a 'dreadful' one. Looking down from the window of her room before the Prince's arrival, she had seen the King go out for a ride in his chaise with the Princess Royal. He gave orders to the postilions and got in and out of the carriage twice with such agitation that her 'fear of a great fever hanging over him grew more and more powerful'. When he returned, Miss Burney's fears were temporarily dispelled. The Princess Royal came in 'cheerfully and gave, in German, a history of the airing and one that seemed comforting'.[32]

Soon afterwards the Prince of Wales arrived, and after a private conversation with the Queen, they went in to dinner. During the course of the meal, the King became more and more agitated until, the conversation turning to the subject of murder, he suddenly rose from the table and in a delirium of rage seized the Prince by the collar, pulled him out of his chair and hurled him against the wall. The Queen fell into violent hysterics; the Prince burst into tears, and was only prevented from fainting by his distracted sisters who rubbed his forehead with Hungary water. Later he decided, as he invariably did when excessively upset, that he must be bled.

On examining the King after this outburst, Sir George Baker decided that he was now 'under an entire alienation of mind and much more agitated than he had ever been. The pulse was very quick'; so restless were the patient's movements that he could not count the strokes. The next morning the rate was 'at least 120; but after bleeding it fell to 100'.[33] His eyes, the Queen told Lady Harcourt, were like 'black currant jelly, the veins in his face were swelled, the sound of his voice was dreadful; he often spoke till he was exhausted . . . while the foam ran out of his mouth'.[34] He was heard to repeat, in a voice so hoarse and tired that the words were scarcely articulate, 'I am nervous. I am not ill, but I am nervous. If you would know what is the matter with me, I am nervous.'[35]

It was decided that he must be moved out of the Queen's bedroom into a dressing-room next door. He was told that the Queen herself was ill, otherwise he would not have gone; and in the middle of the night he insisted on getting out of bed to satisfy himself that she had not been removed from the house. For half an hour he stood by her bed, staring down at her, the curtains in one hand, a candle in the other.

The next night he again insisted on getting out of bed and going into the room next door. The Queen had now been taken to an apartment further down the corridor, and in her place he found the Prince of Wales and the Duke of York, the physicians, equerries, pages and attendants sitting on chairs and sofas round the walls. He demanded to know what they were all doing there, and then began talking of his dear son Frederick, his favourite, his friend. 'Yes,' he croaked, 'Frederick is my friend.'

Sir George Baker was urged to lead his patient back to bed; but, too timid to lay hands upon him, he merely made a few hesitant suggestions which drove the King to such a fury that he penned him in a corner, upbraiding him for being nothing but 'a mere old woman' who knew nothing of his complaint. By signs and whispers, the Prince tried to get someone else to draw the King away, but no one dared approach him until Colonel Stephen Digby, the Queen's Vice-Chamberlain, who had had some experience of insanity in his own family, took him boldly by the arm and led him back to his room.[36]

From now on the King's condition grew progressively worse. He became more violent and uncontrollable, occasionally overcome by convulsions of his arms and legs and hands. He sweated profusely and 'complained of burning'. He still talked endlessly, one day rambling on 'for nineteen hours without scarce any intermission', and sometimes talking 'much unlike himself', that was to say 'indecently'. He gave orders to persons who did not exist; he fancied London was flooded and commanded his yacht to go there immediately; he persuaded himself he could see Hanover through Herschel's telescope; he composed despatches to foreign courts on imaginary causes; he lavished honours on all who approached him, 'elevating to the highest dignity . . . any occasional attendant'. He had to be forced to have a bath and, after refusing to be shaved for a fortnight, he allowed the barber to attend to one side of his face but not the other. He grew so thin that looking-glasses were either covered with green cloth or removed altogether lest the sight of his emaciated figure should give him a fatal shock.[37]

Sir George Baker being so obviously exhausted and so utterly bewildered by the case – as well as being 'rather afraid' of his patient[38] – it was decided to call in other advice, despite the King's rooted aversion to all physicians. First came the ancient and highly respected Dr William Heberden who was living in retirement at Windsor. Then came Dr Richard Warren, sent by the Prince of Wales 'unknown to the Queen who', as Lady Harcourt said, 'would never have consented to the calling in a physician to whom the King had a particular objection'.[39] It was not only that Warren was the Prince of Wales's physician, he also attended the Dukes of Devonshire and Portland, Charles James Fox and numerous other members of that fashionable society which the King so deeply distrusted. He was accepted with patent reluctance and distaste by the Queen, who was soon describing him as 'that black spirit';[40] while the King, a few days after his arrival, ordered him out of the room, pushed him when he would not go and, 'pale with anger and foaming with rage',[41] turned his back on him. Warren did not take long to make up his mind that the King's life was in the 'utmost danger', that the 'seizure upon the brain was so violent, that, if he did live, there was little reason to hope that his intellects would be restored'. He informed the Prince of Wales accordingly.[42]

Warren, whose arrival at Windsor was as eagerly welcomed by the other doctors as it was angrily condemned by the King and Queen, was soon followed by yet another consultant, Dr Henry Revell Reynolds, when it was feared that His Majesty was about to die. Ten days later when that crisis was passed, a fifth doctor was summoned, Sir Lucas Pepys.

It was sadly evident that none of them had the least idea what their patient's illness was, nor how it should be treated. Pitt, who was summoned to a conference at Windsor by the Prince of Wales in the second week of November, found them all wholly mystified, incapable of determining whether the illness was one 'locally fixed on the brain' or a 'translation of a disorder from one part to another'.[43] They agreed that 'on the whole there was more ground to fear than to hope', but it would be at least a fortnight before they could 'venture even to pronounce' a tentative prognosis.[44]*

---

* The King's malady has recently been diagnosed as a particularly virulent form of a rare hereditary metabolic disorder known as porphyria, endemic in the Stuarts and transmitted to the Hanoverians by the Electress Sophia, granddaughter of James I and mother of George I. Its victims suffer from abdominal pain, discoloured urine, weakness of the limbs, neuritis and mental derangement leading to rambling speech, hallucinations and to symptoms of hysteria, paranoia and schizophrenia which a layman might loosely term madness. (Macalpine and Hunter, 172–6). The diagnosis has been questioned (*The Times Literary Supplement* 8, 15, 22, 29, Jan. 1970) by a few historians and various experts in prophyria research, but most historians of the period have found it convincing.

7

The Regency Crisis
1788-1789

*

'The Prince has taken command at Windsor'

The inability of the doctors to diagnose the patient's illness, and the equivocal reports that consequently emanated from Windsor, led to constant speculation in London. 'His recovery is hopeless,' Sir Gilbert Elliot told his wife, and others were confidently assured that his death was imminent.[1] Captain John Willett Payne, one of the Prince's most intimate friends and a frequent visitor to Windsor, was presumed to have inside information about what was happening at the Queen's Lodge. He provided his friends in London with garbled accounts of the King's condition, told Sheridan, on the evidence of the Duke of York, that his Majesty's situation was 'every moment becoming worse', his pulse 'weaker and weaker', and said it was impossible that he could survive much longer.[2]

Indeed, so 'extremely current' were reports of his death within the next few days that on 11 November the *Morning Chronicle* was induced to print a categoric denial. But the rumours continued to circulate as wildly as ever, and even if the King were not yet dead, it was 'a probability amounting almost to certainty', so the Marquess of Buckingham was informed, that the insanity was now 'fixed'.[3]

This belief was reinforced by the Prince of Wales's physician, Doctor Warren, who confidentially informed Lady Spencer, the Duchess of Devonshire's mother, in Latin on 12 November that '*Rex noster insanit*'. Warren subsequently gave Pitt his opinion that there was 'every reason to believe that the disorder was no other than direct lunacy', and that the King might 'never recover'.[4] Not all the other doctors, however, were as

82

gloomy in their prognoses as this. Although Baker told Pitt that the patient was 'in a perfectly maniacal state',[5] on the same day Sir Lucas Pepys reassured Fanny Burney that 'there was nothing desponding in the case', and that the King would 'certainly recover, though not immediately'.[6] Another doctor who was called in for consultation towards the end of the month expressed himself as being 'favourable as to a possibility, and even a prospect of recovery'.[7] This was Dr Anthony Addington, Pitt's family doctor and a former keeper of a private madhouse at Reading – a town which, he claimed, without giving his reasons for an assertion that cannot have much endeared him to its inhabitants, contained an unusually high proportion of lunatics.[8]

Contradictory as were the opinions of the doctors as expressed in private conversations and letters, their public accounts which were sent each day to St James's were equally confusing. Well aware that their statements were not only of vital political importance but were read by the royal family at the time and would be seen by the King himself if he recovered, they could scarcely be blamed for their cautious and non-committal bulletins. Nor could they be surprised that their evasions and inconsistencies increased public unrest to such an extent that Sir Lucas Pepys feared for his life if the King did not recover. He and his colleagues received threatening letters by every post; and Sir George Baker's carriage was stopped by the mob who demanded to know what the King's present condition was. On being told it was a bad one, they cried out, 'The more shame for you!'[9]

The widespread alarm, the rapid fall in the value of stocks, the sudden popularity of the King now it appeared that his son would succeed him, were all, as Lord Bulkeley said, 'very little flattering to the Prince'.[10] Yet the Prince's conduct so far in the crisis had not been exceptionable. To be sure, there were stories that, being denied access to his father's room for fear lest he increase the patient's agitation, he had spied on him. Sheridan's sister said that he tiptoed into the room and peered at his father through a hole in a screen. The King looked up, saw the eye and called a page, whereupon the Prince hastily withdrew. 'I have seen my son,' the King said. They assured him he had not. 'However he persisted, and when he found they still denied it, gave no other answer but a most significant glance at the screen.'[11]

It was also alleged by William Grenville that the Prince had taken his friend Lord Lothian into the King's room when it was darkened so that he could 'hear his ravings at a time when they were at their worst'.¹² And Thomas Rowlandson, in an unusually offensive print entitled 'Filial Piety', depicted the Prince leading two drunken companions into the King's bedroom and calling out, 'Damme, come along. I'll see if the old Fellow's – or not.' But the Prince's sympathizers told different stories which were closer to the truth.

Sir Gilbert Elliot said that he was 'under greater restraint in his behaviour and way of life' than he had ever been since he had been his own master; he had given a most favourable impression by his attention to his father. His behaviour had been 'exemplary'.¹³

Lord Loughborough agreed that it had gained the applause of all men, even of those who were secretly glad that he remained so unpopular.¹⁴ Lord Sheffield asserted that his conduct at Windsor had gained him 'great credit'.¹⁵ Sheridan testified to the 'universal sentiment of warm and respectful approbation of the whole' of his Royal Highness's conduct 'during this critical and arduous trial'.¹⁶ And Colonel William Fullerton, Member of Parliament for Haddington Burghs, fulsomely told Captain Payne that the 'general applause and admiration' which the Prince had excited 'in the mind of every man by the superior manner of his acting in such trying scenes [was] considered by the nation at large as affording the best grounded expectations and prognostications of his future government'.¹⁷

This government, to which Fullerton and Payne and all their friends looked forward with such eager anticipation, seemed to draw closer and closer as the month of November ended. There appeared so little improvement in the King's condition that it was decided he must be removed to Kew, where he might take exercise in the garden 'without being overlooked or observed', and where the doctors might attend him with less inconvenience to their various London practices. Since it was known that the King would strongly resist being moved to Kew from his beloved Windsor, the Cabinet was summoned to the Castle on 27 November by the Prince of Wales to approve the move and to hear what the physicians had to say about the present state of the King's illness.¹⁸

The Cabinet decided that the advice of the physicians 'ought to be followed', and it was settled that the King should be moved to Kew on 29 November. When told of this decision, the King 'strongly objected' to it, refusing to get out of bed. The doctors could not persuade him, nor could Pitt, who returned to Windsor that morning to ensure that all went well. Nor could the King's Groom of the Bedchamber, General the Hon William Harcourt; nor could his Equerry, Colonel the Hon Robert Fulke Greville, whom the Prince of Wales sent into his room with instructions to urge his Majesty to prepare himself for the journey. At this last interruption the King became 'very angry and hastily closed the bed curtains'.[19] The Prince himself, fearful of the consequences, made no attempt to intervene personally; and when Dr Warren did so, the King jumped out of bed and had to be held back by his pages from assaulting him.

Eventually it was recognized that the King was not to be persuaded, and he was told that, if he continued his refusal any longer, force would be used. Reluctantly he allowed himself to be driven off with three equerries and an escort of cavalry.

On arrival at Kew he once more became violent when he learned that he was not to be allowed to see the Queen and his daughters, although he had been assured that he would be. He attacked one of his pages, pulled another by the hair and tried to kick a third. He continued violent the next day, ate very little, 'refused all medicine and threw what he could away'.[20]

From now on 'the unfavourable symptoms of his disorder' greatly increased. At nights he was 'almost unmanageable' and had to be tied to his bed, and by day he begged his pages to put an end to his miserable life. He swore, and uttered strange indecencies.

Soon after his arrival at Kew, on 3 December, the doctors were again examined on oath by the Privy Council in an attempt to ascertain the present 'situation of the King'. *The Times* that morning had complained of the 'truly ridiculous' contradictions in the reports respecting his health, yet the evidence of the doctors left the members of the Council as much in the dark as they had been before their examination. They all agreed that he was for the moment incapable of public business and that it was impossible to conjecture the likely duration of the illness. But whereas Baker, Pepys, Reynolds and Addington all gave it as their distinct opinion that the King could probably be cured, Warren was far more hesitant. In a confused, halting answer he used the word 'insane'; he mentioned an 'unknown distemper'; he said that on the data available it was impossible for anyone to judge whether or not the King would recover.[21] At the end of the meeting Lord Camden said to the Duke of Leeds, 'Dr Warren is a damned scoundrel, tho' I believe him to be a very able physician, and I dare say you will agree with me in both.'[22]

Able physician or not, Dr Warren was soon to have yet another colleague at Kew who entirely disagreed with both his prognosis and his methods. This was Francis Willis, an elderly clergyman who had been granted a medical degree by Oxford University and had shown exceptional skill in the treatment of symptoms of madness. One of his patients had been Lady Harcourt's mother, whose severe mental disorder he had been given the credit of curing. He was also well thought of by the Lord Chancellor, since several wards of the Court of Chancery had been entrusted to his care with satisfactory results. Not everyone was as convinced of his prowess as Lady Harcourt and Lord Thurlow, however. Lord Sheffield said that he was 'considered by some not much better than a mountebank, and not far different from some of those' that were confined in his mad-house in Lincolnshire.[23] His colleagues at Kew, and Dr Warren in particular, were more inclined to share this opinion of him than Lady Harcourt's. Indeed, Dr Willis was considered both socially and pro-fessionally unacceptable, his qualifications, such as they were – he was not a member of the Royal College of Physicians – being considered to render him fit for a position little more important than that of head keeper.[24]

The King, to whom he was introduced on 5 December, did not take at all kindly to this new doctor, the eighth that had been imposed on him.* He greeted him calmly enough, making a considerable effort to appear composed, assuring him that although he had been ill he was now quite well again. When Willis admitted that he was a clergyman, however, the King became agitated once more. 'I am sorry for it,' he said emotionally. 'You have quitted a profession I have always loved, and you have embraced one I most heartily detest.'

'Sir,' Willis is alleged to have replied, 'Our Saviour Himself went about healing the sick.'

'Yes, yes,' agreed the King crossly, 'but He had not £700 [a year] for it.'[25]

Later he 'launched out in strong invective' against all his physicians and earnestly demanded that Dr Willis should take Dr Warren under his care and go back with him to his madhouse in Lincolnshire.[26] By the end of his first day's attendance, in fact, Willis was as violently disliked by the King as ever Warren had been. When he informed his patient sternly that he was mentally deranged and required 'attention and management', the

---

* The seventh doctor, Thomas Gisborne, a retired physician to St George's Hospital, had been called in at the end of November.

King attempted to assault him as he had tried to assault Warren; but Willis was quite prepared for this. His method, he told Colonel Greville, was to 'break in' his patients as horses were broken. He threatened the King with 'a strait waistcoat' if he did not control himself, and went to get one from the next room to show him what it looked like.[27]

From that day onward Dr Willis, his two sons and three of his keepers who followed him to Kew, ensured that the King was kept firmly in submission. Whenever he refused his food, either because he found it difficult to swallow or had no appetite, whenever he became too restless to lie down quietly on his bed, whenever he sweated so much that he threw the bedclothes off, he was put in the straitjacket. Later, he was confined in a specially made chair – his 'coronation chair' he called it – to ensure his 'compliance with whatever [was] thought proper'. And once when he was tied in the chair to be given a severe lecture on his repetitive and improper remarks about Lady Pembroke, that beautiful and adored woman who had adorned the Court of his youth, Willis stuffed a handkerchief into his mouth to keep him quiet until the reprimand was completed.[28]

Confined in his chair or his straitjacket when he was violent, blistered when it was considered necessary 'to divert the morbid humours' from his head, the King was also doctored with a formidable variety of medicines. He was given calomel and camphor, digitalis, quinine, and, as an emetic, tartarised antimony which made him so sick that he knelt on his chair fervently praying that he might either be restored to his senses or allowed to die.[29]

The weeks went by and, as Fanny Burney said, the patient 'went on now better, now worse, in a most fearful manner', sometimes sweating so profusely that his clothes were drenched, 'very irritable and easily offended' and with a racing pulse, at other times in 'good humour' or 'high spirits', occasionally lying down on his bed and singing, always having to suffer confinement when he was deemed in need of either punishment or coercion. Repeatedly he said that he could 'never more wear the crown, and desired his eldest son might be sent for'.[30]

The Prince of Wales, however, was not sent for. At Windsor he had assumed full responsibility and, as Fanny Burney said, 'nothing was done but by his orders, and he was applied to in every difficulty. The Queen interfered not in anything . . .'[31] The Queen, indeed, was growing daily more morose and sulky, so irritating the Prince with her sullen complaints and grumbles that he felt driven to behave towards her in a way that her Keeper of the Robes described as most heartless and high-handed. He gave his orders 'without any consideration or regard for his mother's feelings', she said, knocking his stick on the floor, condemning everything that had been done before he took control, and retiring from her presence without kissing her hand.[32]

The result of this conflict was, so Lord Bulkeley told the Marquess of Buckingham, that once the Prince took command at Windsor, there was '*no command whatsoever*'.[33] It was consequently resolved that the Prince should be given no opportunity of managing the Household at Kew, a duty which eventually therefore devolved upon the unwilling Queen. It was bad enough, the Queen had cause to complain, to live at Kew at all, for it had never been intended to serve as a winter residence – it was so cold and draughty that sandbags had to be placed against the ill-fitting windows and doors – but to be placed in the position of having to give her consent to measures which she knew could only infuriate the King was intolerable. It was additionally distressing that in his agitated moments the King not only 'talked much of Lady Pembroke' – sometimes indecently – but also 'much against the Queen', eventually coming to the conclusion that 'all marriages would soon be dissolved by Act of Parliament'.[34]

In her unhappiness the Queen grew increasingly resentful at the attitude adopted by the Prince of Wales and by the Duke of York who spent so much of his time in his brother's company. She had been particularly annoyed with them, and indeed had flown into a rage with them when, soon after her arrival at Kew, they had wisely taken it upon themselves to remove to safe-keeping the King's jewellery, money and papers that were lying about on tables and in unlocked drawers. The Queen, whose extreme fondness of jewellery was well known, suspected some ulterior motive and began to abuse her sons. They retorted with equal harshness, insisting upon handing the valuables over to the Lord Chancellor.[35]

Even more intolerable to the Queen was the fact that both her sons accepted the opinions of Dr Warren – who continued to insist that the King was 'in a decided state of insanity' and who supplied them and their friends with reports in support of this belief[36] – whereas the contradictory reports of Dr Willis, in which she herself placed her faith, were condemned by her sons as 'mere fabrications' concocted for a 'sinister purpose'.[37]

The official bulletins which were sent to St James's were certainly fabrications. The doctors could never agree on how they should be worded and the Queen, insisting on the right to see them before they were despatched, asked for alterations in them when she thought them insufficiently discreet. Since they were so unreliable, Warren suggested that he and his colleagues ought at the same time to make independent reports of the King's mind to the Prince of Wales, who was not allowed to see his father on the grounds that the patient's mind would be too much disturbed by the visit. All the other doctors agreed except Willis who informed Warren by letter that such a procedure would be totally against his normal practice.[38] Warren took the letter to the Prince who told him to assure Willis that he was not desired to sign any paper with the other doctors unless he chose to do so, but that the Prince would much appreciate a daily account 'in general terms, without specifying any word or action' that Willis thought should not be mentioned.[39]

While the doctors squabbled at Kew, the political quarrels intensified in bitterness in London where the government lived in fear that the King would be declared incurably insane and that they would consequently be dismissed as soon as his son assumed power. As early as 13 November Pitt had recognized that he would have to introduce a Bill providing for a Regency, and that the Regent would have to be the Prince of Wales.[40] As the *Morning Post* put it that day, 'the malady with which His Majesty is afflicted is of such a nature that the medical gentlemen have their doubts as to future consequences, and if the King continues a few days longer in his present situation a Regency will be appointed, at the head of which will be His Royal Highness the Prince of Wales'. Pitt, well aware of the Prince's dislike of him, realized that this would probably mean the fall of his government and the installation of the Prince's Whig friends in its place; and he reconciled himself to the prospect of returning to his career in the law.[41]

8

The King's Recovery

1789

*

'The acrimony is beyond anything you can conceive'

In expectation of enjoying the powers and privileges of a Regent, the Prince was now widely rumoured to be behaving with scandalous impropriety. It was said that at Carlton House where he gave dinner parties every Saturday and Sunday evening,[1] all the restraint he had displayed at Windsor in the early stages of his father's illness was abandoned, that both he and the Duke of York went so far, when they were drunk, as to imitate their father's gestures and actions.[2] Certainly the Prince could not disguise the excitement he now felt at the prospect of influence and money, and eagerly discussing with Sheridan, Lord Loughborough, Grey and others who was to have what office when the Whigs came to power, he displayed a readiness 'to go to all the lengths to which that party [was] pushing him'.[3]

No one was yet certain, however, what the Prince intended to do when he became Regent or whose claims he favoured. It was common gossip at Brooks's that Fox, who had been on holiday in Italy with Mrs Armistead when the seriousness of the King's disorder became known, had been told to hurry home on the Prince's express instructions;[4] but it was Anthony St Leger's opinion that the Prince's feelings towards Fox had much changed in recent years and 'that his coolness towards him was much increased by Mrs Fitzherbert who would never forgive his public declaration on her subject in the House of Commons, and had taken every opportunity of alienating the Prince's mind from him'. St Leger also thought that the Prince's opinion of Pitt was 'very much altered since the negotiations on the subject of his debts'; he was 'sure' that the Prince would send for both Pitt and Fox 'and endeavour to make his time quiet by employing them jointly'.[5] When the Prince had seen Pitt to discuss the ordering of prayers for the King's recovery on 14 November, however, nothing was mentioned about a possible coalition. The Prince was polite enough but uncommunicative, and Pitt had reason to fear the worst.[6]

Pitt's fears were further increased by the ambivalent attitude of the Lord Chancellor in his administration, Lord Thurlow. He and Thurlow were not on good terms, having quarrelled over the trial of Warren Hastings, and Thurlow was suspected of being so determined to remain in office that he was prepared to come to terms with the Whigs. One day at Windsor, on taking leave of some of Pitt's other Ministers, Thurlow could not find his hat; while he was looking for it a page brought it to him announcing, to his obvious embarrassment, 'My Lord, I found it in the closet of His Royal Highness the Prince of Wales.'[7]

But although suspected of being on the point of deserting them, Thurlow managed to conceal from the government the course of his negotiations with the opposition. Indeed, the opposition themselves were not at all sure that they had secured his support in endeavouring to ensure that the Regency would be granted to the Prince without unwanted restrictions. For this support he had been offered the appointment of Lord President of the Council, but this was not enough for him; he wanted to retain the Lord Chancellorship. This was awkward, for the post had been virtually promised to Lord Loughborough. Thurlow, however, was insistent. So he was given some sort of undertaking that his claim would be preferred and Fox reluctantly agreed to break the unpalatable news to Loughborough, though even then the Prince could not be certain that Thurlow had been definitely won over.

The Times also was in the dark about this. After Loughborough had been told that he must stand aside for the sake of the party, it printed a list of what it supposed would be the new Ministers; in this list Loughborough figures as Lord Chancellor. On 28 November the *Morning Post* printed a similar list. Among the other names mentioned were the Duke of Portland as Prime Minister, Fox and Lord Stormont as Secretaries of State, Sheridan as Treasurer of the Navy and Burke as Paymaster of the Forces.

At Carlton House and Brooks's, at Devonshire House and at the Duke of Portland's mansion, Burlington House, the opposition continued their discussions, their intrigues and their feuds. Grey quarrelled with

Sheridan, who had himself been a contender for the post, over who should be Chancellor of the Exchequer; Sheridan quarrelled with Portland who said that he would not serve in the same Cabinet with him;[8] Sheridan also lost his patience with the Prince, who became so agitated over fears that his marriage to Mrs Fitzherbert might once more be raised in the House, that Sheridan burst out in irritation that he had 'the most womanish mind' he had ever come across.[9]

The Prince of Wales told Lord Sandwich that he could be First Lord of the Admiralty, but neither Fox nor Portland would agree to this appointment. The Duke of Portland himself, although the natural choice as First Lord of the Treasury, as the *Morning Post* had indicated, was hinting that he would not agree to lead the new administration unless the Prince formally apologized to him for the 'very rough' way he had treated him during the negotiations for settlement of his debts;[10] and the Duke was known to be further annoyed by the Prince's constant consultations with Sheridan who, with his wife, had moved into Mrs Fitzherbert's house when evicted by the bailiffs from his own.[11] Meanwhile the Duchess of Portland was suggesting that her husband ought not to accept office unless the Prince himself asked him to do so, and that in any case the Prince, who had recently driven so wildly through the streets with his sisters and Lady Charlotte Finch that he had broken several lamps, was perhaps not quite the man to be Regent at all.[12]

It was an opinion that pamphleteers and caricaturists did all that they could to foster. Readers of *The Crisis* were reminded that the problem of the 'mysterious connection' between Mrs Fitzherbert and the Prince had never been satisfactorily resolved and that the public had a right to know if the heir apparent was 'a Papist or married to a Papist'.[13] Subsequent pamphleteers proclaimed that the public also had a right to expect that, if he were to become Regent, the Prince would dismiss such companions as degraded his dignity,[14] and that the 'sacred privileges of the people' would count for more in his estimation than 'the friendship of the card table or the attachments of the turf'.[15]

The Prince's supporters, notably Sheridan and Fox, were attacked with equal force. Sheridan was a 'needy adventurer ready to bring his ability to the best market', a good enough actor, to be sure, provided he was given enough time to learn his part.[16] Fox, whose whole life had been one of dissipation, devoted to the gaming table and the racecourse, was 'a desperado' who would have 'no remorse in tearing up the constitution by the roots to gratify the raving of his monstrous passions'.[17] Even Louis Weltje, who was believed to be engaged in sinister attempts to bribe the Prince's adversaries, was advised by *The Times* to confine his studies to stewpans, and his influence to his patron's closet, or to go back to keeping a gingerbread stall. He was nothing but an 'itinerant German music-grinder raised from earning halfpence by the discordance of a street-walking concert'. An English Prince who showed a predilection for foreign servants such as this could not be said to love his countrymen; many a British subject of infinite merit 'was out of bread' while 'a great German toad-eater' had 'amassed an enormous fortune in the Prince of Wales's service'.[18]

In answer to these charges, the Whigs paid large sums of money to journalists and newspaper publishers in attempts to secure their support against Pitt. Sheridan supplied a great deal of anti-government material to the *Morning Herald*, and Weltje entered into negotiations on behalf of Carlton House supporters to buy the *Morning Post,* which had been printing items about the Prince's marriage to Mrs Fitzherbert. At the beginning of the following year he did succeed in buying it at a very much inflated price.[19] Meanwhile Whig pamphleteers also attempted to redress the balance by issuing edited accounts of the royal physicians' evidence before the Parliamentary committees illustrative of Dr Willis's 'contra-diction of himself'.[20]

These Whig pamphlets referred to the Prince as 'a true genius', possess-ing 'variety and versatility of talents in the first perfection. . . . Parts more lively and quick, a discernment of characters more acute and keen, and understanding more sharp and comprehensive, no man is blessed with. His conversation is unembarrassed and eloquent; his language pure, without care, and flowing with fluence.' He was, in short, 'the first young man in Great Britain'.[21]

Although even his most ardent admirers recognized that the Prince fell far short of this description, the opposition felt that his support was necessary to them and that they must enlist it at the risk of becoming tainted with his unpopularity. Consequently, a message sent by the Prince, on Sheridan's advice, to the Duke of Portland, offering to 'cancel all former discontents' was immediately accepted. The Duke agreed to forget everything that was past. He was, he said, 'properly touched' by the overture; and on 30 November, when the Prince, charming and agreeable, called on him at Burlington House, offering to shake hands and 'never again think about the dispute they had about the motion for paying his debts', the Duke thought that his manner could not have been kinder.[22]

Other breaches in the opposition's ranks were not so easily healed; but at least, as the time approached when the Regency question would have to be debated in Parliament, all Portland's objections to becoming first minister in the new government that the Whigs hoped to form were now removed.

*

Parliament had reassembled on 20 November when Pitt in the Commons and Camden in the Lords had proposed an adjournment for two weeks so that thought might be given to the measures which would have to be adopted if the King's condition failed to improve. By the time of the delayed meeting of Parliament at the beginning of December, both Dr Addington and Sir Lucas Pepys felt able to assure the committee appointed to examine the physicians that there were very good grounds for hope that the King would recover, thus contradicting the far less sanguine views of Warren, who reiterated his belief that the King was not delirious but insane, and of Sir George Baker who was now inclined to agree with him.[23] None of the doctors, though, was as certain of the case as Willis, who flatly contradicted the evidence of Warren and Baker – henceforward known as 'the "opposition" physicians'. Willis confidently asserted, after twenty-eight years' experience 'of the particular species of disorder with which His Majesty [was] afflicted', that there was every reason to suppose that he would be restored to health. After giving this opinion Willis reported privately to the Queen that he felt sure that he had now 'knocked up' all the hopes that the opposition had entertained of coming into power with the Prince of Wales's appointment as Regent.[24]

The opposition, however, were far from convinced that their hopes were dashed. In the heated debate that ensued in the Commons on 10 December, both Sheridan and Burke vehemently defended Warren against Pitt's accusation that, while his 'general skill was generally known and acknowledged', he had 'comparatively little' skill in dealing with mental disorders. Burke demanded to know how Warren, 'the first physician in this country', was 'likely to have given a false, precipitate and ill-grounded account of his Majesty on oath'; and Sheridan declared that it was 'ridiculous to stand upon idle ceremonies and trifling etiquettes; he would speak out. . . . When he heard [Dr Willis] roundly declare what every other of his Majesty's physicians pronounced it impossible to speak to, he must assert that Dr Willis was a very hasty decider and a random speaker.'[25]

Fox, looking ill and astonishingly thin after his exhausting rush home from Italy, cut across the argument about the credibility of the respective doctors and roundly declared that the Prince of Wales, as heir to the throne, of full age and capacity, had 'as clear, as express a right' to assume the exercise of royal power as he would have if the King were dead.[26] This was an extravagant claim, and although it was supported by Fox's supporters in the Commons at the time, it was afterwards felt that he had gone much too far for the opposition's good in putting forward so high a Tory doctrine. As Pitt listened to it, he is said to have smiled, slapped his thigh in triumph and proclaimed that he would '*un-Whig* the gentleman' for the rest of his life.[27] The Prince certainly had a *claim* to the Regency, but hardly an *inherent right*. To assert such a right, Pitt argued, amounted to an unwarranted interference with parliamentary privilege. It was almost treason to the constitution of the country.[28]

Fox's speech was as strongly condemned outside the Commons as in it. The *St James's Chronicle*, in a characteristic commentary, observed that the once firm friend of the Constitution now appeared 'desirous by one stroke to level this most glorious fabric to the dust'.[29] Fox, however, did not seem much concerned by the storm he had raised. As he told his 'dearest Liz', he expected that there were yet further 'hard fights' in the Commons to come and in some of them the opposition would probably be beaten; but he thought it certain that in about a fortnight the Prince would be Regent and his friends would come to power.[30]

He was encouraged in this belief by the number of uncommitted Members who were coming over to the Whig side. Admittedly, Thurlow had shown his hand at last by emotionally declaring in the House of Lords, 'When I forget my Sovereign, may my God forget me.' But Fox was glad to be rid of that particular encumbrance and was thankful that the way now stood clear for the faithful Loughborough, although the Prince of Wales still continued to hold long discussions with Thurlow whose support Sheridan considered crucial. Of the other waverers – about thirty in the Commons and twenty, including the Duke of Northumberland and Lord Rawdon, in the Lords – several were believed to be ready to vote in the forthcoming debates with the opposition who had been lavish in their promises of honours, perquisites and titles as soon as they came to power.

The debates were long and passionate. Both Fox and Pitt spoke brilliantly, while Burke harangued the House in defence of the Constitution as he understood it, with such emotion and lack of restraint, describing Pitt as one of the Prince's competitors and his policy as nothing less than usurpation, that he had to be called to order at least four times.[31] Dr Addington's son Henry, the Member for Devizes and soon to become Speaker, told his father that Burke 'was violent almost to madness';[32] and George Selwyn thought it a most lamentable affair that the King should be in a straitjacket while Burke was walking about at large.[33]

At the end of each debate, the arguments were continued with comparable fury outside the House. 'The acrimony is beyond anything you can conceive,' Lord Sydney told Lord Cornwallis. 'The ladies are as usual at the head of all animosity and are distinguished by caps, ribands, and other such ensigns of party.'[34] Supporters of the King and the government wore what they called 'constitutional coats'; ladies displayed their approval of the Prince and the opposition by sporting 'regency caps' decorated with three feathers and inscribed '*Ich Dien*'. Lists of future Ministers were discussed; bishops were nominated, peerages promised, and courtiers chosen. It was a foregone conclusion that the Duke of York would become Commander-in-Chief, that Mrs Fitzherbert would be made a duchess, and that something equally splendid would be done for the Duke of Cumberland who supported his nephew and the opposition – though his brother, Gloucester, did not.[35]

At the prospect of having such patronage in his hands the Prince became more excited than ever. Fearing that his prospects were endangered by his connexion with Mrs Fitzherbert, he even began to hint that, although he was still on friendly terms with her, she had no influence over him any more for he was in love with someone else; in any event there was no reason for concern about her.[36] Some of his letters were scarcely coherent. 'You may easily conceive I am excessively anxious in the event of the day,' he wrote to Sheridan on the eve of the debate upon 16 December. 'What are your apprehensions about numbers? For God's sake explain yourself, *who is false,* who is staunch, *who deceives us,* pray remark will you, and for Heaven's sake send me word and relieve my uneasiness. Do you think that any . . . will desert us? . . . Pray send word immediately. God bless you . . .'[37]

Almost as agitated as the Prince, the Duchess of Devonshire – whose husband had been invited to accept the office of Lord Privy Seal – sat up till four o'clock in the morning to hear the result of the final debate, in spite of a terrible headache. At last her brother and the Duke of Bedford came to Devonshire House 'like Priam's messengers' with the long-awaited news:[38] by a majority of sixty-four, the opposition had been defeated.

Although most of the waverers joined forces with the Whigs, the opposition's bid failed not only on the issue of the Prince's inherent right to the Regency, but also on the questions of the restrictions to be imposed upon his powers if he *were* to be appointed. Pitt, who had clung to office with great tenacity, had conducted his delaying tactics with admirable skill; and the comfortable majorities which he was able to command were greeted with the most profound satisfaction and relief by the great majority of his countrymen.

The Prince, who had earlier told the Duchess of Devonshire that he would not agree to a restricted Regency, had now to accept that, if he were to be nominated, he would be unable to create peerages outside the royal family and would also, with a very few exceptions, be debarred from awarding any pensions, offices or honours. Nor would he have the disposition of the royal Household, as the King was to be entrusted to the care of the Queen.

In a letter drafted by Burke and amended by Sheridan and Loughborough, the Prince protested to Pitt against these restrictions.[39] But it was unavailing. If the Prince were to be Regent at all, he would have to be so on Pitt's terms. On 12 February the Regency Bill passed the Commons, and the Lords were on the point of passing it also when the news that Dr Willis had long predicted arrived from Kew.

*

The official bulletin on 10 February had described the King as having passed 'the day before in a state of composure'. The next day he was said to be 'better this morning than he was yesterday', and on the 12th he was 'in a progressive state of amendment'. Two days later Sir George Baker for the first time spoke hopefully of the case to Dr Willis, and on 15 February even Dr Warren said that if His Majesty continued through the day in the same state in which he had seen him that morning, 'he might be said to be well'. The next week the Lord Chancellor announced that the intelligence from Kew was now so favourable that 'it would be indecent to proceed further with the Bill when it might become wholly unnecessary'.[40]

Anxious to make sure for themselves that the King was as well as the doctors claimed he was, the Prince of Wales and the Duke of York – who had jointly informed Prince Augustus two months before that their father was now 'a compleat lunatick'[41] – arrived at Kew on 17 February. But Dr Willis, with the prior agreement of the Chancellor, asked them not to go into his room as 'such a step might be of the utmost mischief to the King'.[42]

Continuing to hear progressively better accounts of their father, the Prince and the Duke repeatedly went to Kew and were invariably refused admittance although, as they knew, the Chancellor and others had been allowed to see him.[43] At length, on 20 February, they wrote a formal letter to their mother asking that a day might be named on which they might be permitted to throw themselves at the feet of their father and pour forth their 'respectful joy in his Majesty's presence'. Failing this, they asked that the physicians should give reasons for their refusal in writing.[44] On receipt of this letter the Queen made an appointment for her sons two days ahead, as the King wanted to have the opportunity of having further discussions with the Lord Chancellor first.[45] The date appointed for their visit was 23 February. They arrived at Kew over two hours late in a state of obvious trepidation.[46]

The King could not at first bring himself to enter the room in the Queen's apartments where they were waiting for him, and stood hesitating on the far side of the door 'crying very much'. After some time he pulled himself together and went into the room, but at the sight of his two sons he began crying again, shedding 'tears on their faces'. They, in turn, both seemed to be 'much touched'.

When the King began to talk he avoided all mention of politics or business, telling them that he had had a chance to improve his Latin and to learn how to play piquet, speaking about horses to the Prince of Wales and about his regiment to the Duke of York. The Queen, who was plagued with toothache, was also present, Sir Gilbert Elliot said, 'walking to and fro in the room with a countenance and manner of great dissatisfaction, and the King every now and then went to her in a submissive and soothing sort of tone, for she has acquired the same sort of authority over him that Willis and his men have'.[47]

After an hour's conversation, the Queen's dinner was announced, and the two sons took their leave. Though fully persuaded of their father's complete recovery about which they expressed their great satisfaction to Greville,[48] it was alleged that when they got back to Brooks's almost as a matter of course 'they amused themselves with spreading a report that the King was still out of his mind, and in quoting phrases of his to which they gave that turn'.[49]

Hearing stories like this, the Queen grew ever more resentful of her sons' collusion with the Whigs during the past miserable months. They, in turn, grew ever more exasperated by her petulant ill-temper and her unbending refusal to entertain any thoughts of reconciliation. The mutual resentment flared into a blazing quarrel in which the Prince of Wales accused the Queen of plotting with his enemies and of entering 'into plans for destroying and disgracing him'. She had, he said, 'countenanced misrepresentations of his conduct to the King and prevented the explanations which he wished to give. She was violent and lost her temper.'[50]

When it was decided to give a concert at Windsor to celebrate the King's recovery, the sons were invited, but the Queen, grown so excessively thin that it was said her stays would go round her twice, reminded them in her invitation that the entertainment had really been arranged for those who had remained loyal to his Majesty and herself on the late occasion.[51] The Duke of Portland told Fox that he thought the Queen's comment was 'offensive', and that the Prince and the Duke had every reason to be 'hurt and offended' by it.[52]

Both of them, however, attended the Windsor concert at which their mother's behaviour towards them was more forbidding than ever. It seemed she was determined to make them feel that their conduct merited their being treated as unwelcome outcasts, unworthy of their parents' affection or regard. It was an overtly political occasion. The ladies of the Court wore Tory colours; the musical programme contained numerous party allusions; the elaborate confections served at supper were decorated with Tory slogans. The King behaved politely enough, but the Queen remained 'sour and glum', keeping a stern eye on her daughters to make sure that there was no unseemly fraternization between her male and female offspring. The Prince left Windsor in the most peevish of tempers.[53]

With the help of Burke, Sheridan and others, he wrote letters to the Queen endeavouring to 'counteract the impressions' which his enemies, who had daily access to the King, gave of the part he and his brother had taken 'in the late important occurrences'.[54] Similar letters were prepared for the King, and Sir Gilbert Elliot was asked to compose a long, detailed and thorough exculpatory memorial.*[55]

But complain as he would that he was being treated as though he were beneath contempt, that he had only learned of his father's intention of resuming government 'by common report', the Prince could gain no satisfaction from either of his parents. As Burke said, everything possible was done 'to disgust' both him and the Duke of York and to keep them from visiting Windsor and Kew. They endured and persevered, but were made to feel wholly unwelcome.[56] When he heard by chance that the King had suffered a bad fall from his horse, having turned abruptly in his saddle to hear something Colonel Goldsworthy said, the Prince wrote angrily to the Lord Chancellor to demand why he had been kept in 'perfect ignorance' of the circumstance. It was *'perfectly indecent'*, yet unhappily only 'too consonant to the *general system*' now adopted towards him.[57]

This general system was clearly exemplified when the Duke of York was almost killed in a duel on Wimbledon Common with Colonel Charles Lennox, nephew of the third Duke of Richmond. Lennox, whose mother, a daughter of the Marquess of Lothian, was one of the Queen's Ladies, had publicly insulted both the Prince and the Duke of York. The Duke returned the insult. Lennox issued a challenge, and the Duke accepted it. In the consequent duel, the ball from Lennox's pistol whistled past the Duke's ear, slicing off a curl from his wig. But when his mother heard of his narrow escape, she displayed not the least emotion, merely remarking that it was more likely to be Frederick's fault than Lennox's. Later, despite the protestations of the Prince of Wales, she insisted that Colonel Lennox should be invited to the King's birthday party at St James's where she welcomed him warmly.[58]

---

* The decision to compose this memorial was prompted by a 'most harsh and unnatural letter' which the King wrote to Prince William abusing him for associating with his brothers during his father's illness. This letter, the Prince claimed, was the 'first direct intimation' he had received that his conduct and that of the Duke of York, during his Majesty's 'lamented illness had brought on [them] the heavy misfortune of [his] Majesty's displeasure' (RA 31942-4). In fact, Prince William had been at sea during the crisis; but it was widely rumoured that he had been hoping to be appointed First Lord of the Admiralty in the event of a Regency, and *The Times* falsely alleged that he had actually returned home from America, without permission, in expectation of this appointment. In May 1789 when he was created Duke of Clarence, the King is said to have wearily remarked that he well knew that this was yet another vote 'added to the Opposition' (Wraxall, v. 171).

The Prince also attended the party and, noticing his fellow-guest on the ballroom floor during a country-dance, led his partner, the Princess Royal, out of the dance to a chair by the side of the Queen. The Queen said, 'You seem heated, Sir, and tired.'

'I am heated and tired, Madam,' the Prince replied, 'not with the dance, but with dancing in such company.'

'Then, Sir, it will be better for me to retire, and put an end to the ball.'

'It certainly will be so, for I never will countenance insults given to my family, however they may be treated by others.'[59]

When Fox heard of this new development in the quarrel, he told Liz Armistead that the Queen seemed to him 'to go beyond the worst woman we ever read of'. 'Liz would not be such a mother if she had a son,' he continued, 'and with such a son as the D[uke] of Y[ork] I do not believe, except the Queen, there is another in the world that would be. . . . Friend and enemy, except only his father and mother, agree in praising the Duke of York to the greatest degree.'[60]

The general public, however, took a less favourable view of the conduct of the King's two eldest sons. On 10 March their coach was stopped by a jam of other carriages in a narrow street. 'The mob soon knew the Princes. They called "God Save the King!", while the Prince, letting down his glasses, joined them in calling very heartily, and hallooed, "Long Live the King!" and so forth with the mob. But one man called out to him to cry "Pitt for ever! or God bless Pitt!" ' This was too much for the Prince who bravely responded to the demand by shouting 'Fox for ever!' At this 'a man pulled the coach-door open, and the Prince endeavoured to jump out amongst them in order to defend himself; but the Duke of York kept him back with one arm, and with the other struck the man on the head, and called to the coachman to drive on, which he did at a great pace, the coach door flapping about as they went'.[61]

After the opera the Prince insisted on walking home to Carlton House, and, as though admiring him for his courage, the crowds along Pall Mall 'called "God bless your Highness!" which he was much pleased with. They also called "Long Live the King!" which he always joined in as loud as any of them. At St James's he fell in with a gang of butchers, with marrow-bones and cleavers, who knew him, and began immediately to play before him; and he found it impossible to get rid of them. They accordingly cleared the way for him, playing and shouting all the way up St James's Street. When they came to Brooks's they gave him three cheers; and the Prince in turn hallooed out, "Long Live the King!" and gave them three cheers himself. He then sent them ten guineas to drink.' This sort of thing, Sir Gilbert Elliot commented, 'is to the credit of his spirit and natural manners; and he is out of luck for not being extremely popular, for a tenth part of his popular qualities, and indeed of his good qualities, has made the fortune of many princes and favourites of the people'.[62]

How far the Prince was from being a favourite of the people was demonstrated the next month, on 23 April 1789, when a service of thanksgiving for the King's recovery was held at St Paul's. Although the Whigs had their supporters in the crowds that lined the streets, it was obvious to all that the King and Pitt were the real heroes of the day. 'What pleased us most', Mary Frampton told her sister, 'was that the populace huzza'd Mr Pitt, but hooted and hissed Mr Fox – at least, the greatest number did so. Mr Fox, in consequence, sat quite back in his coach, not to be seen.'[63]* Pitt, indeed, had never been 'in such high estimation'; he had 'reached the summit of human glory'.[64] The King, too, had never been more popular. In Datchet the month before, the people had gone down on their knees to welcome him; and in Windsor the military guard had been reduced to tears at the joyful sight of his homecoming. Now in London, the public buildings were decorated and illuminated in his honour, and people put candles in their windows and decorated their houses with crowns, the letters 'G.R.' and the words 'Rejoice' and 'God Save the King'.[65] Shouting their congratulations on the King's recovery, they abused those 'rats' who had deserted him, notably the Duke of Queensberry, the Marquess of Lothian and Lord Rawdon, and broke the windows of houses that were not illuminated.[66] 'The King's recovery gave me the most heartfelt satisfaction,' wrote Lord Cornwallis expressing a widespread contentment. 'I rejoiced very sincerely on his own account, and I cannot wish to see poor old England in the ravenous jaws of the Buff and Blue Squad.'[67]

The Prince, who was driven to the Cathedral to the accompaniment of the jeers and catcalls that now almost invariably greeted his coach, was reported to have further antagonized his critics by entering into a whispered conversation with his brother and uncles during the service, by

* Fox was recognized as his coach passed through Temple Bar, *The Times* confirmed, 'and received an universal hiss which continued with very little intermission until he alighted at St .Paul's' (*The Times*, 24 April 1789).

munching biscuits during the sermon, and by making some observation to the Duke of York that made his brother laugh so much he had to cover his face with his hands.[68] Another observer contradicted this by reporting that 'throughout *this* day' the Prince behaved well.[69] Party spirit similarly coloured the reports of the King's behaviour during the service. The Dean of St Paul's wrote of his 'earnest and uninterrupted devotion'; and *The Times* described his demeanour as being truly religious. Sir Gilbert Elliot, on the contrary, thought that he seemed 'wholly indifferent' to the proceedings. 'He looked about with his opera-glass and spoke to the Queen during the greatest part of the service, very much as if he had been at a play.'[70] But however the King and his son may have behaved on this particular day, it was universally agreed that the Prince's future prospects and those of the Whig party were bleak indeed.

9

The Bottle and the Turf
1789-1791

*

'A voluptuary under the horrors of digestion'

It was partly in an effort to provide fresh encouragement to the dispirited Whigs of the north that the Prince and the Duke of York now set out on a trip to Yorkshire. It was an unexpected and undoubted success. The Prince behaved with charm and dignity, responding to his welcome with a pleasure all the deeper because of his unpopularity in London. The 'elegance and *condescension* with which he behaved upon all occasions' during his stay in York earned him, one observer ventured to hope, 'the most *zealous affection* of all its inhabitants'. He gracefully accepted the freedom of the city in a speech as well received as it was delivered. He distributed charity, and attended balls, concerts and dinners. From the portico of Lord Fitzwilliam's mansion, Wentworth House, wearing his blue, red and gold Windsor uniform, he addressed 'a delighted multitude' of twenty thousand people by the light of roaring bonfires, and held up to their admiring cheers the three-year-old Lord Milton, heir to the estates. At Castle Howard, his host decided that he was really 'very good company'. He returned to London expressing his 'uncommon satisfaction at the whole of his Yorkshire journey'.[1]

The excursion was the 'happiest thing imaginable', Edmund Burke told Captain Payne in an enthusiastic letter, 'and the best adapted to dispel prejudices in that county which was cruelly poisoned with them. I hope his R.H. has been pleased; indeed, I ought not to doubt it, because I know the benevolence of his character, and that he could not be indifferent to the happiness he gave to so many people. I spent a good part of the evening yesterday in reading a long letter from Lord Fitzwilliam, and two others from a gentleman and a lady, relative to the Prince's Yorkshire visit. They are, with different details, all expressive of the infinite satisfaction given by his R.H. to them and to everybody who saw him. They all describe his behaviour as having the ease, grace, and pleasantness of what flowed from pure nature. . . . In particular, it is said that he was properly attentive and civil to those who were adverse in their politicks, so as rather to please than to offend them without losing a marked preference to his friends . . .'[2]

Even *The Times*, no friend to the Prince, gave him credit for gaining 'great affection from all ranks of people wherever he has been'. 'Those gentlemen attached to his interest will reap the benefit of it at the next general election', *The Times* added. The opposition had been 'at a very low ebb' in Yorkshire, but they seemed 'now to revive'.[3]

Back in London the Prince found himself as unwelcome at St James's and the Queen's House as ever; and when he went to Windsor he would dine at the White Hart, spend the night in his apartments in the Castle and return to Carlton House without troubling to call on his parents who he felt sure would not want to see him. His father, whose health was improving daily, virtually ignored him; his mother, continuing to express her high opinion of Mr Pitt and, in the words of Lord Hawkesbury, President of the Board of Trade, talking 'violently and even indiscreetly against all the members of opposition', seemed almost to hate him; his every act was 'deemed censurable'.[4] He would love to have been of consequence, but his ambitions were thwarted at every turn. His occasional interventions in public affairs were dismissed, even by his own political supporters, as meddling. He was condemned in the columns of *The Times* as a hard-drinking, swearing, whoring man 'who at all times would prefer a girl and a bottle, to politics and a sermon'; his only states of happiness were 'gluttony, drunkenness and gambling'.[5] The more he was accused of being such a wastrel, the more inclined he felt to behave like one, and the more, indeed, he *did* behave like one. Deprived of the acclaim to which he had so spontaneously responded in Yorkshire, he wilfully provided his numerous enemies in London with fresh evidence of his self-indulgence. In June that year Lady Susan Leveson-Gower reported him as being 'drunk as possible' and behaving 'very ill' at Boodle's and as having to be 'dragged out' of Ranelagh.[6]

Gillray's most frequently reproduced caricature of the Prince dates from this period. It shows him, 'a voluptuary under the horrors of digestion', picking his teeth with a fork as he recovers from the effects of an immense meal at Carlton House, his huge belly bursting from his breeches, his florid face threatening apoplexy.* Beneath his massive thighs are empty wine bottles, discarded on the carpet; beside his feet, next to an upturned dice-box, are lists of 'debts of honour unpaid' – an unfair allegation: he was no longer a gambler and 'allowed no play in his house'.[7] At his back are more bills for which an overflowing chamber-pot acts as paperweight. On a console table behind him are numerous medicines including preparations 'for the piles', 'for a stinking breath', and two famous cures for venereal disease, Veno's Vegetable Syrup and Leeke's Pills.†

To those who accepted this caricature as a true likeness of the Prince of Wales, it seemed entirely appropriate that he should include so many reprobates among his closest friends, and that the two most notorious dukes in England, Queensberry and Norfolk, should be frequent guests of his at Brighton.

The ninth Duke of Norfolk was sixteen years older than the Prince, the fourth Duke of Queensberry thirty-eight years his senior; and both of them had been celebrated drunkards while he was still a baby. Norfolk, an extraordinarily ill-educated man, though of considerable native intelligence, was said to be not only one of the most drunken but also one of the dirtiest gentlemen in the country, so averse to the use of soap and water that he had to be washed by his servants when too drunk to restrict them. Queensberry was cleaner, but a good deal more depraved, a 'little, sharp-looking man, very irritable, and swore like ten thousand troopers'.[8] A dedicated whoremonger, he had made himself thoroughly detested at Court by spending his evenings during the Regency crisis drinking champagne at Carlton House although a Lord of the Bedchamber, a post from which he was immediately dismissed on the King's recovery.

In the company of Norfolk and Queensberry it was natural to find the

---

* According to the huge scales in the Old Coffee Mill (now Messrs Berry Bros and Rudd, the wine merchants) in St James's Street, the Prince's weight in December 1797 was 17 stone 8 pounds (*Farington Diary*, iv, 98).

† The Prince was so dismayed by a subsequent Gillray print, *L'Assemblée Nationale*, which disparagingly featured Mr and Mrs Fox, Mrs Fitzherbert, Lady Bessborough and the Duchess of Devonshire, as well as himself, that he paid a large amount of money for the destruction of the plate (George, *English Political Caricature, 1793–1832*, 76). He was, however, a regular customer of Mrs Humphrey and her successor at whose shop in St James's Street Gillray's prints were displayed and sold (RA 27094–28394).

various wild members of the Barrymore family – the seventh Earl of Barrymore himself, a young man rapidly dissipating a fortune worth over £20,000 a year, known to all and sundry as 'Hellgate'; his brother, the Hon and Rev Augustus Barry, a compulsive gambler ever on the verge of imprisonment and consequently known as 'Newgate'; his youngest brother who, in acknowledgement of a club foot, was called 'Cripplegate'; and his sister whose savage temper and foul language combined to render 'Billingsgate' an entirely appropriate soubriquet. Her sister-in-law, the Countess, whom the Earl had married at Gretna Green, was the daughter of a sedan-chairman and the niece of that alluring courtesan, Letitia Lade, who had numbered the Duke of York amongst her numerous lovers. Sir John Lade, Letitia's husband, an amusing, disreputable fellow, the inheritor of a large brewery fortune, who gave occasional advice in the Prince's racing stables, was another welcome guest at his table.

With the Lades and the Barrymores, with Norfolk and Queensberry, with other such dissipated companions as George Hanger and the Duke of Orleans whose inflamed, scorbutic face, rising above the dark green collar of his coat, was a familiar sight in Piccadilly and on the Steine, the Prince of Wales spent much of his time during the months that followed his father's recovery. Stories of the escapades of his friends were continually retailed in drawing-rooms and taverns and filled column after column in the newspapers. The Barrymores, in particular, were regularly in the news. Everyone had heard tales of how they raced down to Brighton in their coach, sometimes stopping to uproot or displace signposts, at other times screaming 'Murder! Rape! Unhand me, villain!' and how, when the coach was overtaken and forcibly stopped by law-abiding travellers, they jumped out to insult and lay about their would-be saviours. In Brighton, calling themselves the 'Merry Mourners', they went about at night with a coffin, knocking on the doors of middle-class citizens and tradesmen, announcing to terrified maidservants that they had come to take possession of the family corpse. One of them, 'Cripplegate', rode his horse up the staircase of Mrs Fitzherbert's house and into the garret where he left it to be brought down by two blacksmiths; another, 'Hellgate', dressed in the skirts and bodice of his cook at three o'clock in the morning, sang a serenade to Mrs Fitzherbert beneath her bedroom window.[9]

A scurrilous publication, *The Jockey Club, or a Sketch of the Manners of the Age,* gave an audacious but not altogether inaccurate account of the activities of the 'chosen companions and confidential intimates' of the Prince of Wales, the 'very *lees* of society'. 'If a man of the most depraved, the vilest cast were, from a vicious sympathy, to choose his company, it were impossible for his choice to fix anywhere else.' When the heir to the Crown chose such company, affording such proof of his tastes and attachments, then the people had a duty 'to think seriously for themselves'.

The Prince's connexion with Mrs Fitzherbert was a matter of serious national concern, *The Jockey Club* continued. His debts were equally a national disgrace. By his dissipation and his extravagance he had set decency at defiance and scorned public opinion. As soon as Parliament had voted him money on his hypocritical assertion that he would in future live within his means, he had revived his turf establishment in a more ruinous style than ever and contracted fresh debts to an enormous amount. 'Had a private individual acted in like manner he would have become the outcast of his family and the whole world [would have] abandoned him.'

Nor was the Prince alone singled out for condemnation. The Barrymores, George Hanger and Sir John Lade were 'creatures with whom a man of morality or even common decency' could never associate. Lady Lade was nothing more than 'a common prostitute'; the Duke of York a lecher who spent most of his time 'amongst the nymphs of Berkeley Row'; Louis Weltje, 'a brute'; Lord Clermont, 'another brilliant ornament' of the Prince's Court, 'remarkable only for his profligacy', was 'a hardened incorrigible veteran in every species of iniquity'.[10]

Protest as he would against this 'most infamous and shocking libellous production that ever disgraced the pen of man', demand as he would that these '*damnable doctrines* of the *hell-begotten* Jacobines' ought to be 'taken up in *a very serious manner by Government* and prosecuted',[11] the Prince could enlist scant sympathy. Those who knew him best knew that he was a good-natured fellow at heart, far from being the vicious scoundrel depicted in pamphlets and prints, that he disapproved of the more heartless practical jokes of his companions and compensated their victims. But it could not be denied that his behaviour was frequently as irresponsible as theirs, nor that on occasions he seemed to have thought for nothing except his own pleasure.

*

In August 1789, on the occasion of his birthday – an event of which his parents declined to take any official notice – there were long and rowdy celebrations in Brighton. The church bells rang; the town was illuminated; various ludicrous sports including jack-ass races were held in a field outside the town; bonfires were lit; an ox was roasted whole and hunks were sliced off with a broadsword; hogsheads of ale were opened on the green; there were sailing races; and there were boxing-matches at which the Prince awarded prizes to the winning contestants.

The Prince took a particular interest in the ring, though after seeing a man killed at Brighton he settled an annuity on the bereaved widow and said that he would never watch another fight again. But his chief delight was the turf, to the pleasures of which he had been introduced by the Duke of Cumberland. Indeed, one of the grooms at Carlton House remarked that horses, of which the Prince was genuinely fond, were the one and only subject of his thoughts. He regularly attended Lewes and Brighton Races, and went racing elsewhere whenever he could. In 1786 his stud had been broken up in accordance with his proclaimed intention of leading a more economical life, but he had gradually built up a new racing establishment at Newmarket, and between 1788 and 1791 his horses won no less than one hundred and eighty-five races. On 20 October 1791, however, there was a scandal at Newmarket when his famous horse, Escape, a fine animal purchased by the Prince two years before for £1,500, was beaten by two outsiders.

Escape was ridden by Samuel Chiffney, a jockey whose high opinion of his own exceptional talents was well justified. He had won the Oaks four times, and in 1789 had won the Derby for the Duke of Bedford. In July 1790 he had been engaged as 'rider for life' by the Prince of Wales who paid him a salary of two hundred guineas a year. His failure on Escape on 20 October was followed the next day – at odds of 5 to 1 against – by an easy win which resulted in the loss of large sums of money by numerous punters and, so it was alleged, handsome profits for himself. It was also alleged that Warwick Lake, Gerard's younger brother and the Prince's racing manager who disliked and distrusted Chiffney, had made some indiscreet remarks about Escape's performance, and that the Duke of Bedford had made some equally derogatory remarks, declaring in the course of them that Chiffney ought to be dismissed. There were further allegations that Escape had been winded just before his failure on 20 October by being given a bucketful of water.

At the subsequent Jockey Club inquiry, however, both Lake and Bedford denied the remarks attributed to them, Bedford adding that he had not even been at Newmarket that day; while Chiffney said that his bet on the second day had amounted to no more than twenty guineas. Nothing was proved against jockey, owner or trainer; but the Jockey Club was clearly not satisfied.

Outraged by the insinuations made against him, the Prince declared that he would have nothing more to do with Newmarket. And to demonstrate his belief that Chiffney had been quite innocent of the charges brought against him, he publicly announced his intention of continuing to pay him his two hundred guineas salary for the rest of his life.[12]*

Charles James Fox, an inveterate racing man, believed that although some of the Prince's people had been guilty of an 'absolute cheat', the Prince himself was 'quite innocent'. Nevertheless, his behaviour was 'very injudicious' since he did not seem displeased with his jockey, yet was 'very much so with Lake for telling him he was sorry he had won, by which Lake only meant to say . . . that he was sorry a thing had happened which would cause disagreeable conversation to the Prince. . . . People will suspect.'[13]

People *did* suspect; and, although there was no cause for supposing the Prince guilty of any impropriety, Sir Charles Bunbury, an influential member of the Jockey Club who had once been unhappily married to the King's beloved Lady Sarah Lennox, expressed a common view when he told him that if he were ever to let Chiffney ride for him again, no gentleman would allow a horse of his to start in the same race.[14] 'I was never more vexed in my life,' Fox concluded in a letter to Liz Armistead, 'and I consider it as putting an end to amusement here [at Newmarket] most completely because there were always people enough inclined to do wrong, and an example of this sort is sure to encourage them.'[15]

*

As in sport, so in politics, this was a most unfortunate period in the Prince's career. His perfunctory and half-hearted attempts to form a

* The Prince's stud was accordingly sold at Tattersall's in March 1791 for prices ranging from twenty-five to 270 guineas. The principal purchasers were Lord Grosvenor, the Duke of Bedford, and – to the annoyance of *The Times* which thought that he ought to have followed his brother's example and have 'seen the imprudence of keeping up a very large turf establishment' – the Duke of York. Chiffney published a spirited defence of his conduct under the characteristically immodest title, *Genius Genuine by Samuel Chiffney of Newmarket*. He left Newmarket for London in 1806 when he sold the Prince's annuity for £1,260. He died in poverty the following year. The Prince never patronized Newmarket again (Mortimer, *Jockey Club*, 46).

party against the detested Pitt, 'Old Billy' as he called him, met with little success. When, for instance, he and his brothers, the Dukes of York and Clarence, tried to get an opposition candidate, Lawrence Dundas, elected as one of the Members for Cambridge University they were soundly defeated. The Prince had told the Duke of York that he and William had 'the most sanguine hopes';[16] but as Pitt was one of the three candidates for the two seats and Lord Euston, the elder son of the Chancellor of the University, the Duke of Grafton, was the other, no one else rated Dundas's hopes very highly. In fact, he received no more than 207 votes against a total of 993 cast for his opponents.

It was for the Prince a typical humiliation. He was 'little respected', the Duke of Portland had to confess; while Sir Gilbert Elliot was now of the opinion that if anything could make a democracy in England it was the behaviour of the Prince and his tiresome brothers. Tory supporters of the government voiced similar views in stronger terms.[17]

The Times – whose founder, John Walter, received secret service money from the Treasury for supporting the government and for publishing items in disparagement of the opposition – ensured that this low opinion of the Prince and his brothers was kept well before the public. The insincerity of their joy at their father's recovery, *The Times* assured its readers, was quite obvious. 'Their late unfeeling conduct would ever tell against them, and contradict the artful professions they thought it prudent to make.'[18] Although John Walter was fined and imprisoned for a subsequent libel on the Prince, a few months after its appearance he published yet another. For this he was punished by a second term of imprisonment from which he was released before completing the sentence through the generous intervention of his victim. The Prince, however, received little credit for this, and *The Times* continued to report his activities with undisguised disdain.[19]

References to him in private correspondence were equally unflattering. He continued to give splendid levees and 'admirable dinners' at Carlton House, it had to be admitted. Lord Harrowby was assured that he still fascinated everybody there, with his 'natural ease and elegance'.[20] Yet he consistently annoyed his guests by keeping them waiting. At one levee in February 1790, the Prince maintained 'his character for want of punctuality, and kept a vast crowd waiting in a very cold room above an hour before he admitted them. As patience and waiting are essential accomplishments at his Court, this perhaps was done by design.'[21] At a subsequent levee he 'made people wait till near four o'clock'. 'During the interval,' James Hare, Member of Parliament for Knaresborough, told the Duchess of Devonshire, 'there were, I hear, frequent comparisons made between him and his father not much to his advantage.'[22]

Gradually, however, despite the sorry condition of his financial affairs, relations between the Prince and his father began to improve. On 10 August 1790 he wrote to the Duke of York from Brighton asking him to find out from the King whether or not his birthday was to be celebrated, as the '*only reason*' for his not having paid his respects the previous year was his not having received 'the smallest intimation on that head'.[23] The King signified that he was at last ready to receive him once more.

He was again at Windsor for the King's birthday the following 4 June and, according to the *St James's Chronicle*, he had never made a more splendid appearance. He wore 'a bottle-green and claret-coloured striped silk coat and breeches, and silver tissue waistcoat, very richly embroidered in silver and stones, and coloured silks in curious devices and bouquets of flowers. The coat and waistcoat embroidered down the seams and spangled all over the body. The coat cuffs the same as the waistcoat. The breeches were likewise covered with spangles. Diamond buttons to the coat, waist-coat, and breeches, which with his brilliant diamond epaulette, and sword, made the whole dress form a most magnificent appearance.'[24]

That year the Queen wrote in good time from Windsor to assure him that she and his father 'certainly' expected him in order to keep his own birthday on 12 August, 'which,' she added, 'none will do with greater pleasure than, my dearest son, than [*sic*] your very affectionate mother and sincere friend'.[25] The assurances of affection and sincere friendship were to some extent formalistic, but at least the breach between mother and son which had seemed permanent eighteen months before was now evidently bridgeable.

Certainly the ball held at Windsor on 12 August 1791 was a distinct success. The following day even *The Times* praised the charming manners of the Prince, once more reconciled with his parents. 'Perhaps no heir to the Crown since the days of Edward the Black Prince', *The Times* went so far as to suggest, 'has been more generously admired for his amiable man-ners than the Prince of Wales; and the very happy and substantial recon-ciliation that has taken place between H.R.H. and his august parents, contributed in no small degree to add to the pleasures and festivities of the day.'[26]

IO

The Prince's Brothers

1792-1793

*

'The common cause of all the Princes of Europe'

A few months after that surprisingly successful ball at Windsor, *The Times* had further cause to praise the greatly improved Prince of Wales for the well-delivered maiden speech he made on 31 May 1792 in the House of Lords during a debate on the 'seditious writings' of the extreme reformers.[1] No one knew of his intention of taking part in the debate, not even his two brothers between whom he was sitting, when he suddenly rose and spoke in so 'manly, eloquent and . . . persuasive a manner' that he gained both 'the attention and the admiration of the House'.[2] Captain Payne was overjoyed by the effect that this forceful speech had had. It was 'more, *infinitely more*' than he had dared to hope for. The 'moment lost at the Regency' was now recovered and could 'easily be maintained by constant perseverance'.[3]

In his speech the Prince spoke fervently of his undying attachment to the principles of England's 'great and sacred' Constitution, which he had 'very early in life imbibed' and which, to the latest hour of his existence, he would 'glory in professing'.

England's 'present happy and perfect' Constitution seemed all the more precious to him now that the French Revolution had unleashed the dreadful doctrines of those hell-begotten Jacobins on an innocent world. And when, in February 1793, the French revolutionary government declared war on England, where 'in open defiance of all law and decency' infamous propagators of republican principles had long been active, the Prince recognized that his own future depended upon the successful prosecution of the war. 'THE VERY EXISTENCE OF EVERY PRINCE AT THIS MOMENT,' he wrote to the Duke of York, underlining each word with heavy strokes, 'IS CONCERNED AND DEPENDS ON THE TOTAL ANNIHILATION OF THIS BANDITTI, who are a disgrace to the human species.'[4]

To the Duke and to others he professed an eager desire to take a personal, active part in their defeat. He badly wanted to serve abroad, Sir Gilbert Elliot said, 'and to have his share of the glory' that was going. It riled him that he was kept at home while his brothers 'and all the Princes of Europe' were 'acting personally in their common cause'.[5] It was not that he was jealous of the Duke of York's military reputation, he insisted; indeed, he was willing to serve under him; but he did not want to be disregarded while other members of his family achieved popularity and respect.

The Duke of York, in recognition of his military training in Hanover, was, at his father's insistence, appointed commander of the British army and despatched to Flanders to co-operate with the Austrians, though he had no practical acquaintance with war and had necessarily to rely on the advice of his more experienced staff. He was to prove a less than competent military commander, and, as Gillray cruelly emphasized, he energetically embraced the pleasures and dissipations of life in the officers' mess. His bravery, however, was never questioned.

His younger brothers, Prince Ernest and Prince Adolphus, were also given opportunities to display their physical courage. And even his cousin, Prince William, the Duke of Gloucester's son, who had entered the army with the rank of Colonel in the First Foot Guards at the age of thirteen, was enthusiastically if ineffectually serving with his regiment in Flanders five years later and was a major-general before he was twenty.*

Prince Ernest, a handsome, very tall, well-corseted young man, had always been destined for a military career. In 1786 he had been sent at the age of fifteen to the University of Göttingen where military subjects

---

* Prince William had been born in 1776 in Rome where his father had chosen to reside following his banishment from Court as a result of his improper marriage. The marriage, which had not weathered well in Italy, came close to collapse when the Duke embarked on an affair with one of his wife's attendants, Lady Almeira Carpenter. After this the Duchess's behaviour towards her husband became so 'grossly indecent', in the words of one of his letters of complaint to the Prince of Wales, that he considered it essential that their daughter Sophia Matilda should be provided with a governess 'to keep her clear of the Duchess but at meals and in the evening society', and that Prince William should be allowed to finish his education at Cambridge. After some hesitation the King agreed to this, granting his brother an additional pension to defray the cost. The Prince accordingly entered Trinity College and, although his intellectual powers were severely limited, he received the degree of MA in 1790 when he was fifteen (RA 54374–8, 54384, 54387).

1. King George III by Gainsborough
2. Queen Charlotte by Stroehling
3. Queen Charlotte in her bedroom at
   the Queen's House (Buckingham House)
   with the Prince of Wales and Prince
   Frederick. From the painting by Zoffany

4. Princesses Charlotte, Augusta,
Elizabeth by Gainsborough, 1784

5. The Prince of Wales as a child by Brompton

6. The Prince of Wales, aged eighteen, on horseback by Stubbs

8. Georgiana, wife of the 5th Duke of Devonshire by Reynolds

7. Mary Robinson by Reynolds

9. Mrs Fitzherbert by Gainsborough

ANTI-SACCHARRITES, _ or _ JOHN BULL and his Family leaving off the use of SUGAR.
To the Masters & Mistresses of Families in Great Britain, this Noble Example of Œconomy, is respectfully submitted

10. 'Anti-Saccharites – or – John Bull and his
family leaving off the use of sugar.' The
move to boycott sugar as a protest against
the slave trade gives the parsimonious King
and Queen an opportunity for petty saving.
'O delicious! delicious!' says the King, while
the Queen tells her six daughters, 'O my
dear creatures, do but taste it! You can't
think how nice it is without sugar: – and
then, consider how much work you'll save
the poor Blackeemoors by leaving off the use
of it! – and above all, remember how much
expense it will save your poor Papa! – O its
charming cooling drink.' In 1792 when
Gillray produced this caricature, Charlotte,
the oldest princess, was twenty-six,
Amelia, the youngest was nine.

11. 'A voluptuary under the horrors of digestion.'
Gillray depicts the Prince, aged twenty-nine,
after a heavy meal at Carlton House.

12. Gardeners at work in the grounds of the original Marine Pavilion, Brighton, as designed by Henry Holland

13. A view of Brighton in 1804 showing the Prince riding along the Steine

14. *(above left)* John Willett Payne by Hoppr

15. *(above right)* Charles James Fox by Hicke

16. *(below left)* The Earl of Moira by Reynol

17. *(below right)* Colonel McMahon by Lawr

18. The Race-Ground at Brighton by Rowlandson

19. 'His Royal Highness the Prince of Wales, with a Lady of Quality, going to Ascot Races'

20. *(above left)* Prince Frederick, Duke of Yo[rk]
    by Reynolds
21. *(above right)* Prince Ernest, Duke of
    Cumberland, by Beechey
22. *(below left)* Prince Edward, Duke of Ke[nt]
    by Edridge
23. *(below right)* Prince Augustus, Duke of
    Sussex, by Beechey

4. (*above left*) Prince William, Duke of
   Clarence, by Lawrence
5. (*above right*) Princess Amelia by Beechey
6. (*below left*) Princess Mary, later Duchess of
   Gloucester, by Beechey
7. (*below right*) Princess Sophia by Beechey

28. The Prince of Wales in 1794. A chalk drawing by John Russell

29. The Prince of Wales in the uniform of the 10th Light Dragoons by Beechey

30. Princess Caroline by Lawrence

31. Princess Charlotte by Lawrence

32. The Marriage of the Prince of Wales, and Princess Caroline at St. James's Palace
on 8 April 1795. By Graham. The Archbishop of Canterbury, John Moore,
is seen blessing the bride and bridegroom. The King is on the left, and the Queen
on the right with the Duke of York and four of the Princesses behind her.

33. Carlton House. Henry Holland's portico on the north front

34. The Dining Room at Carlton House

35. Frances, Countess of Jersey by Hoppner

36. Isabella, Marchioness of Hertford by
Downman

37. The Royal Stables at the Marine Pavilion, Brighton

38. The Chinese Corridor at Brighton

39. The Prince of Wales by Hoppner

40. The Prince of Wales aged forty-five
by Hoppner

formed a major part of his curriculum; and he was still abroad, training with the Hanoverian Army, in 1792. He was certainly not averse to a career in the Army, but his father's rigid policy of keeping him, and all his other five brothers, out of England and as far away from the baneful influences of Carlton House for as long as possible, was very irksome. 'No man ever desired more to return to his family, to his country than I do,' he wrote to the Prince of Wales from Hanover in February 1792. He had been kept abroad for almost six years and had 'not seen a single one out of England except Frederick'. 'I should even be pleased if my father would permit to my coming over to you if I even was only to stay there but a short time. Nothing can equal the pleasure I should have of seeing you all again; that we all should be again together there I do not believe will ever happen again.'[6]

It certainly was not to happen yet. The next year Prince Ernest was serving at the front with his regiment, the 9th Hanoverian Hussars, of which he was Colonel. And in 1794 his renewed request that he might be allowed to come over to England on a fortnight's furlough to see his family after an absence of eight years – and to protest at his transfer from the dashing 9th Hussars (the 'finest' in the service, officered by 'Gentlemen, many young noblemen') to the less dangerous Heavy Dragoons (officered by 'blackguards') – was again refused by his father.[7] A few months later, however, severe wounds, which eventually lost him the use of his left eye and almost the use of an arm, brought him home to England at last, his good looks lost forever. It was but a short stay. Before he was fully recovered he was back on the Continent once more, proving himself as talkative, opinionated and brave as ever.

Prince Adolphus had also gained a reputation for bravery. He, too, had attended the University of Göttingen and had trained with the Hanoverian Army. And he, like Ernest, had been wounded, had come over to England to convalesce and had soon afterwards returned to his regiment. He was the only one of the brothers not to become entangled in debt.

Although condemned to fight on a more remote and disagreeable front, Prince Edward also saw action in the war. At an early age he had decided on a military career, and after completing his education in Germany had been gazetted Brevet-Colonel in May 1786 when he was eighteen. The following year, having overspent his allowance in Hanover, he had been sent in disgrace to Geneva with his severe military tutor, Colonel Baron von Wangenheim.

Prince Edward had hated Geneva. It was the 'dullest and most insufferable' of all places, he had told the Prince of Wales, and he had been kept there for month after miserable month 'without a single line from the King and only one from the Queen'.[8] He had constantly asked to be allowed to return home and for enough money to settle his debts; but receiving no answer to his petitions, he had given von Wangenheim and his other 'bear-keepers' the slip, and had returned home without leave in 1790.

The King was furious. He granted him an interview which lasted a bare five minutes and packed him off to the army in Gibraltar where he was to be 'strictly disciplined'. Prince Edward disliked Gibraltar even more than Geneva. It was fearfully hot; there was nothing to do; of his male companions some were 'stupid, others low'; and there were almost no women to be found. He carried out his duties as commanding officer of the Royal Fusiliers punctiliously, proving himself a pertinacious stickler for the rigidities of discipline and military etiquette; but the Governor felt constrained to report his wild extravagance and his 'unbounded ideas of [his] independence'.[9] Soon he made up his mind that he could not survive the frustrations of life upon the 'solitary Rock' without a mistress. Despite the difficulties put in his way by von Wangenheim, who had kept him so short of money in Switzerland that he was scarcely able to 'enjoy those indulgences not only Princes but private gentlemen enjoy at a certain age', he had contrived in Geneva to enjoy the favours of a Mrs Rainsford with whom he had fallen in love. To find such another mistress as Mrs Rainsford in Gibraltar being impossible, he despatched a trusted friend to find him one in France. While awaiting her arrival, he lapsed further into debt by not only redecorating and refurnishing his apartments in the most expensive taste but by recruiting an orchestra and ordering four new carriages from London. When the chosen lady, Thérèse–Bernardine Mongenêt, known as Mlle de St Laurent, arrived from Marseilles he was ready to receive her in style.

She proved an excellent choice as mistress. She shared his liking for music; she was intelligent; she was good-tempered; she had 'above all, a pretty face and a handsome person'.[10] Excellent as were her qualities, though, her arrival in Gibraltar, well publicized in the Press, frustrated any chance that there might have been of her lover's hoped-for return to England. The King would not for a moment consider it, and would not even answer his son's letters. Instead of returning to England, Prince

Edward was sent to Canada. To make his exile more tolerable, Mlle de St Laurent agreed to go with him.[11]

Even with the solace of Mlle de St Laurent's company Prince Edward found Canada worse than Geneva and Gibraltar. It was 'the most dreary and gloomy spot on the face of the earth', he wrote to the Prince of Wales from Quebec. While his brothers were 'employed on the brilliant field on the Continent', he was left to vegetate there, ignored by his parents, denied the opportunities granted to his younger brothers, Ernest and Adolphus, and kept for eight and a half years away from home without 'the most distance chance' of seeing active service upon which his *'own Regiment* of Hannoverian guards' was employed under the Duke of York in Europe.[12]

The Prince of Wales, though he had never really been fond of Edward and was to grow to dislike him thoroughly, took pity on his plight. He exerted his influence on his behalf in London, and in January 1794 Prince Edward delightedly wrote to return his 'most hearty thanks' for his brother's help in having him promoted Major-General and placed on the staff of Sir Charles Grey, Commander-in-Chief in the West Indies. Two months later he arrived at Martinique and took an active part in the reduction both of that island and of St Lucia for which he was honourably mentioned in despatches.

*

Although four of his brothers – Frederick, Ernest, Adolphus and Edward – were all fighting in the war, the Prince of Wales could at least take some small comfort from the fact that the other two, William and Augustus, were not.

For years Prince William had been as distressed by his father's attitude towards him as his younger brothers had been. While he was still a child the King had decided that he should join the Navy, and in May 1779, before he was fourteen, he had been despatched aboard Captain Robert Digby's flagship with orders from his father that he was to be 'received without the smallest marks of parade' and to be treated with 'no marks of distinction'. In January 1780 he was rated midshipman and took part in the relief of Gibraltar. Thereafter for the next ten years he was, like his brothers, kept out of England, returning only for brief periods and then sent away again by the King who learned with horror of his debts and brawls, his drinking and his women. A moderately competent naval officer, as determined to maintain strict discipline in his ship as Prince Edward was in his regiment, he was promoted Captain of the frigate *Pegasus* at the early age of twenty in 1786. Nelson judged it one of the 'best disciplined' frigates he had seen, though the Prince's own officers found their captain far too rigid and obstinate, far too taken up with stringent etiquette to make service under him any sort of pleasure.

His own pleasures in the Navy would have been much enhanced had his father allowed him more money and more freedom. What could be the use of 'our worthy friend our near relation keeping us so close?' he asked the Prince of Wales in exasperation in 1786. 'Does he imagine he will make his sons his friends by this mode of conduct? If he does, he is sadly mistaken. He certainly wishes us all well and thinks he is doing his best. I am convinced he loves me by his way of receiving me last. I cannot but regard him, and would do anything to please him, but it is so difficult to satisfy.'[13]

'I understand the old boy is exceedingly out of humour,' Prince William wrote in another characteristic letter in 1788 when he had begun to wonder if the King really did love him after all. 'I am in hourly expectation of a thunderstorm from that quarter. Fatherly admonitions at our time of life are very unpleasant and of no use; it is a pity he should expend his breath or his time in such fruitless labour. I wonder which of us two he looks upon with least eyes of affection.'[14]

At the time that Prince Edward had been lamenting the dreary life he was made to endure at Geneva, Prince William had been complaining about the frustrations of being cooped up at Plymouth. 'Dulness rules here altogether,' he had mournfully told the Prince of Wales, 'but what is worse than all, not a woman fit to be touched with the tongs, not a house to put your head in after dark. . . . If it were not for the duty of the ship I should perhaps hang myself.'[15]

A few months after this letter was written, however, Prince William, or the Duke of Clarence as he now was, found just the woman he was hoping to find in Dorothea Jordan, a beautiful, generous and good-natured Irish actress, who, three years younger than himself, already had four illegitimate children by two previous lovers. She was later to have ten more, five sons and five daughters, by the Duke of Clarence whose enforced retirement from active service in the Navy was rendered less unpalatable by the prospect of this pleasant domesticity. To compensate him for his early retirement from the sea, which both his limited talents and his closeness to the throne rendered advisable, he was appointed Ranger of Bushey Park; and it was in Lord North's former house at Bushey that he settled down with Mrs Jordan, much to the distress of her many admirers who resented her frequent absences from the stage which were rendered necessary by the long succession of little Fitzclarences.

The determination of the King and the Admiralty not to allow the Duke of Clarence to resume his naval command was finally fixed when he began in 1793 to make some extraordinary speeches in the House of Lords. The spirited defence of the slave trade, which he made in a long speech in April 1793 soon after breaking his arm falling down the slippery steps of Mrs Jordan's house in Somerset Street, was not widely considered objectionable – certainly not on Merseyside where it earned him the freedom of Liverpool – even though he himself felt obliged to apologize later to William Wilberforce for having suggested that he was either a fanatic or a hypocrite.[16] Indeed, the Prince of Wales deemed it a *'most incomparable speech'*, if, perhaps, 'in the comprehension *of some people* rather too severe on Wilberforce'.[17] But a subsequent speech delivered by the Duke in June, in which he declared to an astonished House that the objects of the war having been achieved, peace should now be concluded, was generally condemned as highly irresponsible. And what was quite as bad was his constant abuse of his Majesty's Ministers, principally Pitt, to anyone who would listen to him. The Prince of Wales, as ready to lambast Pitt as the next man, agreed that his brother went much too far; but then, as he told the Duke of York, William was not to be taken too seriously. He was as good-natured a fellow as existed; he meant no harm; but he paid 'not the smallest regard to truth'.[18]

While the Duke of Clarence was kept out of the Navy in England, his younger brother, the delicate and artistic Augustus, was kept out of the country altogether. Prince Augustus, who had accompanied Ernest and Adolphus to the University of Göttingen, had not been able to follow them into the Hanoverian service owing to a chest complaint which necessitated his seeking the warmer climates of Switzerland and Italy. He was still in Italy in October 1792 when he wrote to the Prince of Wales from Rome to complain of his homesickness. He longed to be allowed to return home 'after an absence of so many years'. 'I have frequently wrote to his Majesty on this subject,' he said; 'the physicians have also informed the King it would be highly advantageous to my health – not a line on the subject nor even a hint. . . . Perhaps a word thrown in by you on a favourable occasion might have the desired effect – the more so as he knows my wish is not to remain near the Metropolis, from which both physical and political reasons drive me. Happy in being a quiet spectator of the prosperity of my country I should be glad to retire into some quiet corner of it when I might give myself up to the recovery of my health and the forming of my mind.'[19]

It would have been better had the King allowed Augustus to come home, for in April the next year at the age of twenty he secretly married in Rome Lady Augusta Murray. The plain and rather bossy second daughter of the fourth Earl of Dunmore, she was a woman almost ten years older than himself whose mother seems to have benignly countenanced the ceremony though well aware of its illegality.

One of the Prince's attendants informed the King of the marriage, and soon afterwards Augustus received orders to return home immediately. He took the pregnant Lady Augusta with him; and for fear lest objection might be raised against the previous ceremony on the grounds that, although it had been performed by an Anglican clergyman, it had taken place in the Papal states, he married her a second time at St George's, Hanover Square on 5 December. He signed the register as Mr Augustus Frederick and the bride signed it as Miss Augusta Murray.

As soon as the King heard of this ceremony, he ordered the marriage to be declared null and void under the provisions of the Royal Marriage Act of 1772. The Prince, who had returned to Italy soon after Christmas, was forbidden to see his wife or to correspond with his sisters. His father thereafter ignored his existence, as from time to time he had chosen to ignore the existence of others of his disobedient children. He pronounced himself bitterly disappointed in a son whose good sense he had once dared to hope would eventually 'prove conspicuous'.[20] By the end of October 1794 Prince Augustus was miserably asking his brother to 'cast one moment of compassion on a unhappy being . . . wandering among the ruins of Ancient Rome'.[21]

*

While Prince Augustus had been denied the opportunity of serving his country on account of his health, and the Duke of Clarence on account of his conduct, the Prince of Wales's repeated requests to take a more active part 'in the military line' had at last been answered. In the middle of January 1793 the King agreed to appoint him Colonel Commandant of the 10th (or the Prince of Wales's Own) Regiment of (Light) Dragoons – a regiment shortly to be officered almost entirely by the Prince's personal friends and protégés.

His excitement at the prospect of getting into the splendid uniform of his regiment was boundless. In an almost incoherently effusive letter – for the characteristic 'prolixity' of which he begged her indulgence – he told his mother that his heart was overflowing so much with gratitude to his *'good and gracious* father' that his words and language were too weak to express 'the most disstant idea' of his feelings. His 'joye' was 'boundless'; his head was *'almost turned'*; he must ask her to tell the King that he was so overwhelmed by his goodness that he was totally unfit for society but that the next day at whatever hour would be 'the properest and most convenient' he would come to the Queen's House to throw himself at his father's feet. He feared he almost expressed his feelings 'in a tone of insanity'. 'The King has already given me life, but now he has done more, for he has not only given me life, but the *enjoyment of life* and is that not *the greatest* of all blessings? I am not equal to meeting you this evening overpowered with the shocking events of France [where Louis XVI had been executed three days before] and with the species of sentiment towards *my father* which surpasses all discription.'[22]

A few days later the Prince received official notification of his appointment from the War Office, together with the additional good news that his commission was to be dated 19 November 1782 in order that he might take rank above all the present colonels in the Army.[23] Filled with ideas of military glory, he now wrote to Vienna requesting permission to serve, in the Imperial Army, *'la cause commune de tous les Princes et Souverains de l'Europe'*.[24] The Emperor raised no objection, but the King would not allow it. Nor would he agree to the Prince of Wales being granted the kind of rapid promotion enjoyed by his four younger brothers in the Army, all of whom were, or were soon to become, generals. The Prince must never aspire to become a general himself; he must be content to be and to remain the 'first Colonel at the head of a Regiment'.[25]

In this capacity he joined the 10th Light Dragoons in camp near Brighton where he spent his thirty-first birthday, his father having decided that it would be 'against all military rules' to allow him to come to Windsor for the usual celebrations.[26]

Denied the opportunity of distinguishing himself abroad, the Prince did not take his military duties in England too conscientiously. As *The*

Times announced on 5 August, the Prince's intention was to dine in the mess every day that the Regiment was encamped ('in a delightful spot by the sea side'); but he did not intend to be separated from his comforts. His tent, an extremely elaborate construction with three separate sections for cooking, dining and sleeping, was furnished with the most elegant chairs and a superb square bed, its fringed and tasselled hangings being 'of a very delicate chintz, a white ground with a lilac and green cloud', and its four corners ornamented with the Prince's feathers and motto.[27] Nor did he remain in camp for long. Within a month he was back living amidst the grander pleasures of Carlton House, though more concerned than ever that unless there was soon a dramatic improvement in the state of his finances those pleasures could not much longer be enjoyed.

Fresh Debts and New Mistresses

1793-1794

*

'Lady Jersey's influence'

The Duke of York had solved his own financial problems by getting married. For a time he had entertained thoughts of marrying the rich, young and good-looking widow of the fourth Duke of Rutland who, after her husband's death, had become the mistress of Colonel John St Leger. The Duchess seemed not unwilling, but the Prince of Wales and others of the Duke's friends persuaded him, if only for St Leger's sake, to abandon the project. Far better, the Duke was advised, to consider one of those German princesses whom his father considered so eminently desirable as daughters-in-law. Fortunately there was one of these who did appeal to him. This was Princess Frederica, eldest daughter of Frederick William II of Prussia. She was very small, not at all pretty and had poor teeth; but the diplomat, Lord Malmesbury, as Sir James Harris had now become, thought that although she was indeed far from 'handsome', she was 'lively, sensible and very tractable' and that she would make him happy.[1]

The Duke for his part had little doubt of it. He assured the Prince of Wales that – having renewed his friendship with her – he had 'grown more attracted to her' than he could possibly describe; that he was, in fact, 'over head and ears in love'.[2] John St Leger, who had accompanied the Duke to Berlin, confirmed their fondness for each other. 'I never saw two people so compleatly in love as the Duke and Princess are,' he told the Prince of Wales. 'It is beyond anything I ever saw or heard of. I think your R.H. will like your belle sœur very much: Elle est très aimable et remplie de talents: très bonne musicienne et chantante comme une ange.'[3]

Her parents were delighted with the match. They had not been too hopeful of arranging one as satisfactory as this for so dumpy and plain a girl, and one who was moreover nearly twenty-four. Her mother cried for joy when the marriage was announced, and her father told her contentedly that although she had had to wait a long time she had now won the great prize.

Anxious to get married as quickly as possible – both to enjoy his bride and the additional £18,000 a year which would help to solve his money problems – the Duke appealed to the Prince of Wales to do all he could to hasten the arrangements. He was to see to the ordering of carriages, and at least £20,000 worth of diamonds, to find his bride a good hairdresser, to buy her smart fans and shoes (not easily obtainable in Berlin), and to negotiate for a suitable house, preferably Melbourne House in Piccadilly.

His own house, York House in Whitehall, which he had bought in 1787, was too small; so was Cumberland House which his brother suggested. If Lord Melbourne could be persuaded to exchange his Piccadilly mansion for the smaller but elegant house in Whitehall that would be ideal.

So the Prince went on his brother's behalf to see Lord and Lady Melbourne who said that provided they were not 'any how loosers' – they were hard-pressed themselves for ready money at the time – they were prepared to do anything the Duke wished. It was accordingly agreed that 'His Royal Highness Frederick Duke of York and Albany [should] exchange with Peniston Lord Viscount Melbourne the ... premises ... at ... Whitehall and the furniture therein', and that Lord Melbourne should 'on payment of £23,571 grant and release' to the Duke of York the premises in Piccadilly.[4]*

The Duke was further indebted to his brother for taking the trouble to consult the royal shoemaker, Thomas Taylor, in the matter of Princess Frederica's shoes, though the outcome of this errand, through no fault of the Prince's, was less happy. The Duke sent the Prince one of the Princess's shoes with instructions that Taylor make six 'very neat' new pairs, warning him that the sample shoe 'was about a quarter of an inch too long, and too wide every way'.[5] Taylor was naturally apprehensive, so he told the Prince of Wales that his shoes might not fit the Princess very well

* The Piccadilly house for a time became known as York House and then, after its subsequent conversion into 'residential chambers for gentlemen', as Albany which is still its name today though it has opened its doors to married, widowed and divorced women as tenants as well as men. The Whitehall house, built by James Paine in 1754–58 and improved by Henry Holland in 1787, became Melbourne House when the new occupiers moved in. Subsequently it became Dover House and is now the Scottish Office.

until he had seen her foot and measured it himself. However he set to work and soon the shoes, and the apparent delicacy of the Princess's tiny feet, became objects of the greatest curiosity.

Their owner arrived in England, having married the Duke in Berlin, on 19 November 1791 and was greeted with the utmost enthusiasm. A second ceremony at the Queen's House was all the more warmly welcomed since it was the first acknowledged marriage in the immediate royal family since that of the King himself. Although they were scarcely able to eulogize the Duchess of York's beauty, newspapers contained column after column praising her charm and animation, her neatness and amiable manner. Copies of her famous shoes were sold in their hundreds. Later models, of fine purple leather five and a half inches long and studded with diamonds, were described at length in the Press and even depicted in engravings which, according to the *Public Advertiser*, were acquired by the 'major part of John Bull and his family'.[6] It soon 'became the fashion for every one to squeeze their feet without mercy, in order to be like her Royal Highness, and as she wore heels to her shoes, so did the rest of the world'.[7] The rage for the Duchess's shoes became so excessive, in fact, that Gillray was induced to bring the whole inflated business down to earth in a rude caricature, 'Fashionable Contrasts', which showed the Duchess's minute feet encased in her slippers lying, heels downwards, on the edge of a bed with the Duke's massive shoes lying, heels upwards, between them.

The Prince of Wales welcomed his sister-in-law into the family most warmly and appeared to be 'extremely fond of her'. Mary Noel thought it delightful to see them dancing together; he exerted himself 'to the very best of his power' and behaved towards her 'more like a lover than a brother'.[8]

*

Now that the Duke of York by marrying his little Princess had raised his total income (including the revenues of the Bishopric of Osnaburgh which his father, as ruler of Hanover, had bestowed on him when he was a child) to some £70,000 a year, it was borne ever more strongly on the Prince of Wales that the only solution to his own financial chaos might well lie in the choice of a princess for himself. To pay for the continuing improvements at Carlton House (for which over £60,000 was still needed in 1789), for his racing establishment (which still cost over £30,000 a year) and his several other extravagances, he had made numerous efforts to raise loans from all manner of sources in England and abroad. This gave much concern not only to Pitt and other members of the King's government but also to the opposition who, as Sir Gilbert Elliot said, were a good deal dissatisfied with him for 'soliciting loans in Holland and elsewhere, on usurious terms, and to be repaid at the King's death'.[9] Some of his efforts to raise money were successful, others were not. Towards the end of 1789 he and the Dukes of York and Clarence had borrowed 350,000 guilders at 5 per cent from a Jewish banking firm at the Hague and had ruined the firm by failing to repay the loan or even to pay any interest.[10] Later on negotiations were entered into with a firm at Antwerp for raising the sum of £300,000 which became necessary when other creditors called in a loan for a similar amount.[11]

Appeals were also made to the English bankers, Thomas Hammersley and William Morland, and to Thomas Coutts who, having lent the Prince £60,000 in 1793[12] and after 'straining every exertion to the utmost so as to preclude all *power of going further*', was driven sincerely to hope that his Royal Highness would 'rigidly adhere to the system' of never asking him for any further advances of money which he would be obliged to refuse.[13] Appeals were then made to the Duke of Orleans, who was induced to part with £20,000 to each of the three brothers;[14] to the Landgrave of Hesse-Cassel, who indicated that he might be willing to lend £100,000 to £150,000;[15] and to the Duke of York's father-in-law, the King of Prussia. 'I cannot help for all our sakes pressing you a little bit,' the Prince wrote to the Duke of York. 'Pray do you think that your beau père would not do a little something in the loan-way. . . . My dearest Frederick you must for all our sakes strain every nerve. . . . I hope you will not lose sight of this as it is of too much consequence to be neglected and that you will prove yourself an able negotiator.'[16] But nothing was forthcoming from the King of Prussia. Lord Malmesbury, who relieved the Duke of York of the embarrassing task of negotiating for a loan in Berlin, reported that 'it would not be easy for [the King] at the moment to find the means to the extent that [was] wanted'.[17]

So the Prince's solicitor, Charles Bicknell, and other less reputable envoys, were despatched to Germany, to Holland, to Belgium and, in desperation, to Ireland. And some of these envoys, including Louis Weltje and Annesley Shee, a man who had formerly run a lottery office near Carlton House, expended on his behalf considerable sums which they had difficulty in recovering. Recourse was had to all manner of devices. Attempts were even made to raise loans from men who were to be rewarded by titles as soon as the Prince had power to confer them.[18]

But the sums raised were never enough. He owed Leader, the coachmaker, £32,777; Choppin, the horse dealer, £7,200; White and Thomas, the breeches makers, £1,875; his various tailors, Weston, Schweitzer and Davidson, Louis Bazalgette, and Winter & Co., a total of £31,919. He was in debt to most of his friends – more than £15,000 to the Earl of Moira – while members of his Household had not been paid for months.[19] The Prince knew he could expect nothing from 'the Great Billy', who would certainly not risk his popularity or injure his career by advocating an increased allowance in Parliament. Nor could the Prince look for help to those who had been his supporters during the Regency crisis. The Whig opposition, severely mauled at that time, was being virtually broken up by the controversies raging over the French Revolution and the war. Fox's sympathetic attitude towards the Revolution had widened the breach between himself and the Prince – a breach which Mrs Fitzherbert was at pains to keep unbridged in the face of contrary efforts by the Duchess of Devonshire – and yet, without the support of Fox and his friends, the more moderate Whig party, which was led by the Duke of Portland and included Burke, was powerless to assist him.

Unable to enlist the help of the politicians, the Prince was also unable to turn with any hope of success to the King who was now, as Fox had to admit, 'quite master of the country'.[20] The King's answers to his son's requests were always the same.

It was Lord Loughborough's opinion that 'in these times of democratic frenzy it was necessary to support the splendour of Courts and Princes'.[21] The King, however, was more disposed to take the view of Lord Thurlow that 'in this painful situation' the only wise and honourable line which the Prince could pursue was 'to determine to make every practicable reduction in his expenditure, and to allot a large portion of his income to the discharge of his debts'.[22] The Prince would be well advised, Lord Thurlow considered, to go to live quietly for a time at the country house, Kempshot House near Basingstoke in Hampshire, which he had taken for the hunting to be enjoyed there, and drastically to reduce his establishment.

The trouble with Thurlow's scheme was that the Prince now owed so much that even the most severe retrenchment would not save sufficient money to satisfy his creditors. He shut up Carlton House once again; his racing establishment was more or less dismantled; but these economies were not enough. His situation was becoming so deplorable that tradesmen began to refuse to execute his orders and even stopped him in the street to demand the settlement of their bills. The workmen laid off at Carlton House went so far as to petition the Prime Minister, who immediately passed their petition back to him. In desperation he offered enormous rates of interest to money-lenders but they would no longer help him. So many bonds had had to be dishonoured in the past that his undertakings were now thoroughly discredited. Those few friends who could have helped him were reluctant to do so since they knew that anyone to whom the Prince owed money was never welcome in his company.

So he was forced to turn once more to the solution he so much dreaded. He would have to get married.

*

By the time the Prince came to this unhappy decision, he was already separated from Mrs Fitzherbert. For over a year they had been growing less and less devoted to each other.

Lady Anne Lindsay recorded instances of their quarrels at the dinner-table, of the Prince parrying her accusations until at last he was provoked into making a reply that drove her from her chair with 'angry tears'. After she had left the table on one occasion, the Prince begged leave to talk to Lady Anne and 'regretted her temper, but in terms so kind, so lenient' that Lady Anne was convinced that the fault was more hers than his. 'Ah,' he said, 'if she loved and considered me as much as I love her, we should not quarrel so often as we do.' Lady Anne was 'sorry to hear it was becoming a habit, but was not surprised'.[23] There were stories of quarrels at Brighton where Mrs Fitzherbert was ill at ease in the company of the Prince's more raffish friends. It was said that the Prince would often arrive late at night at her house with various drunken companions, and that 'she would seek a refuge from their presence even under the sofa, when the Prince, finding the drawing-room deserted, would draw his sword in joke, and searching about the room would at last draw forth the trembling victim from her place of concealment'.[24]

It was true that Mrs Fitzherbert usually forgave him for these escapades and that the Prince, for his part, came to her help so long as he could when she was in trouble with her creditors. As her allowance from him was most erratically paid, she was often in debt. On one occasion the bailiffs arrived at her house in Pall Mall with a writ for a debt of almost £2,000 and the threat that if she did not settle it by the next day she would be taken to prison. Since she had no money and the bailiffs would not allow any of her possessions to be carried out of the house to the pawn-brokers, she had to rely upon the Prince to save her. Unable to raise any money himself, he was obliged to send to Carlton House for his jewels which were, so it was said, immediately taken round to the pawnshop.

The Prince also, it was admitted, took Mrs Fitzherbert's side if she was treated slightingly by any member of his family. When the diminutive Duchess of York, who was proving to be rather more aloof and formidable than had been expected, showed that she intended to treat her with the dismissive cold civility which would have been appropriate at the Prussian Court, the Prince strongly remonstrated with his brother.[25] The Duke of York protested that he could not make his wife behave in a more friendly way, but the Prince argued that he ought at least to try. They fell out over the issue; the Prince talked 'coldly and unaffectionately' to Lord Malmesbury about the Duke and his wife,[26] and it was some time before the former friendship between the two brothers was resumed.[27] Lord Malmesbury added a note in his diary that at this time – June 1792 – the Prince 'was more attached to Mrs Fitzherbert than ever'.[28]

Yet, as the months went by and his debts increased, their quarrels became more frequent and more lengthy. Earlier disputes had soon been settled. Edward Jerningham, the poet, had told his niece, Charlotte, that 'the tittle-tattle of the town' in the summer of 1791 had all been 'of the separation of the Prince and Mrs Fitzherbert'.[29] But this squabble had soon been forgotten and the relationship had continued as before. Very often these early disputes had been over women. There had been an un-successful attempt on his part to seduce a lovely and tiresomely virtuous daughter of Lady Archer; there had been a subsequent and more reward-ing attempt upon Lucy Howard whose child, George Howard, supposedly the Prince's son, died in its second year and was buried at Brighton.[30] There had also been an affair with Mrs Anna Maria Crouch, a singer of mixed Welsh and French descent who had scored a triumph as Polly Peachum in the *Beggar's Opera*. A beautiful and fascinating woman, Mrs Crouch had been living in a *ménage à trois* with her husband, who was an impecunious naval officer, and Michael Kelly, the Irish actor and opera singer. The advent of a second lover, in the stout shape of the Prince of Wales, had been too much for Lieutenant Crouch who had taken the opportunity of leaving his wife and living more conveniently and contentedly on an allowance she made him. Her affair with the Prince had been a brief one. Indeed, some reports had it that, after making out a bond for £12,000 and settling about £400 a year on her husband to prevent his bringing an action against him, the Prince made love to her on only one occasion.[31] Certainly Mrs Crouch soon returned to the more lasting affection of Michael Kelly, agreeing to sell back the Prince's bond. An emissary went to her house in the Haymarket to collect the bond from her, taking with him a bag containing one thousand guineas. In his coach, in the care of footmen, were two other bags containing a further thousand guineas each should the first offer not tempt her. Fortunately she settled for a thousand guineas, leaving the Prince free to seek – and to receive – the forgiveness of Mrs Fitzherbert.[32]

Mrs Fitzherbert had long since recognized that the Prince, in Sheridan's words, was 'too much every lady's man to be the man of any lady'. But although ready to forgive him in the past for his casual affairs, she was by now exasperated by his selfishness, his careless accusations that she no longer loved him whenever she had cause to complain of his behaviour, his absurd contentions that she was conducting a secret affair with the royalist emigré, the Comte de Noailles. The Duke of Gloucester told Lady Harcourt that the Prince had 'much consideration' for Mrs Fitzherbert, but that the offhand way in which he 'had his amusements elsewhere' led to her being 'sometimes jealous and discontented'.[33]

Never was Mrs Fitzherbert more jealous and discontented than when she realized that the Prince was falling in love with the Countess of Jersey. She had not taken his other affairs too seriously. Indeed, John St Leger said that she had treated the Crouch affair 'with ridicule'.[34] But Lady Jersey was a far more serious threat. Her husband, an elderly gentleman of the most courtly manners and fastidious dress, known as the 'Prince of Maccaronies', had held various appointments in the King's Household, and Lady Jersey herself was on friendly terms with several ladies about the Court, in particular with Lady Harcourt. Although there were rumours of more than one lover in the recent past, she was also on friendly terms with the Queen, who listened with pleasure to her skilful playing of the harp and who noted with satisfaction that her father, the Rt Rev Philip Twysden, was a bishop of respected lineage. A mother of two sons and seven daughters, some of whom had already provided her with grandchildren, she was nine years older than the Prince, a woman of mature charm and undeniable beauty. Sir Nathaniel Wraxall spoke of her 'irrestible seduction and fascination'.[35] Mary Frampton described her as 'clever, unprincipled, but beautiful and fascinating'.[36] The Prince – on whom her allurements were exercised with the practised care of an ambitious, experienced, sensual, though controlled and rather heartless woman – was captivated. He had known her for years and had always been rather attracted by her, but it was not until now, when she was in her early forties, that he was forcibly struck by the peculiar strength of her appeal.*

So fond of her did he become that he abandoned Mrs Fitzherbert's company entirely for hers; and to the dismay of their mutual friend, Lord Hugh Seymour, wrote a letter under his new mistress's direction to say that he had now found happiness elsewhere.[37] Lady Jersey assured him that the connexion with Mrs Fitzherbert had never been wise, that her being a Roman Catholic was the cause of his unpopularity, that if it were not for her he would have no difficulty in settling his financial affairs satisfactorily, that she was not really fond of him, that she had been heard to declare that it was not so much the person of his Royal Highness that she loved but his rank.

Attracted as he was by Lady Jersey, the Prince did not find it easy to live without Mrs Fitzherbert who, as he well knew, was largely innocent of the charges brought against her. He wanted both women at once. He wrote to Mrs Fitzherbert seeking her forgiveness once more. At first she declined to give it. How could he still love her when for months he had 'given his time to another', and had behaved to her with 'the greatest cruelty'? At length, however, having received 'messages of peace in numbers', she gave way and they were friends again.[38] But there were intermittent quarrels still, and her temper on these occasions, so Lady Harcourt alleged, was 'violent'.[39] The Duke of York also wrote of 'Mrs Fitzherbert's unfortunate temper', and advised his brother 'not to bear with it any longer'; he would be better to be 'out of her shackles'.[40]

Threatened by the Prince's infatuation with Lady Jersey, Mrs Fitzherbert's position was further endangered by the decision of the Court of Privileges that Prince Augustus's secret marriage to Lady Augusta Murray was null and void. If Lady Augusta, a Protestant who could trace

---

* Their names had been linked together in the newspapers as early as 1782, when Lady Jersey professed that she had no feelings for the boy. 'If he is in love with me I cannot help it,' she wrote. 'It is impossible for anyone to give another less encouragement than I have' (Hickleton Papers, A1.2.7).

her descent from Henry VII of England and Charles VII of France, from James II of Scotland and the eleventh-century Marquis of Este, was not acceptable as the wife of a royal prince, how could she, a Roman Catholic, hope to have her own marriage judged legal in the unlikely event of it ever being acknowledged as having even taken place?

The decision of the Court of Privileges was not so unwelcome to the Prince of Wales. Although it did not alter his moral obligations to Mrs Fitzherbert, all remaining doubt about his legal obligations were thus removed. He was definitely free to marry. In June 1794, on the same day that he sent her a note explaining that he had been called away suddenly to Windsor from Brighton, addressing her as 'dear love' and declaring himself 'ever thine', he sent her a subsequent letter to tell her that he could never see her again. Not then knowing of his decision to get married, she naturally attributed this cruel letter to her rival for whom the Prince had recently built a new staircase leading to her apartments at the Marine Pavilion at Brighton. Mrs Fitzherbert endorsed the letter, 'Lady Jersey's influence'. Having done so she left home without making any reply. It was believed that she had gone abroad. The Prince, regretting having dismissed her so abruptly, tried to find out where she had gone and to persuade her to come back, but he could not find her. She did not write; and he, using her silence as an excuse to suppose that she did not truly love him, decided that there was now no longer any possible reason to delay his marriage and the consequent settlement of his bills.

In August 1794 he went to see his father who was on holiday at Weymouth and told him 'very abruptly' that he had severed all connexion with Mrs Fitzherbert and was ready to enter 'a more creditable line of life' by getting married.[41]

PART TWO
1794-1811

12

Princess Caroline
1794-1795
*

'There, dear brother, is a woman I do not recommend at all'

For years, so the Duchess of Brunswick said, every possible contender for the hand of the Prince of Wales, with one exception, had been assiduously practising her English in the Protestant Courts of Germany. The exception was her own daughter, Caroline, whose chances of marrying the heir to the English throne were considered negligible. In the first place Princess Caroline was first cousin to the Prince, and the King of England was known to disapprove of marriages between such close relations.[1] The Duchess of Brunswick was his eldest and only surviving sister, Augusta; the Princess's great-grandmother, moreover, was his own great-grandfather's sister. There were other reasons, too, why Princess Caroline was not considered a likely candidate as a bride for the Prince of Wales. It was rumoured that she was a young woman of far from impeccable character, that as a girl she had had an illicit affair with a man of low birth, that she was exceedingly indiscreet.

Diplomats and soldiers who had been brought into contact with the Court in Brunswick agreed that the Princess would not be a suitable choice. Arthur Paget, British envoy extraordinary in Berlin, thought that it would be injudicious to put down on paper a sketch of her character, but 'could not avoid saying this much': that the proposed marriage was far more likely to 'ensure the misery of the Prince of Wales, than promote his happiness'.[2] Lord St Helens, who had spent most of his adult life on the Continent in the diplomatic corps, wrote guardedly of a 'stain' upon her reputation;[3] Major Toëbingen, an immense officer in the King's German Legion whom Mary Frampton knew very well, wore 'a very large amethyst stud or pin, reported to have been presented to him by the Princess Caroline';[4] while Lord Holland said that any young English traveller who had been through Germany on the Grand Tour would, if asked, have told the Prince that the character of his intended bride was considered 'exceedingly loose', even in that country 'where they were not at that period very nice about female delicacy'.[5]

When her name began to be mentioned in England, the Queen immediately indicated that she did not approve of it, insisting that Caroline, for reasons she did not care to specify, was totally unacceptable. Tearfully she told Prince Ernest that she had never liked the Duchess of Brunswick, and, while she would treat the daughter well, she declined to talk about her. 'Her opinions she could not give,' Prince Ernest told the Prince of Wales, 'as she never intended to speak about it. . . . God knows what is the matter with her, but she is sullen. I sounded her tonight about you, but no reply soever was made.'[6] Yet although she would not talk about Princess Caroline's disadvantages to her family in England, the Queen did write to her brother to confide her fears in him.

'The fact is, my dear brother,' she wrote, 'that the King is completely ignorant of everything concerning the Duke's [Brunswick's] family, and that it would be unseemly to speak to him against his niece. But it is not at all unseemly to tell you that a relative of that family, who is indeed very attached to the Duke, has spoken to me of Princess Caroline with very little respect. They say that her passions are so strong that the Duke himself said that she was not to be allowed even to go from one room to another without her Governess, and that when she dances, this lady is obliged to follow her for the whole of the dance to prevent her from making an exhibition of herself by indecent conversations with men, and that the Duke as well as the Duchess have forbidden her, in the presence of this person from whom I heard all this, to speak to anyone at all except her Governess, and that all her amusements have been forbidden her because of her indecent conduct. . . . There, dear brother, is a woman I do not recommend at all.'[7]

The King, however, when told of his son's choice, was happy to accept it. Forgetting all previous prejudices against marriages between first cousins, evidently ignoring the unfortunate reports that two of her brothers were mad and that her own mother thought that their sister was not much saner herself, he expressed himself much gratified that his niece had been selected. 'Undoubtedly she is the person who naturally must be most agreeable to *me*,' he wrote to Pitt after the conversation with his son at Weymouth on 24 August 1794. 'I expressed my approbation of the idea.'[8]

The Prince did not express any approbation himself. He was marrying, he allowed it to be supposed, because he could not get his debts settled in any other way, and because his plan of allowing the Crown to descend to the children of the Duke of York was now foiled by the Duchess's failure to bear any children and her doctors' belief that she never could have any. The Duke of Clarence appeared to have settled down permanently with Mrs Jordan; Prince Edward showed no signs of growing tired of Mlle St Laurent; Prince Augustus was still languishing in Italy worrying about Lady Augusta Murray; Prince Adolphus, at twenty, could obviously not be expected to get married when he had no wish to do so; Prince Ernest, for the moment, appeared to take little interest in women.

So, if *he* were to provide an heir and if he were to become solvent again, he had no alternative but to marry. For this purpose he seemed to think that any German princess would do. He made few inquiries about Caroline or any of her possible rivals. It seemed almost as though he chose the Brunswick Princess, hastily, sulkily and petulantly, as a peevish protest against having to choose any wife at all. The choice, it was said – by Lord Holland among others – was not in the least unwelcome to Lady Jersey who actively encouraged the Prince to make it. Being unable to marry him herself she had no objections whatsoever to his marrying a woman of supposedly 'indelicate manners, indifferent character, and not very inviting appearance, from the hope that disgust for the wife would secure constancy to the mistress'.[9]*

*

The envoy chosen to go to Brunswick to make a formal request for the hand of Princess Caroline was the tactful, wily Lord Malmesbury who

---

* 'Lady Jersey made the marriage,' the Duke of Wellington later told Lady Salisbury, 'simply because she wished to put Mrs Fitzherbert on the same footing as herself, and deprive her of the claim to the title of lawful wife to the Prince.' (Oman, *Gascoyne Heiress*, 207).

was received most cordially by the Duchess on 28 November. It was made obvious to Malmesbury immediately on his arrival that there was going to be no trouble with the mother. She was rather silly and inquisitive, indiscreet and undignified, but 'all good nature'; she talked 'incessantly' about her daughter's future expectations. The Duke on the other hand was, 'as usual, civil, but reserved and stiff'.

The first impression created by the Princess herself was not altogether unfavourable, though her head seemed rather too big for her body and her neck too dumpy. She was short, Malmesbury noticed, 'with what the French call "des epaules impertinentes" '; her figure was 'not graceful'; her teeth could be described as no better than 'tolerable', and they appeared to be going bad; her eyelashes were white. But she had 'fine' eyes and 'good' hands, and attractive fair, abundant hair. John Hoppner when painting her portrait after her arrival in England decided that her person was 'very bad – short – very full chested and jutting hips'. Her face, however, with which she herself appeared to be 'very well pleased', was not unattractive, and Malmesbury agreed that it was quite pretty, though 'not expressive of softness'. She was 'much embarrassed' upon being presented to the English Lord, yet 'vastly happy' about his mission. She was twenty-four years old.[10]

Lord Malmesbury's initial opinion of Princess Caroline improved on further acquaintance. She was 'gay and cheerful' and loved laughing; she understood a joke and could make one; she appeared to listen attentively to the advice he gave her as to how she should behave in England; she was obviously goodnatured and generous, and was 'certainly not fond of money as both her parents' were.[11] Yet it had to be admitted that with this cheerfulness and good nature went many faults. Her father, an intelligent, cautious, suspicious and evasive man, was well enough aware of them himself. He was most anxious on his daughter's behalf and much afraid of what might happen to her in England; he 'dreaded the Prince's habits' and the tactless way in which his daughter might react to them. Entreating Malmesbury to be her constant adviser, he 'hinted delicately, but very pointedly at the free and unreserved manners of the Duchess' who had never provided a good example for the girl. Caroline was not stupid, he insisted, but she had no judgement; she was always asking personal questions and expressing imprudent opinions about people and affairs in general; one needed to be strict with her; it must be impressed upon her that when the Prince took a fancy to another woman she must not show any jealousy. He had told her all this himself and written it down in German; but he urged Malmesbury to repeat it.

The next day after dinner the Duke's mistress took Malmesbury aside and confirmed all that he had been told: Caroline was not ill-disposed but very impressionable, easily led, and she had '*no tact*'. It was important that Malmesbury should speak to her as, although she respected her father, she was afraid of him and considered him 'as a severe rather than an affectionate' parent.[12] Later Mlle Hertzfeldt added that the Princess did not have a '*cœur depravé*'; she had never done anything bad, but she always spoke before she thought. 'I repeat,' Mle Hertzfeldt impressed upon Malmesbury, '*elle n'a jamais rien fait de mauvais, mais elle est sans jugement et on l'a jugée à l'avenant.*' It would be necessary to be extremely strict with her, to govern her by fear, '*par la terreur même*'.[13]

The longer Malmesbury remained in Brunswick the more certain he became that the Princess was much in need of all the good advice he could offer her. She was always so talkative at supper and usually indis-creet. And after supper when playing cards – at which she was 'very *gauche*' – she was far too free and easy with the ladies about the Court, calling them '*mon cœur*', '*ma chère*', '*ma petite*', even those whom she scarcely knew, gossiping with them, chattering away without a thought as to what she was saying, making 'the most improper remarks', being very 'missish' and taking pride in being able to find out about everything, whom people liked and disliked.

Frequently Malmesbury, in his firm yet delicate way, reminded her that she could not behave like this in England, that she really must learn to consider the effects of what she felt inclined to say before she spoke. He advised her that popularity in England would not be attained 'by *familiarity*, that it could only belong to respect, and was to be acquired by a just mixture of dignity and affability'. He suggested that she should follow the example of the Queen in this respect. But the Princess said she was afraid of the Queen and felt sure that her Majesty 'would be jealous of her and do her harm'. All the more reason then, said Malmesbury, to be attentive to her, holding up as a model the Duchess of York whose discretion and conduct were much admired in England. The Princess strongly disliked the Duchess, and so this piqued her – as Malmesbury intended it should.[14]

Usually, though, she did listen carefully to what he said, particularly when he urged her 'on no account to show that she was jealous' if she detected any signs of her husband being unfaithful to her. Wisely he advised her that 'reproaches and sourness never reclaimed anybody', that he knew enough of the Prince to be quite sure that this sort of reaction 'would probably make him disagreeable and peevish, and certainly force him to be false and dissembling', whereas if she attempted to recover a 'tottering affection' by 'softness . . . and caresses', he 'could not withstand such a conduct'.[15]

The Princess had heard about Lady Jersey, for her mother, with what Malmesbury described as 'her usual indiscretion', had shown her an anonymous letter, 'evidently written by some disappointed milliner or angry maid-servant', in which the writer had tried to frighten her 'with the idea she would lead her into an affair of gallantry' and would be ready to offer her services in finding a willing lover.

'This did *not* frighten the Princess, although it did the Duke and Duchess,' Malmesbury noted significantly in his diary, 'and on my perceiving this, I told her Lady [Jersey] would be more cautious than to risk such an audacious measure; and that, besides, it was *death* to presume to approach a Princess of Wales, and no man would be daring enough to think of it. She asked me whether I was in earnest. I said such was our law; that anybody who presumed to *love* her was guilty of *high treason*, and punished with *death*, if she was weak enough to listen to him: so also would *she*. This startled her.'[16]

Princess Caroline was also shocked when her mother showed her another letter which had arrived in Brunswick. This was from her future father-in-law, who had written to express the hope that his niece would not prove to be vivacious, that she was prepared to lead in England a life both 'sedentary and retired'.[17]

Lord Malmesbury was convinced by now that Princess Caroline's temperament was not in the least suited to such a life. He had no reason to alter his conviction that she was well-meaning and well-disposed, that she had 'great good humour and much good nature – not a grain of rancour'. But when summing up her character to himself in a series of jottings in his diary, he felt bound to conclude that she had 'no judgment; caught by the first impression, led by the first impulse . . . loving to talk, and prone to confide and make missish friendships that last twenty-four hours. Some natural, but no acquired morality, and no strong innate notions of its value and necessity; warm feelings and nothing to counterbalance them.

... Fond of gossiping, and this strengthened greatly by the example of her mother, who is all curiosity and inquisitiveness, and who has no notion of not gratifying the desire at any price. In short, the Princess in the hands of a steady and sensible man would probably turn out well, but where it is likely she will find faults perfectly analogous to her own, she will fail.'[18]

None of these reservations about the suitability of Princess Caroline as a wife for the Prince of Wales was made known in his letters to England, as Lord Malmesbury's instructions had been merely to demand her hand in marriage and to convey her to London. Indeed, the letters the Prince received were uniformly encouraging. His aunt Augusta, his future mother-in-law, assured him, 'Caroline is so happy with your picture and her future situation.'[19] His uncle William, Duke of Gloucester, confirmed how 'much much satisfyed with the conduct of her daughter' his sister, Augusta, was; and he added, 'she strongly recommends that her daughter's cloaths should be chiefly white, as that becomes her most: in short, she is quite delighted, as I heartily hope you will be when you see your beautiful bride'.[20] Lord Malmesbury wrote to say that on being introduced to the Princess she had replied in the most graceful and dignified manner: her words had conveyed everything the Prince could wish to hear; Lord Malmesbury would not repeat them as he hoped his Royal Highness would soon hear them from her own mouth; it was impossible to describe the appearance of delight on her countenance when he had handed her his Royal Highness's portrait. She had immediately fastened it round her neck where it had remained ever since.[21]

The next week Malmesbury wrote again to report that he had been 'ordered by the Princess to say everything that is respectful, grateful and affectionate to your Royal Highness. She has received a box from England with English dresses and it is amazing how much they become her.'[22]

*

Other reports about Princess Caroline that continued to arrive and to circulate in England were, however, more disturbing. Lord Liverpool believed that, if proper inquiries had been made, it would certainly have been discovered how 'very loose' her conduct was;[23] and Lord Holland said that 'unfavourable reports of the person, and yet more of the manners and character of the destined bride came pouring in from Germany after the articles were signed and it was too late to recede.'[24]

Lord Malmesbury himself discovered some additional unpleasant faults in the Princess when he was thrown into closer contact with her during the journey to England. Although the Marriage Treaty was signed on 3 December, the journey did not begin until the 30th owing to the difficulties of making safe travel arrangements in time of war; and, due to French victories and a very severe frost that prevented the British ships sailing into harbour, it was not until 28 March that Lord Malmesbury was able to get his charge safely aboard H.M.S. *Jupiter* in the River Elbe off Stade.

In those two months Lord Malmesbury's poor opinion of the character of the Duchess of Brunswick was fully confirmed. She had agreed to accompany her daughter as far as the coast, but at Osnabruck she wanted to go home to Brunswick for fear lest she be captured by the French. 'If I am taken,' she said to Malmesbury, 'I am sure the King will be angry.'

'He will be very sorry,' Malmesbury replied, 'but your Royal Highness must *not* leave your daughter till she is in the hands of her attendants.'[25]

She argued; but Lord Malmesbury would not give way, and she was at length persuaded to remain with the party. Both Malmesbury and her daughter could have done without her company. Sometimes she was 'very disagreeable about the cold, peevish and ill-mannered . . . troublesome about choosing her apartment'. At other times she told indiscreet stories about the Queen and the Duke of York, neither of whom she liked, and about the King with whom she had been made to share a bed as a child. That had been as disagreeable as possible, she said, as he used to wet it until their 'father [the late Prince of Wales] cured him of his fault by making him wear the blue ribbon [of the Order of the Garter] with a piece of china attached to it which was *not* the George'.[26]

Lord Malmesbury could scarcely blame Princess Caroline for not respecting such a mother, but he felt obliged to reprimand her for showing her disdain so openly, for treating her rudely and actually laughing at her. He also felt compelled to talk to her upon a more serious matter that had become of concern to him: the delicate question of her personal cleanliness.

The Princess did not wash often enough, and her underclothes – which were uniformly coarse – as well as her thread stockings were frequently dirty and far too rarely changed. She was actually 'offensive' from the neglect; and it seemed remarkable to Malmesbury how 'amazingly' her education had been neglected in this respect, 'how much her mother, although an Englishwoman, was inattentive to it'. Malmesbury urged her to be more fastidious. The Prince himself was 'very delicate' and expected 'a long and very careful *toilette de propreté*'. What was too intimate for him to mention himself, he got one of her ladies to tell her, and this lady executed her commission well, for the next day the Princess appeared 'well washed *all over*'.

This was characteristic of her. There was no denying how amenable she was, how good-natured. As he sailed down the Elbe past Gluckstadt, Malmesbury thought that it would be impossible to be more cheerful, more accommodating, 'more everything that is pleasant' than the Princess was – 'no difficulty, all good humour'.

Yet what could the future hold, he had due cause to wonder, for a young woman who so prided herself on the quickness with which she got dressed that she neglected to wash, who cheerfully described how sick she was at sea without the least regard to the delicacy of her language, who, when she had a tooth pulled out, sent a page down with it to Lord Malmesbury for his inspection?[27] Such conduct would never do for the bridegroom awaiting her in London.

13

The Second Wife
1795-1796
*

'It was like Macheath going to execution, and he was quite drunk'

Blissfully unaware of the reception likely to be accorded so unrefined a young woman, Princess Caroline walked about the deck of the *Jupiter* in happy mood, charming the sailors by her friendliness and leading the officers to declare that 'they would have had more trouble with any London lady than her Royal Highness'.[1] She was 'always contented and always in good humour', in the words of Mrs Harcourt, who had been sent across with Captain Payne as her official chaperone, 'shewing such pleasant, unaffected joy at the idea of her prospect in life that it does one's heart good to see anybody so happy'.[2]

Her happiness was soon overcast. On landing at Gravesend she was escorted to Greenwich, but there was no one there to meet her, other than the staff and inmates of the Hospital who poured out of the chapel 'before the service was half over' to catch a glimpse of her. There was an hour of apprehensive waiting during which the Princess made one of those silly, thoughtless, flippant jokes that were to grate upon the Prince's nerves. 'What,' she said, looking at the crippled pensioners in the Hospital grounds, 'is every Englishman without an arm or a leg?' At last there arrived at Greenwich the cause of the delay: Lady Jersey.[3]

Lord Malmesbury had heard from Captain Payne a few days before that his charge would be subjected to the humiliation of being greeted in England by the woman who was supposed to be the Prince's mistress. Payne had told him that Lady Jersey, who with the approval of the King and Queen had been appointed one of the Princess's Ladies of the Bedchamber, had already made a great nuisance of herself by her 'very far from proper behaviour', by her tricks to get aboard the yachts. Now not only did she keep the Princess waiting at Greenwich by not being ready at the time appointed for the coaches to set out, but when at length she did arrive with Lord Clermont and Mrs Aston, one of the Princess's other Ladies, she immediately and impertinently expressed herself 'very much dissatisfied with the Princess's mode of dress, though Mrs Harcourt had taken great pains about it'. Then, having insisted that she should take off her muslin gown and blue satin petticoat and change into a less becoming white satin dress which she had brought with her, she said that the Princess, whose cheeks were of a naturally high colour, ought to use some rouge to bring them to life. Finally, she complained that to ride in a carriage with her back to the horses would upset her, and she hoped, therefore, that she would be allowed to sit facing forwards, next to the Princess.

To this last suggestion Lord Malmesbury strongly objected and, intimating that if she really were likely to be sick when riding with her back to the horses she ought not to have accepted the appointment of Lady of the Bedchamber, he suggested that she join himself and Lord Clermont in their carriage. 'This of course settled the business,' Lord Malmesbury recorded. 'She and Mrs Harcourt, according to the King's direction, sat backwards, and the Princess sat by herself. There was very little crowd, and still less applause on the road to London, where we arrived and were set down at St James's (the Duke of Cumberland's apartments, Cleveland Row) about half past two.'[4] On the journey Princess Caroline behaved in exactly the kind of way Lord Malmesbury had advised her not to do. Provoked by the evident disdain of the sophisticated, haughty, good-looking and well-groomed women opposite her, she began to chatter about her own experiences in the world, of her having been very much in love once with a man from whom her high birth had made it necessary to part. This story which was, of course, soon related to the Prince of Wales did nothing to endear him to his bride.

Although the Prince, in a letter written at the end of November, had *'vehemently'* urged Lord Malmesbury 'to set out with the Princess Caroline *immediately'*, now that she was in England he had not shown any particular anxiety to see her; and when he did see her, he did not appear at all taken with the sight.

He came into the room where she and Malmesbury awaited him,

approached her, and, as she tried to kneel to him in obedience to Malmesbury's instructions, 'he raised her (gracefully enough) and embraced her'. But, apparently, being so close to her was most distasteful to him. He spoke scarcely a word, turned round and, immediately withdrawing to a far corner of the apartment, called Malmesbury towards him. 'Harris, I am not well,' he said. 'Pray get me a glass of brandy.'

Malmesbury replied, ' "Sir, had you not better have a glass of water?" – upon which he, much out of humour, said with an oath, "*No*. I will go directly to the Queen," and away he went. The Princess, left during this short moment alone, was in a state of astonishment.'

When Malmesbury joined her again, she said to him in French – since English, despite her recent hurried lessons, did not yet come naturally to her – 'My God! Does the Prince always act like this? I think he's very fat and he's nothing like as handsome as his portrait.'

Malmesbury said that His Royal Highness was naturally 'a good deal affected and flurried at this first interview, but she certainly would find him different at dinner'. The Princess would have said more, but Malmesbury excused himself on the grounds that he must now report to the King.

His Majesty's only question was, 'Is she good-humoured?' to which Malmesbury could honestly give a favourable reply. But it was clear to him when the King commented, 'I am glad of it', and then fell into silence, that he had already heard from the Queen what their son thought of the person of his bride.

At dinner that evening Princess Caroline's behaviour was as distressingly embarrassing as Lord Malmesbury had ever known it. It was 'rattling, affecting raillery and wit, and throwing out coarse vulgar hints about Lady [Jersey] who was present'.[5] The Princess later excused herself on the grounds that it was the sight of the Prince and Lady Jersey together that made her behave like this. 'To tell you God's truth' (a favourite expression) . . . 'I knew how it all was,' she told Lady Charlotte Campbell in her fractured and peculiarly accented English, 'and I said to myself, "Oh, very well!" I took my partie . . . Oh, mine God, I could be the slave of a man I love; but one whom I love not and who did not love me, impossible – *c'est autre chose*.'[6] On a subsequent occasion, she demonstrated what she meant by this when, on her husband's drinking some punch from Lady Jersey's glass, she snatched a neighbour's pipe and puffed out smoke at him.[7]

Listening to her vulgar, impetuous, defensive chatter, while Lady Jersey remained loftily silent, the Prince, Malmesbury noticed, was 'disgusted'. This unfortunate dinner fixed his dislike of her; and the longer she persisted in her 'attempts at cleverness and coarse sarcasm' in her misguided efforts to show the Prince that she did not care about her rival, the more bitter that dislike became.

It was all the more galling to the Prince that, although the Princess had not been welcomed into London with nearly as much enthusiasm as the *Annual Register* later suggested, the people were prepared to like her, certainly to sympathize with her; for it was known that, apart from the King, who greeted her affectionately with 'tears of joy . . . as if she had been born and bred his favourite child',[8] no one in the Royal Family was in the least well-diposed towards her. The Queen was cold; the Princesses were wary; the Prince virtually ignored her. It was rumoured that Lady Jersey had gone so far as to deposit some evil-smelling substance in her hair to increase the Prince's distaste, had put Epsom salts into the pastry which she had for supper, and had dropped strong spirits into her wine to make the Queen think she was a drunkard.

An outcast, lonely and *gauche*, she enlisted the people's sympathy from the beginning. When a crowd gathered to see her she showed herself to them at a window, made a short speech in praise of the 'brave English people – the best nation upon earth', and 'bowed exceedingly . . . till the Prince shut the window and made excuses of her being fatigued. Everybody speaks most favourably of her face as most pleasing,' Horace Walpole reported, 'though with too much rouge. She is plump and by no means tall.'[9]*

The Prince, too, had his sympathizers. It was no wonder that he was disgusted by his 'sloven' of a bride, thought Lady Hester Stanhope, Pitt's niece; he had always been used to women of such perfect cleanliness and sweetness.[10] Whereas the Princess was, so Holland said, 'utterly destitute of all female delicacy'.[11] 'She did not know how to put on her own clothes,' Lady Hester added, '. . . putting on her stockings with the seam before, or one of them wrong side outwards.'

At the time of his wedding it was only natural that the Prince's thoughts

---

* The newspapers were most flattering about the Princess: 'Teeth as white as ivory, a good complexion, a beautiful hand and arm, and may certainly be deemed a very pretty woman'. (*London Chronicle*, 4–7 April 1795). The *Annual Register* described her voice, with its strong German accent, as being 'replete with melody and delicacy of tone' (*Annual Register*, *1795*, 15).

should turn to that very different woman he had married nearly ten years before. When he had separated from her the previous summer he had agreed that Mrs Fitzherbert's £3,000 a year allowance should be continued as though no break had occurred; in the autumn he had requested that all his friends should continue to show her the same attention that they had done in the past; in December he had asked Lord Loughborough to obtain the King's word that her allowance should be regularly paid throughout her lifetime in the event of his own death.[12] Now, on the very eve of the wedding he sent her a message that she was the only woman he would ever love; and he was said to have ridden out to Richmond himself and passed by her house as though anxious to prove it.[13] Before the ceremony he gloomily remarked to the Duke of Clarence, who had been instructed by their father not to leave his brother's side throughout the day, 'William, tell Mrs Fitzherbert she is the only woman I shall ever love.' And on his way to the chapel he said to the Earl of Moira, who was sitting opposite him in the coach: 'It's no use, Moira, I shall never love any woman but Fitzherbert.'[14] In later years the Princess herself was to tell Jack Payne that she thought Mrs Fitzherbert was 'much more' her enemy than Lady Jersey.[15] Certainly Mrs Fitzherbert was never to refer to her as the Princess of Wales, merely as Princess Caroline.[16]

The wedding took place on the evening of 8 April 1795 in the Chapel Royal at St James's. The bride, whose extremely rich dress was so heavy that she almost fell over, was led into the chapel by the Duke of Clarence and attended by Lady Mary Osborne, Lady Charlotte Spencer, Lady Charlotte Legge and Lady Caroline Villiers.* She approached the altar confidently and stood there chatting away to the Duke of Clarence with characteristic gusto as she awaited the arrival of the bridegroom.[17] When he came, supported by the unmarried Dukes of Bedford and Roxburghe, he was seen to be extremely nervous and agitated. He had obviously been drinking; and at the beginning of the ceremony the Duke of Bedford, who had seen him swallow several glasses of brandy, had

---

* They were the daughters respectively of the fifth Duke of Leeds, the third Duke of Marlborough, the second Earl of Dartmouth and, of course, the fourth Earl of Jersey. They had been selected by the Prince, and the King, so the Queen said, had approved 'greatly of [the] choice' (RA 3898, 36422: Asp/P, ii, 493). The King had not, however, approved the requests of Prince Ernest, Prince Adolphus and Prince William of Gloucester who had all asked to be allowed to come home from the Continent for the wedding as their troops were going into winter quarters. 'The Army,' the King thought, 'was the only place where an officer ought to remain, *particularly* when he commanded a regiment' (RA 36425: Asp/P, ii, 501).

difficulty in preventing him from falling over.[18] Lord Melbourne, who was in waiting, said that 'the Prince was like a man doing a thing in desperation; it was like Macheath going to execution; and he was quite drunk'.[19]* He scarcely glanced at his bride, though the Duke of Leeds noticed that he was 'perpetually looking at his favourite Lady Jersey'.[20] One of his equerries told Lady Maria Stuart that he was so 'agitated during the ceremony that it was expected he would have burst out in tears'.[21] At one point he suddenly stood up in the middle of a prayer. The Archbishop of Canterbury, John Moore, paused for a moment until the King stepped forward and whispered something to his son who then knelt down again. When the Archbishop came to that part of the service in which he had to ask the question whether or not there were any impediment to lawful matrimony, he 'laid down the book and looked earnestly at the King, as well as at the bridegroom, giving unequivocal proof of his apprehension that some previous marriage had taken place. . . . Not content with this tacit allusion, the Archbishop twice repeated the passage in which the Prince engages to live from that time in nuptial fidelity with his consort. . . . The Prince was much affected, and shed tears.'[22]

After the ceremony the King and Queen held a drawing-room in the Queen's apartments to which the Prince conducted his bride almost in silence. The Duke of Leeds, who was walking in front of them, 'could not help remarking how little conversation passed between them during the procession, and the coolness and indifference apparent in the manner of the Prince'.[23] When the Prince appeared in the Queen's apartments, so Lady Maria Stuart said, he looked 'like death and full of confusion, as if he wished to hide himself from the looks of the whole world. I think,' she added, 'he is much to be pitied. The bride, on the contrary, appeared in the highest spirits when she passed by us first, smiling and nodding to everyone. . . . What an odd wedding!'[24]

Towards the end of the reception, the Prince recovered his composure, and became 'very civil and gracious', though he was 'certainly unhappy' and still rather drunk.[25] When the Earl of Harcourt came to hand back the hat which he had held for him during the ceremony, the Prince insisted on his keeping it, though it was a very valuable hat 'ornamented with a most beautiful and costly button and loop of diamonds'. The Duke of Leeds thought that this ostentatious gift confirmed the 'unfortunate

---

* Queen Victoria, who was told this by Lord Melbourne's son, the second Viscount, was also assured that her uncle was '*extremely* DRUNK' by King Leopold of the Belgians (RA Y71/63).

suspicion' that Lady Jersey was the Prince's mistress, since the Earl of Harcourt's wife was Lady Jersey's most intimate friend.[26]

The Prince's drunkenness increased as night approached, so his bride afterwards recounted; and when he did eventually make his way into her bedroom, he fell insensible into the fireplace where he remained all night and where she left him. In the morning he had recovered sufficiently to climb into bed with her.[27]

*

The first few months of the marriage were not quite as unpleasant as this disastrous beginning led people to expect and as her biographers have suggested. Four days after the wedding the bride was seen on the Terrace at Windsor looking perfectly happy on the arm of her father-in-law who escorted her up and down with evident 'delight' and 'entire gratification'.[28] Her sisters-in-law, although far from sharing their father's enthusiasm, seemed prepared to like her after all and to wish her well. Princess Elizabeth, to whom she spoke of her 'present happiness', praised her 'perfect good temper' and flattered herself that she would 'turn out a very comfortable little wife'.[29] Two months later Princess Elizabeth wrote again to her brother to assure him that his wife was full of 'professions of regard and love' for her husband.[30] The husband himself wrote to his mother from Brighton to tell her that, despite the 'execrably bad' weather, his wife was 'extremely happy' with the place which agreed with her 'most perfectly'. She was in the 'best health and spirits possible', and they were 'very comfortable'.[31] His mother was herself happier than words could express at this unlikely and welcome news.[32]

When she heard that her daughter-in-law was pregnant she was delighted and wrote to say that she hoped she would take 'all possible care of herself'; she was 'extremely glad' to hear that she was going 'on so well in her present situation'.[33] As the time of the birth approached the 'sisterhood' at Frogmore were 'in a constant state of anxiety', jumping and flying to the windows whenever the house bell rang.[34] Princess Elizabeth said that they were all sure that their brother was 'upon the *high fidgets*', walking about the room, pulling his fingers and 'very anxious'. They did not expect to see him at Windsor, being certain he would not want to leave the Princess till she was 'safe in bed'.[35]

The Prince, indeed, was anxious. For 'two whole nights' he stayed up, 'much agitated', waiting for news of the safe delivery of the child,[36] and was evidently much relieved when, at a quarter to ten on the morning of 7 January 1796, he was able to give the Queen the good news: 'The Princess, after a terrible hard labour for above twelve hours, is this instant brought to bed of an *immense girl*, and I assure you notwithstanding we might have wished for a boy, I receive her with all the affection possible. ... I long to see you and to press you to that affectionate heart which you never can know how much it loves you. Pray have the goodness to apologise to my dear sisters for my not writing to them, but I am so fatigued . . .'[37]

Thanking God that both the mother and child were quite well 'and likely to continue so', he wrote a separate letter to his father who replied that he was 'highly pleased' and 'indeed had always wished' that the first child should be a girl: 'You are both young and I trust will have many children and this newcomer will equally call for the protection of its parents and consequently be a bond of additional union.'[38]

That some such bond of union was now necessary the King was only too well aware. It was clear to him by now that the early hopes of a satisfactory marriage were not likely to be realized. Despite the encouraging reports received at Windsor and the Prince's evident concern during his wife's confinement, the couple were ill-matched in every way. However correctly she managed to conduct herself at Windsor, at the Queen's House and with the King, the Princess could not forbear to behave in her husband's presence in the very way that Malmesbury had warned her he would find insupportable. Incited to pert sarcasm, outrageous comment and tiresome petulance by her husband's unconcealed preference for Lady Jersey and his evident distaste for her own more flamboyant sensuality, she irritated him beyond endurance. One evening at Carlton House after she had, in Malmesbury's words, behaved 'very lightly and even improperly', the Prince demanded to know of his guest how he liked such manners and why on earth he had not been warned what she was like. Malmesbury's explanation that his orders from the King had not required him to express any opinion as to her character was gloomily accepted by the Prince; but it naturally did not please him and 'left a rankle in his mind'.[39]

Soon the Prince's dislike turned to positive hatred, and his consequent treatment of his wife, who enjoyed the people's sympathy, became common gossip. It was said that, infuriated by the unsuitable company she entertained, he had had all the furniture removed from her dining-room with the exception of two common chairs; and that he had taken back from her a pair of pearl bracelets which had formed part of her wedding jewels and which he had given to Lady Jersey who, having 'no happiness without a rival to trouble and torment',[40] did not hesitate to wear them in the Princess's presence.[41] Believing that she spoke contemptuously of him to her various companions, and might already be unfaithful to him with one or other of the various men who – for reasons which to him were inconceivable – found her physically attractive, he forbade her to entertain anyone without his approval. 'She drives always alone,' the lawyer, Charles Abbot, noted in his journal, 'sees no company but old people put on her list. . . . She goes nowhere but airings in Hyde Park. The Prince uses her unpardonably.'[42]

'She is, I am afraid, a most unhappy woman,' another sympathizer agreed. 'Her lively spirits which she brought over with her are all gone, and they say the melancholy and anxiety in her countenance is quite affecting.'[43]

'I do not know how I shall be able to bear the loneliness,' she wrote to a friend in Germany, 'the Queen seldom visits me, and my sisters-in-law show me the same sympathy. . . . The Countess [of Jersey] is still here. I hate her and I know she feels the same towards me. My husband is wholly given up to her, so you can easily imagine the rest.'[44]

Her husband, indeed, spent as little time in her company as he possibly could. Leaving her at Carlton House, he spent weeks on end in the country, either at Northington Grange near Alresford in Hampshire which, having given up Kempshot Park, he had rented for £900 a year from Henry Drummond, the banker, at the Pavilion in Brighton where, according to Lord Auckland, Lady Jersey now had her bed in his dressing-room, or at Bognor where she was as often seen in his company as she was on the Steine. In London they saw each other at card parties at the Queen's House, where, so Charles Abbot said, 'in the course of the evening the Prince of Wales repeatedly came up to her table, and publicly squeezed her hand'.[45]

As Lady of the Bedchamber to the Princess she spent a great deal of time in her company, too, and, as the Princess knew, gave malicious reports of her behaviour to her husband and the Queen. When some indiscreet letters which the Princess had written to Brunswick were handed to her by a messenger who was unable to go to Germany as planned and consequently could not deliver them, she read them, noted the rude remarks about herself and the Royal Family – in particular about 'Old

Snuffy' or 'de old Begum' as the Princess alternatively referred to the Queen – and immediately handed them to her Majesty whose growing dislike of a daughter-in-law she had never favoured was thus permanently confirmed.[46]

In April the Princess decided she would stand no more. In French she wrote to her husband asking to be excused from ever dining alone again with, as she put it, 'a person whom I can neither like nor respect and who is your mistress' – a person later identified in a characteristically ungrammatical and misspelled letter as 'Lady Jerser'. 'Be as generous as your nation is,' she pleaded, 'and keep your word as every good Englishman, since such is the character of the nation. Forgive me, my dear Prince, if my expressions are too strong, believe that it is a heart wounded by the most acute pain and the most deadly sorrow which pleads for your help.'[47]

The Prince replied angrily: 'You must allow me to answer in English your letter of this morning as you sufficiently understand the language, because it is essential for me to explain myself without any possible ambiguity upon the subject of the unwise, groundless and most injurious imputation which you have thought fit to cast upon me.... Let me remind you, Madam, that the intimacy of my friendship with Lady Jersey ... *my mistress, as you* indecorously term her ... under all the false colour that slander has given it, was perfectly known to you before you accepted my hand, for you yourself told me so immediately on your arrival here.... I then took the opportunity of explaining to you that Lady Jersey was one of the oldest acquaintances I had in this country and that the confidence resulting from so long a friendship had enabled her to offer advice which contributed not a little to decide me to marriage. You will recollect, Madam, that you have seven ladies in your family besides Lady Jersey, any, or everyone, of whom it is in your power to summon either for dinner or for company at any hour of the day.... If the choice be not more extensive it is not my fault, but it is the consequence of the etiquette existing from all times for the situation of the Princess of Wales.... We have unfortunately been obliged to acknowledge to each other that we cannot find happiness in our union.... It only remains that we should make the situation as little uncomfortable to each other as its nature will allow.... I have been solicitous that you should have every gratification which the nature of the times, the manners of this country and the established customs of your rank would admit, with a due regard at the same time to the pecuniary difficulties I so cruelly and unjustly labour under. . . . Let me therefore beg you to make the best of a situation unfortunate *for us both*, which is only to be done by not *wantonly* creating or magnifying uncomfortable curcumstances.'

Commenting on his wife's reference to the generosity of the English nation and the implied unfavourable contrast with his own, the Prince expressed the fear that these references had been inserted for an ulterior motive: that the Princess intended to use her letter – with its false insinuation that she was forced to keep company alone with Lady Jersey – as part of an appeal against the Prince to the nation at large. He recommended her to consider exactly what result she might expect from such an appeal.[48]

This reply elicited a further, longer and even more ungrammatical letter from the Princess in which she regretted the 'coldness and great contempt' of his conduct towards her, made further complaints about his intimacy with Lady Jersey, and repudiated any idea that she was attempting to make an appeal to the sympathies of the English people. She had always admired the wise withdrawal of the Queen from anything that could be called political intrigue and would follow her example. If she could obtain her husband's friendship, it would be very precious to her; however, she dare not ask for it at present by any other right than that of the mother of his child.[49]

The Prince, who felt a 'few words' of reply – 740 words – were exacted by her letter, protested that if she wished for more of his company she would do well not to make his own house 'obnoxious' to him, and to consider whether 'the captious tone' she adopted towards him was calculated to make him feel at ease in her society. He hoped that, as well as following the Queen's example by not meddling in politics, she would be like her also in studying her husband's disposition and promoting his comfort; this was 'not to be effected by irritating insinuations or fretful complaints'. He hoped, finally, that this unpleasant correspondence might now cease.[50]

The Princess, unfortunately, was not ready to put a stop to it yet. In the longest and most incoherent letter she had written to him so far, she replied that she would like the orders governing her conduct to be given to her in writing so as to avoid all misunderstanding, and that if it was right for *her* to follow the good example of the Queen towards the King there was even more reason why *he* should follow 'the steady and correct behaviour of the King towards the Queen'.[51]

'I really am tired to death of this silly altercation,' the Prince complained to her Chamberlain, the Earl of Cholmondeley, on receipt of this letter. But since the Princess desired it, he would give her her orders in writing, although he had made quite clear to her already 'the latitude allowed by her situation respecting her mode of life'. If she wished to live on civil and friendly terms with him, she had only to say so.[52]

The Princess then reiterated her request to be given in writing the exact terms upon which they were in future to live. In particular, she wanted to be assured that if they were henceforward to be man and wife in name only, he would never again, not even in the event of the death of their daughter, make any attempt to produce another heir. The Prince, accordingly, writing in French so that there should be no possibility of her misunderstanding him, gave this undertaking: 'Nature has not made us suitable to each other. Tranquil and comfortable society is, however, in our power; let our intercourse therefore be restricted to that, and I will distinctly subscribe to the condition which you required through Lady Cholmondeley, that even in the event of any accident happening to my daughter, which I trust Providence in its mercy will avert, I shall not infringe the terms of the restriction by purposing, at any period, a connection of a more particular nature. I shall now finally close this disagreeable correspondence, trusting that as we have completely explained ourselves to each other, the rest of our lives will be passed in uninterrupted tranquility. I am, Madam, with great truth, very sincerely yours, George P.'[53]

The Princess, however, was still not yet prepared to close the correspondence. Protesting that his letter did not make it clear that the proposal for a separation came in the first place from him and not from her, she felt it her duty to give the King, her only protector, an account of what had taken place between them. Deeply perturbed by this threat, and hoping to forestall the trouble that he felt impending, the Prince immediately wrote to his mother to say he would come down to Windsor first thing in the morning so as to be there as soon as church was over and discuss with her the best course of action.[54]

The Queen was not encouraging. She knew the King well enough, she thought, to be fully persuaded that he would never agree to any open rupture.[55] And this, indeed, when the Prince made a formal request for a 'final separation' in an extremely long letter on 31 May,[56] was the King's reply: 'You seem to look on your disunion with the Princess as merely of a private nature, and totally put out of sight that as Heir Apparent of the Crown your marriage is a public act, wherein the Kingdom is concerned; that therefore a separation cannot be brought forward by the mere interference of relations.' The public would have to be informed of the whole business, and the public were 'certainly not prejudiced' in the Prince's favour. Parliament would also have to be informed, and Parliament would think itself obliged to secure out of his income the jointure settled on her in case of her husband's death. The King was 'certainly by no means inclined to think the Princess [had] been happy in the choise of conduct' she had adopted; but if the Prince had 'attempted to guide her, she might have avoided those errors that her uncommon want of experience and perhaps some defects of temper' had given rise to.[57]

14

The Broken Marriage
1796
*

'The vilest wretch this world ever was cursed with'

Denied his father's agreement to a formal separation, and tormented by the enthusiastic support which the public so readily accorded his wife, the Prince's detestation of her became more virulent than ever. It was bad enough when *The Times* took her side to condemn the vices of her unjust husband and his 'most disgraceful connexions',[1] and when the *Morning Chronicle* reported that everyone pitied her and execrated him.[2] It was worse when the *True Briton* lavished compliments upon 'the amiable and accomplished personage' who had been 'the object of so much unmerited ill treatment', and dismissed the Prince as 'incorrigible', a man with '*a total disregard* to the opinions of the world', whose 'conduct favoured the cause of Jacobinism and democracy in this country more than all the speeches of Horne Tooke'.[3] It was intolerable that the Princess, on going to the opera, 'electrified the house by her presence', and that 'before she could take her seat, every hand was lifted up to greet her with the loudest plaudits, crying out Huzza!...'[4]*

---

* 'Every woman as well as man, in every part clapped incessantly', Horace Walpole confirmed (*Walpole Correspondence*, xii, 186). And the Duke of Leeds recorded, 'I was in my box at the Opera when the Princess of Wales arrived. The pit and some of the boxes began to applaud, and the whole House almost instantly rose and joined the applause. I looked down at her box, and seeing her appear agitated, immediately went down to see her.... After repeated curtseying to the audience she sat down.... She said ... she supposed she could be guillotined ... for what had passed this evening' (*Leeds Memoranda*, 221). The more popular his wife became, the more disliked was his mistress. 'Lady St Asaph told Lady Beaumont that she was at a very large assembly at the Duchess of Gordon's to which Lady Jersey was invited – when Lady Jersey came the ladies made a lane for her and let her pass unspoken to' (*Farington Diary*, i, 199–200)

It was all made much worse for the Prince by the fact that most of his family, unnerved by the public reaction, seemed to think that he ought to attempt some sort of public reconciliation. The Duke and Duchess of York – although the Princess, in turn, loaded them with 'cruel calumnies'[5] – appeared inclined to sympathize with her; while his sister, Princess Elizabeth, confessed, 'We are one and all very miserable about you, and what we have suffered passes all powers of expression. . . . Friends and foes are all of opinion that a *resignation must* take place for the sake of the *country* and the whole royal family, for if you *fall* all must fall, and then with your excellent heart how could you bear the distress and misery of your own family. I am sorry, very sorry, to write these severe and cruel truths, but alas! . . . if you could see the agony of mind of our poor mother and the distress she is in I am sure you would not be able to stand it and would make a sacrifice for her sake.'[6]

Then, making the whole affair even more exasperating, there was the attitude of those of his erstwhile friends who were numbered among Lady Jersey's countless enemies, notably Lord Hugh Seymour, who referred to her as 'that bitch',[7] Jack Payne, whose conduct towards Lady Jersey and himself since his marriage had been 'infamous',[8] and Thomas Tyrwhitt, his Private Secretary, who, like Payne, was dismissed from his service for taking the Princess's side against her.[9]* None of them appeared to realize

---

She was the cause of all the rage against the Prince, the Bishop of Waterford told Lord Charlemont: 'She ought to resign her office and retire; she will not. He ought to dismiss her; he will not.' Meanwhile, the Princess, on account of her supposed ill treatment, was 'the greatest favourite with people of all ranks' (HMCR, Charlemont MSS, ii. 273).

* Some years later, after his dismissal of Lady Jersey, the Prince was equally displeased with people who continued to visit her, and worked himself up into 'a passion' with Lady Bessborough who had gone to see her son when he was very ill (*Granville Leveson Gower Correspondence*, ii, 121). He was constantly quarrelling with those who remained on good terms with people with whom he himself had fallen out. As Lord Melbourne told Queen Victoria, he 'never could bear anybody to be friends with those he disliked and consequently my father and mother who knew Mrs Fitzherbert very well, continued her friends and [the Prince] never would see them; and then all of a sudden, when he came back to her, there he was back at Whitehall and came in just as if nothing had passed, and if he had seen them just the day before' (RA Queen Victoria's Journal, entry for 12 January 1838). Thomas Tyrwhitt was reinstated as Private Secretary in 1797 as though the Prince had never quarrelled with him, and remained in that office until 1804. In 1805 he became Lord Warden of the Stannaries. A tiny, bustling, florid man, a great favourite of Princess Elizabeth, the Prince referred to him affectionately as 'our little red dwarf', or occasionally, after he received his knighthood in 1812, as 'The 23rd of June', he being – as he elaborately explained to his mother who might not otherwise have understood the 'ingenious pun' – the 'shortest (k)night' (RA 21295; Asp/K, i, 384).

what a 'very monster of iniquity' his wife was. She was '*a fiend*', an 'infamous wretch', 'a worthless wretch', the 'vilest wretch this world ever was cursed with', the most 'unprincipled and unfeeling person of her sex'; there was 'no end to her wickedness, her falsity, and her designs'.[10]

He besought the Queen to make the King realize what a dangerous woman she was. In letters, whose language became almost hysterical, he pleaded with his 'dearest, dearest, dearest mother', his 'most beloved mother', his 'ever best and dearest mother', to persuade the King 'to take a firm line in defence' of his son, otherwise the '*fiend*' would prove the ruin of the whole royal family. 'The King must be resolute and firm, or everything is at an end,' he begged her to believe. 'Let him recall to his mind the want of firmness of Louis 16. This is the only opportunity for him to stemm the torrent. . . . I know you will fight for me to the last, and I will for you, and by you till the last drop of my blood, but if ever you flinch, which I am convinced is impossible, I shall then despair. . . . My best love to all my dear sisters. I hope they remain stout, for without it, we must all sink. God bless you, ever dearest mother. I am so overpowered with unhappiness that I feel quite light headed. I know not where to turn for a friend now but to you. . . . I wrote at considerable length to the King yesterday to tell him that nothing but his resolution and support can bring *us all* through at this moment. . . . *If I* fall *all* must fall also; but we must *all rise* victorious if the King will but take a *decided tone* to the Princess, to his Ministers and to the world in general, but if half measures are adopted there is an end of everything. Nothing can equal what I go through nor can anything paint it strong enough for your imagination. I have retained Erskine besides my own lawyers to prosecute every paragraph, every pamphlet that can be construed into a libel. By the by I see by Ernest's letter that the Princess has been at the Queen's House. For God's sake let me know everything that has past, tell me nothing, or conceal nothing from me. I suppose she has made the best of her own story and told her lies as usual. . . . The thought makes me quite frantic. . . .'[11]

Appalled by the thought of what she might say about him privately, the Prince professed himself equally horrified by his wife's public conduct. When Fox, from whom he was still estranged, was re-elected for Westminster on 13 June, his supporters, headed by 'fifty bludgeon-men', carried him in procession past Carlton House where they expressed a wish to see the infant Princess. Whereupon she not only carried 'the poor little girl to the window' in order to 'make her also an instrument against her poor injured father', but 'actually afterwards drove in her carriage through the mob, to pay her devoirs to Mr Fox after such a speech too as he made, and to get herself applauded'. Surely the King must now see the Princess 'in her true colours, how false, how mischievous, how treacherous' she was, how much she was made the tool 'of the worst of parties at this moment, the democratick'.[12]

The King, however, tended still to believe that his niece was more sinned against than sinning, and that if she received proper guidance all would yet be well. He supposed that if Lady Jersey retired from her service, harmony could be restored. Certainly Princess Caroline herself led him to believe so. For months she had been insisting that 'so long as Lady Jersey' held the place she occupied in her Household there could be no peace between herself and her husband; and in this determination she had the King's sympathy. Towards the end of June the Princess had her way. It was agreed, as the Queen confirmed to her in writing, that the Countess of Jersey should leave her service and should not again be admitted to her private company. The Queen added that the Princess ought now to show that she was willing to have a 'complete reconciliation' with her husband and to refrain from all reproaches.

In obedience to the wishes of her parents-in-law, the Princess then wrote to her husband in her bad French to say that she looked forward to the moment which would bring him back to Carlton House and would 'finally put an end to a misunderstanding which had ceased to exist' so far as she was concerned. If he would do her the honour of seeking her company in the future, she would do everything in her power to make it agreeable to him. If she had ever displeased him in the past, would he please be generous enough to forgive her?[13]

To this warm letter, the Prince delivered the curt reply: 'Madam, I have had the honour of receiving your letter this day and propose having the pleasure of being at Carlton House some time in the course of Monday.'[14]

When he arrived he was as formal as this message threatened he would be; and, as soon as he had finished dinner, he left and went to spend the evening with Lady Jersey.[15]

Although forced to give up her place in the Princess's Household to Lady Willoughby de Eresby, Lady Jersey was determined not to give up the Prince. She wrote a rude letter to the Princess, saying that she had only continued in a situation 'rendered impossible' for a person of her rank, 'or indeed for anyone possessing the honest pride and spirit of an Englishwoman', by her 'duty and attachment' to his Royal Highness, the 'same duty and attachment which she would be ever proud in possessing'.[16]

Far from breaking with Lady Jersey, as the King had hoped he would do, the Prince saw more of her than ever. He entertained her at the new country estate, Critchell House, near Wimborne Minster, Dorset, which he had rented for £1,120 a year from Charles Sturt, having given up Northington Grange. In the late summer he went down to spend some weeks with her at Bognor; and he installed her in a house adjoining Carlton House which he had altered for Jack Payne but which was now vacant owing to Payne's disgrace. The Queen, distressed by reports of Lady Jersey's having moved into Jack Payne's former house, was reassured by her son, who wrote an extraordinarily detailed account of how the move had taken place entirely for the benefit of the Earl of Jersey, the Prince's (as yet unpaid) Master of the Horse. For Jersey 'could not be answerable to bring the whole expenditure of the stables within the sum allotted by Parliament unless he was perpetually upon the spot, which he could not be had he to run eternally two or three times a day to and from Grosvenor Square'.[17]

Since the Prince was free to move about the country in the wake of the 'old sorceress', Lady Jersey, the Princess of Wales deeply resented the fact that her own movements and activities were so strictly regulated. When she asked permission, through Lord Cholmondeley, to spend a couple of days in the country, the Prince indignantly refused to consider the request. He warned the Queen of the '*dangerous consequences*' of allowing her an opportunity of '*repeating her tricks*', especially as she still persisted 'in the line of conduct she so artfully and maliciously [had] adopted' of endeavouring to draw popularity to herself at his '*expense* and at the expense of the whole family'. He would not hesitate to give his '*most decided negative*' to the 'idea of a Princess of Wales travelling all over England'; but, perhaps, the Queen would show the letter Lord Cholmondeley had received to the King for his concurrence.[18]

The King did not want to become involved in the matter; but he agreed that the Prince might refuse the request on his own responsibility.[19] The Prince immediately did so, telling Lord Cholmondeley that he was hurt, 'in the most sensible way possible' that such an improper proposal should ever even have been put to him in the first place. At the same time he complained to Cholmondeley of the Princess's having invited company to dinner composed of others besides her Household and of her 'having encreased her *evening parties* beyond the list ... officially transmitted to the Ladies of her Bedchamber'. 'Any infringement of these rules I never can nor will admit to whilst the Princess remains under my roof, as it would lead to consequences subversive of all order and arrangement,' he reminded Cholmondeley sharply. 'You will therefore of course write to Lady Willoughby to explain this matter thoroughly to her.'[20]

The Princess was 'very sorry' to receive this answer to her request to go to the country for two days; she had not thought it would have been a breach of Court etiquette as the Queen sometimes went to spend a day or two with Lord and Lady Harcourt; she was the 'more disappointed' as the Prince had promised that she might 'enjoy uninterrupted those innocent pleasures consistent' with her rank.[21]

The Prince remained adamant. The Queen, he admitted, did make occasional visits to the Earl and Countess of Harcourt at Nuneham Courtenay, but she never went *alone*; she attended upon the King when *His* Majesty was graciously pleased to honour them with a visit. As to the innocent pleasures suitable to her rank, 'it always was and must be understood that those pleasures can never be admitted or thought of at the expense either of etiquette or precedent'. The Prince hoped that in future the Princess would avoid making such applications which were totally inconsistent with her situation as well as with his own.[22]

Both Lord Thurlow and the Duke of Leeds thought that the extraordinary way in which the Prince of Wales treated his wife could be attributed only to madness; and the second Viscount Melbourne later told Queen Victoria, who loved talking about her strange uncle, that he, too, thought the Prince's conduct towards the Princess was nothing but madness. ' "George IV never was popular," Lord M. said,' so Queen Victoria recorded in her journal. 'And whatever [Princess Caroline] did, had no weight with the people, for, they said, it was all his fault at first. ... It was quite madness his (George IV) conduct to her; for if he had only separated, and let her alone, that wouldn't have signified; but he persecuted her, and "he cared as much about what she did, as if he had been very much in love with her," which certainly was very odd. ... The way in which he treated her immediately after the marriage was beyond everything wrong and foolish. Considering the way *he lived* himself, Lord M. said, he should never have attacked *her* character.'[23]

Melbourne admitted, however, that her character was not all that the public liked to suppose it. This, indeed, was what the Prince found so unendurable. Here was the Princess spreading the most humiliating stories about him and behaving, he was convinced, in the most scandalous way; yet to the public *she* was a martyr, innocent and wronged, while *he* was considered such 'unfit company for gentlemen' that 'persons of rank (afterwards indebted to him for advancement in it)' refused to meet him at dinner at Holland House.[24]

Princess Caroline certainly showed little restraint when talking about the Prince. She had no hesitation in making it known how drunkenly he had behaved on their wedding night, nor how, when they had gone to stay shortly afterwards at Kempshot Park, where Lady Jersey was the only other woman in the party, all the men had got drunk and had gone to sleep, snoring with their dirty boots up on the arms of sofas. The whole scene 'resembled a bad brothel' much more than a Prince's court. Her husband, she claimed, had made her smoke a pipe, and when she had discovered she was pregnant, he had announced that the child was not his.[25]

She told Lord Minto, almost the first time she met him, that they had lived together for only two or three weeks, and 'not at all afterwards as man and wife'. 'If I can spell her hums and haws,' Lord Minto wrote to his wife after this conversation with the Princess, 'I take it that the ground of his antipathy was his own *incapacity*, and the distaste which a man feels for a woman who *knows* his defects and humiliations.'[26]

The thought of this dreadful, mocking wife of his talking intimately to other men horrified, appalled and obsessed him. He would rather, he said, see toads and vipers crawling over his food than even so much as sit at the same table with her, so much did she revolt him, so deeply did he detest her. Yet other men, it was whispered, eagerly sought her out and contrived to be left alone with her. One of these, he believed – and had some reason to believe – was George Canning, at that time the clever young Member of Parliament for Newtown, and one of Pitt's most promising supporters. Even so, it was almost universally felt that the Prince ought either to have her back to live with him or, if they were to live apart, to give her more freedom – though people might not have thought so had they known that her own father had warned that she must be kept very strictly otherwise she would 'certainly emancipate too much'.[27] The Prince's brother, the Duke of Clarence, while offering him sympathy in private,[28] said to a lady at a ball at the Castle Inn, Richmond, 'My brother has behaved very foolishly. To be sure he has married a very foolish, disagreeable person, but he should not have treated her as he has done, but have made the best of a bad bargain, as my father has done. He married a disagreeable woman but has not behaved ill to her.'[29]

The Prince, though, was not prepared to make the best of a bad bargain. Nor was he prepared to make any relaxation of the rules he had imposed on his wife. It was all very well, he told Lord Cholmondeley, for her to complain of the 'solitary hours' that she passed; this was 'a circumstance entirely depending upon her own pleasure'; she always had, or ought to have had, at her immediate call the two Ladies who were in waiting upon her, and besides them the other Ladies who composed her Household ought always to be ready to obey her commands.[30] He agreed that the Hon Gertrude Vanneck, a huge, masculine woman, should be replaced as the Princess's Keeper of the Privy Purse by the more companionable Miss Hayman, but the Princess was not to suppose that this would entitle Miss Hayman to live in her house for this was 'quite out of the question'.[31] No persons whatever, he repeated, could ever be received or entertained by the Princess unless they had previously been approved of by him.

When the Princess again objected to this rule and declined to obey it until she was told to do so directly by the King, the Prince appealed to his father who wrote his daughter-in-law a letter confirming that it was his opinion, too, that 'she could not receive any society but such as the Prince approved of'.[32]

On receiving the King's letter from Lord Cholmondeley, the Princess said she would immediately go to the Prince's apartments at Carlton House and have it out with him. Lord Cholmondeley dissuaded her, saying that the Prince was too busy at the moment but that he would tell him of her wish for an interview. When the Prince heard that his wife wanted to see him '*alone*', he instantly refused the request, indicating that he would see her only in the presence of a third person and that he would, in accordance with her wish to speak to him, present himself at her apartments with Lord Cholmondeley.

Immediately he entered her room the Princess reminded him abruptly in French that in two and a half years of marriage she had been treated '*ni comme votre femme, ni comme la mère de votre enfant, ni comme la Princesse de Galles*'. 'I give you notice here and now,' she continued, 'that I have nothing more to say to you and that I no longer regard myself as subject to your orders or your rules.'

'The Princess then stopped,' the Prince told his father, 'upon which the

Prince said, "*Est-ce-que c'est tout, Madame, tout ce que vous avez à me dire?*" to which she replied, "*Oui.*" The Prince then bowed and withdrew.' He thought it 'highly unnecessary to offer at this moment to his Majesty one single comment on this most extraordinary conduct on the part of the Princess'.[33]

A few weeks later, however, he wrote to his father to say that he had told the Princess that he 'could not help inferring from her conduct that she could have no other plan than to live in a separate house', and that, so far as he was concerned, no objection would be raised to this. But the King continued to refuse to consider any kind of formal separation. She might take a small house outside London – she did, in fact, take the Old Rectory, Charlton, near Blackheath – but she was not to give up her apartments at Carlton House.

As the Lord Chancellor said, the Prince was already so unpopular with the people that any step which might increase that unpopularity could not be taken without danger to 'the publick safety'; it was, therefore, of the 'utmost moment' to preserve 'even the outward appearance of cohabitation'; a formal separation would be 'incompatible with the religion, laws, and government' of the Kingdom.[34] This was the King's view entirely, and he informed his son accordingly.[35]

*

The Prince's situation was rendered the more unendurable by the fact that, although he had married for money, his finances were in almost as sorry a state as ever. It had been proposed that his income of £73,000 a year should be increased to £138,000 and that a capital sum of £52,000 should be allowed to cover the costs of the wedding and for finishing Carlton House. But when it became known that his debts had reached the immense sum of £630,000 in the eight years since the arrangements made in 1787, it was immediately accepted by the government that part of his increased income must be set aside for their settlement. Pitt proposed that the proportion of the Prince's income which came from the Duchy of Cornwall – about £13,000 a year – should be reserved for this purpose, and that in addition £25,000 a year should be deducted from the rest of the income. This meant, however, that the debts would not be liquidated for twenty-seven years, and the storm of protest that greeted Pitt's suggestion made it clear that the government would have to be sterner with the Prince than this.

The Prince had taken little part in politics during the past few years and now had virtually no political friends, while his unpopularity with the country at large was so great that even the King, so well liked upon his recovery in 1788, was now contaminated with it. On his way to the House of Lords in October 1795 the state coach was stoned and shouts of 'Down with George!' filled the air.

Those who had supported the Prince at the time of his earlier financial crisis were not so ready to do so now that he had shown himself to be so incurably, incontinently extravagant. Fox and Sheridan proposed the sale of various crown estates; the Earl of Lonsdale suggested that the frontages of Hyde Park, which did not form part of the Crown estates, should be sold off to builders who would readily pay two guineas a foot for it, thus realizing over £800,000.[36] Others, including Grey, felt that in war time and at a period of so much political agitation and popular distress, the Prince should not have his income increased to anything like the amount that the government proposed. An increase to £113,000 would, in Grey's opinion, be quite sufficient.

So strong, indeed, did feelings run against Pitt's proposals that it seemed for a time that the government would have to resign; and only when the Prince himself agreed to £65,000 a year instead of £25,000 being deducted from his income for the repayment of his debts, was it saved. The Prince also had to agree to the appointment of commissioners for the future conduct of his financial affairs.

Blaming the '*infamous deceit of Pitt*' for having had to agree to a settlement that left him as badly off as ever, the Prince once more set about reducing his expenses and the numbers of his Household, expressing the hope that he would one day soon be enabled to 'resume the appearance' due to his birth.[37]

Disappointed in his expectations of a more generous income, the Prince was disappointed, too, in his hopes of promotion in the Army. In February 1795 he was dismayed to read in the *London Gazette* that he had once again been passed over, several colonels far junior to him being promoted major-general, including his nineteen-year-old cousin, Prince William of Gloucester with whom, and with whose father, he had been on bad terms for several years.[38] He wrote an impassioned letter of complaint to the Queen who entered 'most sincerely' into his feelings and saw 'with great sorrow the effect' his disappointment had upon his mind; but she strongly warned him not to let his anger at it drive him once more into opposition and into the ranks of the Foxite Whigs. 'Every opposition to the Crown, headed by a branch of the Royal Family,' she wrote, *'lessens the power of the Crown!* and I am sure it cannot be your interest to assist in that. . . . After all, who is the Crown to look up to for staunch supporters? Certainly the Royal Family!'[39]

Henry Dundas, Secretary for War, gave him the same warning: 'It is impossible that your Royal Highness, after a moment's cool reflection on the subject, can put any consideration whatever in competition with those important interests which are now at stake.'[40] The Earl of Moira wrote in similar terms, ardently hoping that the military rank he had so much set his heart on would be granted him but conjuring him 'not to let any fretfulness seduce' him into the opposition's camp if his Majesty persisted in rejecting the application.[41]

He took their advice, but with ever greater urgency he pleaded with the King to let him have his way, earnestly supplicating for the promotion that his younger brothers had been granted. If the country were to be invaded he might be employed, he wrote, in 'a real and important trust', professing that since there were so many other alternative heirs to the throne his own life was 'of little political importance'.[42]

But the King refused to depart from what he had always thought right. 'My younger sons,' he repeated, 'can have no other situations in the State . . . but what arise from the military lines they have been placed in. You are born to a more difficult one, and which I shall be most happy if I find you seriously turn your thoughts to; the happiness of millions depend on it as well as your own.'[43]

The Prince, feeling that the Duke of York – who had been promoted Field Marshal on his return from the Continent in 1795 – was not doing all he might to help him, had a furious quarrel with both his brother and the Duchess, and for a time would not speak to either of them.[44] Then, when hoping that at least he might be made Colonel of the Royal Horse Guards, an appointment upon which he had long since set his heart and which the government had indicated he might have, he was thrust into deeper gloom by a message from the Queen to the effect that the colonelcy had been given to the Duke of Richmond.[45]*

For a time the Prince resigned himself to his disappointments until, in

* When the Duke of Richmond died in 1806, the Prince generously waived his claim to succeed him so that the Colonelcy could pass to his friend the Duke of Northumberland (Alnwick MSS: Asp/P, v, 383).

1797, he renewed his application with more urgency than ever. The King, however, remained adamant. He had given the Prince command of a cavalry regiment because his son had rightly pressed him to place him in a situation in which he could 'manifest his zeal in defence of his country'; but he resisted 'every idea . . . of the Prince of Wales being . . . considered as a military man'.[46]

So the Prince had to display his military virtue as a cavalry colonel, or not at all; and when an opportunity to gain distinction seemed to present itself with a report of a French fleet sailing towards the south coast, he seized it with the utmost enthusiasm.

He was given this report as he was returning to Critchell House after a day's hunting. It was brought by an officer of his regiment who was stationed at Wareham. Immediately he announced that he was going to join the regiment and galloped off towards Dorchester in the hope that he and his men would give the enemy a warm reception. Stopping at Blandford on the way he ordered a squadron of the Bays who were in quarters there to hold themselves in readiness. Then he rode off again, arriving in Dorchester after dark. The place was quiet, and the major-general in command of the district had gone to bed. The King, who received his son's hasty message that he was 'instantly' joining his regiment early the next morning, could not credit the report of a French fleet in English waters; and soon it was, indeed, confirmed that the supposed French fleet was not a French fleet at all but an English one.[47]

Through no fault of his own, the Prince had been made to look a fool. Inevitably he had cause to complain that his 'poor efforts to meet the danger' had been turned 'into ridicule' by the 'language of some of the Ministers and the hirelings employed by them'.[48]

He was more than ever anxious now to obtain the promotion so long – and, as he thought, so unjustly – denied him. To remain '*a mere Colonel* of Dragoons', he bitterly complained to the Lord Chancellor was 'wholly below the dignity' which his 'birth and station' gave him in the country.[49] 'Only think of [Prince William of Gloucester's] being a Major-General attended by two aides-de-camp, on account of *his* rank as the *Duke* of Gloucester's son,' he exclaimed in exasperation to his mother, 'and the *Prince of Wales, eldest son* of the King only a simple Colonel, and under the command of such a dull stupid boy' as his stupendously boring cousin, 'Silly Billy'.[50]

Yet his father would not be moved. In a final effort to persuade him to change his mind, the Prince consulted several leading lawyers who assured him that the laws and constitution of the country contained nothing which might prevent his accepting any command that his Majesty might think fit to confer upon him.[51] The King's answer, however, was sadly familiar: 'The command I have given you of the 10th Regiment of Light Dragoons, should the enemy succeed in their intentions of invading this island, will enable you at the head of that brave Corps to show the valour which has ever been a striking feature in the character of the House of Brunswick.'[52]*

---

* The King invited William Beechey to paint a portrait of himself reviewing this 'brave Corps'. On the Queen's authority, apparently, but without the King's knowledge, Beechey included a portrait of the Prince of Wales in the picture. The King was so angry when he saw what had been done that he ordered the canvas to be thrown out of the window. Fortunately, the order was not carried out; and some time later, father and son being on rather better terms, the picture was hung at the Royal Academy. Nevertheless, when the King had a copy made to present to Henry Addington, he gave instructions that the figure of the Prince should be left out (Roberts, *Beechey*, 57–63; *Farington Diary*, i, 226; Alnwick MSS: Asp/P, v, 128–9).

15

The Return of Mrs Fitzherbert
1796–1801
*

'You know you are my wife, the wife
of my heart and soul'

Three days after the birth of his daughter, the Prince, feeling suddenly and alarmingly ill and protesting that he felt himself about to die, wrote out in his own hurried hand his 'last' will and testament. It was a document of extraordinary length, extending to over three thousand words. In it he mentioned, with 'the truest affection', his friend Jack Payne, 'though, from some unfortunate misunderstandings and circumstances', he had not seen him for some time. He also mentioned his friend, the Earl of Moira, whom he appointed his executor; Mrs Fitzherbert's companion, Miss Isabella Pigot, upon whom he had already settled £500 a year; and his old and faithful servant, Santague, recommending him, together with those other domestics, who had been 'in the habit of constant attendance' upon his person, to 'the King's gracious protection' in the hope that they would not be allowed to starve. He went on to take particular notice of his 'dear parents' whose forgiveness he asked for any faults he may have ignorantly and unguardedly been guilty of, and his infant daughter whose care he entrusted, in the event of his father's death, to his 'dearest and most excellent mother', in conjunction (if she wished it) with his brothers, the Duke of Clarence, Prince Edward and Prince Ernest and his sisters, Augusta and Mary. The child's mother – though he forgave her 'the falsehood and treachery of her conduct' towards him – must in *'no way either be concerned in the education or care of the child, or have possession of her person'*, since it was incumbent upon him *'both as a parent and a man to prevent by all means possible the child's falling into such improper and bad hands as hers'*.

168

The will, however, was principally concerned with Maria Fitzherbert, his 'beloved and adored Maria Fitzherbert', to whom he bequeathed all his estates, all his property, all his monies, all his 'personalities of whatever kind or sort', all the contents of all his houses which were listed in the most exact detail down to cabinets, girandoles and clocks, pier glasses, china, wine and liquors, jewels, plate, plans, maps, prints, drawings, trinkets, watches and boxes. He addressed her, the 'wife of his heart and soul', 'his true and real wife', his 'second self', in the most extravagant, not to say, hysterical terms. She was dearer to him, even millions of times dearer to him, than that life he was now about to resign. Her person, her heart and her mind were, and ever had been since the first moment he had known her, 'as spotless, as unblemished and as perfectly pure' as anything could be that was human and mortal.

'I desire I may be buried with as little pomp as possible,' he wrote, 'that *my constant companion, the picture of my beloved wife, my Maria Fitzherbert* may be interred with me suspended round my neck by a ribbon as I used to wear it when I lived and *placed right upon my heart*; I likewise will and decree and entreat of *my adored* Maria Fitzherbert to permit that whenever she quits this life and is interred, my coffin should be taken up and placed next to hers wherever she is to be buried, and if she has no objection, that the two inward sides of the two coffins should be taken out and the two coffins then to be [soldered] together.... *To thee therefore my Maria, my wife, my life, my soul, do I bid my last adieu; round thee shall my soul forever hover as thy guardian angel, for as I never ceased to adore thee whilst living, so shall I ever be watchful over thee and protect thee against every evil. Farewell, dearest angel ... think of thy* DEPARTED HUSBAND, *shed a tear o'er his memory and his grave and then recollect that no woman ever yet was so loved or adored by man as you were and are by him....'*

He signed his name and then, remembering something else, turned over the sheet: 'I forgot to mention that the jewels which she who is called the Princess of Wales wears *are mine, having been bought with my own money*, and therefore ... I bequeath [them] to my infant daughter as her own property and to her, who is called the Princess of Wales, I leave one shilling....'[1]*

Despite his protestations as to how deeply he adored his beloved Maria,

* The relief that he felt when he had at last come to the end of this diffuse and enormously long document – so he professed four years later – 'certainly did restore one in a manner to life after a dangerous and precarious illness' (RA 50225–6: Asp/P, iv, 100).

and despite his insistence on how greatly he longed for her to return to him, she did not respond to his blandishments. Apart from all her other reservations about the advisability of a reconciliation, she was far from convinced that the Prince's liaison with Lady Jersey was at an end; and she had good reason for holding this belief. Although the Prince did his best to avoid Lady Jersey, to whose full-blown charms he had long since grown averse, this determined lady was not easily put off. She was removed from Jack Payne's former house adjoining Carlton House in June 1799;[2] and six months later her husband was formally dismissed from his appointment as the Prince's Master of the Horse on the grounds of economy, though he had in fact been most erratically paid.[3] Yet she declined to be brushed aside, refusing to acknowledge any change in the former relationship, in spite of the broadest hints which were given to her by the Prince's friends and emissaries. He sent Edward Jerningham to see her and to suggest to her that the affair must be considered as finished; but she refused to accept the message. 'Damn you!' she was supposed to have said to Jerningham. 'I wish you well of your new trade.'[4] Later the Prince sent Colonel John McMahon, soon to be appointed Vice-Treasurer of his Household, to call on her after she had met him on the stairs at the Opera House and had followed him down to talk to him. McMahon told her emphatically 'that it was the desire of the Prince that *she would not speak to him*'; but she refused to accept the rebuff, said that there was 'a popish combination against her', and spoke bitterly of McMahon 'for having submitted to carry such a message'.[5]*

While the Prince was taking pains to avoid Lady Jersey, Mrs Fitzherbert was equally concerned to avoid him. She gave up going to Brighton; she sold the lease of Marble Hill, and went to live quietly in a smaller house at Castle Hill, Ealing, where she remained for several months, reluctant to consider the possibility of a reconciliation. 'The link once broken could never be rejoined,' she said, confiding in Prince Ernest;

---

* John McMahon, who became Keeper of the Prince's Privy Purse in 1804 and his Private Secretary in 1806, was a loyal and useful servant. He was said to be the illegitimate child of a chambermaid and a butler who had later kept an oyster shop in Dublin. He had been a very bright child, and become a clerk, then an actor, then a soldier in a regiment commanded by Lord Moira who recognized his talents and artful resource, helped him to buy a commission and eventually brought him to Carlton House (Huish, i, 404–8). His bustling little figure and red, spotty face were to be regularly seen in London as he hurried about upon his master's more dubious errands. From 1802 to 1812, through the influence of the Prince's friend, the Duke of Northumberland, he was Member of Parliament for Aldeburgh.

even if they were to make it up, they would 'not agree a fortnight'.[6] The Prince, nevertheless, pursued her assiduously, sending his brothers and Miss Pigot to her with innumerable messages, assuring such mutual friends as the Duchess of Rutland that 'there *never was an instant*' in which he did not feel for her (though she 'never felt' for him) and that everything was '*finally at an end* IN ANOTHER QUARTER'. His letters to her were nearly as long as his will and even more vehement. He sent her presents which included a locket containing a miniature of one of his eyes painted by Cosway and a bracelet engraved with the words '*Rejoindre ou mourir*'.[7] He worked himself up into such a frenzy that his family and friends feared he might be near to losing his reason.

When the Prince heard that Mrs Fitzherbert was seriously ill he became frantic, and a newspaper report that 'SHE *had died* at Bath' so overwhelmed him that he could 'neither feel, think, speak'. He thought he was going mad, he said, and became so ill that he could not hold a pen in his hand. He was afterwards convinced that if he had not been 'thus bereft of all sense' he would have killed himself.[8] He took quantities of laudanum, and insisted on constant bleeding, losing in one three-day period no less than thirty-six ounces of blood from the arm. He grew so thin that people failed to recognize him; and Lady Holland recorded in her journal that he was 'supposed to be dying'.[9]

'Save me, save me, on my knees I conjure you from myself,' he implored Mrs Fitzherbert in one impassioned, fervent, scarcely coherent letter in which almost every word is underlined with two or more heavy strokes. 'IF YOU WISH MY LIFE YOU SHALL HAVE IT . . . OH! GOD! OH, GOD, WHO HAS SEEN THE AGONY OF MY SOUL AND KNOWEST THE PURITY OF MY INTENTIONS HAVE MERCY ON ME: TURN ONCE MORE I CONJURE THEE, THE HEART OF MY MARIA, TO ME, FOR WHOM I HAVE LIVED AND FOR WHOM I WILL DIE. . . . YOU KNOW YOU ARE MY WIFE, THE WIFE OF MY HEART AND SOUL, MY WIFE IN THE PRESENCE OF MY GOD . . .' He broke off in tears at two o'clock in the morning, and continued again at four: '*The wretched experiences of the last five years have* MADE LIFE ONLY DESIRABLE IN ONE SHAPE TO ME, AND THAT IS IN YOU. I AM WRAPPED UP IN YOU ENTIRELY . . . NOTHING CAN ALTER ME, SHAKE ME OR CHANGE ME. ALIKE YOURS IN LIFE AND DEATH. THE CHRYSIS IS COME AND I SHALL DECIDE MY FATE, THAT IS TO SAY YOU SHALL FIX MY DOOM . . .'[10]

He threatened that if she did not return to him he would announce their secret marriage to his father and the world. 'You know not what you will drive me to FROM DISPAIR . . . I WILL *prove my marriage*, RELINQUISH EVERYTHING FOR YOU, RANK, SITUATION, BIRTH, AND IF THAT IS NOT SUFFICIENT, MY LIFE SHALL GO ALSO . . . THANK GOD *my witnesses are living*, your uncle and your brother . . . Oh! my heart, my heart. . . .'[11]

Frightened by this letter, Mrs Fitzherbert asked for time to consider her position; and, while she tried to make up her mind, both her own family and the Prince's urged her more strongly than ever to agree to a reunion. Princess Augusta and Princess Mary both actively encouraged it;[12] so did Prince Ernest who assured his brother that Mrs Fitzherbert had 'a very sincere regard' for him;[13] so did Prince Edward who, home from Canada for a time, undertook to conduct the negotiations. On 17 July 1799 Prince Edward had a 'very long tête à tête' with her. He afterwards assured his brother that if he was 'any judge at all of the business' his wishes would 'ere long be accomplished'. There was just the matter of her religious scruples to be cleared up.[14]

This was not done without difficulty, and entailed the Rev William Nassau of the Roman Catholic church in Warwick Street being commissioned to go to lay her case before the Pope. While waiting for his decision, she went to stay in Wales out of reach of the Prince's further importunities,[15] and he vainly sought permission to go abroad to Lisbon or Madeira 'for a recovery of his health'.[16]

At length the papal decision was made known. It was a favourable one. Mrs Fitzherbert might rejoin the Prince who was her lawful husband in the eyes of the Church. So, by the summer of 1800, they were 'once more inseparables', the Prince subsequently deciding that Roman Catholicism was the 'only religion for a gentleman'.[17]

In June Mrs Fitzherbert gave a 'public breakfast' for the Prince of Wales as a way of announcing to society that a formal reconciliation had taken place.* She hardly knew how she could 'summon up resolution to pass that severe ordeal', she later told a relative, Lord Stourton, 'but she thanked God she had the courage to do so'.[18] Some of her staider friends

---

* According to *The Times* there were no fewer than four hundred guests, including most of the ladies of fashion in town. 'Our fashionable dames', the newspaper commented, 'continue to endeavour to outvie each other in the expence, stile or peculiarity of their entertainments.' But Mrs Fitzherbert beat all her rivals 'by the eccentricity of her entertainment and the *length* of it. . . . In the gardens three marquees were erected for the accommodation of the company who met about two o'clock and dined at seven. The entertainment did not conclude till past five o'clock yesterday morning' (*The Times*, 18 June 1800).

were rather shocked by her behaviour, all the more so when it became known that she had not relinquished the generous allowance which she had accepted at the time of the Prince's marriage to Princess Caroline. Lady Jerningham, who considered the whole affair 'very incomprehensible', and revised her former opinion of Mrs Fitzherbert as 'a woman of principle', was grateful that a '*bad* cold' gave her a good excuse not to attend the breakfast.[19] A guest at a subsequent breakfast given by the Duchess of Devonshire was even more disapproving. This was Lady Jersey who coasted round the Prince as he stood by one of the bands in the garden talking to Dr Charles Burney. 'The Prince was quite annoyed with her and eyed her askance; but she is resolved to plague him; she professes it to be her resolution.'[20]*

Mrs Fitzherbert, however, now confidently disregarded Lady Jersey and settled down to what she described to Lord Stourton as the happiest years of her connection with the Prince. They were 'extremely poor, but as merry as crickets'.[21] They spent the greater part of their time in each other's company, visiting friends for long periods in the country, nearly always together in London where the Prince remained with her most evenings until midnight when he returned home to Carlton House.

'He is so much improved,' she told Lady Anne Lindsay contentedly, 'all that was boyish and troublesome before is now become respectful and considerate ... We live like brother and sister. I find no resentment though plenty of regret that I will have it on this footing and no other, but he must conform to my stipulations or I will have nothing to say to him. I did not consent to make it up with the Prince to live with him either as his wife or his mistress.'[22]

---

* Lady Jersey fulfilled her resolution, taking pride in the 'look of the utmost disdain' which she bestowed upon him when they found themselves at the same party (Rogers, *Table-Talk* 218). She was to succeed in making trouble for the Prince with both Princess Caroline and Princess Charlotte. By 1814 the Prince was only too well acquainted with 'all the wickedness, perseverance and trick of that infernal Jezabel Lady Jersey, and of all her Jacobinal set of connexions' (RA 21560: Asp/K, i, 513). After various direct and indirect requests for a pension she was granted one (RA 20388-9, 20802-3, 21236: Asp/K, i, 216, 281, 344). Despite this she was so violent a supporter of Queen Caroline during her trial in 1820 that she was 'at daggers drawn even with the Holland family', and wore the Queen's portrait round her neck (*Lieven*, 51, 69). She grew very impatient with other 'opposition ladies' who thought it prudent to await the outcome of the trial before leaving their names at the Queen's house. She was 'longing to fly into her arms', the Countess of Harrowby told her son, 'and to pay her every possible honour and attention' (Harrowby MSS, 24 October 1820). Afterwards she went abroad. On her return she retired to her husband's seat, Middleton Park, where, so she said, she cared for the details of country life and nothing else. She died at Cheltenham in 1821.

Her poverty was more imagined than real. In January 1801, having given up her house in Pall Mall at the time of the separation, she bought the Earl of Aberdeen's handsome house at the corner of Tilney Street and Park Lane for £6,000;[23] and, the Prince having increased her allowance from £3,000 to £4,000 a year, she sold the lease of her house in Ealing to Prince Edward and took a larger one on Parson's Green, Fulham.[24] Her happiness was only interrupted by the Prince's 'bitter and passionate regrets, and self-accusations for his conduct, which she always met by saying, "We must look to the present and the future, and not think of the past." '[25]

For the Prince, though, the present was not without its worries and the future did not look too promising. He was more 'comfortable' now that he had got Mrs Fitzherbert back again, even though he was apparently not allowed to make love to her; yet his other problems which had seemed insignificant compared with his almost demented longing for a reconciliation now returned to haunt him once more.

In the first place, there were his debts. He managed to raise yet another loan of £40,000 without interest from the Landgrave of Hesse-Cassel,[26] but this did not go far; and soon after receiving the money he felt compelled to make further economies in his Household, abolishing the offices of Chamberlain and Master of the Horse, though Lord Cholmondeley had never received any salary for performing the duties of the one and Lord Jersey was still owed several hundred pounds for carrying out those of the other.[27] Indeed, few of those who worked for the Prince received their salaries with any regularity. Before General Gerard Lake left for India as Commander-in-Chief, for instance, he was owed four years' salary as the Prince's Gentleman Attendant; and the allowance of the Prince's dentist, Charles Dumergue, whose skills were supposed to merit regular fees of a hundred guineas a year, was over five years in arrears by 1805. Tradesmen were kept waiting for even longer periods. Payments to numerous firms and individuals, on claims agreed in 1795, were still continuing up till October 1806. One of these creditors, the overcharging jeweller Nathaniel Jefferys, who was at one time owed over £89,000,[28] published damaging advertisements of his alleged losses, threatened to bring his outstanding claim before the House of Commons, and in an open letter to Mrs Fitzherbert – who had offended him by not thanking him gracefully enough for helping her to pay off a pressing debt – wrote that the nation's feelings towards her were of 'EXTREME DISGUST'.[29]

174

Ignoring his unsettled debts, the Prince continued to incur others at as fast a rate as ever, as though he were constitutionally incapable of restraint or retrenchment, spending, for example, £2,166 on new table linen, £3,419 on chandeliers.[30] His wardrobe bills, which amounted to a total of £591 in one representative quarter, make revealing reading. A week rarely passed without one or other of his various tailors, usually Messrs Schweitzer and Davidson of 12 Cork Street or John Weston of 27 Old Bond Street, receiving a substantial order. In the course of a period of less than three weeks he was capable of placing five separate orders with John Weston for a total of twenty waistcoats of various styles, colours and shapes from 'fancy lilac double breasted' to 'brown nankeen striped Marseilles quilted', the same firm having supplied him with '18 fine Marseilles waistcoats' and '24 fine printed Marseilles waistcoats' only a month or so before. He almost invariably ordered his clothes in similar bulk. In one short summer, between 4 July and 14 September, he was supplied with seventy-four pairs of gloves; in a subsequent year, within a period of six months, he bought 'ten dozen pairs of white long gloves'. 'Superfine cambric handkerchiefs marked with coronets' came to Carlton House in batches of three dozen; 'rich gold spotted muslin hand-kerchiefs' arrived in smaller parcels, but they cost twelve guineas each. Everything, naturally, had to be of the highest quality, from his black silk drawers and stockings and his prime doeskin pantaloons (with corsets) to his 'superfine scarlet flannel underwaistcoats lined with firm calico', his 'fine white beaver morning gown double-breasted lined throughout with flannel with a belt made extra wide and very long', his 'black astrakhan Polish caps', and his 'fine white coating bathing suits, jackets, vests and trousers lined throughout with fine Welsh flannel'.

He spent an immense amount on fur. Pelisses, of which he had an enor-mous number, cost anything up to £150 each. Muffs, which he ordered scarcely less often, were almost as expensive – three 'rich muscovy sable muffs' cost a hundred guineas each. Swords were another expensive item; in eighteen months he bought four steel and gold sabres from John Prosser of Charing Cross, including 'a very superb elegant steel and gold sabre embossed with trophies and laurels' at a total cost of £236. Then there were his uniforms (a Dragoon's regimental coat alone cost £29), his costume for masquerades, his black silk masks and 'character masks made to order', his fancy-dress clothes for appearances as Henry V (£16.10s) or Leontes (£27.1s) supplied by Martin Gay, the Drury Lane theatrical costumiers, his 'tartan masquerade jackets' (£17.10s each), his 'mandarin of war's court dress' (£52.10s), his plumes (£36), his perukes (£33), and his various 'pairs of false curls'.[31]

The Prince's perfumers, Bourgeois Amick and Son, Urania Devins, and other firms, received orders with as unfailing regularity as his tailors, bootmakers, drapers, hatters, hosiers, mercers, lace merchants and furriers. He spent over £20 a week on cold cream and almond paste, perfumed almond powder and scented bags, lavender water, rose water, elder flower water, jasmin pomatum and orange pomatum, eau de Cologne, eau Romaine, Arquebusade, essence of bergamot, vanilla, eau de miel d'Angleterre, milk of roses, huile antique and oil of jessamine. He bought them all in huge quantities – perfumed powder was delivered in amounts of up to 36 lbs at a time; tooth brushes came by the three dozen.[32] But then he bought almost everything in huge quantities: in need of a few walking sticks, he bought thirty-two in one day.[33]

The costs of running Carlton House and of entertaining there in the grand style expected of him were, of course, enormous. Apart from the various gentlemen of the Household, the Treasurer (£500 a year), the Keeper of the Privy Purse (£500 a year), the Vice-Treasurer (£300 a year), two clerks (£150 and £100 a year), the Prince's surgeon (Thomas Keate, £150 a year) and the surgeon to the Household (John Phillips, £100 a year), apart from four Pages of the Backstairs, three Pages of the Presence, two Grooms of the Chamber, and seven musicians, there were in 1806 no less than forty indoor servants. These included a housekeeper, a wardrobe keeper, a maître d'hôtel, an inspector of Household deliveries, nine housemaids, four cooks, three watchmen, two kitchen boys and a kitchen-maid, two confectioners, two cellarmen, two coal porters, a coffee-room woman, a silver scullery woman, and a table decker. Their wages, which ranged from £300 a year for the maître d'hôtel down to £15 a year for the kitchen boys, came to almost £3,000, the rest of the Household adding a further £3,700 to the annual bill.[34] In a representative month just under £500 was spent on general groceries, meat and fish, while the wine merchant's account came to £1,118, including the cost of fifty dozen bottles of vintage port.[35]

Generous as he was with himself, the Prince was equally generous with his friends and family.* His accounts are full of bills for clothes for his

---

* The Duchess of Devonshire, who was frequently in debt owing to her passion for gambling and jewels, was one of those who had reason to be thankful for the Prince's generosity. She was

sisters and his mother, for toys for children, for Brussels lace dresses and cloaks, for hats, stockings, ribbons and tippets. One day Messrs W. & G. Bicknell sent an account for '48 pairs of women's fancy white silk hose with laced clocks'; another day Messrs Beamon & Abbott requested payment of £126 for 'a superb Persian scarlet shawl'; later an account arrived for an admiral's dress coat which had been made 'with rich gold epaulettes' for the Duke of Clarence at a cost to the Prince of £143.[36]

*

The Prince remained on good terms with the Duke of Clarence as he did, for the moment, with his other brothers, though he had occasional differences and quarrels with all of them.

Clarence considered the Prince his 'best friend' for the support he gave him in his unavailing efforts to obtain some sort of employment. He repeatedly and vainly asked the Board of Admiralty for a command at sea; he even asked his father to appoint him First Lord of the Admiralty in succession to the ailing Lord Spencer;[37] but – as he 'rather expected' – he was met with a firm refusal. He was also sharply rebuffed when he asked to be placed in command of the fleet in the Mediterranean, and he had to be content with the command of the militia.[38]

The Prince's next brother, Edward, created Duke of Kent in April 1799, was also disappointed in his hopes of a higher command in the Mediterranean area. He had arrived back in England from Canada at the end of 1798 with Mlle, or, as he now called her, Mme de St Laurent, and had been received by his parents with more cordiality than he had

---

constantly writing to thank her 'dearest, dearest brother', as she called him, for helping her out of one of her 'most terrible scrapes', or to ask for a further £2,000 or £3,000 'without it being known'. 'There never was anything equal' to his kindness, she assured him; she trembled to think of the sums she had cost him; it was 'quite shocking' of her to torment him as she did when she dared not approach her husband. Her 'whole heart and life' were devoted to him; she felt more than she could express. Her requests for help were often prefaced by piteous accounts of how her difficulties had brought her to a 'state of terrible weakness' and such 'nervous palpitations' that she thought she was going to die. She did not write, she once disingenuously assured him, with the 'most distant idea' of his being able to be 'of any use' to her; but she had kept her sorrows so long to herself that they preyed upon her; she relied so much on his friendship and had such confidence in him that it was a relief to open her heart to someone whose affection she had 'uniformly' cherished in her heart for many years. She never seems to have made such pleas in vain. She entreated him not to tell anyone of her financial plight – she was '*most afraid*' of Weltje, Payne and Sheridan – and he complied with her wishes. Sometimes he put money into her account without telling even her that he had done so (RA, Add. 27/71/40–41, 50, 71; Chatsworth MSS).

expected;[39] but on his return to Canada, he found that his continued liaison with Mme de St Laurent was considered to render him unsuitable for a more desirable appointment nearer home. 'I am the last person in the world to preach or to wish to meddle in your private happiness or connections,' the Duke of York admonished him, writing to him not only as an elder brother but as Commander-in-Chief at the Horse Guards, 'but at the same time I must fairly say to you you can have no idea how much the world talked of the public manner in which you went everywhere accompanied by Madame de St Laurent. I am perfectly well aware that this may be done abroad, but you may depend upon it that it cannot be done at home, and therefore I advise you as a friend to consider this subject well over. . . . A great deal depends upon appearances in this world. . . . Ministers would feel a delicacy in venturing to recommend to his Majesty to appoint you to [a command in England, Scotland or Ireland] under your particular circumstances at this moment.'[40]

In May 1800, however, the Duke of Kent was obliged to return home owing to illness, and two years later he was appointed Governor of Gibraltar where it was hoped his known reverence for military discipline would help to restore order to a lax and unruly garrison.

The enthusiasm with which he set about this task, closing drink-shops, getting the troops out of bed before dawn, issuing innumerable instructions in the minutest detail about uniforms, saluting, hair-cutting and even shaving, eventually drove the garrison to a mutiny in which several men were killed. In his meticulous script, the Duke wrote long letters to the Prince justifying his conduct. He insisted that, had he met with support from his subordinates, the garrison would have been 'brought to a degree of perfection' beyond his most 'sanguine expectations', and he expressed the deepest concern that the Prince might be misled into supposing that he had had the slightest responsibility for 'those events' which had almost broken his heart and which 'cast an indelible stain upon the troops concerned in them'.[41] The Duke's excuses, however, were wholly discounted in Whitehall. He was recalled home in disgrace, and, in a stormy interview in which both brothers lost their tempers, the Duke of York condemned his conduct 'from first to last as marked by cruelty and oppression'.[42]

The Prince of Wales, supposing his brother to be not so much cruel and oppressive as misguided and unimaginative, offered him his sympathy as he had offered it to the Duke of Clarence, and promised that as soon as he was in a position to do so, he would see that justice was done to him.[43] The Duke was duly grateful, thanking him in the most heartfelt terms for the 'unvaried friendship' shown to him 'throughout life, but more especially on the present *most trying* occasion' when everything that was dear to him, his character as a soldier and as a man, was 'at *stake*'.[44]

The Prince's other brothers, Adolphus and Augustus, were also in need of his sympathy. Adolphus, created Duke of Cambridge in 1801, had fallen in love with his cousin, Princess Frederica of Mecklenburg-Strelitz, the young widow of Prince Louis of Prussia. He asked her to marry him and she accepted, but when he sought his father's permission the King refused to consider it until the war was over. The Princess sought comfort in the arms of a German princeling whom, to Prince Adolphus's bitter consternation, she secretly married, having become pregnant.

Prince Augustus and his problems were even more of a trial to the Prince of Wales than were those of Adolphus. For Augustus's entanglement with Lady Augusta Murray had now been complicated by the birth of a son which was followed later by that of a daughter.

Prince Augustus, still languishing on the Continent where his asthma showed no signs of improvement, was scarcely in a position to bring up the boy; nor was Lady Augusta, whose meagre pension was most irregularly paid. So, with characteristic generosity, the Prince undertook to take charge of him himself, at the same time urging his brother to abandon all hope of establishing the legality of his marriage, for the King's determination on the point remained an 'insuperable and invincible' obstacle.[45] Prince Augustus, however, refused his brother's offer, ignored his advice and compounded his folly by returning home to England without the King's permission. Sent back to the Continent, he settled gloomily in Lisbon whence he wrote the Prince miserable letters about the 'melancholy stinking place', the falsehood of reports that he had turned Roman Catholic, and the inadequacy of his allowance of £8,500 a year.[46] Meanwhile Lady Augusta, left behind in England, also complained mournfully and at length to the Prince about her 'distressed situation in point of pecuniary matters'.[47]

By the beginning of 1802, Prince Augustus, who had at last been raised to the peerage as Duke of Sussex the year before, had grown as exasperated with Lady Augusta as were the other members of his family, and as they were with him. When she came out to Lisbon to insist that he come home with her to proclaim their marriage in the face of all opposition, the Duke refused to allow her into his house; and on her return she immediately wrote an extremely long letter of protest to the Prince about the treatment she had received at his brother's hands, 'the utmost of insult and ill usage a woman could receive – never admitted to his presence – driven from his abode – the sport of his mistress and dependents'. 'Your brother, Sir,' she continued in rising anger, 'has accustomed me to hardship – has inured me to injury – has oppressed me with vexation – has steeped me in calamity – (let him remember what *was* my situation in society when we first met – and what it *is* now. This sad reverse, Sir, is his work).'[48] As well as badgering the Prince of Wales, Lady Augusta badgered the King and the government, demanding money and a peerage, threatening to publish all the letters and documents she possessed unless justice were done, insisting upon being known as Princess Augusta, endeavouring to buy the title from the Emperor of Austria and returning, unopened, letters addressed to her as Lady Augusta Murray.[49] The Duke decided that although his conduct had always been 'delicate' towards her, she 'certainly did not deserve it'.[50]*

On his return to England, the Duke of Sussex followed his brothers' example in pressing the Prince to support his application for an important military or civil appointment, preferably in Jamaica where the climate would suit him, or at the Cape, as Civil Governor. The Prince did support him, but the government were naturally reluctant to place so sickly and inexperienced a man in a position of responsibility; and their persistent refusal of his request, combined with his creditors' threats of an 'execution upon all the little property' that he possessed, dismayed Sussex to such an extent that the Duke of Kent feared it might actually 'derange his intellect'. Unless some means were found to accomplish something '*forthwith*' for their brother, Kent warned the Prince, it would be 'impossible to answer for the consequences'.[51]

* It was finally agreed, in 1806, that Lady Augusta should have her debts paid and be provided with an allowance on condition that she stopped claiming to be the Duchess of Sussex. She took the name d'Ameland by royal licence. The two children were given the surname D'Este, both their mother's family and the House of Hanover being descended from the Italian House of Este, rulers in Italy in the Middle Ages. Augustus Frederick D'Este (1794–1848) joined the Army in which he achieved the rank of Colonel in 1838. He died unmarried, having failed in his protracted claims to be declared legitimate on the grounds that 'as the marriage took place in Rome it was outside the Royal Marriage Act' (Grey Papers (Durham) Box 43). His sister, Augusta Emma D'Este married, as his second wife, Sir Thomas Wilde, who as Lord Truro became Lord Chancellor in 1850. There were no children of the marriage.

Prince Ernest, Duke of Cumberland since 1799, was another trial to the Prince of Wales, who had by now decided that he thoroughly disliked him and was constantly induced to complain of the way in which he gossiped about him behind his back. The Duke, a reactionary of the most vehement kind, accused his brother of consorting with Whigs – whose views 'threatened the very foundations' of the monarchy and the Constitution – and of all manner of radical excesses which, as the Prince complained to his mother, were 'without the shaddow of a ground' and which 'none but a *fool* would credit and none but a *scoundrel* propagate'.[52]

The Prince's disagreements with the Duke of Cumberland were not as bitter, however, as his quarrel in 1804 with the Duke of York with whom, for many weeks, he was not on speaking terms.

The cause was the Prince's perennial disappointment at his inability to gain any sort of responsible command in the Army in which his younger brother had now reached the highest rank. In 1801, in the following year, and again in 1803 – when, a French invasion appearing imminent, the King announced his intention of commanding the defending army in person and of sending his wife and daughters to be cared for by Bishop Hurd at Hartlebury Castle[53] – the Prince renewed his requests to the King, repeating his former arguments in ever more impassioned terms: 'It would therefore little become me who am the first and who stand at the very footstool of the throne to remain a tame, an idle, a lifeless spectator of the mischief which threatens us . . . I am bound to adopt this line of conduct by every motive dear to me as a man and sacred to me as a prince. Ought I not to come forward in a moment of unexampled difficulty and danger? Ought I not to share in the glory of victory when I have everything to lose by defeat?'[54]

No, the King still thought, decidedly he should not; and 'desired no further mention should be made to him on this subject'.[55] Undeterred by the repetition of this familiar rebuke, the Prince approached his brother as Commander-in-Chief: was it not 'a degrading mockery to be told that the only way he could display his zeal was at the head of his regiment?[56] The Duke of York did not agree. 'Surely you must be satisfied,' he replied, 'that your not being advanced in military rank proceeds entirely from his Majesty's sentiments respecting the high rank you hold in the State, and not from any impression unfavourable to you.'[57] The Prince was certainly not satisfied: 'I must *emphatically* repeat, "*That idle inactive rank was never in my view*," but that military rank with its consequent command was never *out of it*.'⁵⁸ He knew he was incapable of commanding an army, he admitted to the Duke of Devonshire, but he could collect 'the best generals around him and they might in fact command and direct him'.⁵⁹

Everywhere he went he talked about his grievance until, as Lady Bessborough said, he could talk of nothing else. He remained for hours on end with those who felt obliged to listen to him recounting his wrongs, and became, as he always did on such occasions, exasperatingly tedious and boring.⁶⁰

It was all to no avail, and in resentful desperation he decided that the whole correspondence on the subject ought to be published. It was a decision taken against the advice of nearly all his more responsible friends, notably the Duke of Northumberland who thought that the Prince could do nothing but 'submit in silence to the orders' he had received; any further step would not only be 'unbecoming his dignity but . . . unavailing'. Ignoring this advice, the Prince allowed the correspondence to be published, on 7 December 1803, in the *Morning Chronicle*, the *Morning Herald* and the *Sun. The Times* was also offered the material but declined it because of 'the delicacy of the subject'.⁶¹

The Prince denied that he himself had been responsible for the publication, assuring both the Earl of Moira and Sheridan that he had had 'nothing to do with the business'.⁶² But few believed him, and certainly the King did not. 'See what he has done,' he was heard repeatedly lamenting, in a hoarse and hurried voice, 'he has published *my* letters.' For weeks, during which father and son did not meet and the Prince was ostentatiously absent from his parents' Drawing-Rooms, the King referred to him as 'the publisher of *my* letters'.⁶³

Worse was yet to come. Some time later the Prince's regiment was withdrawn from its front-line encampment close to the Sussex coast, where the French were expected to attempt an invasion, and sent inland of Guildford. This humiliating withdrawal, carried out at the moment of alarm upon instructions from the Horse Guards, was an indignity the Prince could 'never pass by', the Duke of Clarence assured their sister, Amelia, in his usual tactless way: it would 'produce an irreparable breach for ever' between the two brothers.⁶⁴

Goaded by the Duke's remarks, which had been reported to him by Colonel McMahon, and infuriated by what he took as a personal insult, the Prince threatened that he would never again speak to the Duke of

York, particularly as he himself had loyally defended him after his igno-minious failure as commander of the expedition to the Helder in 1799. Once again the placatory Duke of Northumberland urged restraint, advising the Prince to behave as though not in the least provoked; he must 'endeavour to disguise his feelings'.[65] The Prince could not disguise his feelings. He was furious with his brother and he did not mind who knew it. The Duke presented himself frequently at Carlton House to explain his reasons for the regiment's withdrawal, but the Prince refused to listen to them or even to ask him in. On making a final attempt, the Duke was handed a curt note by one of his brother's pages: 'The Prince of Wales is extremely concerned that the Duke of York has given himself the trouble of calling so frequently of late at Carlton House. But one moment's recollection and reflection must convince the Duke of York that it is im-possible for the Prince of Wales, whatever may be his regret, to receive the Duke, after *all* that has so *recently* passed.'[66]

16

The King's Relapse

1801–1804

*

'We sat till past eleven and the Prince talked the greater part of the time'

Although the Prince's relations with the Duke of York soon improved, he was never able to keep on good terms with his father. Whenever a happier relationship between them seemed likely, a family dispute, a political quarrel, a disagreement over money or over the Prince's employment in the Army or the State would drive them apart again.

In 1797 the Prince had entertained hopes of being appointed Lord Lieutenant of Ireland, an idea suggested to him by the Irish Whigs.[1] But the King had dismissed it out of hand; and the Prince had drawn closer once more to the opposition, giving dinners at Carlton House for Fox, Sheridan, the Duke of Norfolk and other leading opponents of Pitt's government.* For a time it had even seemed possible that a new government might be formed under the aegis of the Prince by some of these opponents and various disgruntled members of the present administration; but the Prince's widespread unpopularity, much intensified by his rejection of Princess Caroline, had stood irremovably in the way. Indeed, even if the Prince had been a far more popular figure, it was doubtful whether the

---

* Some of these dinners went on until four o'clock in the morning with the Prince's oratorical powers declining with each bottle of wine consumed. Lord Glenbervie records William Fawkener having told him that he 'never heard worse reasoning in better language, that the Prince would sometimes put two or three tolerable sentences together, but could not maintain that tone and fell into mere balderdash without expression or argument, but always with a sort of emphatic speechifying manner and in tirades'. Fawkener, adds Lord Glenbervie, 'has no high opinion of the Prince's understanding but says the Prince thinks highly of it and that he conceives himself particularly to have great penetration into characters and great quickness and readiness in learning men's private histories and views, and their particular passions and foibles. With this vanity he will be a most difficult master for any Minister' (*Glenbervie Journals*, i, 343).

Whig opposition were strong enough to form the nucleus of an acceptable government. The Prince's Private Secretary, Thomas Tyrwhitt, thought that their standing in the country had never been so low; Charles Grey agreed that they were 'without numbers or power'; and Fox considered that the old party was 'too much routed and dispersed to be rallied again'.[2]

At the beginning of 1801, however, Pitt felt obliged to resign over his thwarted intention of bringing in a Relief Bill for the benefit of the Irish Roman Catholics, a measure to which the King – persuaded that to agree to the Irish claims would be to violate his Coronation Oath – was rigidly opposed. As Pitt's successor, the King selected Henry Addington, the Reading doctor's son who had been Speaker of the House of Commons since the outbreak of the French Revolution. Addington, a modest man of limited competence, was reluctant to accept the appointment. But the King would consider no one else; Addington was honest, reliable and, above all, his attachment to the Church of England, as his Majesty assured Bishop Hurd, was as sincere as his own.[3] 'Lay your hand upon your heart', the King said to him, 'and ask yourself where I am to turn for support if *you* do not stand by me.'[4]

Addington said he would go to Pitt and try to get the Prime Minister to change his mind about the Catholic Relief Bill; but Pitt was as implacable as the King, and told him, 'I see nothing but ruin, Addington, if you hesitate.'[5] So Addington reluctantly gave way. On 5 February he wrote accepting office, and on the 10th went to see his Majesty who embraced him as he entered the room, saying, 'My dear Addington, you have saved your country.'[6]

That week, while out riding with one of his equerries, the King confessed to feeling unwell; he had been sleeping badly and was 'very bilious'.[7] Soon he was displaying all the symptoms that had characterized his former serious illness in 1788; and by the end of the month, his physical condition having alarmingly weakened and his conduct having become 'very extravagant', the Willises – with the exception of the father who at eighty-three had become 'rough and violent' – were once more in attendance upon their difficult patient, helped by four 'keepers'.[8]

It being feared that his father might even die, the Prince of Wales summoned both Pitt and Addington to Carlton House, Addington as *de jure* Prime Minister, Pitt, since he still held the seals of office, as Prime Minister *de facto*.

Pitt, stiff and unaccommodating as he usually was with the Prince, told him that it seemed a Regency might be necessary and that, if there were to be one, he would have to insist upon its being limited as had been proposed in 1789. The Prince, apparently rather mortified by this suggestion, replied that he would have to have time to think it over; but, strongly urged by the Earl of Carlisle and Lord Egremont amongst others to accept any restrictions that Parliament might want to impose, he agreed to it, and seemed prepared to abstain from the kind of reckless political intrigue in which he had become involved at the time of his father's previous incapacity.

He had his critics, of course. Mrs Harcourt said that, as usual, his conduct was 'very bad'; it was no wonder that he could not get to see the King since he always called when he knew his father was too ill to receive him. One day he went to the Queen's House just after his Majesty had taken his medicine, 'and on being refused, sent word to Lord Uxbridge, with whom he was to dine, by Jack Payne, that as the King would not see him, he really felt too much to think of dining in company. Sad grimace.'[9] Lord Malmesbury agreed that the Prince's conduct was most unseemly at the beginning of his father's illness; he was 'in great agitation of mind and spirits' as he had been during the last Regency crisis. He went about 'holding language in the streets as would have better become a member of opposition than heir to these Kingdoms', saying his father's mind was 'completely deranged'; and on the 'second day of the King's illness . . . he went in the evening to a concert at Lady Hamilton's and there told Calonne (the rascally French ex-minister), "*Savez vous, Monsieur de Calonne, que mon père est aussi fou que jamais?*" ' Malmesbury admitted, though, that 'he became more decent soon after this'.[10]

Certainly when he set about making provisional plans for a possible new administration, he did so discreetly. He cautiously approached the Duke of Devonshire, the Marquess of Buckingham and Lord Spencer; he tentatively offered the Viceroyalty of Ireland to the Duke of Norfolk with the idea of introducing a Catholic Relief Bill; he considered Shelburne (now Marquess of Lansdowne) for the office of Foreign Secretary, Grey for that of Secretary of War, Sheridan as Chancellor of the Exchequer, and Fox – though there would be difficulty with Mrs Fitzherbert over this appointment – as Home Secretary. Meanwhile there were 'great flockings of minor politicians into Carlton House'.[11] The Dukes of Clarence and Kent hung about the Prince in the hope of better employment, though the

Duke of York remained aloof at the Horse Guards, sharing his father's and the Duke of Cumberland's views on Catholic relief and supposing his future to be more secure with his father as King than with his brother as Regent.

Various names were canvassed for Prime Minister. Neither Fox nor Grey wanted so high an office at present, and, in any case, Fox could scarcely hope to attain it now that Mrs Fitzherbert had been returned to favour. Pitt was not in the running owing to the Prince's dislike of him. Addington, however, was considered a possibility; and certainly the Prince spent much of his time in private conversations with him. Subsequently the Earl of Moira emerged as a strong candidate.

But it was extremely difficult for the Prince to judge how necessary it was to consider the merits of any candidate, since he could get no reliable information about the King's condition. Even the Queen and the Princesses were not allowed to see him after 24 February, so the Prince had to rely upon what information he could glean from the doctors, Gisborne, Reynolds and the Willises. On 27 February, Dr John Willis told him that his Majesty was so confused that, if he were disposed to read, he would be unable to make out a single letter;[12] yet later Willis and his brother expressed much more optimistic opinions and spoke of a recovery 'within three weeks'.[13] On 1 March Reynolds reported the patient 'worse last night than ever'; and the next day he was so ill, with a pulse rate of 136, that the Prince was summoned to the Queen's House where he waited, with other members of the Royal Family, outside the sick-room expecting at any moment to be told of the King's death.[14] But, after a strong dose of musk, his Majesty grew a little better; and although he remained for some time alternating between 'insensibility and stupor' and such 'extreme nervous irritability' that they feared a 'paralytic stroke', by 5 March he had sufficiently recovered to be able to feed himself again. A few days later the Prince was at last permitted into his room to see him, accompanied by the Rev Thomas Willis, the doctors' brother, who had achieved considerable influence over the entire Household, and had, as the Queen put it, 'gained everybody's approbation'.[15]

The Prince, whose conduct, even Malmesbury admitted, was 'right and proper' now, found his father pale and very thin.[16] They had a perfectly coherent conversation; and the next week the King was well enough to receive Pitt and to accept back from him the seals of office, a ceremony which Pitt found 'particularly distressing' since it was being rumoured, notably by the Duke of Cumberland and by the Rev Thomas Willis, that the King's illness had been induced by his agitation over the intended Catholic Relief Bill.[17]*

Despite the King's recovery the Prince was not again admitted to his presence until 14 April, the day upon which the Willises' 'keepers' were dismissed. But on that day, so the Prince told the Earl of Carlisle, he was received with 'every mark of love and fondness'. His father 'began with the happiness he felt at being able the same day to embrace his son and dismiss Dr Willis's keepers, that being the first day since his illness that any one of his own servants had been permitted to attend him. The Prince was delighted to find that his mind was not poisoned on his account, but on the contrary [the King] did him ample justice for his correct conduct during the whole of the malady. He continually and repeatedly talked of himself as a dying man, determined to go abroad to Hanover [which no one had dared to tell him had been occupied by the Prussians at the instigation of Bonaparte, a man dismissed a few years before as 'a Corsican adventurer'[18]]. He made the Prince sit down to dinner with him, and expressed pleasure that once in his life he should have to say he dined *tête-à-tête* with his beloved son. He ate little – a small piece of mutton, a little beetroot, a small piece of cheese, and the contents of a small apple tart. He drank three glasses of wine, and all to the Prince's health. He talked of all his children in terms of the greatest affection – in terms to move to tears; but particularly so when he dwelt upon his little granddaughter. . . . He insisted much on the Prince accepting a white Hanoverian horse, laying the most vehement stress upon the Prince of Wales's right to mount such a horse, his joy, his pride; and this went to very incorrect discourse. . . . He then ran off, and talked of the device he used, by some position of his wig, to make the Council believe him in better looks and health. Here [he] was very wild.'[19]

* Cumberland took full credit for having persuaded the King to appoint Addington in Pitt's place, and was constantly urging his father to stand firm against Catholic relief. While the Prince of Wales was denied access to the sick-room by the Rev Thomas Willis, Cumberland was allowed in to play on his father's fears and prejudices. To the Duchess of Devonshire, the Prince of Wales expressed his 'disgust' at the conduct of the Duke of Cumberland 'who had broke with him during the King's illness and sided with the Duke of York' (Chatsworth MSS). His own conduct, he considered, had been exemplary. 'I have had the good approbation of the country,' he assured his friend, Arthur Paget, 'though one must always expect there will be in this world a certain number of grumblers, though there have been fewer upon this occasion than ever yet have been known upon any circumstances which has so interested the public mind' (*Paget Papers*, I, 343).

It was clear, then, that although he was very much better, the King was still far from being cured. He went out on 18 April, having said a thankful good-bye to the Willises, to fulfil an urgent desire to see his baby grand-daughter who was on a visit to Princess Caroline at Blackheath. Yet the next day Thomas Willis received a letter from Princess Elizabeth who told him how nervous she and her sisters and mother were at the prospect of being left alone with the King while he remained in such an uncertain state.[20]

Willis and his brothers were only too eager to respond to the call, and Thomas Willis appealed to Addington for his authority to take his Majesty into their care once more. Addington said that they could do so provided the Queen agreed; but the Queen, fearful of her husband's reaction to being again put into the hands of the Willises, whom she her-self had begun to find intolerably managing, refused to be responsible for giving her consent without ministerial approval. Addington, for his part, did not like to act without the agreement of Parliament. Eventually the Queen reluctantly gave way on the understanding that she would 'not be named or supposed to know anything that was intended'.[21]

The Willises, impatient of the delay, had already decided to take action. Unwilling to forsake the task they had 'undertaken when great credit was at stake', the Rev Thomas Willis confessed, they determined upon a 'cruel scheme', 'frightful as it was'. They planned no less than to seize the King and detain him by force.

They did so in the Prince of Wales's apartments at Kew where their erstwhile patient had gone to convalesce. When Thomas Willis entered the room, the King attempted to escape from it, but was prevented by Willis who insisted on the necessity of his being brought 'immediately under control again'. 'Sir,' said the King, sitting down and turning very pale, 'I will never forgive you whilst I live.' He again tried to escape, but Dr John Willis and four stalwart 'keepers' barred his way.[22]

From that moment he was kept more closely confined than ever, separated from his family, bled, cupped and purged, only occasionally being allowed out to take a few turns round Kew Green with one or other of the Willises in close attendance. His wife and daughters were permitted to see him for a short time on 19 May, but the Prince was not.

The Prince, supposing that his father had now suffered 'a severe relapse', took advice on what he should do. Lord Carlisle advised him that the first step was to remonstrate with Addington and Lord Eldon, the

Lord Chancellor, for their 'supinely suffering the King's health to be tampered with by persons who [could] hardly be called physicians'.[23] It was the King himself, however, who succeeded in getting rid of them by the simple, effective method of refusing to do any work unless he were allowed to show that their continued presence at Kew was quite unnecessary. He took 'a solemn declaration that unless he was allowed to go [on the Queen's birthday, 19 May] to the house where the Queen and his family were, no earthly consideration should induce him to sign his name to any paper or to do one act of government whatever'. The threat of a royal strike was taken seriously; and when the King walked over to the Queen's apartments on her birthday no one presumed to prevent him.[24]

Soon afterwards the King left to continue his convalescence at Weymouth where, as he told Bishop Hurd, sea bathing 'had its usual success'. Lord Eldon urged him to retain the services of Dr Robert Willis 'at least for the present . . . as a regular physician'. But the King replied that he was 'quite satisfied with Dr Gisborne', and in Gisborne's absence he would consult Sir Francis Milman. He would not and could not bear the idea of consulting Dr Robert Willis or, indeed, 'any of the Willis family'.[25]

*

For a time during his father's illness, as in 1788–89, the Prince had fallen out again with his mother. The Earl of Malmesbury said that at the Drawing-Room on 26 March, when her Majesty looked pale and the Princesses 'as if they had been weeping', the Prince behaved 'very rudely' to his mother. He suspected her, not unjustly, of plotting with the Dukes of York and Cumberland and the Rev Thomas Willis to ward off the threatened Regency by allowing it to be supposed that the King's illness was less severe than it was. But the Prince was soon on as good terms as ever with the Queen once more, and on much better terms with the King than he had been for years. 'As Heaven's my witness,' he told Lady Bessborough with tears running down his cheeks, 'I love my father to my heart, and never think of his sufferings without tears.' And she believed that he really meant it. The Prince had 'great faults', she knew, but they were more of the head than of the heart. She had 'never heard the Prince at any time mention the King but with respect and affection'.[26]

The Prince's relations with the new government were also satisfactory, for he got on much more easily with Addington than he had ever been able to get on with Pitt.* And once the Preliminary Articles of the Treaty of Amiens had been signed in October, Addington felt able to open negotiations for a possible coalition with some of the Prince's Whig 'friends'.

Although these negotiations were far from universally welcomed by members of the administration – Charles Yorke, the Secretary of War, for one, dreaded 'a connection with the Prince and his friends' – and although they eventually broke down, there was no doubt that the Prince was now considered, both in government circles and at Court, as a more responsible man than he had ever been in the past.

At last it was possible to raise once more the delicate question of his financial position, and to put forward a claim to the arrears of the revenue of the Duchy of Cornwall. These amounted, so Pitt estimated, to £234,000 which had been withheld from him until he had reached the age of twenty-one, although, as his lawyers undertook to prove from historical precedents, the income ought to have been his from birth.

The Prince's claim to the Duchy arrears – which had been appropriated by his father to settle his own debts – was due to be raised in Parliament on 31 March 1802; but not all the Prince's 'friends' felt able to vote in support of the motion. Grey, for one, 'was not quite convinced of his right', and when he met the Prince by chance on the street and was greeted volubly as a sure supporter, he felt obliged to say so. The Prince was 'evidently a good deal struck' by what Grey said, but 'bore it very well'.[27] The motion was defeated by 160 votes to 103.

Next year, however, a compromise was reached. In order to re-establish the Prince in 'that splendour which belonged to his rank', as Addington put it, it was proposed that he should be given an additional income of £60,000 for three years to enable him to pay off his outstanding debts. For this settlement the Prince was prepared to abandon his claims to the Duchy's arrears, not because he did not consider himself entitled to them, he hastened to make clear, but because he did not want to provoke any disagreement with the King with whom he was on uneasy terms again.

* The relationship between Pitt and the Prince was even more unfriendly after Pitt's resignation. Colonel McMahon complained to the Duke of Northumberland about Pitt's 'reprobate behaviour' in insolently neglecting the Prince while he was staying near Brighton in the summer of 1801. 'He rode daily into town and afforded the solitary instance of being the only man of any consideration in life that did not offer his duty and leave his name at the Pavilion' (Alnwick MSS: Asp/P, iv, 307). The Duke of Northumberland agreed that 'the indignities and insults offered to the Prince by that arrogant and insolent man [had] been such as [could] neither be overlooked nor forgiven'. The Duke trusted in God that his Royal Highness would 'never consent to any coalition with Mr Pitt' (RA 40073-4: Asp/P, iv, 489).

Despite Pitt's contention that the government's proposal was 'highly indecent' and that 'any further vote for the Prince ought on every account to be resisted', the Annuity Bill was passed. The majority was so small, however, that the Prince, in sending a message to Parliament to thank Members for what they had voted to do for him, felt it prudent to add that he could not think of increasing the country's financial burdens now that England was once more at war with France.* Lord Malmesbury commented that there was 'general disapprobation of the way in which Addington [had] managed the Prince's business', and that the 'division ... being so near run impressed the public that his ministry was a weak one'.[28]

Indeed, a year later, in February 1804, it seemed on the verge of collapse when the King once again fell ill with symptoms that threatened another attack of his distressing malady. Addington immediately sent for the Willises who responded promptly and, to the horror of the royal family, presented themselves at the Queen's House 'with the intention of their being introduced into the King's apartment to attend him'. The Dukes of Kent and Cumberland were fortunately there to bar their way; and faced with this firm opposition by the royal family, who had given solemn undertakings to the King never to allow any member of the Willis family near him again, Addington sent instead for the physician to St Luke's Hospital for Lunatics.[29]

The methods of this physician, Samuel Foart Simmons, differed little from those of the Willises and he soon had his patient wrapped up in a straitjacket. As on previous occasions, the Prince found it impossible to discover the true state of his father's condition. Simmons's reports were optimistic but qualified; his bulletins reported that the patient was 'going favourably', though 'any rapid amendment was not to be expected'. A month later it was reported that 'a short time' would 'perfect his recovery', but, as Mrs Harcourt told Lord Malmesbury, while he seemed well enough in the presence of his Ministers with whom he made great efforts to appear normal, 'towards his family and dependants his language was incoherent and harsh, quite unlike his usual character'. Mrs Harcourt added that Simmons 'did not possess, in any degree, the talents required to lead the mind from wandering to steadiness', and that the King, sus-

* 'The Prince's business comes on again today, but I shall again be an absentee,' Lord Harrowby was informed by his son in a letter which reflected the views of many other Members. 'I cannot vote for a bill which grants £60,000 a year for no public purpose whatever; as we know the Prince will not resume his establishment at present and will probably make his debts a pretence for not resuming it at all' (Harrowby MSS, 9 March 1803).

picious of the doctor and cantankerous with everyone, had made all sorts of changes in the Household, dismissing servants 'without a shadow of reason'. All this 'afflicted the royal family beyond measure; the Queen was ill and *cross*, the Princesses low, depressed and quite sinking under it'. After Mrs Harcourt had left Lord Malmesbury, Lord Pembroke was shown into his room where the two men 'dwelt on the very serious consequences to which [the King's condition] might lead, and in vain sought about for a remedy'.[30]

The Prince of Wales had already decided that he must provide the remedy himself. Once again he set about planning a new government in agitated consultations with various advisers, including Lord Thurlow, Lord Moira and Sheridan – whom he appointed Receiver-General of the Duchy of Cornwall (on the death of Lord Eliot) forgetting that he had formerly promised the post to General Lake. He would have preferred Moira as Prime Minister; but he said that he was prepared to consider other candidates, even Pitt, who was now certainly eager to return to office and who might easily, so the Earl of Darnley assured the Prince, 'be converted into a firm and certainly a most useful friend'.[31]

Pitt, however, shared the opinion, once expressed by Lord Thurlow, that the Prince was 'the worst anchoring ground in Europe'. He did not trust the Prince's friendship, and doubted his sincerity in letting it be known that he was prepared to call upon men of any party or faction provided they enjoyed the country's confidence. 'With respect to the Prince's intentions,' Pitt warned, 'I fear no very certain dependence is to be placed on any language which he holds.'[32] He refused to consider the Prince as a reliable or valuable ally, virtually disregarding his influence.

Under continued attack from Pitt, from the followers of Grenville and Fox, and deserted by many of its former supporters amongst the county and Scottish members, the government's majority fell in vote after vote until Addington felt obliged to resign. The King, distressed beyond measure by his resignation, became more difficult and cantankerous than ever with his family. When he learned that Pitt wanted to include Fox as well as Grenville in the new coalition ministry, he refused in any circumstances to countenance Fox's appointment, all the more strongly because the Prince, having forgiven his former friend for his attitude towards the French Revolution and Bonaparte, was now on good terms with him again. And without Fox, Pitt was unable to form that strong, broad-based government which he had hoped would be able to conduct the impending war with the spirit that Addington and his ministers had so conspicuously lacked. For it was decided on 7 May at meetings at Lord Grenville's London house and at Carlton House that if Fox was not to be appointed to the new government then none of his supporters, none of Grenville's, nor any 'friend' of the Prince's would accept office either.[33]

Both Lord Moira and George Tierney strongly deprecated the Prince's involvement with the Foxites and the Grenvilles, believing that if only the Prince had rallied to Pitt he would have become reconciled to the King, to the great benefit of the monarchy. As it was, the King and his son were now likely to become more estranged than ever, particularly as the Prince – evidently much gratified to have so formidable a body of political friends and delighted, as he told Lady Elizabeth Foster, that he and Fox were once again so intimate[34] – took to giving large dinner parties for Pitt's opponents at Carlton House where he talked at inordinate length on all manner of subjects, political and otherwise.

'We sat till past eleven and the Prince talked the greatest part of the time,' Charles Grey told his wife after one of these Carlton House dinners. 'There was no lack of length or repetition.' It was a good thing, Grey added, that the guests met elsewhere before going on to Carlton House for 'when we meet His Royal Highness there is in general an end of everything but speeches from him'.[35]

The Prince's loquacity was confirmed by Thomas Creevey, an enthusiastic Whig and Member of Parliament for Thetford, a pocket borough in the gift of the Duke of Norfolk. One evening at this time Creevey attended a Carlton House dinner at which were present about thirty members of the opposition including Fox, Grey, Sheridan and the Duke of Clarence. 'The only thing that made an impression upon me in favour of the Prince that day (always excepting his excellent manners and appearance of good humour),' Creevey wrote, 'was his receiving a note which he flung across the table to Fox and asked if he must not answer it, which Fox assented to; and then, without the slightest fuss, the Prince left his place, went into another room and wrote an answer, which he brought to Fox for his approval, and when the latter said it was quite right, the Prince seemed delighted, which I thought very pretty in him, and a striking proof of Fox's influence over him.

'During dinner he was very gracious, funny and agreeable, but after dinner he took to making speeches, and was very prosy as well as highly injudicious. He made a long harangue in favour of the Catholics and took occasion to tell us that his brother, William, and himself were the only two of his family who were not *Germans* – this too in a company which was, most of them, not known to him. Likewise I remember his halloaing to Sir Charles Bamfyld at the other end of the table, and asking him if he had seen Mother Windsor [a notorious procuress] lately.'[36]

What the Prince frequently spoke about was the state of his father's mind and the continued difficulty he experienced in getting information about it. He felt sure that he was 'as mad as ever', but the doctors declined to say so. There were persistent reports of the King's agitated, uncontrollable conversation, his rambling, repetitive talk about future plans, his indecent, even obscene behaviour in front of the servants, his writing of passionate love letters to a seventy-year-old lady who attended his Drawing-Rooms, his rudeness to the Queen who was finding him more and more intolerable, and who herself was becoming so insufferably ill-tempered that the Princesses were 'rendered quite miserable' by her.[37]

By June he was considerably better, so the Duke of Kent reported to Carlton House. He was not entirely reconciled to his family, particularly to the Queen whom he repeatedly blamed for the reappearance of the 'mad doctor', Simmons, and the 'keepers' into the house, but at least he was now 'coolly civil' to her. His behaviour to his daughters and to Kent himself was 'particularly kind, in a proper not in an outré way. So far for the fair side of the picture. On the *other* hand' his physical health was 'unusually bad'; his face and eyes were 'a livid yellow'; his right leg was 'much swollen and there was a tremor in his limbs'; he was very bilious and his tongue was 'furred half an inch thick'. 'There was also a singular catch in his throat' and 'an uncommon deficiency of sight and hearing'.[38]

Helped by Grey, Grenville and others, the Prince wrote letter after letter to the Lord Chancellor, Lord Eldon, complaining of the injustice of his being kept in the dark as to the King's true condition. As his eldest son and heir to the throne, he ought to be the first to be informed of it. If the King were ill, why was he being burdened with 'the full exercise of the royal functions'? If he were well, why did 'Dr Simmons and people of his appointment continue in attendance?'[39]

The Chancellor called on the Prince on 3 June to explain the position in person. 'With great agitation, and occasionally with tears, he acknowledged that the King had been in a very unpleasant way at Windsor, and went on to express his readiness at all times to bear testimony to the propriety and forebearance of the Prince's conduct, and promising that if anything of the same sort recurred, the fullest information should be laid before His Royal Highness.'[40]

The physicians had, he added, signed a document to the effect that although the King was 'sufficiently recovered to be capable of exercising his high functions', there were 'still certain symptoms remaining' that made them apprehensive of a relapse. 'Medical guidance' was, therefore, absolutely necessary. The document was signed not only by Simmons, but by Sir Francis Milman, Sir Lucas Pepys and Drs Reynolds and Heberden.[41]

The Prince was still not satisfied. He wrote to the Chancellor again on 19 June to complain of the conduct of his Majesty's Ministers in making no communication, either with the Privy Council, Parliament or the Prince of Wales, about the medical treatment to which the King had been subjected for the past five months. He strongly criticized the manner in which Ministers 'alone [had] decided that under the British Constitution the King's Commands [might] legally be received on the highest matters of his Government, at the very time when his person and all his ordinary action[s] [were] subjected to controul. Under such circumstances [the Prince could] no longer forbear to express his entire disapprobation of *principles and measures* which he sees to be full of danger to the British Monarchy.'[42]

But the time for formal protest had by now passed; the King's condition was improving day by day; and on 26 June the Chancellor, to his evident relief, felt able to avoid answering the Prince's charges by declaring briefly that 'in the judgement of the physicians' his Majesty was quite well.[43]

So far recovered was he, indeed, that it was felt both by Pitt and the Queen and her children that he was capable of standing up to an interview with the Prince during which, it was hoped, a formal, public reconciliation might take place. The absence of the Prince from recent Drawing-Rooms had been conspicuous. When the King had been present, the Prince had not; when the King had not been present, the Prince had still not attended them either, because the Duke of York had been there or because the Princess of Wales had been. The King had not attended the most recent Drawing-Room held on 4 June to celebrate his birthday; but on learning that the Princess of Wales would be there the Prince drove along Pall Mall sitting prominently on the driving-box of his barouche while the guests were on their way to St James's.[44]

It was, in fact, the King's constant and increasingly cordial attentions to Princess Caroline, to whom he had granted the profitable Rangership of Greenwich Park, that angered the Prince above all else. It was one of the principal reasons why he was so reluctant to suppose that an interview with his father could possibly improve relations between them.

*

Another main cause of the Prince's ill feeling towards his father was his continued failure to obtain active employment in the Army. As a means of circumventing the King's determined stand on this point, Lord Moira had suggested that the Prince should be given command of a specified Military District, for which he would be directly responsible to the Commander-in-Chief. In the event of a French landing he would surrender command of this District, and present himself at the King's headquarters where he would assume the nominal responsibilities of a second-in-command. But nothing came of this curious plan which was soon forgotten; and thereafter the Prince resignedly gave up all idea 'of any military rank or command whatever'.[45] The disappointment still rankled, though, while the Prince's anger at the King's evident attachment to the Princess of Wales burned more fiercely than ever.

Eventually, however, the Prince was persuaded to make the opening move towards a reconciliation. Fox strongly supported the idea;[46] so did Sheridan;[47] while the Duke of Kent wrote, 'the Queen and all my sisters *wihout exception,* Adolphus to a *certainty,* and Ernest, *at least to all appearances hitherto,* are full of nothing but the urgency of bringing you together *without* delay'.[48] So, on 4 July, the Prince wrote to the Queen to say that he lamented heartily not paying his duty to the King. 'Were this allowed me,' he said, 'I should fly to throw myself at the King's feet, and offer to him the testimony of my ever-unvarying attachment. I have long grieved that misrepresentations have estranged his Majesty's mind from me.'[49]

Despite this submission the King, insisting that no good would come of it, remained as reluctant to see the Prince as the Prince was to see him. The publication of the King's letters refusing the Prince's requests for promotion in the Army had never been forgotten nor forgiven;[50] and there was also the Prince's more recent misfortune in becoming indirectly involved in the election as Member for Middlesex of the radical Sir Francis Burdett; at a dinner for Sir Francis the toast had been 'The Prince of Wales' rather than 'The King'.

But in the end the King gave way to the persistent pressure of Pitt and Lord Eldon, on condition that his son came to Kew and not to Windsor, that 'no explanation or excuses' were made by the Prince, and that the Queen, the Princesses and 'at least the Duke of Cambridge' were present throughout the interview.[51] 'I will not see him at Windsor for there he will stay,' the King protested. 'I will see him at Kew for there he must go about his business when it's over. I know him. . . . Yes, yes, I'll see him, and I'll be very civil to him; but I'll never forgive his publishing my letters, and I'll never correspond with him.'[52]

As the day fixed for the interview, 22 August 1804, approached, the Prince became less and less inclined to go through with it. In addition to his earlier objections, there were now reports that the King's mind was weakening again. The Duke of Kent warned the Prince that there was 'an astonishing change for the worse, as his manner was so much more hurried, his conversation so infinitely more light and silly, his temper so much more irritable, besides a strong indication of fever on his cheek, a return of that dreadful saliva, of the strong bilious eye, and of numberless symptoms that manifested themselves last February and were the forerunners of the serious attack'.[53] From other sources came reports that he had become so elated since the 'horrid doctor', Simmons, had left that he gave vent 'to very improper expressions' and was 'so violent with his family that they all dread him beyond description, without having any power to sustain him'. Colonel McMahon was told on good authority that he was 'quite outrageous' with the Queen to whom he manifested the 'greatest aversion', stating publicly that he would have nothing more to do with her; that he was going to fit up the Great Lodge in Windsor Park and install Lady Pembroke there as his mistress; or if the invitation to this lady – which he had made through his surgeon, David Dundas – should not be accepted, he would have the Duchess of Rutland; failing her, he would take Lady Georgiana Buckley. McMahon was further told by one of the royal Dukes 'that on going to see the lodge the other day with two of the Princesses he accidentally met a housemaid called Sally and appeared in ecstasies at seeing her – that he desired the Princesses to stay above stairs when he came down and went into the room where she was and locked himself in with her for three quarters of an hour'.[54]

All these 'proofs of madness and insincerity' induced the Prince to write to the Lord Chancellor saying that 'the information he had recently received' had persuaded him that it would be prudent to avoid an interview which might only 'irritate' the King's mind. Lord Eldon, however, declined to submit such an excuse to the King and urged him merely to plead illness. This the Prince, whose 'extreme agitation' at the prospect of the interview had, indeed, led to a severe attack of diarrhoea, was quite willing to do.[55]

When the King was handed the Prince's letter, he looked at the cover and seeing that it came from Carlton House, did not immediately open it, 'evidently seeking to command himself'. After reading it, he announced, 'The Prince is ill'; then, having made some remark about the illness being probably caused by apprehension, he declared that the interview would have to be put off until his return from Weymouth.

At Weymouth the King's behaviour was alarming. On his yacht he let fly against Roman Catholics and, in the presence of the sailors, declared his hatred of all reforms. At the theatre, when he was not sound asleep, he talked as loudly as the actors. Once, being awake, he vigorously applauded some slighting reference to Members of Parliament; and on another occasion, he woke up to find the Queen was not in the box. Where was she? he wanted to know. Princess Augusta whispered where she had gone. 'The King then cried out "Why did she not take with her all the play bills?"'[56]

He frequently threatened to keep a mistress, and several times declared that if Lady Yarmouth did not yield to his solicitations he would make love elsewhere. He even made improper suggestions 'with peculiar emphasis and strength of voice' to one of the Queen's most respectable Ladies. 'The other day he went into the markett and bought himself six mulletts, talking so incoherently at the same time to [the fishwives] that they scarcely believed they had their own senses.'[57] His headaches were so very severe that Sir Francis Milman warned the Queen that he apprehended 'an immediate apoplexy'.[58]

Hearing reports of the King's disconcerting behaviour at Weymouth, the Prince more and more dreaded the forthcoming interview with his father, which at length took place on 12 November.

The King, looking extremely thin and worn, and accompanied by the Queen, the Princesses and the Dukes of Cumberland, Kent and Sussex, met him at the door. 'You have come, have you?' he said, and taking out his watch expressed himself pleased that his son, who was not renowned for punctuality, had arrived five minutes early. But he did not embrace him or even take his hand, treating him 'much as he would a foreign minister'. The conversation was entirely devoted to such topics as the weather and to scandal, 'a great deal of the latter, and *as the Prince thought*, very idle and foolish in the manner and running wildly from topic to topic [dwelling a good deal upon the reports of Mrs Siddons's elopement with Thomas Lawrence], though not absolutely incoherent'. The King monopolized the conversation, scarcely waiting for and certainly not listening to the Prince's replies, and once working himself up into a formidable rage. Yet the Duke of Cumberland thought the affair went off well enough; and the Duchess of Devonshire was told that the King's conversation 'though a little hurried' was never deranged. The Queen and the Princesses all kissed the Prince affectionately, and Amelia, overcome with joy to see her 'beloved brother' again, was in tears.[59]

It was all 'highly interesting and gratifying', the *Morning Post* commented. 'From the result of this endearing interview which has taken place, we are induced to entertain the fond hope that a most sublime display of patriotic co-operation will ere long be presented to an anxious public.'[60]

That weekend the family were all together at Windsor. William Fremantle, who had been the Marquess of Buckingham's private secretary, was also at Windsor and thought that the King 'seemed infinitely better and less irritated'. The Prince, on the contrary, 'was evidently very much out of spirits and in ill humour – hardly spoke a word to anybody and looked very ill'. It appeared to Fremantle 'quite impossible' that the reconciliation could last.[61] Certainly it was not likely to do so while the King continued to make his regular and lengthy visits to Blackheath to see Princess Caroline and his darling little granddaughter, nor while the quarrel over Charlotte's upbringing, which had broken out earlier on in the year, remained unresolved.*

---

* The King was again at Blackheath a few days after the interview with his son. When she heard that he was coming, Princess Caroline wrote a characteristic letter to him: 'I am this moment Honor'd with your Majesty gracious intention of coming to Black-Heath; and beg leave to express how much I feel myself gratified of the very distinguish'd, and condsending mark of your Majesty favour and goodness towards me and my dear Daughter. my future Conduct will I trust proof to your Majesty, my gratitude and sincere devotion with which sentimens of Dutyful Respects, Veneration and truly attachment, I have the Honor to remain my whole like Sir your Majesty most humble and obedient Servant Niece and Subject Caroline' (RA 42397).
To Lady Glenbervie, her Lady of the Bedchamber, the Princess subsequently complained that the King's behaviour to her, 'when he was represented as recovered from his insanity and used to visit her alone and dine with her at Blackheath', was far from being as agreeable to her as her letters to him suggested. 'She says [Lady Glenbervie told her husband] the freedoms he took with her were of the grossest nature, that those visits always put her in terror, that she could not refuse to see her uncle, her father-in-law and King alone in her room, without declaring that he was still mad, while the Ministers . . . wished it to be understood that he was in his senses' (*Glenbervie Journals*, ii, 55).

17

The Delicate Investigation
1804–1806
*

'There was strange goings-on'

Princess Charlotte was now eight years old. A bright, excitable girl, with blue eyes, very blonde hair, well-shaped hands and a skin badly pitted by smallpox, she had up till now been in the care of a Governess, the Countess of Elgin, widow of the fifth Earl of Elgin and daughter of Thomas White, the London banker. Lady Elgin had at first been assisted by Frances Garth, a niece of General Thomas Garth, a modest, retiring, young woman who had been brought up by her grandmother 'in a very plain and solid way'.[1] Unfortunately 'poor Miss Garth', as the Prince referred to her, had been unable to control her spirited charge and she had had to be replaced by Miss Hayman, 'a very lively, entertaining person', whose character was more suited to the upbringing of a 'pepper-pot'.[2] Miss Hayman, who had met the Prince 'full butt in the doorway' as she was crossing the hall at Carlton House, was delighted by the appointment, never having, in all her life, met anyone with 'such captivating manners' as the child's father.[3]

The King, in turn, was increasingly entranced by his pert little grand-daughter. He used to say that 'there never was so perfect a little creature'. He talked of her endlessly and, so Princess Elizabeth told the Prince, whenever he saw her he was in 'extacys of joy'.[4] The Queen, too, was charmed by her. 'The dear little girl behaved like an angel,' she informed her son after one of Charlotte's periodic visits to Windsor from Warwick House, the dark gloomy mansion in a cul-de-sac near Carlton House where she lived in London. 'She delighted the King with singing Heart of Oak, as also with her reluctance of leaving us.'[5] She pleaded often, 'Me go again to Grandpapa'.[6]

She was a 'remarkably firm, thriving child, very lively, intelligent and pleasant . . . amazingly clever and engaging . . . really one of the finest and pleasantest children I ever saw,' confirmed the Earl of Minto, who saw her one day at Blackheath where she had been taken by her Governess to see her mother. 'The ladies played on the pianoforte and the little girl danced, which she likes as well as possible. She also sang *God Save the King* and *Hearts of Oak*. I wish my girls were so accomplished.'[7] She was also a clever mimic, like her father. 'She tears her caps,' Miss Hayman reported, 'with showing me how Mr Canning takes off his hat as he rides in the park.'[8]

The Prince confessed that when she was little he 'doated upon her',[9] wrote frequent letters to Lady Elgin asking her to bring the 'dear little girl' to see him, and gave her instructions as to her care and education, accompanied by perpetual warnings about the dangers of exposing the child to evil influences 'from a certain quarter'.[10] He did not know 'what would become of the *dear* infant' if it were not for Lady Elgin's diligence in ensuring that she was spared as much as possible the *'continual bad examples'* provided at Blackheath.[11] In the strict and elaborate rules he made governing her care he laid special emphasis on the importance of ensuring that no unauthorized persons were ever allowed into her presence.[12]

As Princess Charlotte grew up, the Prince continued to receive favourable reports of her character and attainments. She was rather delicate it appeared, and was finding it difficult to rid herself of a slight stammer which became painfully bad when she was excited; but she was growing 'much more engaging every day' in the Queen's opinion, and her aunts agreed that she remained a 'perfect delight'. 'She is quite an angel,' Princess Amelia wrote from Weymouth, 'and I never enjoy anything so much as her being with us.'[13] She was taken to Weymouth each summer, staying in apartments rented for her and her extensive Household on the Esplanade, and going out every day to bathe, to ride about in her carriage and to pick up shells on the sands at Portland. She was, so Lady Elgin said, 'perfectly well, good and happy'.[14]

It could not be denied, however, that she was also excitable and temperamental, liable to fits of sudden temper. Her Governess recorded an account of her behaviour one day when she had become almost hysterical with delight at the present of a watch. 'The happiness was inconceivable, jumping and frisking like a little lamb. The letter [accompanying the present] was kissed over and over and the Governess half smothered.' Later

Charlotte wanted to show the watch to one of her tutors, Mr Watson; it was clipped on to her dress under a fur cape, so she went to her governess, for her cape to be taken off. 'Unfortunately, not understanding the intention, the Governess took [the watch off] to lay it on the table – which was sadly contrary to her meaning, and the fire was kindled. The storm was violent – declaring her poor governess very cruel and at last that she would never do anything right again, etc. Mr Watson, meekness itself, was perfectly astonished . . . I stood still and let her go on, and when she stopt I said, quite calm, "Sir, I am sorry you have seen this sad scene, you could not have supposed it". "No, Madam, I could not and I grieve I have seen it." '15

Her father, too, grieved when he heard of such scenes, and felt more than ever determined that his daughter must be kept out of the hands of her mother from whom, he felt sure, she had inherited her emotional instability. Her grandfather, on the other hand, thought that the child was not often enough with her mother; and now that Charlotte was eight, and new arrangements for her future education would have to be made, he hoped that she would be allowed to see her more often.

He proposed that the child should in future live at Windsor and be brought up under his eye and protection. The Prince agreed to this provided that the King was to have 'sole and exclusive' care,16 intending by this phrase to convey his wish that Princess Caroline should have nothing to do with her upbringing.

The King's intentions were different. On 18 August 1804 he wrote to his daughter-in-law from the Queen's House telling her that he could not set out for Weymouth without first seeing her and his 'ever dear granddaughter'. Would they both, therefore, meet him at Kew, the following Monday? 'I trust,' the King added, 'I shall communicate that to you that may render your situation much more happy than you have as yet been in this country, but not more so than your exemplary conduct deserves. Believe me ever with the greatest affection. . . .'17 In her excitement at receiving the flattering and promising communication, the Princess replied with even less regard to the rules of her adopted language than usual: 'This moment I have received your Majesty most gracious letter, which the contents mak's me so happy that I am afraid at will be impossible for me to express my sentiments of gratitude upon papar. . . .'18

The meeting took place as arranged, though Lady Elgin was horrified to find when she got to Kew with her charge that the King was there quite alone. He 'was waiting to receive Princess Charlotte and took us into the dining-room,' she reported. 'Yet when he said *he* was alone, and had come merely to see the Princess of Wales and Princess Charlotte I was quite stupified. He then added he was to take Princess Charlotte to himself, as the Prince wished it, but he could say nothing yet. His Majesty was going on when the Princess of Wales came.'

Princess Caroline had driven down separately, her suggestion that her daughter should travel with her in her carriage being overruled by the Governess who had thought it better that the child should not. Princess Charlotte, she explained, was 'so nervous' that she ought to remain quiet, otherwise 'she would be agitated from her joy'.

The King took his daughter-in-law and his 'little darling' into an inner apartment. After a moment the child came out again, carrying the King's private key to the garden gate, saying it was his wish that she and her Governess should go for a walk while her mother and grandfather had a talk. When Princess Charlotte and Lady Elgin returned, all four of them had dinner together, the King eating his pudding and dumplings with a good appetite, but 'overexerting' himself. He was '*still weak*'.[19]

The Prince was appalled when he learned what his father had done, and now threatened to refuse his consent to entrusting the child to his care. After lengthy negotiations – which had to be conducted through the Lord Chancellor as the King still refused to write letters to his son himself – it was eventually agreed that Princess Charlotte should live at Windsor from June to January and remain at Warwick House for the remaining four months of the year. Her mother was to be allowed to see her at regular intervals but only as a visitor.

John Fisher, Bishop of Exeter and later of Salisbury, whose opinions of Popery and Whiggism coincided with the King's,[20] was appointed Superintendent of Education at a salary of £600 a year; Lady de Clifford, a widow of impeccable character, succeeded Lady Elgin as Governess and was also paid £600 a year; and Mrs Alicia Campbell reluctantly accepted the post of Sub-Governess at £400 a year, an appointment to which the Prince agreed very sulkily as the King had made it without consulting him.[21] A Sub-Preceptor (the Rev George Frederick Nott) was to teach the Princess Latin, English, ancient history and religion; another clergyman was to instruct her in French, belles lettres and modern history. German, writing, music and dancing completed the subjects on her curriculum which was regulated by a strict and rigorous timetable:

From 8 to 9	.	.	.	.	Prayers and Religious Instruction
From 9 to 10	.	.	.	.	Breakfast and Walk
From 10 to 11.30	.	.	.	.	French and Modern History
From 11.30 to 12	.	.	.	.	Walk
From 12 to 1.30	.	.	.	.	English, Latin, Ancient History
From 1.30 to 2	.	.	.	.	Dressing
From 2 to 3	.	.	.	.	Dinner
From 3 to 5	.	.	.	.	An airing in the Carriage
From 5 to 7	.	.	.	.	Writing, Music, Dancing
From 7 to 8	.	.	.	.	Amusement[22]

A figure of £12,000 – increased to £13,000 a year in 1805[23] – was allotted to the expenses of the Princess's Household which, as well as the Governesses, Preceptors and tutors, a dresser and an under-dresser, included a coachman and postilion, three footmen, a page, a porter, an errand-boy, a gardener and six maids.[24]

No expense or efforts were to be spared in the education and upbringing of this girl who could hope one day to become Queen of England; and her father expected to receive, and was given, regular reports of her progress which, from the neat letters she herself wrote to him, appeared to be most satisfactory. 'If you find any alteration in my conduct,' she dutifully wrote to him soon after her tenth birthday, 'I owe it to dear Lady de Clifford . . . and Mr Knott who have all laboured to bring me to a sense of my duty, which I hope I shall feel more and more as I grow up. I can but repeat the same to you again, that I shall ever feel the sincerest love, regard, respect and attachment to you, my dearest papa; and that I shall endeavour all in my power to deserve your affection and approbation more and more. . . .'[25]

*

Those who knew Princess Caroline well had little reason to feel surprised that the Prince should be so determined that she exercise no influence over their daughter's upbringing. For the reckless indiscretion of her behaviour at Blackheath was becoming notorious.

Outwardly her Household at Montague House, to which she had by now moved from The Old Rectory at Charlton, appeared to be conducted well enough. In 1801 the Prince had had cause to complain about the 'excess in her expenditure'. He had sent the Duke of Kent to remonstrate with her, and to point out that 'she could hardly expect a larger allowance than she had while the Prince's continued so reduced'. She accepted this 'with great good humour', readily agreed to all requisite economies, and promised to be more 'guarded in future' about 'the great number of company' invited to the house and about the amount of money she spent upon alterations and decorations.[26] It was, both Lady Charlotte Campbell and Mary Berry thought, money ill-spent, for Montague House was 'all glitter and glare and trick ... tinsel and trumpery ... altogether like a bad dream', 'the dining-room, *à la Gothique*, very pretty, but the rest of the house in abominable taste'.[27]

By 1802 the salaries of her establishment, which had been running at about £5,000 a year, had been reduced to just over £4,000. She was still, however, able to live in style and comfort. As well as a Vice-Chamberlain, a Privy Purse, a Mistress of the Robes (the Marchioness Townshend) and two Ladies of the Bedchamber (the Countess of Carnarvon and the Hon Lady Sheffield), she was attended by three Bedchamber Women, two Pages of the Backstairs and one Page of the Presence. The staff included a maître d'hôtel, a chef, a coffee-room woman, a gardener, six maids, two boys, a porter and a dairyman.[28]

Guests at Montague House had no reason, therefore, to complain of the service; but what did strike many of them as eccentric, to say the least, was the Princess's conduct. They had to agree that her conversation was 'certainly uncommonly lively, odd and clever' – but what a pity it was, one guest lamented, that she had 'not a grain of *common* sense', that she had a 'coarse mind without any degree of moral taste'. They had also to agree that she was an easy, friendly hostess, but what a shame it was, as Lady Charlotte Campbell said, that her 'low nonsense, and sometimes even gross ribaldry' were so shockingly disconcerting.[29] Miss Hayman, formerly Princess Charlotte's Sub-Governess and now Privy Purse at Montague House, had the kindness to tell her so. She suggested to the Princess that according to the manners and modes of English society her practice of taking some man downstairs to the Blue Room and remaining there with him for some hours after dinner, while the other gentlemen were with the ladies upstairs in the Drawing-Room, could be considered highly improper. The Princess 'received this hint very ill' and told Miss Hayman that she 'neither desired nor liked' advice and was not in the least improved by it.[30]

Certainly she disregarded it. Her private life, she insisted, was her own affair. It was nothing to do with anyone else that she loved babies, and – deprived of having any more by her husband – that she adopted several orphans and foundlings and placed them in the care of local foster-mothers who regularly brought them to see her. 'It is my only amuse-ment,' she explained to Lady Townshend, 'and the only little creatures to which I can really attach myself – as I hate dogs and birds – and every body must love something in the world. I think my taste is the most natural and whoever may find fault with it may do it or not.'[31]

Nor was it anything to do with anyone else, the Princess thought, that she liked the company of young men and entertained them in private; that she liked to sit on the floor and talk scandal to her Ladies, or go for pic-nics and eat raw onions and drink ale (pronounced oil), or flirt with any presentable man who came to the house.

Almost every guest at Montague House had some story to tell of her arch flirtatiousness. Walter Scott, whose *The Lay of the Last Minstrel* had made him famous at thirty-three and whose politics appealed to the Prin-cess as much as his poetry, was one of these guests. Limping behind her down a dark corridor through which she was leading him towards the con-servatory, he had hesitated because of his lameness at the top of a flight of steps. 'Ah! False and faint-hearted troubadour,' she had chided him coquettishly. 'You will not trust yourself with me for fear of your neck!'[32]

Some, including William Lamb, thought that she was more or less insane. The Prince assured Lady Bessborough that he for one believed her so.[33] Bishop Hurd also professed himself 'a perfect convert' to the hypothesis of insanity.[34] And Lord Holland considered that 'if not mad, she was a very worthless woman'.[35]

For years there had been all manner of rumours and scandals about her. The repeated visits of George Canning had been widely discussed. In the autumn of 1801 and again in 1802, there had been reports that the Princess was pregnant;[36] and some time later the Prince had told Lady Bessborough that he himself had been told that she had had a child.[37] But he had chosen to take no public notice of all the stories, until in the sum-mer of 1805 he felt obliged to investigate them by an extraordinary accu-sation levelled against the Princess by one Lady Douglas, wife of Sir John Douglas, a lieutenant-colonel in the Marines who was a Groom of the Bedchamber to the Duke of Sussex.

Lady Douglas was an attractive, socially ambitious, spiteful and 'showy bold' woman whose origins were more humble than she liked it to be supposed.[38] She and her husband lived near the Princess at Blackheath, sharing their house at this time with the gallant and garrulous Rear-Admiral Sir Sidney Smith under whom Sir John had served in the defence of Acre against Bonaparte. It was said that Lady Douglas and the Rear-Admiral had been conducting a long-standing love affair.

The Douglases and Admiral Smith, it appeared, had once been frequent visitors at Montague House, but there had been a bitter quarrel after the Princess had discovered that Lady Douglas had been spreading malicious stories about her behind her back. She had told Lady Douglas that she would be no longer welcome at Montague House and had subsequently, so it was alleged, written her anonymous letters, followed by obscene drawings of 'Sir Sydney Smith and Lady Douglas in an amorous situation'. The Princess had also, it was further alleged, sent Sir John Douglas an anonymous letter with a picture of 'Sir Sydney Smith doing Lady Douglas your aimable wife'. The Douglases had, in turn, accused the Princess of similar offences which they detailed in written statements.

The Prince had hoped that the matter would never come to such a pass. As Lord Erskine told the King, he had taken 'no steps whatever to make it the subject of public investigation; but manifested on the contrary the greatest desire to avoid it is possible'.[39] He now sought the advice of the Prime Minister who told him, 'I do not know, Sir, what your Royal Highness must do; but I do know what *I* must do. I must lay the whole business, Sir, before his Majesty without the smallest delay.' Lord Thurlow was of the same opinion. 'Sir,' he said, 'if you were a common man, she might sleep with the Devil; I should say, let her alone and hold your tongue. But the Prince of Wales has no right to risk his daughter's crown and his brothers' claims. . . . The accusation once made must be examined into.'[40]

The King sadly agreed to be 'entirely guided by his Ministers'. And so, in the summer of 1806, a Commission of Enquiry consisting of Lords Grenville, Erskine, Spencer and Ellenborough, with Sir Samuel Romilly, the Solicitor-General, as their legal adviser, was appointed to consider the strange case of the Princess of Wales.

Lady Douglas's evidence was considered first. It appeared from this that she had first met the Princess in 1801 and had been immediately struck by what a strange woman she was. The Princess had embraced her, and had told her what nice arms she had, that she had 'the sweetest black eyes she had ever seen, that she was a charming woman'. On a subsequent visit to Montague House, where she had found the Princess in bed, consuming 'an immense quantity of fried onions and potatoes and an equal amount of ale', they had talked of Lady Douglas's approaching confinement. The Princess had never seen an *accouchement*, she said, so she would like to be present at this one; she would bring with her a bottle of port and a tambourine to keep up her friend's spirits. She was going to have a baby of her own, she confessed. Her habit of taking unwanted babies into her protection was not as innocent as it seemed. She had started this supposedly charitable work so as to make it no cause for comment when her own baby came to be born and was introduced into the Household. People would merely suppose that it was just another destitute child like all the others she had taken care of. No one would know that she was pregnant as she knew how to manage her dress; by putting cushions under it, it would seem that she was just growing rather fat. If the worst came to the worst and she were discovered, she would 'give the Prince of Wales the credit for it, for she had slept two nights in the year she was pregnant in Carlton House'.[41]

'I have a bedfellow whenever I like,' she added; 'nothing is more wholesome.' Her room was most convenient for the purpose as it stood at the head of a staircase leading directly into the Park. 'I wonder you can be satisfied with only Sir John,' she said to Lady Douglas more than once, urging her to 'amuse herself' with Prince William of Gloucester, who would be quite amenable. She confessed that she had herself lain with Sir Sidney Smith who liked a bedfellow better than anybody else she had ever known. As for herself, she was 'a little devil in petticoats'. Lady Douglas did not know whether or not Sir Sidney Smith was the father of the baby boy to which the Princess told her she eventually gave birth, but she 'rather suspected' that he was.[42]

Sir John Douglas evidently also suspected this to be the case. The Princess of Wales had often been to their house, he deposed in his turn; but she came, he thought, more to see Sir Sidney than himself or his wife. 'After she had been for some time acquainted with us, she appeared to me to be with child,' Sir John said. 'One day she leaned on the sofa, and put her hand upon her stomach, and said, "Sir John, I shall never be Queen of England." I said, "Not if you don't deserve it." She seemed angry. . . .'[43]

Other witnesses called by the Commission deposed that Sir Sidney Smith had often been to Montague House in 1802 and had stayed very late. Robert Bidgood, who had been twenty-three years in the Prince of Wales's service before becoming a Page of the Backstairs to the Princess, said that Sir Sidney had also been seen in the house early in the morning, 'a full two hours before company was usually expected, though the footman had let no one in'.[44] Bidgood's wife, Sarah, said that she had been told in a conversation with Frances Lloyd, the coffee-room woman, that Mary Wilson, one of the housemaids, had once gone into the Princess's bedroom to make up the fire and had found her and Sir Sidney 'in such an indecent situation that she immediately left the room, and was so shocked that she fainted away at the door'.[45] Frances Lloyd herself, who had been nearly twelve years in the Princess's service, deposed that once when she had been in bed with a bad cold, the doctor who had been summoned to treat her had asked her if the Prince ever visited Blackheath; the doctor had been curious to know because, so he had told her, the Princess was with child. Miss Lloyd added that one morning she was called to get the Princess's breakfast ready by six o'clock, which she had never been asked to do before; and when she opened the shutters she saw the Princess and a man walking about in the garden.[46] Sarah Lampert, a servant of the Douglases and wife of their footman, confirmed that the Princess and Sir Sidney Smith used to walk about in the garden together, and sometimes at night in the Park. She said that Sir Sidney used to creep out of the Douglases' house late at night after the master and his lady were in bed, and that in the morning his bed was found not to have been slept in. The Princess's servants had told her, Mrs Lampert added, 'what a quantity of breakfast was eaten in her Royal Highness's bedchamber and what extraordinary things she sent for, for a lady to eat in bed – meat, chicken, tongue, etc.' They were not able to get into the room to clear the meal away 'until quite late in the day'.[47]

Sir Sidney Smith was alleged not to be the only gentleman of whose company the Princess seemed excessively fond. She also spent a great deal of time alone in the company of Captain Thomas Manby of the Royal Navy, particularly during a visit in 1804 to Southend where Bidgood, who grew accustomed to the sight of water-jugs, basins and towels left unused in the morning outside the Princess's bedroom, believed that Captain Manby was inside; for it was common gossip among the other servants that he frequently slept in the house. One day Bidgood, so he claimed, had seen them reflected in a looking-glass, kissing each other on the lips.[48]*

---

* Thomas Manby, at that time in command of the frigate *Africaine*, married in 1810 and had two daughters. Promoted rear-admiral in 1824, he died nine years later in a Southampton hotel from an overdose of opium. George Manby alleged in his *Reminiscences* that his brother had been offered £40,000 by McMahon to support the Douglases' case, an offer which was indignantly rejected (Manby, 127). Lady Douglas accepted an annuity of £200 which was still being paid in 1830 at the time of the King's death (RA 29819-55).

Lady Douglas, in a letter she wrote to the Prince after her examination, also reported that Captain Manby had been seen kissing the Princess. Sir Sidney Smith had told her that he had been to dinner with Manby at Montague House 'when he observed her seek Captain Manby's foot under the table and when she had succeeded put her foot upon Captain Manby's and sat in that manner the whole evening, dealing out *equal attention and politeness above board to them both*; at length she got up and went out of the door, looking at Captain Manby who followed and went behind the door to let him pass through and kissed him behind the door. Sir Sidney saw it and went home immediately.'[49]

William Cole, who had been for twenty-one years in the Prince's service before entering that of the Princess in 1796 as a Page of the Backstairs, agreed that she was 'too familiar' with certain gentlemen, particularly with Sir Sidney Smith and Mr Canning.* Cole gave evidence that one evening, on returning to the Blue Room where he had just taken some sandwiches, he found the Princess and Sir Sidney Smith sitting close together on the sofa 'in so familiar a posture as to alarm him very much'. They had both appeared confused at the sight of him. He added that on a particular occasion he had seen the figure of a man wrapped up in a great cloak enter the house from the Park, and he 'verily believed' it was Sir Sidney Smith. He also declared that the Princess and Captain Manby had been seen constantly in each other's company; and that when Thomas Lawrence was in the house, painting a portrait of the Princess, there had been similar sus-

---

* More would have been heard about Canning in the 'Delicate Investigation', so the Prince suggested to a mutual friend, Lady Bessborough, had he not deleted references to him in the evidence out of respect for herself (*Granville Leveson Gower Correspondence*, ii, 204). In fact, the witnesses made only passing references to Canning, though the Prince's suspicions about him were shared by others. Lord Boringdon, who claimed to have been Canning's earliest adherent in the House of Lords, thought that he was probably guilty; and when Canning himself asked Lady Bessborough if she had heard the stories about him and the Princess and she replied that she had done, 'he neither owned nor denied' them. Lady Bessborough was 'staggered', yet afraid that the stories were 'in great part true' (*Granville Leveson Gower Correspondence*, ii, 205–6). At the time of the separation of the Prince and Princess in 1796, Canning had apparently been with her when she had received her husband's letter agreeing never to propose 'a connexion of a more particular nature' should any accident happen to their daughter. She had asked Canning how she ought to interpret the letter – so he told the Duke of Wellington who, in turn, repeated the story to Dorothea de Lieven, the Russian ambassador's wife – and Canning had 'decided peremptorily that it was a letter giving her permission to do as they liked, and they took advantage of it on the spot' (*Lieven Letters*, 98). Whether or not they were lovers then, there is nothing to suggest that there was anything improper in their relationship after 1800 when Canning fell in love with a married Joan Scott.

picious circumstances, and whisperings in the Blue Room behind locked doors after the Ladies of the Household had all gone to bed.

Cole further deposed that he had been dismissed from the service of the Princess soon after he had disturbed her on the sofa in the Blue Room with Sir Sidney, and that on visiting his former colleagues at Montague House he had been told by Mary Wilson that 'there was strange goings-on; that Sir Sidney Smith was frequently there; and that one day, when Mary Wilson supposed the Princess to be gone into the Library, she went into the bedroom, where she found a man at breakfast with the Princess; that there was a great to-do about it; and that Mary Wilson was sworn to secrecy, and threatened to be turned away if she divulged what she had seen'.

In July 1802, Cole concluded, the Princess was 'very large', though towards the end of the year she was her usual shape again.[50]

All this seemed highly damaging. Yet other servants at Montague House were ready to declare that they had not noticed anything particularly improper in the Princess's behaviour. One maid who had been almost ten years in her employment had never noticed any difference in her shape and, although Captain Manby had certainly been a frequent visitor at Southend, the Princess's bed never looked as though two people had slept in it.[51] Another female servant said she was sure that the Princess, whom she had known for eleven years, had not been pregnant in 1802; and that although the Princess was often alone with both Captain Manby and Sir Sidney Smith, sometimes until two o'clock in the morning, she had never noticed any impropriety.[52] Nor had the footman. Nor had the maître d'hôtel who agreed that Sir Sidney Smith was often alone with the Princess, but then so were Canning and other gentlemen. Nor had the Page of the Presence, Thomas Stikeman, who had been in her service ever since her arrival in England; he had never observed the Princess behaving improperly. Admittedly Sir Sidney Smith was often alone with her until a very late hour, but that did not seem to Stikeman cause for unfavourable comment; after all, she was consulting him about the decoration of some of her rooms which were being 'altered in the Turkish style'. To be sure he had been rather uneasy about Captain Manby staying so late when they had been on holiday at Ramsgate; but he had himself observed nothing improper, even though other servants had seen the Captain in the house earlier than nine o'clock in the morning, and a watchman had once found him 'concealing himself in a dark passage leading to the

Princess's apartments'. 'The Princess,' Stikeman said, 'is of that lively vivacity, that she makes herself familiar with gentlemen. . . . Nothing led me from the appearance of the Princess to suppose she was with child, but from her shape it is difficult to judge when she is with child. When she was with child of the Princess Charlotte I should not have known it when she was far advanced in her time if I had not been told it.'[53]

The Hon Mrs Lisle, a sister of Lord Cholmondeley and one of the Princess's Bedchamber Women, was rather more severe. She did not think the Princess had been pregnant at the time in question. But she had certainly spent hours alone with Captain Manby and other gentlemen, including the Hon Henry Hood, son of Admiral Lord Hood, the Governor of the nearby Greenwich Hospital, with whom she went out for rides in a little whisky. It was in the Princess's nature to do so; she preferred men's company to that of her Ladies. She behaved with them, Mrs Lisle disapprovingly observed, 'as any woman would who likes flirting'. Mrs Lisle could 'not have thought that any married woman would have behaved as her Royal Highness did to Captain Manby'.[54]

The doctor who had attended at Montague House in 1802 and had treated the coffee-room woman's cold, denied he had made any remarks about the Princess's pregnancy. Sir Francis Milman who had also attended the Princess in 1802 said that if she had been pregnant he could not have helped noticing it. Sir Sidney Smith firmly rejected all suggestions that he had not acted with propriety. Captain Manby declared that the story of his having kissed the Princess was a 'vile and wicked invention', nor had he ever slept in a house occupied by her. He assured Lady Townshend that his conversations with her had been devoted to discussions 'relative to the equipment of her protégés who were going as midshipmen' with him.[55] Thomas Lawrence admitted to having slept in the same house as the Princess, but he had never been alone with her behind locked doors and nothing had ever passed between them which he could 'have had the least objection for all the world to have seen and heard'.[56]

This conflict of evidence obviously disturbed the Commission. Most of the hearsay evidence was, of course, valueless; and all the condemnatory evidence that came from the servants who had been in the employment of the Prince before his marriage was, to some extent, suspect. But there was other evidence that could not be ignored. Witnesses who could 'not be suspected of any unfavourable bias and whose veracity in this respect' there was 'no ground to question' had 'positively sworn' to conduct 'such as must, especially considering her Royal Highness's exalted rank and station, necessarily give occasion to very unfavourable interpretations'.[57] The 'circumstances . . . stated to have passed between her Royal Highness and Captain Manby must be credited'.[58] There were far too many stories like the ones Lord Glenbervie told of the Princess – of her having sat next to Captain Manby at dinner, and after dinner on a sofa, of her having 'directed all her *looks,* words, and *attentions* to him', of her having stood up almost immediately he left the room, with the excuse that she had heard a baby crying, and of her going into an adjoining room to which she had a private key and in which she remained for about three-quarters of an hour.[59]

The Commissioners were, however, happy to announce their 'perfect conviction' that there was 'no foundation whatever for declaring that the child now with the Princess [was] the child of her Royal Highness or that she was delivered of any child in the year 1802'.[60]

This child, they decided, was born in Brownlow Street Hospital on 11 July 1802, the son of Samuel and Sophia Austin. The parents had come to London from Somerset to find work some years before; but the father, who suffered severely from rheumatism, had found it difficult to keep any job for long, and at the time of the baby's birth had recently been discharged from his employment at Deptford dockyard. The mother, who knew that poor women were given food in the kitchens of Montague House, went there herself in the hope of charity, taking her baby with her. The footman, Stikeman, suggested that the Princess might adopt the child if the mother could bear to part with it, and advised her to come back another day when her Royal Highness was there to see it. Mrs Austin took the advice, returned to Blackheath some days later, and was shown into the Blue Room. The Princess came in, touched the baby, whose name was William, under the chin, and exclaimed, 'Oh! What a nice one! How old is it?' The mother said, 'Six months.'

The Princess then turned away and spoke in French to one of her Ladies who told Mrs Austin that, if she could bring herself to part with the baby, he would be *'brought up and treated as a young prince'*. After a brief discussion the mother agreed, and when all arrangements had been made she was told to go into the coffee-room for some refreshments before she went home. The coffee-room woman was rather grumpy and disillusioning. 'I don't suppose the child will be kept in the house,' she said. 'I don't know what we shall do with it here; we have enough to do to wait on her Royal Highness.' It would probably be put out to nurse with the Steward's wife who looked after other children who were in the Princess's care.

Worried by these remarks, Mrs Austin returned to Montague House some time afterwards to make sure her baby was being properly cared for. She was invited into the house and told to look through a keyhole into a room where she saw the Princess walking up and down, nursing the baby and talking to him. Since then she had been back to Blackheath to see the child regularly, and to collect an allowance for the education of a younger child. She was quite satisfied that William was being well cared for, and deeply grateful for all the Princess had done for her and for her husband, who had now been found regular employment as a locker in the docks through the Princess's influence.[61]*

*

The Commissioners who had conducted 'the Delicate Investigation' confirmed that Princess Caroline was a kindhearted and generous woman; they had also declared that she was not the mother of the child who lived in her house. But their report had done nothing to abate her reputation as a woman of inveterately rash behaviour. It may well be that Lady Douglas was a mischief-maker and a liar, driven by jealousy and malice to invent the charges she had made in her statement; but it was just as likely that the Princess had, in fact, told her that she was pregnant and made all the remarks about bedfellows which she was alleged to have made. Samuel

* William Austin, or 'Willikin' as the Princess called him, was educated first at a day school at Blackheath, then at a school at Greenwich run by Dr Charles Burney, the son of the musical historian. The Princess later took him with her on her travels on the Continent, bringing him back to England with her in 1820. After her death he returned to Italy where his behaviour became increasingly wild and strange until he was placed in a public lunatic asylum in Milan by the police in April 1830. Later he was removed to a private asylum outside the town; and here he was maintained out of the proceeds of a trust, which had been executed in his adoptive mother's lifetime, amounting to about £150 a year – she left him nearly everything in her will but her estate was insolvent. He was brought home in 1845 to an asylum in England, Blacklands House, Chelsea, where he was periodically examined and found to be 'so lost and imbecile in mind that he requires the attention paid to a child. He occasionally appears cheerful, and attempts to sing, but never enters into conversation.' To the end he remained in 'the same lost and fatuous condition as when admitted' (RA Geo. Box 13). He died in 1849. The Princess paid for one of his two younger brothers to be apprenticed to a firm of piano manufacturers and arranged for the other to be found employment in a solicitor's office where he had hopes of being articled at her expense. She died before his hopes were realized, however; and by 1846, having lost eight of his thirteen children after 'long and expensive illnesses', he had remained an ill-paid clerk for thirty-one years (RA Geo. Box 13).

Lysons, the antiquary, was one of many who held the opinion 'that she endeavoured to make Lady Douglas believe she was with child, and that though Lady Douglas gave some of her evidence apparently inconsiderately yet that what she swore to was her belief'.[62] Her husband, in the opinion of the Rev Robert Finch, was certainly a 'very honourable man'.[63]

It was possible, too, of course, that the Princess had had a child in 1802; there were rumours enough to this effect, it being evidently 'common talk upon the Heath that year that the Princess was with child'.[64] The Earl of Westmorland, who had been the Lord Privy Seal in his friend Pitt's administration, thought it worth while to write to Henry Addington (by this time Lord Sidmouth) to tell him that a friend of his had been told by a reputable attorney that proof existed of such a birth. The proof was in the hands of Richard Edwards of Crane Court, Fleet Street, printer of a book about 'the Delicate Investigation'.[65] Indeed, it was the opinion of that relentless gossip, Lord Glenbervie, that William Austin was certainly the Princess's illegitimate child – this was Mary Berry's opinion, too – and that he was not the only one she had had.[66]

The Princess herself, though she also liked to say that the only *'faux pas'* she had ever committed was going to bed with Mrs Fitzherbert's husband, took pleasure in fostering such rumours. Her daughter believed that one of the foster-children in her care, Edwardina Kent – who was named, 'by way of a good joke', after the Duke of Kent – was her child by Sir Sidney Smith;[67] and during a conversation one evening with Lady Glenbervie, a Lady of the Bedchamber, the Princess murmured in a 'kind of reverie', gazing at William Austin, 'It is a long time since I brought you to bed, Willy.'[68] But another of her Ladies, Lady Charlotte Campbell, was assured that 'Willikin' was not her son. 'No', the Princess said, 'I would tell you if he was. No, if such little accident had happened, I would not hide it from you. He is not William Austin, though; but, *avouez moi*, it was very well managed that nobody should know who he really is, nor shall they till after my death.[69]

In later years the Princess decided to elaborate this story: she confided in Henry Brougham's brother, James, that she had humbugged 'the whole set' of people involved in 'the Delicate Investigation'. William Austin, she now said, was the natural son of Prince Louis Ferdinand of Prussia, a nephew of Frederick the Great, and had been brought over to England 'by a German woman'. She had obtained a child of a similar age and appearance from the Austins, and this baby had been 'taken God knows where but sent away'; the baby from Germany had been substituted in its place and the Princess had contrived to ensure that Mrs Austin did not see it for some time: 'She never knew or suspected that it had been changed' and, of course, 'believed to that hour' that the child was her son. In 1805 or 1806 Captain Manby brought Prince Louis over to England and the Princess had seen as much of him as she could. She insinuated that he had been in love with her all his life until, courting death, he had been killed at Jena. She, for her part, had always been attached to him and, as her heart was 'engaged to him', she had never been able to love the Prince of Wales, though she would have respected him if he had treated her well. She assured Brougham that her mind was much easier after telling him this; he was the only person she ever had told. Subsequently she often asked him whether he thought Austin really looked like a labourer's son, 'whether he did not betray his blood by looking so like a German, and things of that sort'.[70]*

To those who knew the Princess well, these reckless statements seemed perfectly in character. She was constantly making such assertions, repeatedly blurting out remarks that were either incredible or offensive and often both, though sometimes vividly pertinent: 'Prince William of Gloucester would likely to marry me . . . he is the grandson of a washerwoman.' 'The Duke of Kent is a disagreeable man and not to be trusted.' '[The royal dukes] all have pudding faces which I cannot bear.' 'The Duke of Cambridge looks like a sergeant, and so vulgar with his ears full of powder.' The Prince of Wales 'lives in eternal hot water and delights in

---

* This story has been generally discredited; but on her deathbed she repeated the substance of it to Dr Stephen Lushington, one of her counsel during the proceedings in the House of Lords in 1820. Towards the end of his long life, in September 1858, Lushington put the story on record in response to a request by Lord Brougham.

'I will tell you all I know as to W. Austin,' Lushington wrote. 'The Queen on her deathbed informed me that W. Austin was not the person he purported to be, that he was in truth a son of a brother or friend of Brunswick who was dead and that he had been clandestinely brought over from the continent. She then explicitly declared that W. Austin was not her own child. She did mention who the mother was but indistinctly.

·When attending the funeral I was on board a vessel in the Elbe commanded by Capt. Fisher, W. Austin being with him, a German nobleman or General (I do not remember which) asked for permission to see W. Austin; he immediately said you know his history and to my great surprize repeated in substance what the Queen had said to me respecting W. Austin's birth and parentage and he then added that Austin bore a great resemblance to his reputed father.

'I have no recollection of the name of this Consul or General. The enquiries made for him afterwards by order of Lord Liverpool produced no result' (Brougham MSS, 10, 268).

it. If he can but have his slippers under an old dowager's table and sit there scribbling notes that's his whole delight. . . . He has offered me 60,000 if I'll go and live at Hannover, but I never will; this is the only country in the world to live in. . . . [I] ought to have been the man and *he the woman to wear the petticoats*. . . . He understands how a shoe should be made or a coat cut, or a dinner dressed and would make an excellent tailor, or shoemaker or hairdresser but nothing else.'[71]

But if the Duke of Cambridge was vulgar, it was generally agreed that the Princess of Wales herself was even more so. To Lady Hester Stanhope she was 'an impudent woman . . . a downright whore . . . she danced about exposing herself like an opera girl . . . she gartered below the knee: – she was so low, so vulgar'.[72] Others might be amused by her parties at Blackheath where a mechanical doll performed obscene antics, and her adopted, pampered child, 'Willikin', was dangled over the dining-room table to snatch his favourite sweetmeats from the dishes, knocking over the wine in the process. But Lady Hester was disgusted by the child. 'Once he cried for a spider on the ceiling,' she recalled, 'and, though they gave him all sorts of playthings to divert his attention, he would have nothing but the spider. Then there was such a calling of footmen, and long sticks, and such a to-do! He was a little, nasty, vulgar, brat . . . and so ugly. . . . The P[rince]ss used to say to Mr Pitt, "Don't you think he is a nice boy?" To which Pitt would reply, "I don't understand anything about children." '[73]

Lady Bessborough thought the Princess's levity was 'inconceivable';[74] Lady Sarah Spencer and her mother were so distressed to receive an invitation to Blackheath that they fled from Spencer House pleading a 'pre-engagement' with the Dowager Countess Spencer at her country house in Hertfordshire;[75] while Mary Berry, who was presented to her at a ball at Henry Hope's house, wrote of her, 'Such an exhibition! But that she did not at all feel for herself, one should have felt for her. Such an over-dressed, bare-bosomed, painted-eye-browed figure, one never saw. G. Robinson said she was the only true friend the Prince of Wales had, as she went about justifying his conduct.'[76]

Having read the report of the Commission, the Prince discussed it with his elderly, cantankerous friend, Lord Thurlow, who persuaded him that the Commissioners had shown 'too great a degree of lenity to the Princess'. Although, he said, there 'might not be quite sufficient' evidence to 'commence an action for High Treason, still, from the circumstances of her imprudence, amounting nearly to positive proof . . . they ought to follow it up by a recommendation to the King (which he ought instantly to sanction) of bringing in an Act of Parliament to dissolve the marriage'.[77]

The Commissioners, of course, were not prepared to make any such recommendation. They had already gone further than in justice they ought to have done when they declared that the allegations of misconduct ought to be credited until they received some 'decisive contradiction'[78] – which was to say that the Princess was to be presumed guilty until proved innocent, whereas her guilt was very far from being established. Lady Bessborough and Lord Boringdon might well have been right in supposing that Canning was her lover;[79] there might well have been good grounds for the rumours which Richard Ryder, Member of Parliament for Tiverton, heard to the effect that, not content with Canning, she had seduced both the Duke of Cumberland and Sir William Scott;[80] Lord Eldon might well have had reason to believe that Thomas Lawrence had also made love to her;[81] her footman, Roberts, might well have been justified in declaring that the Princess was 'very fond of fucking'.[82] But there was no actual proof of adultery; and the King accepted that there was not.

He did recognize, though, that his niece had been guilty of much 'levity and profligacy' and that he could not protect her from the consequences even had he wished to do so.[83] He told the Queen that the Princess could no longer be received as an intimate of the family, 'and no nearer intercourse [could be] admitted in future than outward marks of civility'. It was not only that she had been shown to be morally unstable, but that she was, what was in his eyes quite as bad, 'a female politician'.[84]

This was undeniably true, although her supporters continued to insist that it was all the Prince's doing.

18

Foxites and Pittites
1806–1809
*
'At the head of the Whig Party'

Ever since the innovation of the Prince's grand political dinners at Carlton House, and the fall of Addington's government the Prince had begun to be 'a very great politician', in the words of Thomas Creevey, and 'considered himself at the head of the Whig Party'.[1] He had become even more influential at the beginning of 1806 when Pitt died at the age of forty-six, worn out by his exertions to win the war and to stay in office. For Pitt's death opened the way for what became known as the 'Ministry of all the Talents', a government less broadbased than its name implied, its most powerful members being friends of Fox. When Lord Grenville, Pitt's successor as Prime Minister, insisted on Fox being included in the Cabinet as Foreign Secretary, the King resignedly remarked, 'I thought so.'[2] Fox's reception at the Queen's House when he went to kiss hands on his appointment was not the ordeal that he had expected. The Queen's civility, in fact, was 'quite marked', especially as she hadn't spoken to him since 1788.[3]

Two of Fox's closest colleagues, Earl Spencer and William Windham, who had now returned to his side from the Portland group, became respectively Home Secretary and Secretary for War and the Colonies. Charles Grey, who was to become Viscount Howick in April and, on his father's death in 1807, the second Earl Grey, was appointed First Lord of the Admiralty; the Earl of Shelburne's son, Lord Henry Petty (later Marquess of Lansdowne) became Chancellor of the Exchequer; Earl Fitzwilliam was appointed Lord President of the Council; Lord Erskine replaced Lord Eldon as Lord Chancellor; and the Earl of Moira came into the Cabinet as Master General of the Ordnance.

Although Moira was the only personal representative of Carlton House in the Cabinet – and although the Prince complained that he had been insufficiently consulted about the ministerial appointments – now that so many of his 'friends' were in office his influence was more considerable than it had ever been before. Indeed, Lord Melville thought it paramount; the power of the Crown had passed from St James's to Carlton House, and the Prince was now 'looked up to as the fountain of office, honour and emoluments'.[4] Certainly both the Prince and Moira made numerous demands on the new government's patronage; and their recommendations, as Lord Holland said, 'were greatly attended to'. More peerages and honours were conferred at the Prince's instigation 'than at that of any other individual, Lord Grenville and Mr Fox alone excepted', though these honours 'were all more calculated to display his influence in procuring favours than to promote the interests of the party, or even his own. They were given to men who never professed attachment to the Whigs or to him, and who, it was foreseen, would take (as most of them subsequently did) the first opportunity of deserting both'.[5]

The Prince was undoubtedly extravagant in his offers of patronage and showed great determination in ensuring that his promises were fulfilled. In the first list of recommendations for baronetcies sent to the King, every name that was not submitted by Fox was put forward either by Moira or the Prince. The Prince pressed one of his claims 'with uncommon earnestness', Grenville said, 'and had, I fear, actually committed himself by a written promise on the subject'.[6]

*

While the Prince had been enjoying the new-found influence which the formation of the 'Ministry of all the Talents' had brought him, Princess Caroline had been drawing ever closer towards her husband's political opponents, declaring that she was 'proud to name herself a Pittite'.[7] Not only Canning and Brougham, but such figures as Lord Castlereagh, Pitt's Secretary of State for War, Lord Eldon, the dismissed Lord Chancellor, Eldon's friend and fellow arch-conservative, the Duke of Cumberland, and Spencer Perceval, who had resigned as Attorney-General on Pitt's death, were now regular visitors at Montague House, where they provided the Princess with their encouragement and advice.

Perceval, Eldon, Canning and Castlereagh all dined with the Princess at Montague House on 15 June 1806 and discussed the action to be taken now that the Commissioners, who had undertaken 'the Delicate Investigation', had condemned her conduct without inviting her to defend it. It was eventually decided that copies of the evidence should be sent to the King together with a long and detailed defence prepared under the direction of Spencer Perceval, who, convinced that the Princess was 'a much injured lady', went about declaring that he would go 'to the Tower or to the scaffold in such a cause'.[8]

The King, as Lord Holland said, 'adroitly' referred Perceval's defence to the Cabinet, saying that he would be guided by their advice. There was then a prolonged delay, the Princess complaining of the 'long weeks of daily expectation and expense' having brought her 'nothing but disappointment',[9] the Prince upbraiding the government for displaying a 'total want of energy and good-will' towards him and for not acting with vigour in his support which, from 'the peculiar formation' of the ministry, he felt himself 'entitled to expect'.[10]

It was not, however, until two days before Christmas that the Cabinet gave their reply, and then it was an indeterminate one. In a dissenting minute the Secretary for War, William Windham, expressed the opinion that the charge originally brought against the Princess was 'as to part directly disproved, and as to the remainder' rested on evidence that could not entitle it to the 'smallest credit'.[11] But the other members of the Cabinet said that they concurred with the conclusion of the Commissioners and humbly submitted that the Princess's request to be once again received by the King and to be assured of his 'satisfactory conviction of her innocence' was a matter 'depending solely' on His Majesty's 'own feelings and persuasion'.[12]

The King, dissatisfied with this vague reply, insisted on a more definite answer. So the Cabinet discussed the case again. They discussed it in Downing Street; they discussed it at the Foreign Office; they argued at length; they broke up and met again. On occasions their ponderous deliberations wandered far from the point at issue and entered into such subjects as the improbable contents of a box which, so Lord Moira had learned, had been entrusted by the Princess of Wales to a gentleman to deliver to Captain Manby. The gentleman, Admiral Nugent, notoriously absent-minded, had left this box in a hackney-coach, and had subsequently asked a friend, Moira's informant, who lived near the hackney-coach stand, to make inquiries about it and to recover it by offering, if necessary, a reward of two hundred guineas. The friend did manage to recover the box and, intrigued by the generous reward he had been authorized to offer, opened it.

Inside were many letters to Captain Manby, several trinkets, ornaments and 'souvenirs'. These last included a letter bag containing several hairs which Moira's informant had been 'married too long not to know came from no woman's *head*'. It being objected that this information could not very well weigh with the Cabinet at this stage of the business and that, in any case, the hairs were 'not of a nature to be produced as evidence even if the examination were to be instituted anew', Lord Ellenborough, the Lord Chief Justice, pleasantly observed that these exhibits *might* be admitted as evidence if the larger 'record to which they were originally attached' were also to be 'examined and compared in the court'.[13]

All this, as the Lord Privy Seal observed, was 'laughable enough', but it did add considerably to the length of the Cabinet's deliberations; and it was not until the end of January 1807 that they reached their conclusion. This was that there was no longer any justification for the Princess of Wales not being received into his Majesty's presence, but that the 'result of the whole case' did 'render it indispensable' that a 'serious admonition' should be conveyed to her Royal Highness.[14] With their advice, the Cabinet enclosed a draft letter which they suggested the King should send to the Princess, telling her that although it was no longer necessary for him to decline receiving her, at the same time he was compelled to express his 'concern and disapprobation' of her conduct.[15]

The King accepted the Cabinet's advice and despatched the letter to his daughter-in-law, merely striking out the words 'concern' and 'disapprobation' in the draft and substituting 'serious concern'.[16] Immediately on receipt of the King's letter, the Princess replied saying that she would come to Windsor on the following Monday. Ever since the beginning of 'the Delicate Investigation' she had been bombarding the King with letters, begging for his 'gracious protection', appealing to his 'sound judgment and great clemency', pleading with him to be restored to his favour, assuring him that the evidence brought against her by 'strong and powerful enemies' was 'most malicious, atrocious and false', longing for 'that happy moment' when she might be allowed to appear again before his Majesty's eyes and to receive once more the assurance from his own mouth that she had his protection.[17]

On receipt of this last letter, announcing that she would come to Windsor on Monday, the King hastened to acquaint her that he would prefer to see her in London and would let her know what day, 'subsequent to the ensuing week', would be convenient for him.[18]

Here the matter ended for the moment, as in March 1807 the so-called 'Ministry of all the Talents' fell. Fox had proved himself an excellent Minister and his authority had been unquestioned; but in the summer of 1806 he had become seriously ill and by September he was dead. Grenville, in hope of gaining greater strength for the government in Parliament, had called a general election. And although over forty more Members believed to be in general sympathy with the ministry had been returned, Grenville's power, now that Fox had gone, had soon been shown to be severely weakened. The new ministry managed to abolish the slave trade, but, falling out with the King over the Roman Catholic Militia Bill, it collapsed in ruins.

The Prince did nothing to try to save it. Annoyed with Grenville for declining to take up the still burning question of his debts, for not supporting him more strongly in his quarrel with the Princess, and for treating him with 'the most marked neglect', failing to consult him in any one important instance, he stood aside, an idle spectator of its dissolution.[19] In any case, as he told Moira, since the death of poor Fox he had 'ceased to be a party man'. In his dear friend's lifetime it had been the pride of his life to acknowledge himself in alliance with him; now that he was dead, he himself was politically 'neutral'.[20] So the Whigs were out of office once more.

*

The government that succeeded the 'Talents', under the uncertain and reluctant leadership of the Duke of Portland, was a sadly divided one. But it included many of the Princess's friends: Canning became Foreign Secretary, Spencer Perceval, Chancellor of the Exchequer, Lord Eldon, Lord Chancellor, and Lord Castlereagh, Secretary for War. And one of the Cabinet's earliest acts was to confirm their predecessors' view that there was no longer any need for the King to decline receiving the Princess of Wales into his presence. The Cabinet suggested that, since the evidence produced against her was 'undeserving of credit', she should be admitted with 'as little delay as possible' and should be 'received in a manner due to her rank and station'.[21] It also noticed in a separate minute dated the same day, 21 April 1807, the Princess's request to be allotted 'some apartments in one of the royal palaces' more convenient to Court.[22]

The King agreed to this request, allowing her apartments at Kensington Palace which the Princess accepted 'under the full confidence' that when an apartment at St James's could be 'made vacant' it would be allotted to her.[23] But, as the King replied to the Home Secretary, Lord Hawkesbury, who sent him the Cabinet's minutes, he felt some little time was necessary for him to prepare for an interview with the Princess which he had not expected to take place so soon and which could not 'in its nature be very pleasant'.[24]

The Prince, for his part, was continuing to insist that the interview ought not to take place at all, and that the only hope of removing 'all chance of future discord' was a formal separation.[25] Despite these protests the Princess was received at Court on 4 June. The Prince, who was also there, did not speak to her, talking to his sisters with his back to his wife so that they could not speak to her either, even if they had wanted to. As the Prince and Princess left, Lady Bessborough noticed that they 'both looked contrary ways, like the print of the spread eagle'.[26]

More than ever determined to have as little to do with her as possible, the Prince went out of his way to ensure that they never met by chance. For fear lest he should see her, he did not make a courtesy call on her mother, his aunt, the Duchess of Brunswick, when she arrived in England in the summer. And when it became so hot that he thought it advisable for Princess Charlotte to leave London earlier than usual, he did not want to send her to Windsor in case her mother should use it as an excuse for frequent visits there, making it impossible for him to visit his family without the risk of meeting his wife.[27] The King and Queen agreed, considering that until all 'unpleasant matters' were past and 'quiet restored', it would be far better to find a house for Princess Charlotte 'near the seaside'.[28]

Although the Princess's behaviour seems to have become rather less open to reproach after 'the Delicate Investigation', it was still far from discreet. She continued to 'dress very ill, shewing too much of her naked person';[29] she still continued happily to flirt with a varied assortment of men of all ages from the elderly pot-bellied lawyer, Sir William Scott, to the much younger Lord Henry Fitzgerald; she encouraged the advances of both John William Ward, afterwards Earl of Dudley, and William Henry Lyttelton, afterwards third Lord Lyttelton of Frankley – though Ward, for one, declared that he had no wish to take advantage of her fondness for him. 'When Ward and Lyttelton first began to frequent Kensington, Ward said to the other, he thought the Princess had cast a favourable eye upon him. Lyttelton replied, "No, I only fan the flame which you have kindled." On which Ward rejoined with one of his arch and malicious looks, "I had much rather be the bellows than the poker." '30

William Eliot, a young Lord of the Treasury, described a 'long, long Friday, Saturday and Sunday' he spent in the Princess's company a few months after she had been received at Court again. As the only other man present was the Princess's Vice-Chamberlain, 'all the whispers, all the glances, all the nods, all the endless etceteras' were directed towards him. 'I certainly never saw nor heard anything at all like the style of proceeding', he wrote. 'Indeed I was perfectly convinced . . . that the poor woman is downright mad. It is quite out of the question giving you any sample of the conversation. . . . One night I had the honour to play at chess with her till 2 o'clock in the morning with [three of her Ladies] gaping in attendance, and all the rest of the world gone to bed.' Another night, Eliot was taken out for a walk alone in the dark with her for he knew not how long; another evening, also for a seemingly endless time, he wheeled her about the grounds in a garden chair. 'Being thus persuaded as I am still that she was quite mad, and that a raving fit might break out from one minute to another,' he concluded, 'I leave you to guess the extent of my misery.'31

To the Prince, what was above all else intolerable about his wife was her continuing popularity. This was much increased by the sympathy felt for her on news of her father's death from wounds received at the battle of Auerstädt. Also, the Prince had been virulently condemned for bringing her to face charges which, it was suggested, he had himself concocted. The *Morning Post*, no longer his supporter, expressed its sympathy for 'a truly *virtuous* and *illustrious female*' who had for many months been 'the object of the most foul and infamous calumny ever advanced by the most unprincipled of men'.32 She no sooner entered a theatre than the audience broke out into tumultuous applause which clearly delighted her as much as it distressed the Prince who was, as Lord Fitzwilliam said, more susceptible to adverse expressions of public opinion than any other man alive.

Those who knew her more intimately than most of the members of theatre audiences, however, had to agree with Lord Minto who regretted that one could never feel sure that she would 'act prudently or honestly for any time'.33 At this stage in her career, for instance, she quarrelled with the men who had previously supported her and were now in power. Spencer Perceval, who no longer had any cause to publish the defence that he had compiled for her when in opposition, and who destroyed all the printed copies he could get hold of, was 'a presumptuous, foolish lawyer'; Lord Eldon was 'a vulgar bore'; all their colleagues were 'drivellers'.[34] On the other hand, the previous Prime Minister, Lord Grenville, who had also been a driveller when supported by the Prince of Wales, was a paragon to her now that he had incurred her husband's displeasure. She was, as Canning observed, naturally given to opposition.

She was also still naturally given to extravagance, if not on the same dramatic scale as her husband. The economies to which she had agreed in 1801 had long since been forgotten. Although she received an allowance of £12,000 a year from the Prince, together with an additional £5,000 from Parliament which had also put up £34,000 for the cost of her house, her admitted debts amounted to £49,000.[35] By 1808 her unpaid tradesmen had become so exasperated that, after an unavailing appeal to Spencer Perceval as Chancellor of the Exchequer, they had threatened to stop all supplies to Montague House.[36]

The government's view was that it was not the public's responsibility to settle the Princess's debts, but that of the Prince, who had an income of the most generous size. The Prince argued that, even if he were willing to settle the debts of so unworthy a woman, he could not possibly do so. Ministers countered with the unpalatable truth that if the Prince did not make it possible for her to pay her creditors, the public's hostility would fall on him not on her, and he was already so disliked that the probability of increased unpopularity would scarcely bear contemplation. To this argument the Prince felt bound to give way. He agreed to pay off her debts by quarterly instalments – though he still could not discharge all his own – and to increase her income to £17,000 a year on condition that any future debts she might incur would be borne by herself.[37]

Even this sacrifice seemed to the Prince not too high a price to pay for the sake of averting further unpopularity. He persevered, as best he could, in his determination to remain aloof from politics, though he could not forbear despatching a two-line reply to Spencer Perceval's rather fulsome letter informing him that he had accepted office as Prime Minister on the Duke of Portland's death.[38] Lord Moira thought he saw 'the very curl' of the Prince's lip when his fancy was 'tickled at giving so civil a rebuff to the advances of the tiny Premier'.[39] He abandoned his open support of Catholic relief, in case, so he said, his continued advocacy might provoke a return of the King's insanity for which his family and the country would blame him. And for fear of becoming involved in the calumny, he even continued in a 'state of neutrality' when his brother, the Duke of York, fell so drastically in the public esteem on being accused of appalling misdemeanours at the Horse Guards.

The charge brought against the Duke by Colonel Gwyllym Lloyd Wardle, the radical Member of Parliament for Okehampton, was that he had used the patronage at his disposal as Commander-in-Chief at the Horse Guards for the benefit of his former mistress, Mrs Mary Anne Clarke, a flamboyant and extravagant actress. It was alleged that Mrs Clarke had accepted money from officers who wanted promotion or employment, and that the Duke not only knew of her activities and agreed to her recommendations but actually shared in the proceeds.

Wardle's charges were eagerly supported by other radicals, including Samuel Whitbread, one of the Members for Bedford. The Prince, seeing in them an attack on the whole royal family, at first declared that he would stand by his brother. As more and more witnesses gave evidence, however, and as the charges against the Duke appeared to be hardening, the Prince gradually began to withdraw his support. There were many who urged him to do so and thought him wise to do so. Lord Temple, later Duke of Buckingham and Chandos, who had been a junior Minister in his uncle Lord Grenville's administration, strongly advised him not to interfere as he might otherwise become identified with the Duke's disgrace. George Tierney, who had also served as a junior Minister under Grenville, agreed that the Prince would be well advised to remain aloof; and so did Thomas Tyrwhitt, now Member for Plymouth.[40]

The Prince obviously felt uneasy in his neutrality, and several times wavered towards his original position of open support. The King sent a message to him asking him to make it clear that he stood behind his brother and the government who supported him, while the Queen pleaded with him to do so for the sake of his father who was beside himself with worry. But the Prince still hesitated. He had never been on cordial terms with the Duke since his failure to gain promotion in the Army and what he took to be the Duke's shifty behaviour during their father's illness in 1804. They were civil to each other when they met, but observers noticed that the Prince's attitude was formal and stiff.[41] As the Duke of Kent said, the Duke of York had always been his father's favourite, the Prince being his mother's, and this pronounced preference, combined with 'various events' which had taken place since the Prince had adopted his early line of opposition in politics, had widened the breach between the two. There was '*apparent* good standing' between them, but it went 'no further than *that*'.[42]

As though to excuse himself for his disobliging attitude over the Clarke scandal, the Prince complained that his brother had never consulted him about the matter, nor had the government, so why should he interfere to save them now? In any case, even if the Duke were not guilty of all the charges, he had not paid the allowance to Mrs Clarke that he had promised her, and this was shabby of him. Nevertheless, the Duke was his brother after all, and he did not want to appear actually hostile. He therefore told McMahon, who was now Member of Parliament for Aldeburgh, to vote for the Duke when the time came, though he refrained from making similar requests of the Dukes of Northumberland and Norfolk who between them controlled the votes of many other Members. 'This,' Fremantle observed disdainfully, 'is only another proof of his great weakness and indecision.'[43] As it happened, these additional votes were not needed. The House decided by a majority of eighty-two that the Duke was not guilty of corruption or of conniving at his mistress's corruption. Since he had obviously discussed his official business with her, though, he was dismissed as Commander-in-Chief.

The Prince emerged from the sad affair with his reputation more tarnished than ever.

19

Princess Charlotte and
Minny Seymour
1806–1809

*

'How aimably polite and fascinating his
manners are on his own ground'

In such unhappy times as these the Prince was thankful to escape to Brighton where he was so much better liked than he was in London.

Brighton had grown and flourished to an extraordinary degree since the Prince's first visit there in 1783; and had become, according to the proud if somewhat ambiguous boast of the *Brighton Directory* of 1800, 'the most frequented [and] without exception one of the most fashionable towns in the Kingdom'. The population had risen to over 7,000 and handsome houses were still being built on every side. The graceful Royal Crescent, begun in 1798, was finished, at last, nine years later, and its builder in celebration of the event had erected a vast statue of the Prince of Wales on the grass in front of it. It represented the Prince in his colonel's uniform making a suitably heroic gesture; but the soft stone from which it was carved was not strong enough to withstand the salt sea breezes, and one of its arms consequently fell off, misleading visitors into supposing that it represented the great Lord Nelson.[1]

West of the Royal Crescent, on the Steine, stood Mrs Fitzherbert's attractive new house – built for her by William Porden at a cost of £6,300[2] – next door to the rather larger one in which, during his occasional visits, the Duke of Marlborough was cared for by a staff of forty servants. Nearby was the Prince's Marine Pavilion, slightly altered in recent years by Holland's nephew and assistant, Peter Frederick Robinson, who had made it appear less classically austere by removing the statues from beneath the cupola and adding green, tent-shaped metal canopies to the balconies. Robinson had also added two oval rooms, one a dining-room, the other a drawing-room, as wings projecting at angles from the eastern front.

Some years before, the Prince had entertained the idea of altering the appearance of the Pavilion in a far more drastic way. In 1801 Henry Holland had made some sketches for a new exterior in the Chinese style which it was estimated would cost £9,500;[3] and in 1805 William Porden, Holland's successor as the Prince's architect, had also made some Chinese sketches. These were never put into effect, however. Porden, who had once been a pupil of Samuel Pepys Cockerell, Surveyor to the East India Company, was deeply interested in the Indian movement in architecture which his master, Cockerell, had applied at Sezincote in Gloucestershire, a large house that he had designed for his brother, the nabob, Sir Charles Cockerell. The Prince also admired Sezincote; and, after seeing it, seems to have discarded the idea of a Chinese pavilion in favour of an Indian one. He asked Humphry Repton, who had laid out the gardens at Sezincote, to come to Brighton 'to deliver his opinion concerning what style of architecture would be most suitable for the Pavilion'. Repton's views coincided with those of the Prince and by 1807 he had finished designs for an Indian pavilion which his patron found 'perfect'.[4]

But although the Prince announced his intention of carrying the work into 'immediate execution', he had for the moment to be content with building stables and a riding house, an immense structure in the Indian style, which was finished at a cost of over £55,000 in 1808 and provided, under a huge central cupola, eighty-five feet wide, stabling for fifty-four horses as well as living accommodation for the ostlers and grooms.[5]*

A great deal of money had also been spent on remodelling and

* The stables and riding house took over three years to build, partly owing to the difficulty of obtaining timber of sufficient size for the vast dome during the French blockade of continental ports, but more particularly because the Prince could not afford to pay the tradesmen at work on it. 'I am harassed with letters from the tradesmen at Brighton,' Porden complained to the Prince's Vice-Treasurer on 22 January 1807. 'The distress of many of these creditors is I believe very great and the clamour against his Royal Highness will be in proportion. . . . The stoppage of money at this quarter has been particularly distressing to me . . . the naked timbers of the roof of the riding house stand exposed to all weathers, a monument of disgrace to his Royal Highness and all concerned (RA 33593–4). In June Porden felt obliged to renew his complaint: 'My workmen complain heavily that they are not paid while the tradesmen employed at Carleton House regularly receive their money; a complaint that I know not how to answer' (RA 33595).

redecorating the interior of the Pavilion itself. Here in 1802 a Chinese gallery had been made for some lovely Chinese wall-papers that had been given to the Prince, and a Chinese corridor had been formed 'of stained glass, of an oriental character, and exhibiting the peculiar insects, fruit, flowers, etc. of China'.[6]

The taste for *Chinoiserie* had become rather less fashionable in England since the Emperor Ch'ien-lung's rebuff of Lord Macartney's mission in 1794; but the Prince's own enthusiasm was unimpaired. He dismantled his Chinese Room at Carlton House and brought its contents to Brighton, together with all manner of Chinese porcelain and furniture, bamboo sofas and lacquered cabinets, weapons and curios, ivory junks and pagodas, lanterns and uniforms. In the Chinese corridor there were even larger-than-life-size figures of Chinese fishermen in flowing silk robes dangling lanterns from their rods.[7]

Lady Bessborough – who was told by the Prince that he had chosen to decorate the Pavilion in the Chinese taste 'because at the time there was such a cry against French things, etc. that he was afraid of his furniture being accused of jacobinism' – thought it all 'really beautiful in its way'. She had had no idea that the 'strange Chinese shapes and columns could have looked so well'. It was in 'outré and false taste', of course, but 'for the kind of thing as perfect' as could be. Mary Berry would not agree with her. The effect, she thought, was 'more like a china shop . . . than the abode of a Prince. All is gaudy without looking gay,' she recorded in her journal; 'and all is crowded with ornaments without being magnificent . . . all is Chinese, quite overloaded with china of all sorts and of all possible forms, many beautiful in themselves, but so overloaded one upon the other.'[8]

In the exotic surroundings of the Marine Pavilion the Prince was to be seen at his most happy, charming and relaxed. Thomas Creevey who was a frequent visitor throughout the autumn of 1805 said that the Prince behaved with the greatest good humour as well as kindness to everyone; 'he was always merry and full of his jokes, and any one would have said he was really a very happy man'. He said repeatedly himself that he would never be as happy when he was King as he was then.[9] Lady Jerningham, who also saw a good deal of him at this time, agreed that he was full of 'affability and good humour'. 'Your father sat by him some time on a couch,' she told her daughter, 'and they were making jokes and laughing most heartily. . . . It is really not to be described how aimably polite and fascinating his manners are on his own ground – the most finished civility, joined to the utmost degree of good-natured affability.'[10]

He had put on weight again, despite the use of a 'vapour bath' which he had bought 'with full equipment' that summer;[11] but he had lost little of his grace, and his charm was as captivating as ever – at least to those who did not presume to become over-familiar with him: as Lord Thomond remarked, he observed 'with nice attention any encroachment upon his importance'.[12]* He still drank a good deal, and liked to get his guests drunk when he could; but he was rarely now drunk himself, though sometimes he appeared a little unsteady when he went after dinner to the Assembly Rooms at the Castle Inn. Here the other guests clambered up on to benches to get a look at him. Sometimes in his own house he had to make excuses to his partner and leave the floor when the wine he had drunk made him too dizzy to dance; and once he was taken violently ill with 'an inflammation on his stomach' which the Duke of Cumberland attributed to his 'drinking hard three days successively' with his guests at the Pavilion. But, under the benign influence of Mrs Fitzherbert, his days of regular, habitual drunkenness were past. He now took trouble to avoid most of those inveterate drunkards who in the past had looked to him for toping company. When the Duke of Norfolk came on his annual visit from Arundel, the Prince made excuses not to drink with him after dinner, pleading that he had important letters to answer, and leaving Norfolk to go on drinking with the Duke of Clarence. Norfolk did not take too kindly to this treatment and showed that he was affronted. So one evening the Prince took another of his guests, Thomas Creevey, aside and said to him 'stay after everyone is gone tonight. The Jockey's got sulky, and I must give him a broiled bone to get him in good humour again.' So Creevey stayed; but, the drink overcoming him, he fell asleep. He woke to find Norfolk snoring contentedly, while the Prince and the Duke of Clarence were deep in an animated discussion as to 'the particular shape and make of the wig worn by George II'.[13]

Occasionally the Prince was sulky himself; but he could soon be brought round, as the Duke of Norfolk could. To one young lady who had given some slight offence he showed that he was displeased by bowing to

* It was owing to such 'encroachment' that the Prince, many years before, had fallen out with his uncle, the Duke of Cumberland, whose 'style was so low that, alluding to the Principality of Wales, the Duke called his nephew *Taffy*. The Prince was offended at such indecent familiarity and begged it might not be repeated – but in vain' (Walpole, *Last Journals*, ii, 405).

her curtly as she arrived and giving her no more than a 'little parting shake of the hand' when she left. The next evening when she arrived she made him a curtsey 'perhaps rather more grave, more low and humble than usual (meaning – "I beg your pardon dear foolish, beautiful Prinny for making you take the pet")'. Immediately he held out his hand, and all was forgiven.[14] One of Sir Philip Francis's daughters recorded an equally characteristic story of the Prince's essential good humour. Her brother, Philip, with whom he often sang at the Pavilion, was rendering with him one evening an Italian hunting song when Francis 'suddenly found the full face of the Prince, somewhat heated by the eagerness of his performance, in immediate contact with his own; and this circumstance, combined with that of the loud bass tones in which his Royal Highness was singing the words, "*Ritornoremo a Clori, al tromontar del dì*", striking him in some ludicrous point of view, he became absolutely unable to resist the effect on his nerves, and burst out laughing. The Prince evidently perceived that his own singing had produced the unreasonable laughter, but, instead of showing his displeasure at a rudeness which, however involuntary would have been resented by many far less illustrious persons, he only called the offender to order with the words, "Come, come, Philip!" his countenance betraying at the same time a strong inclination to join in the laugh himself.'[15]

A friend of Francis's sister, Sarah – whose little daughter could often be seen at Brighton sitting on the Prince's knee and eating sugar plums – was entranced by evenings spent at the Pavilion. 'The Prince's talents for conversation and powers of entertainment' were, she thought, 'truly extraordinary and delightful'. She shared to the full the Francis girls' 'extreme admiration of all his amiable qualities, fascinating manners and uncommon accomplishments', and she, like them, had to acknowledge her '*weakness*' for him.[16]

Dinner at the Pavilion was served pretty punctually at six o'clock, and it was a meal of surpassing excellence. 'The like I never saw, and the like I probably shall not see again,' wrote a highly contented clergyman, who had been flattered to be asked to say grace 'in the best way that ever such an injunction was given'. 'A more cheerful meeting never passed, there was as much decorum as if we had been dining at the table of the most correct among our bishops. Such music, such brilliant conversation, such a profusion of luxuries – the Master of the feast so condescending, and gracious.'[17] A more fastidious guest, Lady Bessborough, agreed that dinner at the Pavilion was always excellent, though she had cause to complain that the dining-room, like the other rooms in the Pavilion, was appallingly hot. There were usually about fifteen guests, one of whom was always Mrs Fitzherbert, who was 'very fat' now, according to Mrs Calvert, though still attractive despite a set of 'not good false teeth'.[18] After dinner Mrs Fitzherbert and one or two others played cards; while the Prince talked to those who – like himself – did not enjoy cards; or listened to his band; or got out his maps to discuss the progress of the war, to find the site of the most recent battle and to display his 'vast powers of recollection in military information', the accuracy of which, so Sir Nathaniel Wraxall said, 'excited astonishment' even amongst experienced soldiers.[19]

Sometimes, having had a little practice shooting with an air-gun at a target fixed at the far end of the room, the Prince would introduce a performance on the organ by his Organist in Ordinary, Charles Wesley;[20] or a pianist would be invited to play upon the 'curious fine-toned six octave grand piano in black ebony case' which he had bought for £680 in 1808.[21]

The band stopped playing punctually at midnight when servants came in with sandwiches and wine.

The Prince went to bed late and got up very late. Most mornings he could be seen sitting on the balcony of Mrs Fitzherbert's house – to which, it was believed, there was an underground passage from the Pavilion – or promenading along the Steine, bowing with varying degrees of elaboration and with a grace 'universally admired' to friends and acquaintances, or greeting a favoured and favourite friend with 'literally open arms'.[22]

The friends were remarkably varied. Sir Philip Francis was so frequently a guest at the Pavilion that the set of rooms he occupied there were named after him.[23] A room was also always available for Sheridan, once again one of the Prince's closest and most indulged companions. Despite his age – he was fifty-five in 1806 – Sheridan still behaved like the wild young man he had once rejoiced in being. He would come into the drawing-room disguised as a police officer and arrest the Dowager Lady Sefton for playing some unlawful game; he would creep amongst the guests during an exhibition of phantasmagoria, and in the darkness sit upon the lap of the haughtiest lady in the room; he would go into the kitchen at any hour that he felt hungry and, by cajoling the servants – making them laugh by telling them that if he were Prince of Wales they would all have much better accommodation than *this* – he would soon have everyone waiting upon him.

Late one night he went in to see if he could find a bit of supper, was soon provided with what he wanted, 'ate away and drank a bottle of claret in a minute', then returned to the ballroom where he was still dancing between three and four o'clock in the morning. The Prince continued to regard him, for all his follies and debaucheries, as 'a man that any prince might be proud of as his friend'.[24]

In marked contrast to Sheridan were the exquisite, meticulous George Brummell and the gruff old Lord Thurlow, both often to be seen in the Prince's company. 'Beau' Brummell, sixteen years younger than the Prince, had established his reputation for social elegance, wit and meticulous appearance while still a schoolboy at Eton and an undergraduate at Oriel College, Oxford. Struck by his manners, his dress and pert self-confidence, the Prince presented him with a cornetcy in his regiment when he was only fifteen, and thereafter their friendship became firm. Occasionally the Prince was put out by some peculiarly sardonic remark of his protégé, whose reputation was such that he was commonly supposed to have disdainfully jilted a woman on discovering that she ate cabbage. The Prince was also offended sometimes by the deep reverence with which Brummell's views on fashion in dress were treated, as if *he* rather than the Prince himself were the arbiter of taste in such matters. However, the Prince's admiration for his young friend was unfeigned. He went to watch him dress and stayed on to dinner. It was said that his graceful way of opening a snuff-box with one hand was copied from Brummell, though the Prince did not really like the snuff which he bought in such large quantities from Fribourg and Treyer (and kept in an astonishing variety of valuable snuff boxes), either brushing his nose slightly with the pinch or dropping it altogether before it reached his nose.[25] It was even alleged that he 'began to blubber when told that Brummell did not like the cut of his coat'.[26]

Thurlow was a man of utterly different cast from Brummell. He was always dressed in bulky, old-fashioned clothes, huge cuffs and buttons, long ruffles and a vast wig. He had the biggest, bushiest black eyebrows that Creevey had ever seen and a voice like 'rolling, murmuring thunder'. The Prince always behaved towards him with the 'most marked deference and attention';[27] and he had good reason for doing so, for although Thurlow was 'the politest man in the world to ladies', he was very rough with men. When he caught them out in some unfortunate slip or ridiculous observation he never let go of them. Creevey, who took care to keep clear of him, had seen 'the sweat run down their faces from the scrapes they had got into'.[28] He did not, of course, mix very well with some of the other guests at the Pavilion. One day during the race week he found himself invited to dinner at the same time as Sir John Lade. 'I have, Sir,' he told the Prince gruffly when informed of this unfortunate juxtaposition, 'no objection to Sir John Lade in his proper place, which I take to be your Royal Highness's coach-box, and not your table.'[29]

*

A far more appealing person to be seen from time to time at the Pavilion was a little girl, Mary Seymour, whose eighth birthday was celebrated on 23 November 1806. She was the youngest of the seven children of Lord Hugh Seymour, a son of the first Marquess of Hertford, and of Lady Horatia Seymour, a daughter of Earl Waldegrave. Lord Hugh, a naval officer, had been appointed Master of the Robes and Keeper of the Privy Purse to the Prince in 1787, and both he and his wife had thereafter become friendly with Mrs Fitzherbert.[30] Knowing of her marriage to the Prince, Lord Hugh had refused to continue to serve in the Prince's Household after the second marriage to Princess Caroline. His wife, however, had remained on intimate terms with Mrs Fitzherbert, who offered to take care of any of her children when Lady Horatia's declining health led her doctors to insist that she should go to live in a warmer climate. The offer had been accepted and after Lady Horatia's departure for Madeira, her baby girl, who was considered too delicate to undergo the long sea voyage, had been entrusted to Mrs Fitzherbert's care. The mother had died in July 1801 shortly after her return to England, and the father had died in Jamaica a few weeks later. In his will he appointed the Earl of Euston, whose wife was Lady Horatia's sister, and Lord Henry Seymour, his brother, as his executors and his children's guardians. The children were all mentioned by name with the exception of Mary who had not been born when the will was drafted. But both executors thought that Mary, or Minny as she was called, ought to be considered as coming within the terms of the will, and they wrote to Mrs Fitzherbert asking her to give the child up to her aunt, Lady Waldegrave. They recognized that it would come as 'an unpleasant proposal' to Mrs Fitzherbert who, they 'really believed', was 'much attached to the child'; but there were good reasons for removing her 'from what hereafter might be thought an *improper* education'.[31]

Mrs Fitzherbert, who had become devoted to Minny, was deeply distressed when she received the letter. She could not bear the thought of parting with the child. She told Lord Thurlow that she would never give her up, saying that if the worst came to the worst she would run away with her.[32]

'The misery I have at the thoughts of having her taken from me is more than I can express,' she protested to Lord Robert Seymour. 'She is now past four years old. I am perfectly certain no person can feel for her as I do. . . . I fairly own to you that I am so totally wrapped up and devoted to that dear child that if I lose her it will almost breake my heart. . . . The child was placed with me by both the parents in confidence that I should treat it as my own. This confidence I accepted and had occasion to renew the promise to her poor mother whilst she was sinking fast into the grave . . .'[33]

She explained how, 'with a heavy heart', she had offered to deliver Mary up to her mother on Lady Horatia's return from Madeira, and how Lady Horatia had replied, 'Don't think I could be so unfeeling as to take her from you. *You are* more her mother than *I am*.' She explained, too, how Lady Horatia had called her back as she was about to leave the room and begged her 'to request the Prince to call upon her as she wished to speake to him'.

'I delivered her message,' Mrs Fitzherbert continued, 'and the Prince accordingly went to her. The next day I saw her and she repeated to me the conversation that passed between them, a great deal relative to Lord Hugh's and her own concerns, and then said "I have been recommending my little Mary to him and have received his promise to be her friend and protector through life." '[34]

According to Lady Euston, Lady Horatia's feelings about the Prince were more ambivalent than Mrs Fitzherbert's letter implied. She recognized that he loved Minny, but she doubted that his reputation and character were those of a suitable guardian. As she told Lady Euston, she wanted him to be kind to her children, yet she could not help feeling that to be too much in '*that* society' might be dangerous for them.[35] She had tried to avoid seeing the Prince, Lady Euston maintained, as such a visit would be 'extremely unpleasant' for her: she had not spoken to him for many years, as their former friendship – broken when he had rejected Mrs Fitzherbert for Lady Jersey and had married Princess Caroline – had never been resumed. She knew that he would attempt to justify his conduct and his subsequent quarrel with Lord Hugh, so she asked her maid to say that she was lying down and could not see him should he call.[36]

But the Prince was undeterred. One day, while Lady Euston was sitting with her, Lady Horatia's door flew open and there he was, walking into the room as though 'visiting an old friend'. He 'started and changed colour' at the sight of her, for she looked so ill; while she was too overcome to speak. 'He took her by the hand,' Lady Euston reported, 'and began to talk as fast as possible, and she once or twice looked at me as if she was quite overcome by his talking. . . . She did not speak to him at all, and as she sat with her head turned towards me she once or twice in a low voice expressed a degree of vexation on his volubility – she grew more and more faint.' Yet, after he had gone and she had recovered, she smiled at Lady Euston and asked her 'whether it did not put [her] in mind of former times when he used to *go off* upon some favourite subject till he *talked himself into believing that all he said was true*'.[37]

That evening she decided that, after all, she was glad that the Prince had been. He had spoken of Lord Hugh and of Minny and their other children with such obvious affection that she could not help but be pleased by it. Lord Hugh would have been pleased as well, for he 'had always been very sincerely attached to the Prince', and, despite their quarrel, was still 'certainly more attached to him than he now liked to acknowledge'.[38]

After his visit to Lady Horatia, the Prince wrote to the executors offering to settle £10,000 on Minny – payable, with interest, when she reached the age of twenty-one or when she married or he himself died – provided that she were allowed to remain with Mrs Fitzherbert who could not, he said, be more attached to her if she had been her own child. The Prince declared 'his ultimate view to be to raise her up as a companion and as he [hoped] a bosom friend of his own daughter',[39] who was about three years older. But Lord Henry was adamant: Minny was perfectly well provided for already; she must be brought up by her aunt.*

The Prince consulted Lord Thurlow, who suggested that he should employ Samuel Romilly to fight the case for him. The resultant court hearing was an extremely long one. Lord Eldon, who appeared for the

---

* The financial provision was made, all the same. In 1815 the Prince asked that the bond, setting forth the terms of the gift, should be lodged with Coutts's Bank, 'in *confidential* trust for Miss Seymour', who was then sixteen. He stipulated that Mrs Fitzherbert, from whom he had by then finally parted, should not be told whence the money came, merely that the deposit had been made (Archives of Coutts & Co.; RA Geo. IV, Box 7).

executors, argued strongly that 'whatever amiable qualities' Mrs Fitzherbert might possess, 'the religion she professed excluded her from the right to retain the custody of a Protestant child'. Romilly and Thomas Erskine, who appeared with him, pointed out that the child was already being given religious instruction by an Anglican clergyman under the direction of the Bishop of Winchester. In an affidavit 'Maria Fitzherbert, widow' swore 'That although she was bred in the Roman Catholic faith she always entertained and expressed the opinion that a child ought to be educated in the religion professed by its parents. . . . That Mrs Fitzherbert had in fact educated a child of inferior condition born in her own house, in that religion. . . . That the Appellant was of a delicate constitution and of a very tender and affectionate disposition, and having no other mother than Mrs Fitzherbert, she was bound to her by as strong ties of affection as she could possibly have been to her natural mother.'[40]

The Prince of Wales also made an affidavit in which he swore that he had called on Lady Horatia a few weeks before she died; that she had told him how fond of him her child was, and how fortunate she was to have such a dear friend as Mrs Fitzherbert to look after her for her; and that she had said to him, 'I have something more, Prince of Wales, to say to you; recollect that it is the last request of a dying mother, and that is that you will take on oath and swear most solemnly that you will be the father and protector through life, of this dear child. . . . Whereupon, his Royal Highness accordingly, without the smallest hesitation, gave his most solemn engagement to her to fulfil to his utmost this request.'[41]

The Master in Chancery considered that the executors had the better case; so did a higher court, presided over by Lord Eldon, who had become Lord Chancellor once more since the case began. Thomas Erskine, Mrs Fitzherbert's counsel, advocated an appeal to the House of Lords; and by the time the appeal was heard by the Lords, Erskine had replaced Eldon as Lord Chancellor, so Mrs Fitzherbert's chances of winning appeared more promising.

Both she and the Prince determined that no opportunity should be lost of ensuring success. They enlisted the support of the Marquess of Hertford, Minny's eldest uncle, who agreed to say in the House that it was painful to have a family matter discussed in front of strangers, and that if their Lordships agreed, he and Lady Hertford would take upon themselves the guardianship of their niece on the understanding that they would be free to deal with her as they thought best.

The Prince then went about energetically from one peer to the next urging them to vote for this solution, even going so far as to hint that he himself was the father of the child to whose care he was bound by 'a promise exacted by her dying mother'.[42] When he heard that Spencer Perceval strongly objected to this behaviour, referring to him as a liar and a cheat, he burst out vehemently 'with most offensive personal abuse, and an oath which cannot be recited, that he felt he could jump on [Perceval] and stamp out his life with his feet'.[43] Many Members of the House of Lords deprecated this interference in their judicial duties as strongly as Perceval did; and Romilly urged Colonel McMahon to endeavour to put a stop to the Prince's unseemly activities which would do his cause more harm than good. But, as it happened, despite the resentment aroused by the Prince's canvassing, the Lords decided by a large majority that the child should be given up to the Hertfords. Only thirteen votes, including that of Lord Eldon, were cast against the proposition. As soon as the result of the voting was known, Lady Hertford asked Mrs Fitzherbert to continue to care for their niece; so the matter was finally settled.

The Prince was overjoyed. Romilly said that he could not have been more anxious that Mrs Fitzherbert should keep the child, if Minny had, in fact, been their own daughter.[44] And naturally it was whispered that she *was* their daughter – the Prince's concern to ensure that she remained with her adoptive mother, Mrs Fitzherbert, being contrasted with his determination that Princess Charlotte should *not* be brought up by *her* real mother.[45]

There could indeed, be little doubt that his love for Minny Seymour was far deeper than the affection he bore his own daughter, whose provenance he could not bear to contemplate. He spent as much time with Minny as he could, gave her regular presents, wrote to her on her birthday, and watched her grow into a pretty, delightful young woman. He sent her gold charms and almanacs, cakes and money, scent and bracelets and earrings; and she wrote back to her 'dear Prinny' – or 'dear Priney' as she spelled the name when she was little – with natural affection, drawing hearts and crosses for kisses at the bottom of her neat little letters, thanking him for 'making us all so happy'. 'Dear Prinny,' she wrote when she was twelve, 'I am much obliged to you for your nice letter and very pretty presents. I soon poked the ten pound note out of the essence box and was very much delighted with it [money was always 'very acceptable', she assured him in a subsequent letter, since sometimes she was 'rather an extravagant personage'].[46] What a naughty personage you are dear Prinny to send me such new years gifts. I opened the parcel very cautiously.'[47]

Lady de Clifford's little grandson, the Hon George Keppel, who was about the same age as Minny, was often taken to play with her, and in later years he confirmed how fond she and the Prince appeared to be of each other. The Prince struck the little boy as 'a merry, good-humoured man', tall and fat, 'with laughing eyes, pouting lips' and a rather turned-up nose. He liked him, as children did, for he was fond of them, took notice of them and knew how to talk to them.[48] 'He wore a well-powdered wig,' Keppel remembered, 'adorned with a profusion of curls, which in my innocence I believed to be his own hair, as I did a very large pigtail appended thereto. His clothes fitted him like a glove; his coat was single-breasted and buttoned up to the chin. . . . Round his throat was a huge white neckcloth of many folds, out of which his chin seemed to be always struggling to emerge.'

As soon as the Prince sat down, Minny would jump up on to his knee, sitting on his leather pantaloons, her little feet dangling by his Hessian boots. Immediately there began an animated talk between them. Sometimes George Keppel was invited to sit on the spare knee 'and to share in the conversation, if conversation it could be called in which all were talkers and none listeners'.[49]*

*

There were no such displays of fond affection between the Prince and his daughter, Charlotte, admittedly a less appealing child than Minny. Hot-tempered, cheeky and acquisitive, she had, as Lady de Clifford had discovered, a very high opinion of herself, 'an unfortunate vanity', which was, her eldest aunt, Charlotte, commented, 'a little in her blood'.[50] Her preceptors and tutors found her a rather tiresome, over-excitable pupil, though shrewd and innately affectionate. She did not much care for her Governess, Lady de Clifford, George Keppel's 'snuffy old grandmother', who had cause repeatedly to reprimand her for her ill manners and lack of consideration, as when she rushed into a room, leaving the door wide open. To her Governess's reprimand, 'My dear Princess, that is not civil; you should always shut the door after you when you come into a room,' she riposted rudely, 'Not I, indeed. If you want the door shut, ring the bell'; and she flounced out again, leaving it open.

---

* Mary Seymour continued to live with Mrs Fitzherbert until her marriage in 1825 to Colonel the Hon George Dawson (later Dawson-Damer), a son of the first Earl of Portarlington. She had five children, and died in 1847 at the age of forty-nine.

Although she was very fond of Mrs Campbell, and was kindly disposed to the Rev George Nott, she heartily disliked her other Governess, Mrs Udney, 'a great goose', and positively detested Bishop Fisher, a pompous, self-important busybody whose interfering fussiness equally exasperated Lady de Clifford. One day, in a sudden access of rage, Princess Charlotte snatched the wig from the opinionated Bishop's head and threw it into the fire. Another day, after she had hit a maidservant who had offended her, the Bishop asked her why she had failed to follow his advice of always saying the Lord's Prayer when she was angry to calm her temper. 'I did, my Lord Bishop,' she replied saucily, 'or I should almost have killed her.'[51] When she was taken into a house she ran as fast as she could to the top of the stairs and down again; when visitors came to see her at Warwick House, she marched them round her father's rooms pulling off the covers and leaving them on the floor; when George Keppel's sisters came to play she was very rough with them, pushing them into beds of nettles and giving them presents if they neither cried nor complained to their governess.[52] Dr Fisher found her quite as tiresome as she found him, complaining of her appalling ill manners, noticing with profound distaste that 'her nose requiring to be wiped, she did not apply her handkerchief, but wiped her nose with her sleeve as vulgar people do'.[53]

Her hoydenish behaviour, her loud and ready laugh, her brash impudence profoundly distressed her father, who was painfully reminded of her mother. He believed that she ought to be controlled more strictly and was very insistent that her visits to Blackheath and Kensington should be severely limited and meticulously supervised by her Governess, who was never to let the child out of her sight for an instant. 'The boy whom the Princess of Wales has brought up and who is certainly not fit company for my daughter,' he instructed Lady de Clifford, sending a copy of the letter to the Princess, 'is not to be brought in Charlotte's society, as I have learned he has been too often produced on these occasions. These regulations I hold to be absolutely necessary, and I depend upon you for their being strictly adhered to.'[54]

The Prince wrote in similar terms to the King, adding, 'the Princess of Wales must never be under the same roof with me. My daughter's present residence cannot but be regarded the same as my own house, there being a communication between that house and mine and a consequent possibility of my meeting the Princess were she to come here.'[55]

The Prince was also concerned that the teaching staff at Warwick

House, who were always squabbling with each other, were not fulfilling their duties properly. He suspected that his daughter was herself responsible for many of their disagreements. Mrs Campbell, whom he had never trusted anyway, being a woman of Tory connexions nominated by the King, had had to be reprimanded for allowing her charge – indeed for 'encouraging' her – to make out a will in which the Princess bequeathed to her her 'three watches' and 'half [her] jewels'. Mrs Campbell, whom the Princess had referred to as her 'adopted mother', had subsequently resigned on the grounds of 'ill health'.[56]

The Rev George Nott, the Princess's Sub-Preceptor, whose 'dutiful daughter by adoption' the Princess liked to consider herself, was also mentioned favourably in this innocent document which decreed that he should be left all her 'best books' and 'papers', together with all her money 'to distribute to the poor'. The Princess trusted that, after her death, the King would make Mr Nott a bishop.

Already the Prince had had occasion to rebuke his daughter's Sub-Preceptor for subscribing himself the Princess's 'most faithful friend' in a letter which he had written to her reproving her for her unpunctuality. Mr Nott, the Prince had sharply reminded Bishop Fisher, was her 'instructor', most certainly *not* 'her faithful friend', 'a footing of intimacy . . . never authorised' and the assumption of which must, of course, be prevented in future.[57] The Prince was all the more concerned because the Bishop – whom he disliked as much as his daughter did – had suggested that his daughter might be allowed to 'pass the evenings' with Mr Nott. This was a suggestion that could not possibly be entertained. The Princess's day was fully occupied from the hour of 'rising till the time of her dinner', so it was only natural that 'the resumption of study instantaneously after dinner' would be 'peculiarly irksome to the child and unprofitable from the impossibility of commanding her attention'. But the Bishop's concern that if she were left 'entirely idle' she would 'fall into a state of listlessness' showed that he was unacquainted with the manner in which her evenings were employed. She was always pleasantly occupied with ladies and governesses, in music, in dancing or in being 'read to out of some amusing but instructive author'. There was, therefore, no reason whatsoever for the singular request that Mr Nott should be allowed into the Princess's society in the evenings. She was now eleven years old. 'I must make it a rule not to be infringed,' the Prince concluded, 'that my daughter shall never be left alone with any of her masters. . . . I repeat to your Lordship that no man is to be of my daughter's private society.'[58]

Soon after this letter was written Mr Nott was the cause of further trouble. It was alleged, supposedly by Mrs Udney, that he had influenced the Princess in unfilial feelings towards her father, and had failed to check the Princess's unfortunate disposition for idle and even malevolent gossip. In consequence of this report, and despite a warm defence of his subordinate by Bishop Fisher, Nott was suspended. Then, in a counter-attack on Mrs Udney – who had been dismissed in Princess Charlotte's will in six words: 'Nothing to Mrs Udney for reasons' – the Bishop accused her of allowing the Princess to read a highly unsuitable book without his permission, an English translation of Ovid's *Metamorphoses*, and even worse, of showing her an obscene caricature of Nelson's mistress, Lady Hamilton, and explaining its meaning to her.[59]

No one ever did discover the truth behind the squabbles at Warwick House. Mrs Udney was apparently not considered blameworthy, for she continued in her appointment, as did Lady de Clifford. But then Mr Nott was evidently not held to have disgraced himself either, for, although suspended – to be succeeded eventually by the Rev William Short – he was later appointed a Prebend of Winchester, an appointment that led to Mrs Campbell's asking for 'some mark of royal favour' which would show that she, too, had not forfeited the King's good opinion of her. She had to wait some time for this approbation, but was eventually appointed one of Princess Charlotte's attendants.[60]

While her instructors bickered amongst themselves, and her father appeared to take the side of those strict ones she did not like, Princess Charlotte felt increasingly less fond of him as the months went by, and also less fond of her aunts whose 'compagny', she said, 'I hate and detest'.[61] Her letters were outwardly dutiful and suitably affectionate. 'O my dearest papa,' she wrote to him on his forty-fifth birthday in her remarkably neat, round script, 'may I become every year more worthy of so kind a father and be a comfort to him when grown up. . . . I assure you, my dear papa, I will struggle to get the better of my lessons and of all my learning and to do everything I can do to please you.' But she felt constrained to add, 'I am ashamed to say but I hope you will forgive me, that I did not always feel the attachment I ought to have felt. I was ungrateful to a father who, tho' he had a great deal of business, I am sure never had me out of his mind, but I was sufficiently punished, for you could not bear your daughter ungrateful and therefore you would not see her.'[62] 'O how I wish I could see more of you!' she wrote in another letter. 'But I hope I shall in time. I am sensible how irksome it must be to you to see me, feeling I can be no companion to you to amuse you when in health; and am too young to soothe you when in affliction. Believe me that I am always truly happy when I do see you.'[63]

His mother and his sisters urged him to try to go to see her more often, for she badly needed, as Princess Elizabeth said, the 'affection and attention of her father'.[64] 'She is very sensible of any the smallest attention shown to her,' the Queen wrote, 'and also, which is very natural, seems to feel very strongly any apparent neglect. . . . She is blessed with an uncommon share of good sense, she has talents and facility to learn any thing, is easily led to follow good advice when treated with gentleness, desirous to oblige when an opportunity offers, and capable of very strong attachment. . . . As to her manners I will not deny they are a little brusque, but more society will correct that. . . . From the bottom of my heart do I wish that she should connect with her filial duty and sincere friendship for you which may be gained by seeing a little more of her, and by making her look upon you as the source of every amusement and pleasure granted to her. In another quarter every possible pains are taken to make her visits the most agreeable and every amusement thought of to gain her affection.'[65]

If the Prince did not go to see Charlotte as often as he could, particularly when he thought there might be a possibility of meeting her mother; if he now summoned Lady de Clifford to bring her to him at most irregular intervals, he always appeared to find time to go to see Minny Seymour. He also found it possible to spend a great deal of time in the company of Minny's aunt, the Marchioness of Hertford, at her house in Manchester Square.

20

The Advent of Lady Hertford
1806–1809

*

'His father's malady extends to him, only takes another turn'

Isabella, Lady Hertford, the daughter of the ninth Viscount Irvine, was a very rich, beautifully dressed, handsome, formal and stately woman of ample, though well-corseted proportions. At first no one had considered the Prince's close friendship with her family particularly remarkable, even though they were the most dedicated of Tories. The Marquess, who had married Isabella as his second wife when he was thirty-three in 1776, was a pleasant, easy-going man, moderately successful as a politician and later as Ambassador in Berlin. He had been appointed Master of the Horse in 1804. Their only son, the Earl of Yarmouth, who – though possibly it is his father – appears as the Marquess of Steyne in Thackeray's *Vanity Fair*, was married to the heiress Maria Fagniani, daughter of the Marchesa Fagniani and of either George Selwyn or the Duke of Queensberry, each of whom, claiming the honour of paternity, left her large sums of money. Both Lord Yarmouth and his father were on excellent terms with the Prince, sharing with him that collector's passion for French furniture which filled Hertford House with the treasures that can still be seen there.

It soon became clear, however, that it was the company of Lady Hertford that principally attracted the Prince to Manchester Square and to Ragley, the Hertfords' country seat in Warwickshire. It was said that the Prince's new-found preference of Cheltenham to Brighton, which he now claimed was 'too cold' for him, was due to Cheltenham's propinquity to Ragley;[1] and that the Marchioness, an ambitious and rather masterful woman, was highly gratified by the Prince's attentions and the opportunities for political influence which they presented. No one for a moment supposed, though, that however hard he might press his suit she would give way to him and become his mistress. She was celebrated for her staid, unresponsive nature; 'stately, formal and insipid', Lord Holland thought her;[2] and now that she was getting on for fifty it was not considered likely that she would suddenly change for the better. Mrs Calvert, while allowing that she was still beautiful, thought her 'the most forbidding, haughty, unpleasant-looking woman' she had ever met.[3] Lord Glenbervie was wholly mystified by the Prince's motives, not understanding his need to be dominated by an authoritarian woman older than himself. The Prince visited her every morning when she was in London, wrote to her every morning when she was not, and often dined *'en famille* with her and Lord Hertford'. Yet what could he find to write about? She had been a grandmother for 'more than twelve or fourteen years'. Lord Hertford had an income of over £70,000 a year, so he could not be said to be conniving at the intimacy between his wife and the Prince for commercial reasons.[4] Also she looked her age; but then, as Lady Stafford commented, 'elderly dames' seemed 'to be to his taste'.[5]

The more firmly she held to her virtue – and Robert Plumer Ward was told by one of the Prince's doctors that she succeeded in keeping it intact[6] – the more emotional were the Prince's feelings for her. He wrote to her more frequently than ever, sitting up all night to do so, Lady Elizabeth Foster said;[7] he fell silent at the thought of her and his eyes filled with tears. A mature, ample, protective, enclosing woman, she could offer him so much, yet stood aloof from him, until he became, as Lady Bessborough said, 'really distracted' and could think of nothing other than *'la bella e grassa Donna che lo signoreggia ora'.*[8] He fell ill; he was feverish; he demanded to be blooded; he lost his appetite; he grew thin. Soon he was seriously ill.

*

All his life the Prince had been subject to such violent and sudden attacks of illness, especially when emotionally disturbed. His usual symptoms, accompanied by 'great agitation of spirits', were high fever, a racing pulse, weakness in the arms and legs, severe abdominal colic and what he himself referred to as 'violent bilious attacks', 'a violent stoppage in the bowels', 'severe spasms on the neck of the bladder', and 'violent inflammatory attacks' on the lungs. From an early age he seems also to have suffered from gout and 'some degree of rheumatism' and these complaints appear to have been exacerbated in times of stress, as in 1789 when, worried to distraction about his debts, his pulse rate was so rapid that Warren could not count it – 'it resembled a machine completely disorganized'.[9] So, too, was the case in 1792 when, distraught by his father's refusal to give him an Army command, he was reported as having been 'threatened with apoplectic symptoms' and as having no more than two more years to live.[10] He insisted upon being blooded with alarming frequency – continuing his practice of opening the vein himself when his doctors would not do so – took a great deal of laudanum accompanied by medicines to make him sweat, and tried cures at Bath and Cheltenham. But he discovered no satisfactory treatment. Every attack was followed by a period of 'extreme weakness and lassitude'.[11] It is possible that, like his father, he was a victim of porphyria.[12]

He himself recognized that his 'mind' was the 'main spring' of his illnesses.[13] In 1791 'numberless causes of vexation' made him 'very seriously ill indeed', and although, as he told the Duke of York, he did all he could to master himself, he 'could not hold up any longer, and sank under feelings which are not easy to be described'. For this 'violent complaint' he had himself blooded five times, yet even so his nerves felt 'but in a shattered state'.[14] Mary Berry said that, having spitted blood, he 'fainted away after his levée' in April.[15] 'He is supposed to have ulcers on his lungs, like the late Duke of Cumberland,' Sir James Bland Burges told his sister in May, 'and was actually blooded four times last week. His physicians have ordered him to live upon French beans and barley-water. He, however, dined on Friday with three hundred officers, made great havoc of sundry savoury meats and much champagne, claret, and burgundy.'[16]

Two years later when war broke out with France he once again, so he informed Sir John Lade, fell 'very ill *indeed*'.[17] And in 1799, when he was in a fever of agitation about Mrs Fitzherbert's application to the Pope for permission to return to him, he became so seriously ill that his doctors decided that the only cure would be to send him to Bath. From there he replied to a letter from Dr John Turton who had written to him because the Queen was worried that he would take the waters 'improperly': 'I have certainly been very unwell since I have been here. . . . *Mine is a very nervous* and so far a *delicate* fibre, consequently the disorders of the body in general *with me* owe their source to the mind. (This God knows has for some time, and a long time too, been too much the case with me, and then any little addition, such as a casual cold, or even any indisposition, no matter how trifling, contributes much to the unhinging the whole system.)'[18]

As though nervously aware that his periodic attacks were similar to his father's, he did not like detailed accounts of them to be generally known. 'I have been between ourselves *very ill indeed*,' he once wrote to the Countess of Elgin, 'and it is little known *how ill*.'[19] Of a later attack his daughter wrote that news of it had been kept 'profoundly' secret until 'all shadow of alarm was over'.[20] More than once he admitted to being 'very unwell', but the admission was made '*confidentially*' and was not to be talked about. He even went so far as to cause it to be known that his symptoms were other than they were, for fear lest some sinister interpretation might be put upon them. The precaution seemed well justified when he learned that during one of his attacks, when he lay '*constantly on his stomach* in bed', complaining 'of violent pain' and 'spasmodic affection', and taking 'a hundred drops of laudanum every three hours', the Duke of Cumberland, making trouble as usual, was going about saying it was 'all sham', that the illness was really '*no other* than that he *was mad*'.[21]

There was no doubt that his agitation was sometimes so extreme that he did, indeed, appear to be in danger of losing his reason. In 1804, when he was so disturbed both about his failure to get on in the Army and about the possibility of a regency due to the King's illness, he was reported to be in 'a fever of uneasiness', to be talking 'all day without ceasing to Mrs Fitzherbert'.[22] At the same time Sheridan told his wife that the Prince, 'just recovered from an illness in which his life was despaired of for two days', was 'so nervous and anxious' that it was 'not easy to thwart him, though he [ran] a great risk of making himself ill again'. He kept Sheridan in his bedroom, talking to him continually till four o'clock in the morning.[23]

Two years later when the Prince was making a tour of the north of England – staying at Doncaster, Aske, Bligh and Ledstone Hall, with Lord Darlington at Raby Castle in County Durham, with the Staffords at Trentham, with Lord Derby at Knowsley, Lord Fitzwilliam at Wentworth Woodhouse, and at Castle Howard, Lord Carlisle's seat in Yorkshire – he fell seriously ill again. This time the attack was attributed to his great distress at the death of Fox.

He was said to have been overcome with grief at Nelson's death. Certainly he mourned Nelson as 'the greatest character England could ever boast of', and claimed to have 'loved him as a friend'. Yet the loss was not really a personal one. Although Lady Hamilton told Alexander Davison, his prize-agent, that Nelson had 'adored' the Prince,[24] this was no more than flattery intended for his Royal Highness's ears. In fact, when Nelson had learned that the Prince was to be invited to the Hamiltons' house he protested in almost hysterical terms. 'Does Sir William want you to be a whore to the rascal?' he demanded. It was 'shocking conduct' to have asked him. If Sir William knew as much of the Prince's character as the world did, he would rather have let the lowest wretch that walked the streets dine at his table than that 'unprincipalled lyar'. Lady Hamilton's 'hitherto unimpeached character' would be ruined; 'no modest woman would suffer it'. The Prince was 'permitted to visit only people of *notorious ill fame*'; it had been reported that he had said he would make her his mistress; he was 'a false lying scoundrel'.[25]*

If the Prince mourned the loss of Nelson as a national rather than personal tragedy, he felt the death of Fox as both.[26] When he heard of it, though he had long been expecting it, he flung himself on a sofa and burst into passionate tears.[27] He professed himself 'overwhelmed with grief'; and as he wrote to Lord Holland from Trentham, where he was staying when the news reached him, his tears still fell so thick that he could not see what he wrote.[28] For days he could not bring himself to speak to anyone except his hostess, Lady Stafford. Both Lord Fitzwilliam and Lord Carlisle reported to Charles Grey that he had utterly lost his appetite and could not sleep, that his strength had quite failed him.[29] He ate little but fish and salad, and drank only barley water, warm milk and soda water; he looked pale and old and wrinkled in the black clothes he wore for months. 'The Prince is here and very unwell,' Lord Fitzwilliam told Lord Grenville on 24 September 1806. 'He has been so during the whole of this tour. He has lost all appetite and even has he for wine. He was deeply affected with the death of Fox, and has never recovered his spirits since. When first I saw him it was very manifest how much he felt on the occasion. But to return to his health. We got Walker, formerly his apothecary in London, but now retired in Yorkshire, to see him. From a strong pulse, he found it quite thin, low and weak. He thinks him seriously unwell and that he required much attention and repose. Whether he will

---

* The King, who strongly disapproved of Nelson's liaison with Lady Hamilton, did not deem it appropriate that the Prince should attend the funeral as chief mourner, as he had wanted to do. This privilege was accorded to Admiral Sir Peter Parker, the Prince attending in a private capacity. To his obvious dismay, he was refused permission by his father to attend Fox's funeral in any capacity at all. He contributed £500 towards its cost (RA 40784: Asp/P, v, 499; BM Add. MSS 51520).

be persuaded to manage himself as he ought to do is more than I feel confidence of.'[30]

Although the King refused him permission to attend Fox's funeral for reasons of 'propriety', the Prince interrupted his northern tour to be in London while 'the melancholy ceremony' was taking place. Lord Fitzwilliam was gratified to find him rather better on his return to Wentworth House, still 'wonderfully abstemious both in eating and drinking', but in a 'wonderful degree of agitation on a variety of subjects'.[31] He had got over the first shock of grief at Fox's death, but he was now 'in the figgets' about the war, the elections and, above all, Princess Caroline.[32]

By the beginning of December it was being suggested in London that he did not have much longer to live, the Duke of Clarence, with characteristic bluntness, putting forward the view that three months would see him out. Joseph Farington, the diarist, heard that 'an eminent medical man' had given it as his opinion that he could 'never recover' from the state he was in; he was drinking the strongest, iced tea to 'allay the internal heat'. Three months later one of his tailors, John Weston of Old Bond Street, confided to a friend of Farington's that he had become so thin that his clothes hung like greatcoats upon him and were 'obliged to be taken in greatly'. Since the death of Fox he had worn nothing but black and within the past three months had ordered only two new suits to add to the 'some hundred suits' he had in his wardrobe. His temper was 'not so good as it was'; he was 'hasty about trifles, about the placing of a button, and peevish'.[33] His servants were much concerned, 'fearing for their situations'. Edward Jerningham found it quite painful to look at him, so greatly had his countenance altered, 'not so much from the reduction of his enbonpoint as from a sallowness and an expression in his eye as if he suffered mental and corporeal pain. He assumed a cheerfulness, but it was visibly put on from his good humour and a desire to please.'[34] On 2 May, when he attended the Royal Academy dinner, everyone noticed how 'very ill he looked'. Farington, concerned to see him eat nothing but fish and salad, a little pudding and one or two radishes, noticed that he had lost all his 'joy and gaiety, and spirit of address'. When the President of the Royal Academy, Benjamin West, proposed a toast to the Prince's health there 'was much *clapping*, which expressed the general feeling that *he wanted it*'.[35]

Towards the end of the year he recovered once more; but by the late autumn of 1807 he was in a more agitated state than ever over Lady

Hertford. Neither McMahon nor Lieutenant-Colonel Benjamin Bloomfield – who had only recently entered his service as one of the Prince's Gentleman Attendants but had known him for some time as a horse-artillery officer doing duty with the Prince's regiment at Brighton – had ever seen him 'in such a state of lowness and depression'.[36] By the middle of December, sunk in melancholy, he was 'immovable' from his room, so Bloomfield told Lord Hertford, 'plunged into a state of apathy and indifference towards himself' which was indescribably alarming. One evening, Bloomfield found him agitated 'beyond all former example. He clasped his hands and, in quick steps, walked up and down his room as if rouzed by some dreadful event, when he exclaimed, "Oh, my dear Bloomfield, a terrible catastrophe was near happening ..." and in the greatest agony continued, "If Lord and Lady Hertford were but here, the only persons to whom I can talk and confide. ... What is now to become of me, of wretched me in this moment of accumulating difficulties and distress, is more than I can support." '[37]

A few weeks before he had tried to regain his health by a course of the waters at Cheltenham, then by a short tour of the West Country and visits to the Hertfords at Ragley and to Berkeley Castle; but he had gained no relief. Indeed, his visit to Berkeley Castle was made a 'martyrdom', so he told Lady Hertford, by 'the mistaken over-attentions and the bourgeois and insufferable vulgarity and ill-breeding of the Maestra del la Casa', Lady Berkeley, a butcher's daughter.[38] His behaviour was certainly very tiresome there and his hostess was thankful when he had gone. 'Having dined there at six o'clock, Lady Berkeley did not ask him to fix an hour the following day but ordered the dinner to be ready at six, and at that hour the Prince was informed that dinner was ready. He sent word that he could not then dine, and the dinner was taken off the table, and they waited till eight o'clock before he made his appearance. He was there on a Sunday and Lady Berkeley asked him whether he proposed to go to Church? To which he answered "That if she desired it, or it would oblige her, he would go." To this she made no reply, and he did not go. At Bristol, at Gloucester and wherever he went the people were dissatisfied with his behaviour.'[39]*

---

* When he was well the Prince was normally a far less troublesome guest. Lord Lonsdale said 'that wherever the Prince went, and under all circumstances, he expects to see such preparation, and such attention and respect as he thinks due to him, but that when this has been shewn, he dispenses with such a continuation of it as would at all affect the comfort of those

He returned home looking 'most wretchedly' and, in Fremantle's opinion, 'very little mended'. At the beginning of 1808 he was so affected by the sight of his old friend, Lord Lake, on his deathbed that he fainted and was 'not restored until a quantity of cold water was sprinkled over his face'. Some months later Joseph Farington's brother, Robert, who saw him at Weymouth, was shocked by his altered appearance, the strongly marked lines in his sallow face; he had a 'shattered look'.[40]

'More or less ever since I quitted you at Ragley,' he wrote in anguish to Lady Hertford, 'I have been persecuted by the most horrible and spasmodick attacks in my head. . . . The agony I suffer is hardly to be credited.' If only she would write to him all would be better.[41]

To unsympathetic observers the Prince's plight seemed only too familiar. 'His health was reported to be bad, and his appearance confirmed the report,' wrote Lord Holland. 'Those, however, who had made a study of his gallantries, recognised his usual system of love-making in these symptoms. He generally, it seems, assailed the hearts which he wished to carry by exciting their commiseration for his sufferings and their apprehensions for his health. With this view he actually submitted to be bled two or three times in the course of a night, when there was so little necessity for it that different surgeons were introduced for the purpose, unknown to each other, lest they should object to so unusual a loss of blood.'[42]

'I really believe his father's malady extends to him, only takes another turn,' concluded Lady Bessborough, who told her lover, Lord Granville Leveson Gower, that the Prince, driven wild by Lady Hertford's rejection of his advances, had thrown himself upon her instead. 'Such a scene I never went through,' Lady Bessborough said. He 'threw himself on his knees, and clasping me round, kissed my neck before I was aware of what he was doing. I screamed with vexation and fright; he continued some-

---

about him, with whom he lives easily and pleasantly. It is not so with some others of the family, particularly [Prince William of] Gloucester, who subjects people where he visits to a tedious attention to ceremonious personal respect to him' (*Farington Diary*, v, 216). At Lord Crewe's, Gloucester 'made them very weary of him by his fastidious pride and the trouble he gave', refusing to allow the port to be passed in front of him at table and insisting on hot suppers every night. 'Miss Crewe and her young friends would sometimes retire from the general apartment to another sitting room and there set down familiarly to work. [Prince William] would come into the room and they according to etiquette would *stand up*, from which he would not relieve them' (*Farington Diary*, iv, 51). Prince William never even 'allowed a gentleman to be seated in his presence', so Lady Shelley said, 'and he expected the ladies of the party to hand him his coffee on a salver – to stand up while he drank it, and then to remove the cup.' (*Shelley Diary*, i, 29).

times struggling with me, sometimes sobbing and crying. . . . Then mixing abuse of you, vows of eternal love, entreaties and promises of what he would do – he would break with Mrs F. and Lady H., I should *make my own terms*!! I should be his sole confidant, sole adviser – private or public – I should guide his politics, Mr Canning should be Prime Minister (whether in this reign or the next did not appear); . . . then over and over and over again the same round of complaint, despair, entreaties and promises, and always Mr Canning . . . and whenever he mentioned him it was in the tenderest accent and attempting some liberty, that really, G., had not my heart been breaking I must have laughed out at the comicality of having [Canning] so coupled and made use of – and then that immense, grotesque figure flouncing about half on the couch, half on the ground.'[43]

But, as Lady Bessborough knew, it was not really herself but Lady Hertford that the Prince wanted. 'He writes day and night almost, and frets himself into a fever, and all to persuade la sua bella *Donnone to live with him – publickly*!! . . . I should not be surprised if he and the ci devant [Mrs Fitzherbert] were to quarrel quite during their meeting at Brighton. . . . She has got irritated, and he bored.'[44]

This was only too true.

*

For a long time now, it had been noticed, both at Carlton House and at the Pavilion, that Mrs Fitzherbert was being pushed into the background, and that Lady Hertford was gradually taking her place. Lady Hertford, so correct in her conduct and manners, declined to dine at either house unless Mrs Fitzherbert were there too; her reputation might thus be protected while her rival was humiliated. And humiliated Mrs Fitzherbert certainly was. The Prince still spent part of his mornings at Brighton with her, but in the evenings when she came to the Pavilion 'he did not even notice her in the slightest manner'. She 'afterwards understood that such attentions would have been reported to her rival'.[45]

She had had many other rivals in the recent past. The Prince was believed to have had brief affairs with the dancer, Louise Hillisberg, with the notorious Harriette Wilson who admitted in her *Memoirs* to having offered herself to him,[46] and with Marie Anne, the French wife of the second Earl of Massereene; and in 1805 he had apparently established another Frenchwoman, Mme de Meyer, in apartments in Duke Street, Manchester Square, where he used to visit her late at night, leaving his carriage in a corner of the Square and walking to her door muffled up in a large greatcoat.[47]*

Mrs Fitzherbert had sensibly disregarded these brief affairs and peccadilloes. But she could not ignore his passion for Lady Hertford. Often she threatened to leave him, yet hesitated to do so for fear lest she might lose Lady Hertford's niece, her beloved Minny. Also, she still loved him. In the summer of 1808 she made up her mind to see no more of him, at least for a time. Her 'sudden and unexpected departure' went to his 'very soul', he wrote in a distraught letter to her companion, Miss Pigot. The tears flowed from his heart; he would take no notice of the letter Mrs Fitzherbert had written to him, as otherwise he would 'verify the very kind accusation which amongst many others' she had laid at his door, namely of his 'always acting a part, and playing to the galleries'. But if she returned to him, he would receive her 'with open arms'.[48] To Mrs Fitzherbert herself he wrote incoherently, 'As it is, my only, only only love, quite out of my calculation by being able to sleep, I may as well employ myself in that what to me is the only pleasant, as well as the only interesting occupation of my life, which is the writing to thee; and though this alas! is but poor consolation, still as I fancy to myself that it is in some degree, or at any rate, a convincing proof . . . I cannot resist the temptation as it affords me not inconsiderable relief of applying to my pen to endeavour . . . to establish within my bosom at least a species of requiem. . . . I am a different animal a different being from any other in the whole creation. . . . Every thought and every idea of my existance and of my life never leave and never quit thee, for the smallest particle of an instant.'[49]

* The Prince, it seems, declined to accept the paternity of a daughter of a Mrs Mary Lewis, a boarding-house keeper whom he had met at Weymouth. He did, however, apparently accept the paternity of three other children. One of these was the son of a Mrs Crowe who lived in Charles Street, St James's Square under the name of Seymour, with an allowance from the Prince of £1,000 a year. The boy was christened George and known as 'Prince' to his mother and his school friends; he was said to be twenty-two in 1820 and to have been provided for in the Army (RA Geo. IV, Box 10; RA 39524–6). Another of these children was William Francis, son of a Mrs Davies, who was modestly provided for on his mother's death when he was eleven and at school at Parson's Green (RA 29957–73). The third child was the son of Eliza Crole, who, as Major G. S. Crole, decided to sell his commission in 1832 being 'heartily tired of the service' and never having had 'much partiality for it'. He trusted, in a letter addressed to the King's Private Secretary, that the purchase price for the lieutenant-colonelcy for which he was tired of waiting, would nevertheless be made available to him (RA 29974–97). Mrs Crole herself received a pension of £500 a year (RA 30370). In discussing the provisions of his will with Lord Eldon in 1823 King George IV 'mentioned that he had a natural son, an officer in the East Indies, to whom he thought himself bound to give a leacy of £30,000' (RA Eldon MSS., quoted in Asp/P, viii. 483).

To such repetitive appeals Mrs Fitzherbert gave way. But she went back to him only to find that he was still as infatuated as ever with Lady Hertford. At length, driven beyond endurance, she wrote to tell him that she could no longer bear to let the present miserable situation continue. 'It has quite destroyed the entire comfort and happiness of both our lives; it has so completely destroyed mine, that neither my health nor my spirits can bear it any longer. What am I to think of the inconsistency of your conduct, when, scarcely three weeks ago, you voluntarily declared to me that *this sad affair* was quite at an end, and in less than a week afterwards the whole business was begun all over again? The purport of my writing to you is to implore you to come to a resolution. . . . You must decide, and that decision must be done immediately, that I may know what line to pursue. I beg your answer may be a written one, to avoid all unpleasant conversations upon a subject so heart-rending to one whose life has been dedicated to you, and whose affection for you none can surpass.'[50]

Unwilling to lose her, yet besotted by longing for Lady Hertford, the Prince made a placatory reply and continued to ask her to the Pavilion. But on 18 December 1809 she gave a firm and final refusal. She could 'not possibly accept the honour' of his invitation; the 'very great incivilities' she had received these past two years had been too keenly felt by her to admit of her putting herself 'in a situation of being again treated with such indignity'. 'For whatever may be thought of me by some individuals,' she continued, 'it is well known your Royal Highness four-and-twenty years ago placed me in a situation so nearly connected with your own that I have a claim upon you for protection. I feel I owe it to myself not to be insulted under your roof with impunity.'[51]

The Prince replied that he would 'never forget those affectionate feelings' he had ever entertained for Mrs Fitzherbert, and signed himself, 'Always with every possible kindness and good wishes towards you I remain, my very dear Maria, ever very sincerely'.[52]

Mrs Fitzherbert knew now that the separation was complete.*

---

* Mrs Fitzherbert's generous allowance was continued throughout the remaining years of her long life. In 1808 the provisions he had made for her under the terms of his will and her existing pension were both commuted for an annuity of £6,000. This was increased to £8,000 a year in 1820, and by 1830 had been increased again to £10,000 a year (RA 29895–29903; RA 30370).

21

The Windsor Nunnery

1797–1810

*

'They were secluded from the world, mixing with few people'

No one was more upset by the Prince's treatment of Mrs Fitzherbert than were his sisters, with whom she had been upon the best of terms. All of them, with the single exception of Charlotte, the Princess Royal, were still living at home, longing for the day when they would be allowed to escape into marriage, growing older and thickset, less good-natured, ever more frustrated by the enclosed life they were required to lead in what they described to each other as 'The Nunnery'.

Throughout their lives their parents had watched over their growth and development with the most attentive concern. In their childhood this had been tolerable and had gone unquestioned. To be constantly chaperoned, to have a governess standing by whenever a man, even a trusted schoolroom instructor, was present, to have every hour of the day rigidly planned, to be unable to pursue any activity outside the normal curriculum without permission, never to be allowed to read a book that had not previously been approved by their mother, all these conditions, rules and regulations seemed acceptable. No other way of life had been known to them.

They had, without undue complaint, got up early, learned their lessons with varying degrees of success, been taken for drives in the country, gone for walks, sometimes with their governesses or ladies, sometimes with their parents also, walking two by two in schoolgirls' crocodile formation. At Windsor, in the summer evenings, they had gone 'terracing', as they called it, promenading up and down beneath the Castle walls with their parents' attendants and guests while the band played appropriate tunes. In their leisure moments they had taken up their knitting needles or their spinning-wheels or drawing-boards, while their mother, who could never bear to see anyone idle, listened to one of her ladies reading from some improving work as she worked away at her needlework. When it was time for bed they would, one by one, kiss their mother's hand, curtsey to her companions, and, accompanied by a female attendant, leave the room.

Occasionally there was a ball or a concert; sometimes there was a visit to the theatre to see an approved or specially censored play; often there was a birthday party when they all had new clothes. But they rarely saw any men other than their father, his pages, equerries and attendants; and even these they did not see at mealtimes, etiquette forbidding any man to sit down in the Queen's presence. The Princesses, in fact, were shown very little of the world beyond the walls of the Queen's House, the gardens at Kew and the slopes of the Castle at Windsor. Once or twice a year they went *en famille* to stay for a few days with such friends of their parents as the Harcourts at Nuneham Courtenay; or they were taken to the races at Ascot. Once they, or at least the three oldest of them, were taken with their mother and father on a formal visit to Oxford University; and once they were conducted round Whitbread's brewery.

Although so constricted a life, it was not an unhappy one when they were young. They were often seen laughing together, and the healthy good looks and pleasant, easy manners which they all possessed were universally admired. Gainsborough, on being commissioned to paint them, confessed that he went 'all but raving mad with ecstacy in beholding such a constellation of youthful beauty'.[1]

The older they grew, however, the more irksome the restrictions imposed on them were naturally felt to be. They had no personal income other than that allowed them by their mother; they were never permitted to go away for a holiday by themselves, even suitably and heavily chaperoned, but were expected to accompany their father to Weymouth, where the Queen usually felt ill and they always felt bored.[2]

Since the King got up at five, so did they; they walked down with their attendants to the bathing-machines; they rode round the grounds of Gloucester House in a donkey-chaise; they walked on the sands; they went to the Assembly Rooms and to public breakfasts given by the local gentry and dignitaries. Night after night they went to the playhouse to see the same piece performed by '*a very bad sort of actors*', because the King enjoyed it and they had, as Princess Mary complained bitterly to the Prince, 'nothing to do but submit and admire his being so *easily pleased*'.[3] Weymouth, in fact, as Mary had to admit in another letter, was 'more *dull* and stupid' than she could find words to express, 'a *perfect stand*-still of *every*thing and everybody except every ten days a very long review'. The review, she was assured, was 'very fine', but as she was '*perfectly unknowing* in those sort of things' she did not find it in the least amusing.[4] Her sisters found life at Weymouth quite as tedious as she did, and Princess Elizabeth added another complaint when she said that whenever she was there she wished 'to lose the sense of smelling'.[5]

In 1797 when she was thirty-one the oldest of the sisters, Charlotte, had managed to find a husband at last. She was an attractive young woman, though clumsier and less self-confident than the younger girls. At her first Court ball one of her shoes fell off as she was curtseying to the Queen; and although her partner, the Prince of Wales, held her hand in his usual 'most graceful' manner while it was being replaced, so that not everyone noticed the accident, others did notice it and it was remarked that the 'Princess was never elegant in exhibition'.[6] Her shyness made her seem on occasions rather arrogant and aloof; and she was, in fact, inclined to be managing by nature. She felt sure, with some justification, that her mother did not love her as she should, and kept her subdued in the background as though she were a little girl.

One day, in their mother's presence, the Prince had made some good-natured jokes about her which she had taken very badly. Afterwards she had asked her brother never to joke with her about the smallest trifle in front of the Queen as he did not know how much she suffered for it later. The Prince had been most contrite and most affectionate, saying it had always been 'the principal object' of his life to do everything he could to make everyone in the family happy; and Charlotte, encouraged by his kindness, had gone on to say that her parents obviously loved all her other sisters better than herself, that they constantly restrained her, 'just like an infant', and made no attempt to find her a husband abroad or give her an establishment of her own at home. In fact, they made her lead a 'perpetual tiresome and confined life' as though she were not a daughter but a slave.

She begged her brother to see what he could do to find her a husband and mentioned as a possibility his friend, the Duke of Bedford. Knowing that their father would never consent to such a match, the Prince wrote a very long letter to the Duke of York, who was at that time in Germany, to ask his advice about the likelihood of a foreign match.[7]

The Duke of York replied that the Prince of Prussia was hoping to marry one of their sisters; but he was not likely to be interested in Charlotte, who was then twenty-five, since he was only twenty-one.[8] The Prince then interested the middle-aged widower, Prince Peter of Oldenburg, in marrying his anxious sister; and Charlotte was seen to blush whenever his name was mentioned; but although her sisters began teasingly to refer to her as 'the Duchess of Oldenburg',[9] nothing came of this suggestion either. And it was not until the Hereditary Prince of Württemberg came to England in 1797 that Charlotte's long spinsterhood was over.

The Prince was very fat – so fat, indeed, that Bonaparte said that God had created him merely to demonstrate how far the human skin could be stretched without bursting – and very plain. Charlotte appeared to be 'almost dead with terror and agitation' at her first sight of him, which was not surprising as there were strong rumours that he had connived at the murder of his first wife. 'Timid and distressed' as she went into the chapel to be married, she was 'a good deal affected on her return'. Her sisters and father all cried; 'everybody kissed her hand and bowed to the Duke of Würtemberg without being spoke to by either'.[10]

Charlotte settled down happily in Germany, however, writing regularly to the Prince, giving unsolicited advice on the education of her little namesake, having good cause to complain – as had all his brothers when they were abroad – that he did not reply to her letters as often as he might, but remaining 'ever most sincerely attached' to him and always grateful for the 'many proofs of friendship' he had shown her.[11]

At the time of the Princess Royal's marriage, Princess Augusta was twenty-nine, Princess Elizabeth twenty-seven, Mary twenty-one, Sophia twenty and Amelia fourteen. Princess Augusta was more self-confident than her elder sister, a lively, cheerful, affectionate woman, amusing and boisterous. In her younger days she had played cricket and even football with her brothers; she was studious, though, as well as energetic, and Fanny Burney was astonished by the range of her knowledge and the sharpness of her insight. Her hopes of marrying had been dashed by the King, who had found fault with the various suitors proposed for her, and in any case had been unwilling to grant permission for her to marry while the Princess Royal remained unattached. Denied the companionship of any suitable young men of her own age, she had at first formed a romantic admiration for one of her father's doctors, the courtly Henry Vaughan (who changed his name to Halford on inheriting the large estate of an elderly cousin), and then had conceived an enduring passion for one of her father's equerries, a dashing Irish soldier, Major-General Sir Brent Spencer. She confided in the Prince of Wales how much she loved the General, and felt relieved when she had done so; but there could be no thought of a recognized marriage so long as the King was capable of preventing it; and by the time that he was not, she was nearly forty-five. She died unmarried.

Her sister Elizabeth's long struggle for a husband was eventually more successful, though for many years it had seemed that she was the least likely of all the girls to get married. She had been very fat as a child and for years had been an invalid. Artistic and emotional, she was, like her eldest sister, rather managing and interfering; she was also, like Charlotte and all the others, strongly sensual. There had been rumours years before of an illicit affair with one of the King's pages and, less believably, of a pregnancy; and at the time of Charlotte's marriage to the Prince of Württemberg she had written to the Prince in the hope that now one of the girls at least had been settled, the turn of the others would follow. Sympathetic as always to his sisters in their plight, he renewed his efforts to help. The possibility of a match with Louis Philippe, Duke of Orleans, was suggested, only to be condemned out of hand by the Queen, who understandably refused even to consult the King knowing perfectly well what his reaction would be to his daughter's marriage to a Roman Catholic, a penniless one at that, and a man whose likelihood of ever becoming King of France – which, in fact, he did do against all the odds in 1830 – seemed then peculiarly remote. Princess Elizabeth then turned once again to her brother, whose promises of future complaisance, when in a position to fulfil them, were evidently so reassuring that she fell 'on her knees with *gratitude*'. The promises he had made would be '*secreted*' in her '*own breast*'; 'volumes would not suffice' to express half of what she felt towards him for his 'unbounded goodness'.[12]

For the moment, though, she understood that she would have to 'go on vegetating' as she and her sister had been forced to do 'for the last twenty years' of their lives. When she mentioned marriage to her mother she was told that that was a subject not to be raised at the moment. So Princess Elizabeth sublimated her longing for babies of her own by looking after other peoples', and in charitable works for orphans. She was, as her mother wished, never idle; she wrote letters for the Queen, and she produced numerous creditable engravings; she amassed an admirable collection of porcelain; she took up farming and kept a set of Chinese pigs in one of the fields at Frogmore. Anxious not to have become undesirable by the time it became possible for her to marry, she drank sugar melted in water at night to keep her temper sweet, and went for long walks at eight in the morning so as not to become more stout than she already was. She told the Prince that all she wanted in the winter of her life were good friends, warmth, a comfortable chair, a book and 'a good fireside with a *kind brother*'. But the Prince knew that what she was really hoping for was something far more exciting than that. In the meantime, what she sardonically described as the '*lively, chearfull* and *gay life*' which she and her sisters led was, he realized, sadly tedious to them all.[13]

Mary, the fourth sister and the Prince's favourite, troubled him less with her problems. She was a kind, affectionate girl, but more self-contained than the others, more remote, more critical. Discreet in her behaviour, she was quite outspoken in her remarks. She offended the Duke of York by drawing attention to his growing corpulence, and excused herself by observing, 'It is so *very visible* that I could not help *making the* remark'. It was tacitly supposed that she would one day marry her cousin, the boring, pompous and conceited Prince William of Gloucester of whom, unaccountably, she seemed quite fond.

No such opportunity offered itself for either of the two youngest Princesses, Sophia and Amelia, both of whom, being denied acceptable suitors, had affairs with gentlemen about the Court much older than themselves. Sophia was generally considered a delightful girl, very pretty, rather unruly, passionate, moody and delicate. Both the Duke of Clarence and the Duke of Kent admitted to the Prince that she was their favourite; and the Duke of Cumberland's deep affection for her was felt to be not altogether healthy. In fact, Cumberland was reported by the Princess of Wales to have fathered a child to which Sophia seems to have given birth in secret at Weymouth in August 1800 when she was twenty-two. It was a report which the Duke of Kent for one seems to have both believed and propagated.[14] The child was more likely, however, to have been fathered by one of the King's equerries, General Thomas Garth, uncle of Miss Frances Garth, Princess Charlotte's former Sub-Governess.

General Garth might almost have been selected by the King for service at Court on the grounds of his appearance. It could hardly have been expected that so unprepossessing a man could have appealed to any of his daughters, impressionable and frustrated though they were. He was very small, and his undistinguished face was badly disfigured by a purple birthmark that covered part of his forehead and surrounded one eye. Charles Greville, the future clerk to the Privy Council, went so far as to describe him as a 'hideous old devil'; but then 'women fall in love with anything – and opportunity and the accidents of the passions are of more importance than any positive merits of mind or of body. . . . They [the Princesses] were secluded from the world, mixing with few people – their passions boiling over and ready to fall into the hands of the first man whom circumstances enabled to get at them.'[15]

Garth, who was thirty-three years older than Princess Sophia and had been in the King's service since she was a young girl, found himself alone with her, apart from the servants, one summer's evening at Windsor when her parents were in London. She had been ill for some time and had been taken from the Lower Lodge to Queen's Lodge where she was put in a bedroom beneath General Garth's. Nine months later she was 'brought to bed', so Lady Bath told Greville on the authority of Lady Caroline Thynne, at that time Mistress of the Robes to the Queen, a 'very simple, natural and true' woman with 'ample means of information'. The King was told that the Princess was dropsical and he evidently believed it, or at least chose to believe it. In any case, it was easy to deceive him now for he was almost blind.[16]

Princess Sophia, the Duke of Kent's 'poor little Barnacles', his 'dear little angel', never fully recovered her health, though she was to survive all her sisters, except Mary, and to live on well into the reign of her as yet unborn niece Victoria. Her invalidism seems, indeed, almost to have become a form of self-indulgence which was pampered by repeated visits and constant presents from her eldest brother, her 'dear love' for whose affectionate attentions she thanked him in letter after fond and tender letter. Occasionally, so Lord Glenbervie said, she saw her son, who had been christened Thomas and left at Weymouth at the home of Major Herbert Taylor, then Private Secretary to the Duke of York and afterwards to the King.[17]* She may conceivably have married the child's father

---

* There is nothing in the Royal Archives either to confirm or to repudiate Glenbervie's story – which he had from that unreliable source, the Princess of Wales – but the young Thomas Garth, as portrayed by Barraud, certainly bears a strong resemblance to Princess Sophia's portrait by Beechey. In 1824 he filed an affidavit in Chancery maintaining that he had come into possession of certain documents which Sir Herbert Taylor had agreed to buy from him in exchange for an agreement to settle all his debts and an annuity of £3,000 a year. Taylor, so Garth contended, was attempting to get these documents removed from the bank where they were deposited without fulfilling his part of the bargain (*Greville Memoirs*, i, 270-1).

in a secret ceremony, for he remained in favour at Court, being promoted Lieutenant-General and then General and appointed to a responsible position in the Household of Princess Charlotte. But Princess Sophia seems not to have much enjoyed her life for all her family's kindness. '*Poor old wretches* as we are,' she wrote to the Prince in her tiny writing, lamenting the lot of her unmarried sisters and herself and thanking him for his kindness to the '*four old cats*' at Windsor, '*poor old wretches, a dead weight* upon you, *old lumber* to the *country*, like *old clothes*. I wonder you do not vote for putting us in a *sack* and *drowning us* in the *Thames*.'[18]

*

By the time she wrote this letter, Princess Sophia's younger sister, Amelia, had died. At the age of fifteen she had contracted tuberculosis. Three years later she was also suffering from erysipelas, and for much of the rest of her life she was in pain. In vain efforts to cure her, the royal doctors bled her, purged her and blistered her; applied leeches to her skin and quills beneath it; immersed her in hot sea-water baths, prescribed beef-tea, calomel and madeira; poured emetics and laudanum down her throat accompanied by a variety of powders, medicines, restoratives and stimulants. Her sufferings, and the patient resignation with which she bore them, aroused the sympathy of all her brothers and sisters whose letters to each other are replete with references to 'poor dear Amelia', the pretty baby of the family, her present condition and the likelihood of its amendment.

The Prince was a constant visitor. She was his godchild, and next to Mary, who nursed her devotedly during her periodic attacks, he loved her perhaps even more than any of his other sisters. In 1798 when she was sent to Worthing to spend the summer in a house by the sea, he rode over to see her almost every morning from Brighton. He suggested that she should be brought to stay with him in the Pavilion, where he would make her comfortable in a pleasant little apartment, but her parents thought it better that she should stay where she was. When he could not visit her, he wrote to her and sent her presents.

She adored him. He was her 'dear angelic brother', her 'dear angel', her 'beloved eau de miel'; she inscribed herself his '*own child*'; she had always loved him, she confessed, better than any of the younger brothers; a new dictionary would have to be invented for her to be able to say just how much she did love him. She longed for his visits which were her 'greatest happiness', and always felt 'as if in a dream' after he had gone. To see him was 'really and truly a cordial', more good to her than any medicine.[19] He was all the more dear to her, for, as her illness progressed, she fancied that the rest of the family were less than affectionate in their attitude towards her, particularly the Queen and Princess Elizabeth, known by her as 'Fatima', whom she believed to be under their mother's influence. Repeatedly Amelia complained of 'the Queen's *ill and cross* looks'; she could 'not feel any pleasure in seeing *her*'; she didn't expect 'much *feeling or pity* in that *quarter*'; her cruelty was 'not *new*' but now she could not stand it; as for Elizabeth, one day or another she should hear her '*mind*'.[20]

On Christmas Eve 1809 she wrote angrily to the Prince, 'to describe *her* [the Queen's] *feelings*, her manner and her visit to me yesterday, *all* I can say till we meet is it was the STRONGEST CONTRAST to the dear King POSSIBLE, but I am too much used to it to feel *hurt* by *it*. But I pity her.'[21] A few days after Christmas she added, 'I hear Gl. F.R. is returned and the Queen *was particularly* cross to *him*'.[22]

This was the trouble. The 'Gl. F.R.' to whom Amelia referred was Major-General the Hon Charles Fitzroy, one of the King's equerries and a man with whom she was passionately in love. He was better-looking than Princess Sophia's lover, General Garth; but whereas Garth had some charm and wit, Fitzroy was generally reckoned to be a dull, sedate, reserved soldier, interested in little apart from his profession, and not likely to be attractive to women, particularly to those, like Amelia, who were over twenty years younger than himself. He was a son of the first Lord Southampton, who had been a Groom of the Bedchamber to the King, and was descended from one of the illegitimate sons of Charles II. The King was devoted to him, so much so that he was referred to at Court as Prince Charles.

The Queen, who had learned of the affair as early as 1803, kept it secret from the King for fear of the consequences, but she repeatedly remonstrated with her daughter about 'this unpleasant business', 'this unfortunate indulgence'. To refer to the love of her life in these dismissive terms was, for Amelia, unforgivable; and her mother never was forgiven. The Queen's 'ill and cross looks' made her ever more determined to marry her 'blessed and beloved angel', her 'precious darling' as soon as she could. She gloried in her attachment to him, she told him. 'O, Good God, why not be together?' she asked him imploringly. 'I pine after my dear Charles more and more every instant. . . . I really must marry you, though inwardly united, and in reality that is much more than the ceremony, yet that ceremony would be a protection.'[23] She liked to suppose that he was, in fact, her husband already, and she assured the Duke of York that she 'considered herself married'. She signed herself dear Charles's 'affectionate and devoted wife and darling'.[24]

Like Princess Elizabeth in similar circumstances, Princess Amelia pleaded with the Prince to help her; and he seems to have made a promise to do so as soon as he could; but nothing could be done while the King was alive.[25] And this knowledge of her father's stubborn intractability gradually eroded the love that once she had felt for him; but out of duty and kindness she hid her feelings from him.

In her last illness in the summer of 1810, when, as Princess Sophia said, her suffering was 'VERY GREAT INDEED',[26] the King came to her room frequently, holding her hand, peering down at her, trying to discern with his failing eyes the features of his favourite child. She gave him a ring into which she had asked Rundell, Bridge & Co., the Court jewellers, to set one of her jewels and a lock of her hair pressed under a little crystal window with the inscription *Remember Me*. She put it on his finger herself, and as she did so he burst into tears.[27]

Her last thoughts were of General Fitzroy. 'Tell Charles,' she murmured at the end, 'I die blessing him.' In her will she bequeathed him everything she had with the exception of a few tokens to the Prince of Wales, to the Duke of Cambridge, whom the Prince had asked her to appoint joint executor with himself, to Princess Mary and, as an afterthought in a codicil, 'something belonging' to her, to her other sisters and 'the dear King'.[28]

In fact, Princess Amelia had little to leave but jewellery and debts. She had been an extravagant young woman, and had borrowed money from both Mary and Sophia, and from her brother, who had once lent her £4,000.[29] The Prince had the jewels valued and presented them to Princess Mary, giving their purchase price to the fund for the settlement of the debts.[30] The unfortunate General Fitzroy, cajoled by the Prince into renouncing his claim, was obliged to content himself with a monetary compensation and a few boxes of worthless effects.[31] Lord Holland thought that, in the circumstances, the Prince could not very well have dealt with the problem of Amelia's will in any other way; throughout the business he had behaved 'with great delicacy and good nature'.[32] Lady Holland thought so, too: 'The Prince behaved throughout with the greatest tenderness . . . with the utmost circumspection and decorum.'[33] Even the King, when his doctors believed him well enough to hear the contents of the will and the action that his son had taken, was said to have commented, 'Quite right, just like the Prince of Wales.'[34] But afterwards the Prince's conscience was much troubled. Three years later, on Amelia's name being mentioned, he 'burst into tears . . . seemed embarrassed and excessively overcome . . . and regretted he could not more fully comply with her last wishes'.[35] So deeply affected was he by her death that after the funeral he was never again able to sleep in a room that was not lit by several wax candles.[36]

22

Approach to the Regency
1810–1811

*

'Mr Perceval has seen the King'

At the time of Princess Amelia's death on 2 November 1810, the King was seventy-two. His past few years had been troubled by a series of national and family misfortunes and calamities that had worried him to excess. The scandal over the Duke of York and Mrs Clarke had been immediately preceded by the retreat of Britain's army in Spain to Corunna and the death there of its commander, Sir John Moore; it had been shortly followed by the disastrous expedition to the island of Walcheren, an attempt to open up a second front in the west against Napoleon, which had also ended in a British retreat and the loss of thousands of British troops. Then, in the summer of 1810, the Duke of Cumberland became involved in an even more unsavoury scandal than the one that had led to the resignation of the Duke of York.

Cumberland, 'alias the *Black Sheep*' as his brother the Duke of Kent referred to him,[1] had become increasingly embittered, increasingly reactionary and increasingly strange ever since his return home from the war in 1796. Granted a most generous allowance of £18,000 a year by Parliament, he had also received some highly lucrative military appointments in England; but his hopes of a command in the Peninsula had been thwarted, and his criticisms of those whom he felt stood in the way of his ambitions grew ever more outspoken and vituperative. He was an intelligent man with a cruel, sardonic humour, 'very sarcastick', as the Prince said, 'very comical though very impudent'.[2] As another of his brothers, the Duke of Clarence observed, if anyone had a corn he was sure to tread on it.[3] The Prince of Wales's feeling for him alternated between the deepest distrust

269

and the closest intimacy. In 1808 the Prince was reported to be constantly in his company, yet he could never forget that the Duke, as an inveterate Tory, espoused the cause of the Princess of Wales; and he could never forbear to warn his sisters against allowing themselves to be left alone in their rooms with him.[4]

His reputation was such that when in the early morning of 31 May 1810, his Corsican valet, Joseph Sellis, was found dead in bed with his throat cut, it was immediately rumoured that the Duke – who was supposed either to have been caught in bed with his wife or to have been blackmailed by him after making homosexual advances – had murdered him.

At the subsequent inquiry the Duke himself claimed that he had been asleep in bed in his apartments at St James's Palace when he had been woken by a light blow on the head which he had supposed had been caused by a bat attracted into the room by a candle burning by his bedside. He sat up and his eyes caught the flash of a sabre blade which he attempted to grab, almost severing his right thumb. He jumped out of bed, and ran for help to the adjoining room of his English valet, Cornelius Neall, crying out 'Neall! Neall! I am murdered!' His assailant pursued him, cutting him superficially on his buttocks and thigh and more seriously on his head, and would have killed him had it not been for the thickness of his night-cap. His cries for help caused the assailant to flee, dropping the sabre on the floor. Neall, wielding a poker, rushed into the room, followed by other servants who later found a pair of slippers belonging to Sellis in a closet. Shortly afterwards 'a guggling noise' was heard coming from Sellis's room; and the valet was found by a Sergeant of the Coldstream Guards, on duty at St James's, lying on the bed with his hands 'straight down and the blood all in a froth running from his neck'. A razor with a white handle lay on the floor about two feet from the bed; Sellis's blood-stained coat lay hanging over a chair; a basinful of bloodstained water stood nearby.[5]

It seemed clear that, after making his attempt upon the Duke's life, Sellis had returned to his room and was endeavouring to remove the evidence of his guilt when the guards appeared in the corridor outside and, rather than submit to arrest, he had killed himself. This was the view taken by the jury at the inquest; and since the foreman of the jury was the honest Radical reformer, Francis Place, there seemed no cause for dissent.

Yet the motive for the attempted murder remained a mystery. Witnesses at the inquest gave evidence to the effect that Sellis and Neall had been on very bad terms, that Sellis had threatened to leave the Duke's service unless he received better wages and the same perquisites as Neall, that Sellis had been heard to express republican sentiments, 'to damn the King and the royal family', and to say it was 'a pity they were not done away with'. Cornelius Neall testified that some months before, Sellis had accused him of theft, an accusation which was investigated and found to be untrue; and afterwards, discovering 'an evil disposition' from Sellis towards him, he 'thought it right to hang a pistol at the head of the bed' for his protection.

Neall's wife, who had known Sellis for almost twelve years, confirmed that he was very obstinate and quarrelsome and would not bear contradiction, that he lived 'very much to himself' and was 'very distant' with all the other servants.

Mrs Sellis said that her husband had 'frequently complained of a giddiness in the head', but she had never heard him make any criticism of the Duke's conduct towards him. A letter from her husband to the Duke was produced in which Sellis complained of the 'unconfortable and most unpleasant way' in which he was made to travel, being placed upon the carriage box, 'the most disagreeable of al grievances', whereas the Prince of Wales's servants were allowed inside the carriage or provided with a post-chaise.

It appeared, however, that Sellis was in general treated well by the Duke who was 'very partial' to him, and that if he had any grievances against him they were more imaginary than real.[6] It was the opinion of Colonel Henry Norton Willis, the well-informed Comptroller of Princess Charlotte's Household, that Sellis, his mind deranged by his illness, had been goaded into fury by the Duke who 'in his violent, coarse manner' taunted him for being a Roman Catholic.[7]*

*

* There is a curious document in the Royal Archives (Asp/P, vii, 373–8) a 'memoir' by Charles Jones, for several years the Duke's private secretary, who 'compelled by some irrisistable power' which seemed to be calling to him from the grave, set down in 1827, when he feared that he was dying, an account of a conversation he had had with the Duke on Christmas Eve, 1815. Having locked the door and sworn Jones to secrecy, the Duke confessed, 'You know that miserable business of Sellis's, that wretch, I was forced to destroy him in self-defence, the villain threatened to propagate a report, and I had no alternative.' This document – found amongst the papers of a descendant of Captain Jones which were purchased by a Manchester bookseller who presented it to the Royal Library in 1899 – appears to be genuine, but whether Jones misunderstood the Duke's meaning or intentionally wished to harm him it is, of course, impossible to say. The Duke may for some strange reason, in keeping with his mysterious character, have wanted to

Following so soon on this unpleasant scandal, and on the humiliating retreats of the armies from Spain and the Low Countries, the fatal illness of Princess Amelia was too much for the King to bear. During the last week of her life, he shocked the Queen's tall, plain and prim companion, Miss Cornelia Knight, by the 'dreadful excitement in his countenance' when he came into the drawing-room. As he could not distinguish faces any more, 'it was the custom to speak to him as he approached' so that he could recognize people by their voices. Miss Knight forgot what she said to him but could never forget what he said to her: 'You are not uneasy, I am sure about Amelia. You are not to be deceived, but you know that she is in no danger.' While speaking he squeezed Miss Knight's hand with such force that she could scarcely help crying out with the pain. 'The Queen, however, dragged him away,' Miss Knight recorded in her memoirs. 'When tea was served I perceived how much alarmed I had been, for my hand shook so that I could hardly take the cup.'[8]

On 29 October when Perceval saw the King, his conversation was 'prodigiously hurried . . . extremely diffuse . . . and indiscreet'[9] and it seemed that another lapse into insanity was imminent. The next day he was slightly less hurried and irritable, but his conversation remained 'unconnected'; that evening he was 'extremely violent', breaking out, 'as in former instances, in most unfit language to the Princesses'.[10] By the morning of 1 November he was quieter again, but his mind was quite vacant, and his doctors felt that they would once again have to enlist the expert help of Dr Simmons.[11] When Simmons, accompanied by his son and four assistants, arrived at Windsor, however, he insisted that he must be given full charge of the case; and since the 'ordinary physicians' refused to agree to this, he marched off 'with his troop immediately'.[12] The next day Dr Heberden summoned the medical officer of St Luke's Hospital and the keeper of a private madhouse in Kensington Gore.[13]

By now it was becoming clear that a new regency crisis was approaching.

---

mislead or shock his secretary or to impose some burdensome secret upon him. What at least seems clear enough is that, whatever he might or might not have said, he did not murder Sellis. According to a confidential report sent to Lord Henry Seymour by one of the Duke's pages 'the drapery of the Duke's bed over his head was very much cut which saved his life. His bed was also covered with blood. The Duke received four blows on his head . . . and as he was escaping into Neal's room, the assassin made a desperate lunge which took off a large splinter off the edge of the door. No traces of blood were found from the Duke's room to Sellis's. The razor was found close to Sellis's bed. The body and bed completely covered with blood' (Seymour of Ragley MSS, CR 114A/277).

On 2 November Canning told his wife, on the information of Lord Wellesley, the Foreign Secretary, that, although tractable, 'poor old Knobbs' was 'just as mad as ever he was in his life'. Wellesley described 'the sight, but still more the *hearing* of him before he went into the room, as most dreadful – a sort of wailing, most horrible and heartrending to hear'. In a lucid moment he exclaimed that this was the fourth time he had been ill, giving his reasons for the three previous attacks and adding: 'And now it is poor Amelia.'[14] The violence of his disorder had reached so 'horrible a height' by 3 November, the day after Princess Amelia's death, that it was necessary to place him in a straitjacket. For a short time after that he showed signs of improvement, accepted the fact of his daughter's death which he had previously been unable to comprehend, began to sleep better, to grow calmer and to eat with evident pleasure his simple meals of bread and cheese and mutton broth with turnips.[15] But then he relapsed once more into his former feverish restlessness and incessant rambling, interrupted by intervals of quiet in which he corrected himself frequently and allowed 'others to correct him'.[16]

The doctors were all obviously puzzled by his case, agreeing that he was without doubt incapable for the moment of attending to government, but varying in their opinions as to when he would be likely to recover. Dr Reynolds, who agreed with his patient in attributing the illness to anxiety on account of Princess Amelia, had seen the King recover from his three previous attacks and saw no reason at all why he should not recover from this one. But the others were less sanguine: the King was an old man now, almost totally blind.

As in 1788, the government held fast to hopes of the King's early recovery, trusting that he would be better before a Regency Bill became necessary, fearing that such a Bill would result in their dismissal in favour of the Prince's Whig friends. Parliament was adjourned for a fortnight on 1 November, and for a further fortnight on 15 November; but Ministers recognized that with Napoleon's armies so dangerously rampaging on the Continent a decision could not much longer be delayed. On 18 December, following an indecisive examination of the doctors by select Committees of the Commons and Lords, Perceval, while continuing to assure the House of Commons that the King would probably soon be better, felt obliged to write to the Prince to inform him that he intended to introduce a Regency Bill, with restrictions on the lines of Pitt's proposed Bill of 1789.[17]

The Prince, remaining faithful to his resolution not to interfere in politics, had so far done nothing to cause offence either to Ministers or the Queen. He had gone down to Windsor immediately on hearing of the onset of his father's malady, had then retired into the seclusion of his apartments in the Lower Lodge and had not only declined to discuss the King's condition with the opposition but had also said nothing of any significance to the members of the government who came down to Windsor to find out from the doctors how their patient was progressing. The Prince's conduct was 'perfectly proper, correct, most dignified', the Duke of Bedford said. Whenever Ministers approached him, the only answer he made to them was that they themselves 'must be the best judges of the line of conduct they ought to pursue'. Any observer could see, 'even with the most prying eye', Colonel McMahon told the Duke of Northumberland, that the Prince gave 'no audience or access to any description of politician whatever'.[18] Lord Holland confirmed that his behaviour had been exemplary, that he had 'conducted himself . . . with great caution, great dignity and great feeling'. There was no doubt, Holland added, that this could 'in some measure' be attributed to his being 'deeply affected' by Princess Amelia's illness and death.[19]

When Perceval elaborated his proposals for the Regency Bill, however, the Prince took strong exception to them. For the Regent's powers were to be severely limited for about twelve months. He was not to have powers to create peers, except in the cases of military or naval commanders who might not survive to enjoy the honour; he was to be allowed to grant pensions and make appointments to public offices only for the duration of the Regency 'and subject, as to their further continuance, to the subsequent pleasure of his Majesty' upon his recovery. Moreover, 'the management of the whole of his Majesty's Household, and the power of appointing the officers and servants of that establishment' were to be entrusted to the Queen.[20]

Immediately on receipt of Perceval's letter, the Prince replied by reminding him of the answer he had given to Pitt's similar letter in December 1788; and he had 'only to declare' that the sentiments expressed in that letter 'admitted of no change'.[21] The Prince then called all his six brothers and his cousin, William, now Duke of Gloucester, to a meeting at Carlton House. They all arrived within a few hours, and at midnight they signed a letter, written by the Duke of York, in which they entered their 'solemn protest' against measures which they considered 'perfectly unconstitutional', as well as being 'contrary to and subversive of the principles which seated [their] family upon the throne of these realms'.[22]

While the interference of the Royal Dukes was widely resented, there was a good deal of sympathy for the Prince in his demand for a regency without restriction. A limited regency might well have been considered appropriate in 1788 when he was only twenty-six and scarcely to be described as circumspect: but he was now over fifty and had recently displayed a far more responsible attitude. Besides the country was at war and a strong government was essential. This view was forcibly expressed by Lord Grey, who contended that 'under the pretence of preserving the rights and providing for the restoration of a King' who could now never possibly be a King in anything but name, Perceval's administration were merely endeavouring to 'secure the Government in their own hands'.

But Perceval remained, in Whitbread's phrase, 'as bold as brass', 'in great vigour of speaking', determined not to give way.[23] To Plumer Ward it seemed 'amazing' how he fought.[24] He gained his point. Voting on an amendment to remove the restrictions on the proposed regency was close; but the amendment was defeated, and by 8 January 1811 the principle of a restricted regency had been accepted by both Houses.

The next day Lord Grey arrived in London from his home in Northumberland and went to Carlton House to confer with the Prince about the formation of a new Whig government. The Prince had already talked his problem over with Lord Grenville and Moira and had discussed the implications of turning the Tory Ministers out. He had recognized that a strong administration was essential and that it might, therefore, be necessary to bring in Canning, despite his association with the Princess of Wales. He had also made clear his wish to reinstate the Duke of York, with whom he was now on good terms again, as Commander-in-Chief at the Horse Guards.

As Grey lamented sadly, the difficulties in making the necessary arrangements were so great as to drive anyone as mad as the King. He himself heartily disliked Canning and did not wish to serve with him, though Grenville thought it would be impossible to command enough support in the House of Commons without his help. Grenville wanted to be First Lord of the Treasury, but said that he could not afford to give up his profitable sinecure as Auditor of the Exchequer, though Grey, Holland and Whitbread thought the two offices quite incompatible. When it was suggested to him that he might become Home Secretary instead of

First Lord of the Treasury, he said that he could only forego the office normally associated with the Premiership if he were to be responsible for the Treasury patronage. He also wanted his brother, Thomas, to be First Lord of the Admiralty, though Lord Grey had promised this appointment to his own brother-in-law, Whitbread.

The Prince asked that Sheridan should be given the Irish secretary-ship, but Grey objected to 'sending a man with a lighted torch into a magazine of gunpowder'.[25] The Prince also wanted his friend, the Duke of Northumberland, in the Cabinet; but Grey disliked Northumberland almost as much as he did Canning; while the Duke of Norfolk's request to the Prince to be appointed Lord Privy Seal was frowned upon by Grenville. The Marquess of Buckingham, who threatened not to support the new government if Whitbread went to the Admiralty, hoped to see his son, Lord Temple, as Secretary of War, an office provisionally allocated to Grey's friend, Sir James Willoughby Gordon. The Duke of Gloucester and the Duke of Kent pressed rival claims to the Master Generalship of the Ordnance, to the dismay of those Whigs who were already opposing the reinstatement of the Duke of York as Commander-in-Chief.[26]

Towards the end of January 1811 it was more or less settled that Grenville would become First Lord of the Treasury, agreeing for the moment to forego the salary of the Auditorship of the Exchequer while retaining the sinecure for his future security. Grey was to be Foreign Secretary; Holland, Home Secretary; Tierney, Chancellor of the Exchequer; Erskine, Lord Chancellor; and Whitbread, First Lord of the Admiralty. But when these names were submitted to the Prince, he seemed unwilling to commit himself to a change of government at all. So long as there was a possibility of the King's recovery he was reluctant to take the drastic step of dismissing his Ministers. Both Grey and Grenville agreed that if the King's recovery really were to be expected within the near future, then it might be better to leave matters as they stood; and they advised the Prince to go down to Windsor straight away to interview the doctors.

The Prince, though evidently very reluctant to do so and, as Grey noticed, very nervous at the prospect, consented to go, saying that he would leave the next morning. When the time came, however, the Prince could not bring himself to go, excusing himself on grounds of illness. 'I do not believe he will have nerves to take the manly and decisive measures which alone can enable him to conduct the Government with effect,' Grey commented resignedly, 'and I am persuaded, if the present reports of the

King's improved state continue, that he will not dare to make any change in the Administration.'[27]

The Prince's hesitation was understandable, for the King was daily getting better. Indeed, on the very day that the Prince had intended going down to Windsor, his Majesty was able to conduct a relatively coherent interview with Perceval in which he learned of the progress of the Regency Bill, expressed himself pleased with the favourable reports of the Prince's conduct during his illness, and said that he was ready to take up the reins of government again if that was required of him. Perceval replied that the doctors did not think he was quite ready for that yet; but it seemed that one day soon he might well have recovered sufficiently to resume his duties.

The Queen implied as much in a letter to the Prince on 29 January in which she wrote, 'You will be glad to hear, my dearest son, that Mr Perceval has seen the King and communicated the state of public business pending in the two Houses of Parliament. His Majesty gave perfect attention to his report, and was particularly desirous to know how you had conducted yourself, which Mr Perceval answered to have been in the most respectful, most prudent, and affectionate manner.'[28]

The Prince felt convinced that this letter had actually been drafted by Perceval and the Queen had merely copied it out, for what woman, he asked, ever used such a phrase as 'the state of public business pending'? It was an artifice, 'too gross to escape detection'.[29] Grey was also sure that the letter was written 'in concert with Perceval'; it evidently, he told his wife, was 'part of a plan in which I think there can be no doubt that that greatest of all villains, the Duke of Cumberland, has had an active part, to intimidate the Prince by the expectations of the King's immediate recovery, from changing the Administration. So bare-faced a plot, and so much of the same character as the proceedings in 1804, ought to have a directly contrary effect. But *I believe it will be successful*.'[30]

There was certainly no doubt that the Duke of Cumberland, very anxious to keep the Tories in office, was extremely grateful to Sir Henry Halford – who had, he said, '*behaved nobly*' – for impressing upon the Prince the delicate balance of the King's mind and the possibly fatal effects of a sudden change of government.[31] There was certainly no doubt, either, that since the Princess of Wales had quarrelled with the Duke of Cumberland over his advice to her not to 'treat little Billy as fit to be brought up with her daughter', the Prince and his brother were almost inseparable.* As Glenbervie wrote, 'the intimacy between the Prince of Wales and the Duke of Cumberland since the rupture between the Duke and the Princess and more particularly since he went to reside at Carlton House, after the attempt on his life, has been a matter of as general notoriety as the Prince's undisguised hatred of him before that time. The Princess says he now entirely governs the Prince and that it is by his persuasion (others say by Lord and Lady Hertford's) that he has determined to make no changes, except probably giving the presidency of the Council or some other great office to Lord Moira.'[32]

*

Swayed by contrary advice from his family and friends, the Prince appeared to change his mind from day to day. When it was hinted that only timidity and nervousness prevented him from turning to the Whigs, he 'launched out in his eloquent, rhodomontading manner', accusing them of 'treating him worse than his avowed enemies' when they had been in office before, and adding 'that he knew they now complained of his not sending for them, but that he would be damned if he did; they accused him of being timid and nervous, but that by God they and the world should see that he was *un homme de nerf*; that he would not be dictated to by the haughty freaks and caprices of any man'.[33] Yet when Lord Holland called at Carlton House he gained the impression – the Prince was always 'very dextrous in conveying an impression ... without saying anything positive' – that 'he would place his government in the hands of the Whigs, but that he would take his own time and way of doing it, and that he had been nettled at the observations to which his delay had given rise, or in which their impatience had indulged'.[34]

Fearful of the consequences of committing himself to the Whigs, the Prince consulted the King's doctors at Carlton House on 30 January. Dr Robert Willis confessed that he could not 'look with any degree of con-

---

* The Prince had provided a sickroom for his brother at Carlton House while the Duke's apartments at St James's were thrown open to the public who entertained themselves by inspecting the splashes of dried blood on the walls. Dr William Cookson had visited the Duke at Carlton House where he had found him in 'a very nervous state, supposed to be owing to the large quantities of laudanum' which he took. 'He suffers much pain,' Cookson had told Joseph Farington, 'and is much afflicted with spasms. One of the servants at Carlton House [said] that the Prince is much affected by the Duke's illness, "more so," he had added, "than either his mother or his sisters appear to be." ' The servant had gone on to say, 'whenever any of the Prince's family are indisposed he feels for them' (*Farington Diary*, v, 70).

fidence to his Majesty's complete recovery within any limited time', but his hopes of an eventual recovery had 'rather been increased of late' and the King's present progress towards that recovery was upon the whole as favourable as Willis had expected.[35]

Sir Henry Halford went further than this by stating that he thought it 'highly probable' that the King would recover 'within three months';[36] and Dr Heberden, though giving his opinion 'without any considerable degree of confidence', agreed that it was more likely than not that the patient would have recovered within three months.[37]

The doctors' reports left the Prince in a more indecisive state than ever; while the anxiety of his mother and sisters about the King's reactions to a change of Ministers weighed heavily with him. Also, neither Grey nor Grenville was particularly anxious for office in the difficult circumstances in which they would be placed by accepting it. 'What has passed,' Grey told his wife, 'has given me such an insight into the probable state of things under a new Government that I much doubt whether any circumstances could ever induce me to take a share in it.'[38]

So, with the female members of his family opposed to a change, with the Whig leaders now reluctant to take office, with the doctors hinting at his father's recovery within three months, and with the Hertfords and the Duke of Cumberland, as well as the Duke of York, urging him to keep the Tories in office, the Prince felt obliged to disappoint those friends who had so eagerly been looking forward to the enjoyment of power, and had been tiresomely pressing their claims.

On 4 February the Prince wrote to Perceval to inform him of his 'intention not to remove from their stations . . . his Majesty's official servants.

'At the same time,' he continued verbosely, in the sanctimonious tone with which he was inclined to burden such communications as this, 'the Prince owes it to the truth and sincerity of character which he trusts will appear in every action of his life, in whatever situation placed, explicitly to declare that the irresistible impulse of filial duty and affection to his beloved and afflicted father leads him to dread that any act of the Regent might in the smallest degree have the effect of interfering with the progress of his Majesty's recovery. This consideration alone dictates the decision now communicated to Mr Perceval.'[39]

Although Grenville was profoundly relieved by the Prince's decision and 'went down to Dropmore lightsome as a bird',[40] the rank and file of the party were furious. 'Shoals' of angry men went down to Carlton House, Plumer Ward reported, and 'the whole of Pall Mall was crowded with knots of opposition'.[41] Moira and Sheridan both warned the Prince 'that his character would be wholly gone . . . Young Lord Devonshire spoke to him very strongly'; and Lord Thanet told him that his decision 'was the greatest calamity that had happened to the country since the death of Mr Fox'. In his reply the Prince implied to Thanet that he had but to wait a few weeks when the whole situation might well be changed.[42]

At twelve o'clock on the morning of 5 February 1811, the bandsmen of the Grenadier Guards, bearing their regimental colours, marched into the courtyard of Carlton House. They pitched the colours in the centre of the grand entrance and then struck up 'God Save the King' as the first of the Privy Councillors arrived for the ceremony of swearing in the Prince as Regent.

Inside the palace, Yeomen of the Guard, soldiers of the Life Guards and the Prince's liveried servants lined the staircase and the grand hall.

Soon after half past two, preceded by the officers of his Household and accompanied by all the royal Dukes, the Prince – 'grown enormously large' again since recovering from his illness in 1809[43] – made his way through the circular drawing-room into the grand saloon where he sat down at the head of an immensely long table which was 'covered with crimson velvet with massy silver inkstands originally belonging to Queen Anne'. One by one the Privy Councillors, all in full dress, entered the room, the Archbishop of Canterbury, the Lord Chancellor, the Archbishop of York, the Lord Privy Seal and almost a hundred others. As each one came through the doorway in correct order of precedence he bowed to the Prince who acknowledged the courtesy with his accustomed grace. When all were seated in their respective places, the Prince stood up to make his oath of loyalty to the King and to swear that he would 'truly and faithfully execute the office of Regent of the United Kingdom of Great Britain and Ireland . . . and . . . consult and maintain the safety, honour, and dignity of his Majesty, and the welfare of his people . . .'

The oaths and declarations, the signings and countersignings all being completed, the Councillors approached the Regent to kneel before him and to kiss his hand. Although none of them could have failed to notice the marble bust of Charles James Fox which had been removed from the Prince's private apartments to its present ostentatiously prominent position '*at* the head of the room', and although some observers thought that he turned his head away rather abruptly when those whom he did not like knelt before him, it was generally agreed that he maintained throughout the long ceremony 'the most dignified and graceful deportment'.

So, with appropriate stateliness and splendour, while the band continued to play triumphant airs in the courtyard and while Princess Charlotte, riding her horse up and down in the garden, peered inquisitively through the windows, the Regency began.[44]

References

For full bibliographical details see SOURCES.

Abbreviations: RA   —Royal Archives
                      BM   —British Museum
                      PRO   —Public Record Office
                      HMCR—Historical Manuscripts
                                Commission Reports
                Asp/P —Aspinall *(Prince's Correspondence)*
                Asp/K —Aspinall *(King's Correspondence)*

*

1 CHILDHOOD AND EDUCATION (pages 1–13)

1 *Northumberland Diaries,* 47
2 *Ibid.,* 48
3 Huish, i, 11
4 *Northumberland Diaries,* 51
5 Wraxall, v, 355
6 *Northumberland Diaries,* 51
7 Walpole *(Last Journals),* i, 125
8 *Papendiek Journals,* i, 28
9 Quoted by Fulford *(George IV),* 19
10 Huish, i, 14
11 *Northumberland Diaries,* 63
12 *Papendiek Journals,* i, 64
13 *Farington Diary,* vii, 191–2
14 Walpole *(Correspondence),* xxvi, 223
15 *Works of Jeremy Bentham* (1843), x, 30
16 Hurd MSS (Hartlebury Castle)
17 RA Prince of Wales's Copy-books; BM Add. MSS 33132 ff 21–45
18 Markham MSS (York)
19 RA 53076
20 RA 15671
21 RA 41735: Asp/P, i, 9
22 RA41752: Asp/P, i, 18
23 RA 36346: Asp/P, i, 5
24 Walpole *(Last Journals),* ii, 19

25 RA 41774–5: Asp/P, i, 33
26 *Recollections of the Early Years of the Present Century by the Hon Amelia Murray* (1868)
27 Walpole *(Last Journals)*, i, 556
28 *Ibid.*, i, 555
29 *Ibid.*, i, 558
30 Asp/P, i, 27
31 *Burke Correspondence*, iii, 269
32 Kilvert, 120–1; Walpole *(Last Journals)*, i, 555
33 Walpole *(Last Journals)*, i, 558
34 Hurd MSS (Hartlebury Castle)
35 *Ibid.*
36 Kilvert, *Addenda*, 372–3
37 Jesse, i, 129
38 *Papendiek Journals*, i, 132–3, 144
39 RA Y171/81
40 Kilvert, 130
41 RA 41748: Asp/P, i, 16
42 *Hamilton Letters*, 83–4
43 Crawford Muniments (Balcarres)
44 Aspinall *(George III Correspondence)*, v, 22
45 RA: 41774–5: Asp/P, i, 33
46 *Papendiek Journals*, i, 91
47 *Ibid.*, i, 159–60
48 *Ibid.*
49 Grey Papers (Durham), Box 43
50 Wraxall, iv, 321; HMCR Carlisle MSS, 575

2 MRS ROBINSON AND MME VON HARDENBURG (pages 14–28)
1 *Hamilton Letters*, 72
2 *Ibid.*, 73, 75–6
3 *Ibid.*, 75–6, 87
4 *Hawkins Memoirs*, ii, 24
5 MS Memoirs of Mary Robinson (Chequers)
6 *Ibid.*
7 *Hamilton Letters*, 88; RA 23456: Asp/K, iii, 135
8 MS Memoirs of Mary Robinson (Chequers)
9 *Ibid.*
10 *Ibid.*
11 RA 43408: Asp/P, i, 56
12 Capell MSS FH/IX/7 M274, FH/IX/5 M280
13 *Ibid.*, FH/IX/2 M277, FH/IX/14 M287, FH/IX/19 M291
14 *Ibid.*, FH/IX/16 M289, FH/IX/23 M295
15 RA Geo IV Box 7

16 Hurd MSS (Hartlebury Castle)
17 RA 41780–1: Asp/P, i, 36
18 Huish, i, 38
19 Wraxall, v, 383; *Georgiana,* Appendix, ii, 290
20 RA 43373: Asp/P, i, 34
21 RA 38051–2: Asp/P, i, 44–6
22 RA 43374: Asp/P, i, 34
23 RA 43475, 43486: Asp/P, i, 76, 79
24 RA 43469–71: Asp/P, i, 75
25 *Ibid.*
26 *Ibid.*
27 RA 43402: Asp/P, i, 54
28 RA 41789–90: Asp/P, i, 60
29 *Ibid.*
30 *Ibid.*
31 Walpole *(Last Journals),* iii, 361
32 Huish, i, 43
33 RA 43404: Asp/P, i, 54
34 *Ibid.*; HMCR, Carlisle MSS 473; Walpole *(Last Journals),* ii, 350
35 *Granville Leveson Gower Correspondence,* ii, 250; Holland *(Journal),* i, 178; Raikes, iii, 7
36 RA 43440–5: Asp/P, i, 65
37 *Ibid.*
38 *Ibid.*
39 *Ibid.*
40 *Ibid.*
41 *Ibid.*
42 *Ibid.*
43 *Ibid.*
44 RA 43458–9: Asp/P, i, 73

3 CARLTON HOUSE AND BROOKS'S (pages 29–43)
 1 RA 41792: Asp/P, i, 86
 2 RA 41794: Asp/P, i, 86
 3 *Fox Correspondence,* ii, 28
 4 Walpole *(Last Journals),* i, 12
 5 Reid, 42
 6 *Ibid.,* 314; Fitzgerald, i, 82
 7 Walpole *(Last Journals),* ii, 496
 8 RA 16366: Asp/P, i, 113
 9 RA 16362: Asp/P, i, 117
10 RA 16360: Asp/P, i, 116
11 BM Add. MSS 38716, 69; 47567, quoted by Reid, 172
12 Walpole *(Last Journals),* ii, 525

13 BB Add. MSS 38716, 71, quoted by Reid, 172
14 BM Add. MSS 47579, quoted by Reid, 173
15 Walpole *(Last Journals)*, ii, 529
16 RA 16391-2: Asp/P, i, 112
17 Colvin, 291
18 *London Survey,* vol. xx, *Trafalgar Square,* ch. viii; Pevsner, 83
19 Wraxall, v, 364
20 RA 25094-6
21 RA 25186
22 *Plumer Ward,* i, 399
23 *Ibid.,* i, 400
24 *Farington Diary,* vi, 244
25 Stroud, 21-6; Millar *(Tudor, Stuart and Early Georgian Pictures)* 31, 96, 103
26 *Farington Diary,* i, 16
27 *George IV and the Arts of France* (Queens Gallery, Buckingham Palace, 1966)
28 *Walpole Correspondence,* xxxiii, 499-500
29 Reid, 178
30 Moore *(Sheridan),* i, 403
31 Wraxall, iii, 350
32 Reid, 204
33 Wraxall, iii, 351
34 HMCR, Rutland MSS, 14th Report, 458
35 RA 54367, 54370; *Paget Papers,* i, 232
36 *Paget Papers,* i, 150
37 *Croker Papers,* ii, 9
38 Raikes, i, 91
39 Macfarlane, 102
40 Rogers *(Table Talk),* 37
41 Brougham *(Life),* ii, 135
42 HMCR, Charlemont MSS, ii, 141
43 *Ibid.,* ii, 98
44 Wraxall, v, 363-4
45 Oliver, 108
46 Cecil, 29-30
47 *Western Letters,* quoted by Marshall, 27
48 Doran, *Annals of the English Stage,* quoted by Richardson *(George IV),* 24
49 Rogers *(Table-Talk),* 36
50 RA 53081; *Walpole Correspondence,* xxxiii, 416, 517
51 D'Arblay *(Memoirs of Dr Burney),* 124
52 *D'Arblay Diary,* iii, 357-8
53 Doran, *Annals of the English Stage,* quoted by Richardson *(George IV),* 24
54 Landon, 124
55 RA 42343: Asp/P, iv, 282
56 RA 43483: Asp/P, i, 78
57 RA 43499: Asp/P, i, 82

58 *Farington Diary*, i, 6; Richardson *(George IV)*, 36; Bell, *Thomas Gainsborough*, 122–3
59 RA 26792, 26829; Geo. IV, Box 7
60 *Sussex Weekly Advertiser*, 13 July 1786, quoted by Musgrave *(Brighton)*, 87
61 RA 43469–71: Asp/P, i, 75
62 Wraxall, v, 25
63 RA 43420–3: Asp/P, i, 62
64 Malmesbury, ii, 128
65 Wraxall, v, 363
66 *Farington Diary*, i, 156
67 *Glenbervie Journals*, 57

4 THE SECRET MARRIAGE (pages 44–59)

1 RA 43659–60: Asp/P, i, 148
2 *Ibid.*
3 *Ibid.*
4 Malmesbury, ii, 124–5
5 RA 41812–3: Asp/P, i, 155
6 RA 16460–1: Asp/P, i, 156–7
7 RA 25050–75
8 RA 16460–1: Asp/P, i, 156–7
9 RA 31885: Asp/P, i, 159
10 RA 16467: Asp/P, i, 160
11 RA 16461, 31888: Asp/P, i, 155, 161
12 RA 41821: Asp/P, i, 162
13 RA 41822–3, 16277: Asp/P, i, 167
14 RA 31858: Asp/P, i, 155; RA 16379
15 RA 43660: Asp/P, i, 148
16 Crawford Muniments (Balcarres)
17 *Frampton Journal*, 14
18 *Noels and Milbankes*, 233
19 *Statutes at Large*, xxix, Pt. 2, 11–12
20 RA 43556: Asp/P, i, 101
21 Langdale, 134
22 *Ibid.*
23 *Ibid.*, 219
24 RA Fitzherbert Papers, 50210
25 RA 54371, 54372, 54374–5
26 Holland *(Memoirs)*, ii, 126
27 RA 50237–58: Asp/P, i, 189–201
28 RA Fitzherbert Papers, 50205–9: Asp/P, iv, 48
29 RA 50237–58: Asp/P, i, 189–201
30 Langdale, 121; Wilkins, i, 54
31 Holland *(Memoirs)*, ii, 126
32 *Noels and Milbankes*, 255

33 *Ibid.* 272
34 Crawford Muniments (Balcarres)
35 *Ibid.*
36 *Fox Correspondence*, ii, 278–85; Derry *(Fox)*, 220
37 Crawford Muniments (Balcarres)
38 *Fox Correspondence*, ii, 278–85
39 The Rev. S. Johnes Knight to Lady Shelley, 28 September 1830, quoted by Wilkins, i, 90–91
40 *Ibid.*
41 Langdale, 142
42 *Georgiana*, 120
43 Holland Rose, 397-8
44 Walpole *(Correspondence)*, xxix, 37
45 Denbigh MSS (Pailton House)
46 *Elliot Letters*, ii, 14
47 HMCR, Rutland MSS, 14th Report, 432
48 *Ibid.*
49 HMCR, Rutland MSS, 14th Report, 437
50 *Jerningham Letters*, i, 33–4
51 *Bury Diary*, ii, 167
52 Wraxall, v, 27
53 Huish, i, 148
54 HMCR, Rutland MSS, 14th Report, 439
55 RA 41850: Asp/P, i, 225
56 RA 41851–2: Asp/P, i, 225; RA 41854
57 RA 31875: Asp/P, i, 231
58 RA 41860: Asp/P, i, 232
59 RA 16387: Asp/P, i, 232
60 Malmesbury, ii, 130
61 *Ibid.*
62 RA 38116: Asp/P, i, 233
63 RA 38118: Asp/P, i, 236
64 RA 43815: Asp/P, i, 262
65 RA 54476: Asp/P, i, 254
66 RA 44714: Asp/P, i, 264
67 RA 38140–3: Asp/P, i, 247
68 RA 38145–6: Asp/P, i, 250
69 RA 38139, 41865–6: Asp/P, i, 247, 251
70 *Morning Post,* 13 July 1786

5 BRIGHTON AND WESTMINSTER (pages 60–70)

1 *Tour through Great Britain* (1724), quoted by Erredge, iv, 218
2 Musgrave *(Brighton)*, 46, 47, 49
3 *Ibid.*, 86

4 RA 43375: Asp/P, i, 43
5 Huish, i, 80
6 Musgrave *(Brighton)*, 88
7 Wraxall, v, 307
8 HMCR, Rutland MSS, 14th Report, 521
9 Horne Tooke *(Letter to a Friend)*
10 *Parliamentary History*, xxvi, 1009
11 *Ibid.*, 1019
12 *Ibid.*, 1048–56
13 Wilkins, i, 184
14 Langdale, 163
15 *Croker Papers*, i, 48
16 *Parliamentary History*, xxvi, 1067–70
17 Wilkins, i, 179
18 BM Add. MSS 47560, f 27, quoted by Asp/P, i, 291; Reid, 229; Derry *(Fox)*, 223
19 Langdale, 170
20 *Croker Papers*, i, 214
21 Crawford Muniments (Balcarres)
22 Langdale, 172
23 *Fox Correspondence*, ii, 288
24 Holland *(Memoirs)*, i, 205; Langdale, 29
25 *Parliamentary History*, xxvi, 1074–80
26 HMCR, Rutland MSS, iii, 387
27 Wraxall, v, 362
28 *Portarlington Papers*, 6 April 1787
29 HMCR, Rutland MSS, iii, 439
30 Wilkins, i, 215; Fitzgerald, i, 103
31 HMCR, Charlemont MSS, ii, 53
32 HMCR, Ailesbury Papers, Diary of Thomas, Earl of Ailesbury, 314
33 RA 38200: Asp/P, i, 313

6 THE KING'S ILLNESS (pages 71–81)
1 Musgrave *(Royal Pavilion)*, 1–8
2 *Ibid.;* Musgrave *(Brighton)*, 95
3 *Morning Herald*, 24 July 1787
4 *Brighton in the old Time, by an Inhabitant Thereof*
5 RA Geo. IV, Box 7: Huish, i, 173
6 Fitzgerald, i, 188
7 RA Geo. IV, Box 7
8 *Frampton Journal*, 14–15
9 RA 43533, 43536, 43554, 43571: Asp/P, i, 91, 100, 106
10 *D'Arblay Diary*, ii, 398
11 *Cornwallis Correspondence*, i, 360
12 *Ibid.*, i, 374–5

13 Baker MSS, quoted by Macalpine and Hunter, 14
14 *Harcourt Papers,* iv, 12
15 Macalpine and Hunter, 14–15
16 *Harcourt Papers,* iv, 12
17 *Fox Correspondence,* ii, 333
18 Baker MSS, quoted by Macalpine and Hunter, 16–17
19 *Elliot Letters, i,* 225
20 *Morning Post,* 31 October 1788
21 *Gentleman's Magazine,* vol. lviii, pt. ii, 928
22 *D'Arblay Diary,* iv, 272–4
23 *Ibid.,* iv, 275
24 *Ibid.,* iv, 277
25 Baker MSS, quoted by Macalpine and Hunter, 19
26 Chenevix Trench, 18
27 Galt, ii, 73
28 Baker MSS, quoted by Macalpine and Hunter, 20
29 Moore *(Sheridan),* ii, 26
30 RA 43904 Asp/P, i, 360; Fulford *(George IV),* 58
31 RA 48905: Asp/P, i, 363; RA 43897
32 *D'Arblay Diary,* iv, 287
33 Baker MSS, quoted by Macalpine and Hunter, 25
34 *Harcourt Papers,* iv, 21–2
35 *D'Arblay Diary,* iv, 289
36 *Ibid.,* iv, 299–300
37 *Fulke Greville Diaries,* 85–90; *Some Particulars of the Royal Indisposition of 1788–89* (1804); Macalpine and Hunter, 35–42
38 BM Add. MSS 34428, ff. 308–9, Auckland Papers, Lord Sheffield to William Eden, quoted by Derry *(Regency Crisis),* 203
39 *Harcourt Papers,* iv, 25
40 Egerton MSS, 2232, f.71, quoted by Asp/P, i, 406
41 *Fulke Greville Diaries,* 101
42 *Harcourt Papers,* iv, 28
43 RA Add. 2 f.2, quoted by Asp/P, i, 367
44 *Buckingham Memoirs, i,* 441

7 THE REGENCY CRISIS (pages 82–89)

1 *Elliot Letters, i,* 239
2 Moore *(Sheridan),* ii, 22
3 HMCR (1892) 13th Report, Appendix, Part 3, vol. i, 366, quoted by Macalpine and Hunter, 36
4 HMCR (1871) 7th Report, 14, quoted by Macalpine and Hunter, 36; *Buckingham Memoirs,* ii, 7, 19
5 Macalpine and Hunter, 42
6 *D'Arblay Diary,* iv, 317

7 *Buckingham Memoirs*, ii, 21
8 RA 38311: Asp/p, i, 397–402
9 *D'Arblay Diary*, iv, 337
10 *Buckingham Memoirs*, ii, 445
11 *Sheridan Journal*, 131–2
12 *Buckingham Memoirs*, ii, 12
13 *Elliot Letters*, i, 239–40
14 RA 38232
15 Fitzgerald, i, 134
16 RA 41922: Asp/P, i, 378
17 RA 38264: Asp/P, i, 380
18 RA 38273: Asp/P, i, 387
19 *Fulke Greville Memoirs*, 111
20 *Ibid.*, 115
21 Macalpine and Hunter, 51–5
22 RA 38305–11; Macalpine and Hunter, 54–5; *Buckingham Memoirs*, ii, 31
23 *Auckland Correspondence*, ii, 256
24 Macalpine and Hunter, 61–2
25 Malmesbury, iv, 317–18
26 *Fulke Greville Memoirs*, 119
27 *Ibid.*, 186
28 Macalpine and Hunter, 54, 78, 79
29 *Ibid.*, 76
30 *D'Arblay Diary*, iv, 302; *Fulke Greville Memoirs*, 123; Macalpine and Hunter, 54–77
31 *D'Arblay Diary*, iv, 304
32 *Papendiek Journals*, ii, 14–16
33 *Buckingham Memoirs*, i, 444
34 *Fulke Greville Memoirs*, 139–40, 161; *Rose Diaries*, i, 94; Macalpine and Hunter, 70, 76, 79
35 *Elliot Letters*, i, 245; *Auckland Correspondence*, ii, 280
36 *Fulke Greville Memoirs*, 149
37 *Some Particulars of the Royal Indisposition*, 69
38 Willis MSS, quoted by Macalpine and Hunter, 67
39 *Ibid.*
40 *Buckingham Memoirs*, i, 449
41 Ehrman, 123

8 THE KING'S RECOVERY (pages 90–103)

1 Wraxall, v, 259
2 William Massey, *History of England under George III*, ii, 388
3 *Buckingham Memoirs*, ii, 37
4 *Devonshire Diary*, ii, 402; quoted by Reid, 233
5 HMCR, *Dropmore Papers*, i, 362–3; Buckingham to Grenville, 11 November 1788; Derry *(Regency Crisis)*, 48

6 *Buckingham Memoirs*, ii, 2–3
7 Stanhope *(Pitt)*, i, 396–7
8 *Auckland Correspondence*, ii, 267
9 Quoted in Asp/P, i, 357
10 *Buckingham Memoirs*, ii, 32
11 Moore *(Sheridan)*, i, 384
12 *Devonshire Diary*, ii, 405; *Buckingham Memoirs*, i, 451; Derry *(Regency Crisis)*, 53–8
13 *The Crisis*, 3
14 *Letters to a Prince from a Man of Kent*, 45
15 Philip Withers, *Alfred . . . with Remarks on the Regency, proving on principles of Law and Common Sense that a certain Illustrious Person is not Eligible to that Important Trust;* Derry *(Regency Crisis)*, 34–6
16 *Ibid.*
17 *Letters to a Prince from a Man of Kent*, 51; *A Solemn Appeal to the Citizens of Great Britain and Ireland*, 26–7; Derry *(Regency Crisis)*, 36
18 *The Times*, 30 January, 31 January, 4 February 1789, quoted by Aspinall, *Politics and the Press*, 270–4
19 Aspinall, *Politics and the Press*, 274–9
20 *Important Facts and Opinions relative to the King: Faithfully Collected from the Examination of the Royal Physicians*
21 *The Prospect before Us*, quoted by Derry *(Regency Crisis)*, 34
22 Broadlands MSS, quoted in Asp/P, i, 391; *Devonshire Diary*, ii, 407; Derry *(Regency Crisis)*, 55
23 Macalpine and Hunter, 54–5
24 *Ibid.*, 57
25 Stockdale, 222
26 *Parliamentary History of England*, xxvii, 707
27 Moore *(Sheridan)*, ii, 38
28 *Parliamentary History of England*, xxvii, 709–10
29 Reid, 240
30 BM Add. MSS 47570, quoted by Derry *(Regency Crisis)*, 89
31 *Parliamentary History of England*, xxvii, 782–1293; Derry *(Regency Crisis)*, 154
32 *Ibid.*
33 HMCR, Carlisle MSS, 660
34 *Cornwallis Correspondence*, i, 406
35 *Buckingham Memoirs*, ii, 65; *Harcourt Papers*, iv, 102
36 Asp/P, i, 357
37 RA 41709: Asp/P, i, 423
38 Chatsworth MSS, quoted by Asp/P, i, 423
39 RA 38341–4: Asp/P, i, 436
40 Campbell, v, 596
41 RA Add. 9/60: Asp/P, i, 405
42 Willis MSS, quoted by Macalpine and Hunter, 82
43 *Elliot Letters*, i, 274
44 RA 38451: Asp/P, i, 491

45 *Buckingham Memoirs,* ii, 120
46 Macalpine and Hunter, 85; *Buckingham Memoirs,* ii, 121–5
47 *Elliot Letters,* i, 275
48 *Fulke Greville Memoirs,* 246
49 *Buckingham Memoirs,* ii, 125
50 *Elliot Letters,* i, 279
51 Derry *(Regency Crisis),* 191
52 BM Add. MSS 47560, f.33, quoted by Derry *(Regency Crisis),* 191
53 Greenwood, ii, 129; *Elliot Letters,* i, 279; Fitzgerald, i, 190
54 RA 38470–2: Asp/P, ii, 8
55 *Elliot Letters,* i, 320–1
56 *Elliot Letters,* i, 322; *Burke Correspondence,* iii, 472
57 RA 38475: Asp/P, ii, 12
58 *Annual Register, 1789,* 208; *Elliot Letters,* i, 314–18
59 Huish, i, 237
60 BM Add. MSS 47570, f.180, quoted, in Asp/P, ii, 14; Derry *(Regency Crisis),* 191
61 *Elliot Letters,* i, 323–4
62 *Ibid.,* i, 305
63 *Frampton Journal,* 21
64 *Granville Leveson Gower Correspondence,* i, 14; Ehrman, 665–6
65 HMCR, Kenyon MSS, quoted by Derry, 190–1
66 *Elliot Letters,* i, 325
67 Cornwallis MSS, quoted in Asp/P, ii, 7
68 *The Times,* 24 April 1789; Hutton Bland-Burgess Papers, quoted by Ehrman, 665
69 *Frampton Journal,* 22
70 *Elliot Letters,* i, 304–5; *Memoirs of William Pitt* (1821); ii, 488–9; Macalpine and Hunter, 93

9 THE BOTTLE AND THE TURF (pages 104–112)

1 *The Tour to Yorkshire;* HMCR, Carlisle MSS, 670
2 RA 38504–5: Asp/P, ii, 34
3 *The Times,* quoted in Asp/P, ii, 31
4 Asp/P, ii, 3
5 *The Times,* quoted in Asp/P, ii, 2–3
6 *Granville Leveson Gower Correspondence,* i, 16
7 *Ibid.,* i, 468
8 Raikes, iv, 50
9 Angelo, i, 117; Fitzgerald, i, 57–9
10 *The Jockey Club, or, a Sketch of the Manners of the Age* [by Charles Pigott]; Asp/P, ii, 286–7
11 RA 41989–95: Asp/P, ii, 284
12 Fitzgerald, i, 114, 250–4; Seth Smith *(Bred to the Purple),* 63–74; Mortimer *(Jockey Club),* 40–46

13 BM Add. MSS 47570, ff.185, 187, quoted in Asp/P, ii, 215
14 Mortimer, 44; Chiffney, 118–24
15 BM Add. MSS 47570, f.187, quoted in Asp/P, ii, 215
16 RA 43928: Asp/P, ii, 69
17 *Elliot Letters,* i, 327
18 *The Times,* 21 February 1789
19 HMCR, *Dropmore Papers,* ii, 34; Asp/P, ii, 68; *History of the Times,* i, 52–60
20 Harrowby Papers (Sandon Hall) G. L. Newnham to Harrowby 26 July 1789
21 *Georgiana,* 167, 169
22 Chatsworth MSS, quoted in Asp/P, ii, 63
23 RA 43932–3: Asp/P, ii, 84
24 *St James's Chronicle,* 4–7 June 1791
25 RA 36386: Asp/P, ii, 177
26 *The Times,* 13 August 1791

10 THE PRINCE'S BROTHERS (pages 113–122)

1 *Parliamentary History of England,* xxviii, 892
2 *The Times,* 1 June and 2 June 1792, quoted in Asp/P, ii, 250
3 Seymour of Ragley MSS, CR/114/A/349
4 RA 44048–51: Asp/P, ii, 348
5 *Elliot Letters,* i, 372
6 RA 47057: Asp/P, ii, 236
7 Aspinall *(George III Correspondence),* ii. 120; RA 47100, 47102, 47110–1: Asp/P ii, 413, 415, 418
8 RA 45776–7: Asp/P, ii, 40
9 Asp/P, ii, 60
10 *Ibid.,* ii, 61
11 Gillen, 89–92
12 RA 45900–2: Asp/P, ii, 375
13 RA 44703–4: Asp/P, i, 220
14 RA 44820–1: Asp/P, i, 336
15 RA 44867: Asp/P, ii, 73
16 *Parliamentary Register,* xxxvi, 161
17 RA 44048–51: Asp/P, ii, 348
18 RA 43981–2: Asp/P, ii, 176
19 RA 47984–4: Asp/P, ii, 318
20 Hurd MSS (Hartlebury Castle)
21 RA 48063: Asp/P, ii, 471
22 RA 42008: Asp/P, ii, 334
23 RA 38784: Asp/P, ii, 336
24 RA 42375–6
25 RA 38784: Asp/P, ii, 336
26 RA 36409–10: Asp/P, ii, 370
27 Musgrave *(Brighton),* 108

References

11 FRESH DEBTS AND NEW MISTRESSES (pages 123-132)

1 Malmesbury, ii, 439
2 RA 43963-4: Asp/P, ii, 167
3 RA 38608-9; Asp/P, ii, 182
4 Birkenhead, 30
5 RA 43089
6 *Public Advertiser*, 23 January 1791
7 *Frampton Journal*, 34
8 *Noels and Milbankes*, 406
9 *Elliot Letters*, ii, 34
10 *The Royal Criterion; or A Narrative of the Transactions relative to the Loans made in London by the Prince of Wales, Duke of York, Duke of Clarence and their advisers* (1814), 19-27
11 RA 38555-6: Asp/P, ii, 95
12 RA Geo. IV, Box 7
13 RA 42011-12: Asp/P, ii, 320
14 RA 31620
15 RA 43953-60: Asp/P, ii, 160
16 RA 43983-4: Asp/P, ii, 178
17 RA 38624-7: Asp/P, ii, 204
18 RA 31587-91, 31610-34
19 RA Geo IV, Box 7
20 BM Add. MSS 47570, quoted by Reid, 293
21 BM Add. MSS 33629, f.2-4. Diary of Thomas Pelham, 2nd Earl of Chichester, quoted in Asp/P, ii, 303
22 RA 7040-1: Asp/K, i, 620
23 Crawford Muniments (Balcarres)
24 Raikes, ii, 29
25 Wilkins, i, 285; Malmesbury, ii, 449
26 Malmesbury, ii, 451
27 RA 38718-19, 44032; Asp/P, ii, 276, ii, 266
28 Malmesbury, ii, 452
29 *Jerningham Letters*, i, 49
30 Huish, i, 262-3
31 *Farington Diary*, i, 280-1
32 Wraxall, v, 357-8
33 *Harcourt Papers*, v, 38
34 Malmesbury, ii, 452
35 Wraxall, v, 36
36 *Frampton Journal*, 84
37 *Granville Leveson Gower Correspondence*, i, 93
38 *Ibid.*
39 *Harcourt Papers*, v, 69
40 RA 44079: Asp/P, ii, 454
41 Stanhope, ii, Appendix, xx

References

12 PRINCESS CAROLINE (pages 133–141)

1 Malmesbury, iii, 155
2 *Paget Papers*, i, 46
3 Asp/P, ii, 407
4 *Frampton Journal*, 85–6
5 Holland *(Memoirs)*, ii, 145–6
6 RA 47130–1: Asp/P, ii, 465
7 State Archives, Göttingen (Translation T. S. Blakeney), quoted in Asp/P, iii, 9
8 Aspinall *(George III Correspondence)*, iii, 42
9 Holland *(Memoirs)*, ii, 144
10 *Farington Diary*, i, 275; Malmesbury, iii, 152–3
11 Malmesbury, iii, 159, 166, 192, 197
12 *Ibid.*, iii, 164–5
13 *Ibid.*, iii, 169–70, 189
14 *Ibid.*, iii, 165, 179, 200
15 *Ibid.*, iii, 168
16 *Ibid.*, iii, 189
17 *Ibid.*; Greenwood, ii, 247
18 Malmesbury, iii, 196
19 RA Geo.IV, Box 7 and Box 8
20 RA 54409: Asp/P, ii, 519
21 Asp/P, ii, 511
22 Asp/P, ii, 517
23 Holland House MSS, quoted in Asp/P, iii, 3
24 Holland *(Memoirs)*, ii, 146–7
25 Malmesbury, iii, 198
26 *Ibid.*
27 *Ibid.*, iii, 201, 204, 207–8, 211–12, 215

13 THE SECOND WIFE (pages 142–154)

1 *Harcourt Papers*, iv, 2
2 *Ibid.*
3 Malmesbury, iii, 217–18; *Annual Register, 1795*, 14
4 *Ibid.*
5 *Ibid.*
6 *Bury Journal*, i, 19
7 RA Geo. IV, Box 8 (Envelope 2); Fitzgerald, i, 291
8 RA Geo. IV, Box 8 (Envelope 1)
9 *Walpole Correspondence*, xii, 139; *Annual Register, 1795*, 15
10 *Stanhope Memoirs*, ii, 311–12
11 Holland *(Memoirs)*, ii, 251
12 RA 50213: Asp/P, ii, 518
13 Wilkins, i, 328
14 Seymour of Ragley MSS, George Seymour's annotations to Langdale's *Memoirs*

15 RA Geo. IV, Box 8 (4 June 1794)
16 Finch MSS e.6 (Bodleian)
17 *Jerningham Letters,* i, 75; *The Times,* 9 April 1795
18 Holland (Memoirs), ii, 148
19 RA Queen Victoria's Journal. Entry for 13 November 1838
20 *Leeds Memoranda,* ii, 39
21 *Jerningham Letters,* i, 75
22 Wraxall, v, 391
23 *Leeds Memoranda,* ii, 41
24 *Jerningham Letters,* i, 75–7
25 Malmesbury, iii, 220
26 *Leeds Memoranda,* ii, 42
27 *Bury Journal,* i, 38–9; Cramford Muniments (Balcarres), Lindsay Memoirs, vi, 52–3
28 Aylesford MSS. Mrs Selina Wilson to Mrs Stapleton, 16 April 1795, quoted in Asp/P, iii, 55
29 RA Add. 11/29: Asp/P, iii, 64
30 RA Add. 11/32: Asp/P, iii, 72
31 RA 42079–81, 42085: Asp/P, iii, 68–70
32 RA Add. 11/32: Asp/P, iii, 72
33 RA 36436–7: Asp/P, iii, 70
34 RA Add. 11/41: Asp/P, iii, 125
35 *Ibid.*
36 *Abbot Diary,* ii, 19, 25
37 RA 49176: Asp/P, iii, 126
38 Aspinall *(George III Correspondence),* ii, 451
39 Malmesbury, iii, 220
40 *Granville Leveson Gower Correspondence,* i, 359
41 *Bury Journal,* i, 23, 160
42 *Abbot Diary,* ii, 89
43 Adeane, *The Girlhood of Maria Josepha Holroyd,* quoted by Richardson *(George IV),* 62
44 Vehse, *Höfed. Hauses Braunschweig,* quoted by Greenwood, ii, 260
45 *Glenbervie Journals,* ii, 13–14
46 Asp/P, iii, 168
47 RA 39169–74: Asp/P, iii, 168
48 Asp/P, iii, 171–2
49 RA 39175–8: Asp/P, iii, 172
50 Asp/P, iii, 174–5
51 RA 39179–80: Asp/P, iii, 176
52 RA Geo. IV, Box 8 (30 April 1796)
53 RA 42113–4: Asp/P, iii, 181
54 RA Add. 11/49: Asp/P, iii, 183
55 RA 42118–22: Asp/P, iii, 190
56 RA 39199–208: Asp/P, iii, 194

14 THE BROKEN MARRIAGE (pages 155-167)

1 *The Times*, 24 May 1796
2 *Morning Chronicle*, 30 May 1796
3 *True Briton*, 2 June 1796
4 *The Times*, 1 June 1796
5 RA 42118: Asp/P, iii, 190
6 RA Add. 11/51: Asp/P, iii, 200
7 RA 39014-15: Asp/P, iii, 16
8 RA 39201: Asp/P, iii, 195
9 Walpole *(Correspondence)*, xi, 149-50
10 RA 42130-3, 39210-15, 49324-5: Asp/P, iii, 197, 204, 55
11 RA 42130-3, 39210-15: Asp/P, iii, 197, 204
12 RA 42168-74: Asp/P, iii, 230
13 RA Geo. IV, Box 8: Asp/P, iii, 242
14 *Ibid.*
15 *Granville Leveson Gower Correspondence*, i, 122-3
16 RA Geo. IV, Box 13 (29 June 1796)
17 RA 422005-5: Asp/P, iii, 273-6
18 RA 42207-8: Asp/P, iii, 281-2
19 RA Geo. IV, Box 8: Asp/P, iii, 282
20 *Ibid:* Asp/P, iii, 283
21 *Ibid:* Asp/P, iii, 284
22 *Ibid.* BM 43727, ff.16-25
23 RA Queen Victoria's journal. Entries for 2 September 1838, 13 November 1838
24 Holland *(Memoirs)*, ii, 148; Holland *(Journal)*, i, 190
25 *Elliot Letters* iii, 14
26 Minto MSS, quoted in Asp/P, iii, 123
27 Malmesbury, iii, 219
28 RA 42156-7: Asp/P, iii, 222
29 *Glenbervie Journals*, i, 71
30 RA 42220-2: Asp/P, iii, 374
31 Asp/P, iii, 375
32 RA 16716: Asp/P, iii, 377
33 RA 42224-6: Asp/P, iii, 378
34 RA 42234-8: Asp/P, iii, 390
35 Aspinall *(George III Correspondence)* ii, 472
36 RA 39191-2: Asp/P, iii, 120
37 RA 42082-5, 39129-30 39182-3: Asp/P, iii, 70, 153, 180
38 BM Add. MSS 47560, ff. 67-8, quoted in Asp/P, iv, 463
39 RA 39041-3, 36429-30: Asp/P, iii, 33, 35
40 RA 39044-52: Asp/P, iii, 36
41 RA 39056-60: Asp/P, iii, 40
42 RA 39061-4, 39069-72: Asp/P, iii, 43-45
43 RA 39076-7: Aspinall *(George III Correspondence)*, ii, 328
44 *Farington Diary*, 29 May 1795

45 RA 42086-7, 36441-2: Asp/P, iii, 77, 78
46 RA 39352-4: Asp/P, iii, 328
47 RA 44136, 39436, 39437, 44137, 44138-9: Asp/P, iii, 404, 406, 407
48 Alnwick MSS, quoted in Asp/P, iii, 407
49 RA 39493-4: Asp/P, iii, 431
50 RA 42253-8: Asp/P, iii, 469
51 RA 39509-10: Asp/P, iii, 438
52 RA 39491

15 THE RETURN OF MRS FITZHERBERT (pages 168-183)
1 RA 50214-24: Asp/P, iii, 132
2 *The Times*, 2 July 1799
3 *Ibid.*, 21 January 1780; RA Geo. IV, Box 7
4 Finch MSS e.6 (Bodleian)
5 *Farington Diary*, ii, 120-1
6 RA 47175: Asp/P, iii, 185
7 Rutland MSS, quoted in Asp/P, iv, 12-13; Leslie *(Fitzherbert)*, i, 784
8 Rutland MSS, quoted in Asp/P, iv, 16
9 Holland *(Journal)*. ii, 49; Asp/P, iv, 106
10 RA 50205-9: Asp/P, iv, 48
11 *Ibid.*
12 RA Add. 10/21, 12/20, 10/23: Asp/P, iii, 501, 478, iv, 67
13 RA 47175: Asp/P, iii, 125
14 RA 45966: Asp/P, iv, 57
15 Wilkins, ii, 8
16 *The Times*, 1 March 1800
17 *The Times*, 4 July 1800; *Glenbervie Journals*, ii, 121
18 Wilkins, ii, 11
19 *Jerningham Letters*, ii, 124
20 *Ibid.*, ii, 132
21 Wilkins, ii, 19
22 Crawford Muniments (Balcarres)
23 RA 39714: Asp/P, iv, 189
24 RA 29872; Wilkins, ii, 23
25 Wilkins, ii, 20
26 Minto MSS, quoted in Asp/P, iv, 91
27 RA Geo. IV, Box 7
28 *Ibid.*
29 *A Letter addressed to Mrs Fitzherbert in answer to a complaint that her feelings have been hurt by the mention of her name in the* REVIEW OF THE CONDUCT OF THE PRINCE OF WALES
30 RA 25276, 25331-3
31 RA Geo. IV, Box 7; Wardrobe Accounts, 29210-29643
32 *Ibid.*

33 RA 29105
34 RA Geo. IV, Box 7
35 RA 32930, 32934
36 RA Geo, IV, Box 7; Wardrobe Accounts, 29210–29643
37 Aspinall *(George III Correspondence)* ii, 486; RA 44908: Asp/P, iii, 500
38 *Ibid.*
39 RA 45569
40 RA 44164–5: Asp/P, iv, 80
41 RA 46032–3
42 RA 46121–6: Asp/P, iv, 416–21
43 RA 46504–5: Asp/P, viii, 70
44 RA 46068–9: Asp/P, iv, 365
45 RA 42290–1: Asp/P, iv, 73
46 RA 48222–32
47 RA 48206–7, 48219–21
48 RA 48236–9: Asp/P, iv, 275–8
49 Grey Papers (Durham), Box 43
50 RA 48253–7: Asp/P, iv, 498–500
51 RA 46319–20: Asp/P, vi, 64
52 RA 42355–8: Asp/P, iv, 293–6
53 Hurd MSS (Hartlebury Castle)
54 RA 42635–8: Asp/K, i, 19
55 Asp/P, iv, 394
56 RA 39968–9; Asp/P, iv, 425
57 RA 40007: Asp/P, iv, 427–8
58 RA 44198–9: Asp/P, iv, 433–4
59 Stuart *(Foster)*, 112
60 *Granville Leveson Gower Correspondence* i, 430, ii, 292
61 RA 40048: Asp/P, iv, 467–8
62 RA 40052–3, 40054–7: Asp/P, iv, 469, 470–1
63 *Glenbervie Journals* i, 367–8; Fitzgerald, i, 360
64 RA 40064: Asp/P, iv, 479
65 RA 40065–6: Asp/P, iv, 481–2
66 RA 44200: Asp/P, iv, 493

16 THE KING'S RELAPSE (pages 184–200)

1 RA 39319–23, 39329–30: Asp/P, iii, 313, 319
2 Asp/P, iii, 187; Reid, 337
3 Hurd MSS (Hartlebury Castle)
4 Pellew, i, 287
5 Sidmouth MSS, quoted by Ziegler *(Addington)*, 93
6 Sidmouth MSS, quoted by Ziegler *(Addington)*, 94
7 Jesse, iii, 245
8 Macalpine and Hunter, iii, 4

9 Malmesbury, iv, 41
10 *Ibid.*, iv, 6, 20, 31
11 Asp/P, iv, 183
12 RA 38479
13 Macalpine and Hunter, 248
14 Willis MSS, quoted by Macalpine and Hunter, 249
15 Hurd MSS (Hartlebury Castle)
16 Malmesbury, iv, 33; Rose, i, 332–3
17 Jesse, iii, 265; *Stanhope Memoirs*, iii, 311; Macalpine and Hunter, 120
18 Hurd MSS (Hartlebury Castle)
19 HMCR Carlisle MSS, 733–4; *Francis Letters*, ii, 475
20 Macalpine and Hunter, 125
21 *Ibid.*, 126
22 *Ibid.*, 127
23 RA 39738–9: Asp/P, iv, 213
24 Macalpine and Hunter, 125–9
25 Macalpine and Hunter, 129
26 *Granville Leveson Gower Correspondence*, i, 454
27 Asp/P, iv, 249
28 Malmesbury, iv, 224
29 Macalpine and Hunter, 132
30 Malmesbury, iv, 318–20
31 RA 40106–9: Asp/P, iv, 522
32 Pitt to Melville, 29 March 1804, quoted by Ziegler *(Addington)*, 209
33 *Rose Diaries*, ii, 124
34 Stuart *(Foster)*, 116
35 Howick MSS, quoted in Asp/P, iv, 26
36 *Creevey Papers*, 47
37 *Glenbervie Journals*, i, 383
38 RA 46198–9, 46200–1: Asp/P, v, 29, 33
39 RA 40182: Asp/P, v, 26
40 Howick MSS, quoted in Asp/P, v, 28
41 RA 40196: Asp/P, v, 34
42 RA 40211–14: Asp/P, v, 36
43 40215–18: Asp/P, v, 39
44 *Abbot Diary*, v, 517
45 HMCR *Dropmore Papers*, vii, 245
46 RA 39892–4: Asp/P, v, 48
47 RA 46270–1
48 RA 46213–5: Asp/P, v, 52
49 RA 42387: Asp/P, v, 49
50 Twiss, i, 462
51 RA 16748: Asp/P, v, 72
52 Alnwick MSS, quoted in Asp/P, v, 90
53 RA 46262–3: Asp/P, v, 247

54 Alnwick MSS, quoted in Asp/P, v, 91
55 RA 49294: Asp/P, v, 80; RA 49295
56 Alnwick MSS, quoted in Asp/P, v, 113
57 *Ibid.*, v, 114, 117
58 Macalpine and Hunter, 137
59 *Fox Correspondence,* iv, 62; *Granville Leveson Gower Correspondence,* i, 477; Asp/P, v, 10, 125
60 *Morning Post,* 14 March 1804
61 Fremantle MSS (Aylesbury)

17 THE DELICATE INVESTIGATION (pages 201–219)
1 RA 36458–9: Asp/P, iii, 142
2 *Glenbervie Journals,* ii, 88
3 Creston, 85; Weigall *(Charlotte),* 39
4 RA Add. 11/48: Asp/P, iii, 148
5 RA 36501: Asp/P, iii, 487
6 RA 36494: Asp/P, iii, 465
7 *Elliot Letters,* iii, 10, 33, 254; Minto MSS, quoted in Asp/P, iii, 385
8 Weigall *(Charlotte),* 55; Creston, 86
9 RA 49219–20: Asp/P, iii, 449
10 RA 49214–31
11 RA 49219–20, 49207–8, 49409: Asp/P, iii, 449, 370, 373
12 Garth MSS, quoted in Asp/P, iii, 146–8
13 RA Add. 14/24: Asp/P, iv, 70; *Glenbervie Journals,* ii, 133–4
14 RA 36506–7, 36508–9, 36515–16: Asp/P, iv, 39, 42, 71; RA 49258
15 RA 49265; Asp/P, iv, 368
16 RA 16744: Asp/P, v, 55
17 RA 16745: Asp/P, v, 69
18 RA 16746–7: Asp/P, v, 69
19 RA 49283–4, 49288: Asp/P, v, 76, 83
20 *Knight Autobiography,* i, 232
21 RA 49536–7: Asp/P, v, 207
22 RA 49489–91: Asp/P, v, 292
23 RA 33264
24 RA 33220
25 RA 49578–9: Asp/P, v, 426
26 RA 46095–6
27 *Bury Diary,* 19; *Berry Journals,* ii, 479
28 RA 32482
29 *Berry Journals,* ii, 388–9; *Bury Diary,* 22
30 *Glenbervie Journals,* i, 260
31 MS letters of Marchioness Townshend, quoted by Richardson *(Disastrous Marriage),* 66
32 Lockhart, ii, 100–1

33 *Granville Leveson Gower Correspondence*, i, 502
34 Hurd MSS (Hartlebury Castle)
35 Holland *(Memoirs)*, ii, 147
36 *Glenbervie Journals*, i, 255–6
37 *Granville Leveson Gower Correspondence*, ii, 203
38 *Farington Diary*, iii, 292
39 RA Geo. IV, Box 8
40 Holland (Memoirs), ii, 150; *Granville Leveson Gower Correspondence*, ii, 204
41 RA Geo IV, Box 8 (evidence of Lady Douglas; 'Lady Douglas's Memorandum';
   and the 'Duke of Sussex's narrative of two conversations at which he was present').
   c.f. *The Book*, Appendix A, 2–7, Appendix B, 49–91, 92–6
42 *Ibid.*
43 RA Geo. IV, Box 8 (evidence of Sir John Douglas): *The Book*, Appendix A, 8
44 RA Geo. IV, Box 8 (evidence of Robert Bidgood): *The Book*, Appendix A, 9–11, 39,
   B, 103–6
45 RA Geo. IV, Box 8 (evidence of Sarah Bidgood): *The Book*, Appendix B, 106
46 RA Geo. IV, Box 8 (evidence of Frances Lloyd): *The Book*, Appendix A, 13–14
47 RA Geo. IV, Box 8 (evidence of Sarah Lampert)
48 RA Geo. IV, Box 8 (evidence of Robert Bidgood): *The Book*, Appendix B, 104
49 RA Geo IV, Box 8 (Lady Douglas to Prince of Wales)
50 RA Geo. IV, Box 8 (evidence of William Cole): *The Book*, Appendix A, 11–12, B,
   98–103
51 *The Book*, 15
52 *Ibid.*, 21–3
53 RA Geo. IV, Box 8 (evidence of Thomas Stikeman) c.f. *The Book*, Appendix A, 17–19
54 RA Geo. IV, Box 8 (evidence of Hon. Mrs Lisle): *The Book*, Appendix A, 42–6
55 MS Letters of Marchioness Townshend, quoted by Richardson *(Disastrous Marriage)*, 62
56 RA Geo. IV, Box 8 (evidence of Thomas Lawrence): *The Book*, 183
57 *Ibid.;* BM Add. MSS 37847, ff. 156–9: Asp/P, v, 401–5
58 RA Geo. IV, Box 8; Asp/P, v, 401–5
59 *Glenbervie Journals*, ii, 107
60 HMCR Lonsdale MSS, 198–9; Asp/P, 401–5
61 RA Geo. IV, Box 8: *The Book*, Appendix B, 112–33
62 *Farington Diary*, vii, 158
63 Finch MSS, e.6 (Bodleian)
64 RA Geo. IV, Box 8; *Elliot Letters*, iii, 22
65 RA Geo. IV, Box 11 (Westmorland to Sidmouth, 24 June 1820)
66 *Berry Journals*, ii, 389; *Glenbervie Journals*, i, 258, 285, ii, 18–19, 21
67 Asp/K, i, 523
68 *Glenbervie Journals*, ii, 21
69 *Bury Diary*, i, 185
70 RA Geo. IV, Box 11 (James Brougham to Henry Brougham, March 1819)
71 RA Geo. IV, Box 8; RA Geo, IV, Box 11; Oman *(Gascoyne Heiress)*, 93
72 *Stanhope Memoirs*, ii, 227

73 *Ibid.*, ii, 234
74 *Granville Leveson Gower Correspondence*, i, 502
75 *Lyttelton Correspondence*, 18–19
76 *Berry Journals*, ii, 379–80
77 RA 42416–19; Asp/P, v, 408
78 RA Geo. IV, Box 8: *The Book*, 3–10
79 *Granville Leveson Gower Correspondence*, ii, 206
80 Harrowby MSS, vol. iv, f.43, Richard Ryder to Harrowby, 5 July 1806, quoted by Gray, 82
81 Williams, i, 260
82 RA Geo. IV, Box 8 (Cole's evidence about Roberts)
83 *Granville Leveson Gower Correspondence*, ii, 203–4
84 *Croker Papers*, ii, 89

18 FOXITES AND PITTITES (pages 220–229)

1 *Creevey Papers*, 62
2 *Annual Register, 1806*, 21
3 HMCR *Dropmore Papers*, viii, 16
4 Asp/P, v, 298
5 Holland *(Memoirs)*, ii, 162
6 Asp/P, v, 300
7 *Ibid.*, vi, 164
8 Gray, 82; *Rose Diaries*, ii, 298; Holland *(Memoirs)*, ii, 151; Asp/P, vi, 12, 45; *Elliot Letters*, iii, 392
9 RA 40871–4: Asp/P, vi, 97
10 RA 40814–16: Asp/P, vi, 40
11 Asp/P, vi, 110
12 Asp/P, vi, 104–6
13 BM Add. MSS 51520, ff. 49–69, quoted in Asp/P, vi, 110
14 Aspinall *(George III Correspondence)*, ii, 149
15 Asp/P, vi, 127
16 Asp/P, vi, 129
17 RA Geo. IV, Box 8 (Princess Caroline to George III, 8 June 1806, 9 July 1806, 12 August 1806, 2 October 1806, 8 December 1806)
18 Asp/P, vi, 130
19 RA 40918–20: Asp/P, vi, 156
20 *Ibid.*
21 Asp/P, vi, 162
22 Asp/P, vi, 164
23 RA Geo. IV, Box 8 (1 June 1807)
24 BM Add. MSS 38564, ff.91, quoted in Asp/P, vi, 164
25 Asp/P, vi, 171–180
26 *Granville Leveson Gower Correspondence*, ii, 251
27 RA Geo. IV, Box 8 (28 February 1807, 5 May 1807)

28 RA 36551: Asp/P, vi, 189
29 *Farington Diary*, v, 117
30 *Glenbervie Journals*, ii, 75
31 St Germans MSS, quoted in Asp/P, vi, 282
32 *Morning Post*, 21 January 1807
33 *Elliot Letters*, iii, 48
34 *Glenbervie Journals*, ii, 35
35 RA 33128
36 RA 33120-4
37 RA Add. 21/179/122; Eldon MSS, quoted in Asp/P, vi, 391
38 RA 41277: Asp/P, vi, 454
39 RA 41289-90: Asp/P, vi, 467
40 Asp/P, vi, 348-9
41 *Creevey Papers*, 63
42 Asp/P, vi, 350
43 *Ibid.*, vi, 349

19 PRINCESS CHARLOTTE AND MINNY SEYMOUR (pages 230-246)
1 Musgrave *(Brighton)*, 124-5
2 Shane Leslie *(Fitzherbert)*, ii, 129
3 RA 33527
4 Musgrave *(Brighton)*, 140-2
5 RA 33553-91; Musgrave *(Brighton)*, 138
6 Brayley, *Palace at Brighton*, 2
7 Musgrave *(Brighton)*, 128
8 *Granville Leveson Gower Correspondence*, ii, 120; *Berry Journals*, ii, 490
9 *Creevey Papers*, 48
10 *Jerningham Letters*, ii, 287-9
11 RA 31759
12 *Farington Diary*, iv, 2
13 *Creevey Papers*, 50-1; *Farington Diary*, ii, 186
14 *Creevey Papers*, 71-2
15 *Francis Memoirs*, ii, 356-7
16 *Francis Letters*, ii, 516; *Francis Memoirs*, ii, 319
17 The Rev. G. H. Glasse, quoted by Musgrave *(Brighton)*, 130
18 Calvert, 162
19 Wraxall, v, 360
20 RA 29010
21 RA 29011
22 *Frampton Journal*, 14; The Rev. G. H. Glasse, quoted by Musgrave *(Brighton)*, 130
23 *Francis Memoirs*, ii, 319
24 *Creevey Papers*, 51, 57
25 RA 33119; *Farington Diary*, iii, 214; *Walpole Correspondence*, xi, 214; *Gronow Reminiscences*, ii, 18

26 Moore, *Memoirs and Journal*, i, 272
27 *Creevey Papers*, 60, 61
28 *Ibid.*
29 Campbell, vii, 289
30 Seymour of Ragley MSS, CR 713/4
31 *Ibid.*, CR 114A/281A
32 Stuart *(Foster)*, 119
33 Seymour of Ragley MSS, CR 114/A/536/1
34 *Ibid.*
35 *Ibid.*, CR114/A/281A
36 *Ibid.*
37 *Ibid.*, CR 114/A/281/A, CR 713/7, CR 114A/284
38 *Ibid.*, CR 114A/283
39 *Ibid.*
40 Wilkins, ii, 69–70
41 *Ibid.*, 74
42 Seymour of Ragley MSS, CR 713/7
43 Brougham, *Statesman*, ii, 63
44 Romilly, ii, 147
45 HMCR, *Dropmore Papers*, vii, 243
46 Brighton Pavilion MSS
47 RA 50914–16: Asp/P, vii, 138, 234; RA 50911–3
48 RA Queen Victoria's Journal
49 Albemarle, i, 238–40
50 RA Geo. IV Box 8; *Farington Diary*, ii, 97; *Berry Journals*, i, 286
51 Creston, 102
52 *Ibid.*, 88–9, 97, 101–4, 106–7
53 *Farington Diary*, iv, 141–2
54 RA 49587–8: Asp/P, vi, 271; RA Geo. IV, Box 8 (19 April 1808)
55 RA Geo. IV, Box 8 (5 May 1807, 19 June 1808, 22 July 1808)
56 RA 49565–6: Asp/P, v, 385
57 RA 49521–2; Blair Adam MSS, quoted in Asp/P, vi, 237
58 RA 49523–4
59 Eldon MSS, quoted in Asp/P, vi, 388
60 RA 16440–1: Fortescue *(Geo. III Correspondence)*, vi, 460
61 Luttrell, 141
62 RA 49582–3: Asp/P, vi, 203
63 RA 49580
64 RA Add. 11/77: Asp/P, vii, 45
65 RA 36571–2: Asp/P, viii, 29

20 THE ADVENT OF LADY HERTFORD (pages 247-257)
1 *Farington Diary*, iv, 191
2 Holland *(Memoirs)*, ii, 72

3 Calvert, 137
4 *Glenbervie Journals,* ii, 5
5 *Granville Leveson Gower Correspondence,* i, 220
6 *Plumer Ward,* i, 319–20
7 Stuart *(Foster),* 158
8 *Granville Leveson Gower Correspondence,* ii, 294
9 Wraxall, v, 362
10 *Elliot Letters,* ii, 13
11 RA 42214–15, 42292–3, 42314, 42334, 49249–50: Asp/P, iii, 301, iv, 74, iv, 132; iv, 192; iv, 160; RA 42278–9
12 Macalpine and Hunter, 229–40
13 Alnwick MSS, quoted in Asp/P, iv, 490
14 RA 43952–60: Asp/P, ii, 160
15 *Berry Journals,* i, 303
16 *Bland Burges Letters,* 170–1
17 RA 42028–9: Asp/P, ii, 352
18 G. de Beer and R. M. Turton, 'John Turton', *Notes and Records of the Royal Society of London,* xii, 1956, 77–9, quoted by Macalpine and Hunter, 232–3
19 RA 49233: Asp/P, iv, 41
20 Aspinall *(Princess Charlotte's Letters),* 244
21 *Ibid.,* 16; Macalpine and Hunter, 230
22 Howick MSS, quoted in Asp/P, iv, 474
23 Rae *(Sheridan),* ii, 249
24 RA 40498: Asp/P, v, 282
25 Fothergill *(Hamilton),* 399–400
26 BM Add. MSS 51520/3–6; RA 40715–8: Asp/P, v, 439
27 Stuart *(Foster),* 152; Rogers *(Table-Talk),* 240
28 Holland House MSS, quoted in Asp/P, v, 428
29 Howick MSS, quoted in Asp/P, v, 455
30 Fitzwilliam MSS (Sheffield); HMCR, *Dropmore Papers,* viii, 356; HMCR, Fortescue MSS, viii, 339
31 HMCR, *Dropmore Papers,* viii, 426
32 Howick MSS, quoted in Aps/P, vi, 41
33 *Farington Diary,* iv, 54, 98
34 *Jerningham Letters,* i, 300
35 *Farington Diary,* iv, 130–1
36 Egerton, MSS, 3262, f. 28, quoted in Asp/P, vi, 232
37 *Ibid.,* f.32, 34, quoted in Asp/P, vi, 232–3
38 *Ibid.,* f.61, quoted in Asp/P, vi, 217
39 *Farington Diary,* iv, 222
40 *Farington Diary,* v, 28–9, 237
41 Egerton MSS, 3262, f.65, quoted in Asp/P, vi, 220–1
42 Holland *(Memoirs),* ii, 69
43 *Granville Leveson Gower Correspondence,* ii, 297–8
44 *Ibid.,* ii, 297, 349

45 Langdale, 133
46 Wilson *(Memoirs)*, i, 7
47 *Ibid.*
48 Brighton Pavilion MSS
49 *Ibid.*
50 Wilkins, ii, 109–10
51 Shane Leslie *(Fitzherbert)*, ii, 133
52 *Ibid.*, ii, 135

21 THE WINDSOR NUNNERY (pages 258–268)

1 Angelo, i, 191
2 RA Add. 12/18: Asp/P, iii, 456–7
3 RA Add. 12/20: Asp/P, iii, 478–9
4 RA Add. 12/19: Asp/P, iii, 464–5
5 RA Add. 11/20: Asp/P, iii, 51–2
6 *Papendiek Journals*, i, 229
7 RA 43953–60: Asp/P, ii, 160
8 RA 43965–7: Asp/P, ii, 169
9 RA Add. 11/36, Asp/P, iii, 85
10 Minto MSS, quoted in Asp/P, iii, 337
11 RA 51724–5, 51722–3: Asp/P, vi, 325, 492
12 RA Add. 11/56: Asp/P, iii, 242
13 RA Add. 11/154: Asp/P, vi, 315
14 *Glenbervie Journals*, ii, 95
15 Greville *(Memoirs)*, i, 270–1
16 *Ibid.*
17 *Glenbervie Journals*, ii, 98
18 RA Add. 13/51: Asp/P, viii, 252
19 RA Add. 14/19, 14/37, 14/38, 14/39, 14/104, 14/127, 14/202: Asp/P, iii, 482, iv, 548–9 vi, 442, vi, 478, vii, 48; RA Add. 14/36
20 RA Add. 14/104, 14/127, 14/118; Asp/P, vi, 442, vi, 478, vi, 466
21 RA Add. 14/147: Asp/P, vi, 502
22 RA Add. 14/139: Asp/P, vi, 517
23 Childe-Pemberton, 220
24 *Ibid.*, 222
25 RA Add. 14/55: Asp/P, v, 125
26 RA Add, 13/44: Asp/P, vii, 30
27 Taylor *(Relics of Royalty*, 1820) 54–5; Cobbin *(Georgiana*, 1820) 13; *Farington* v, 171
28 RA 14203; RA Add. 14/202: Aspinall *(George III Correspondence)*, v, 208–9; Asp/P, vii, 48
29 RA Add. 14/144: Asp/P, vi, 497
30 Alnwick MSS, quoted in Asp/P, vii, 83–4
31 Childe-Pemberton, 224

References

32 Holland *(Memoirs)*, ii, 248
33 Holland *(Journal)*, ii, 266
34 Childe-Pemberton, 233; Fitzgerald, ii, 17; RA Add. 12/171: Asp/P, vii, 218
35 *Knight Autobiography*, i, 276
36 Wraxall, v, 363

22 APPROACH TO THE REGENCY (pages 269–281)

1 RA 46316–18: Asp/P, vi, 125
2 RA 42430–4: Asp/P, vi, 131
3 RA 47204–5: Asp/P, v, 370
4 RA Add. 14/65: Asp/P, v, 484
5 RA 47286–7: Asp/P, vii, 405
6 RA 47340–1, 47242–3, 47244–5, 47247, 47249, 47251–2, 47272–3, 47278, 47286–7: Asp/K, i, 395, Asp/P, vii, 382, 383, 385, 386, 387, 400, 403, 405
7 Col. Willis, MSS, quoted by Jesse, v, 398
8 *Knight Autobiography*, i, 175
9 *Abbot Diary*, ii, 282
10 *Rose Diaries*, ii, 447–8
11 Macalpine and Hunter, 144
12 Buckingham *(Memoirs)*, ii, 463
13 Willis MSS, quoted by Macalpine and Hunter, 144
14 Macalpine and Hunter, 149–51; RA Geo. IV, Box 7
15 RA 44982–3: Asp/p, viii, 386
16 *Rose Diaries*, ii, 460–1; *Abbot Diary*, ii, 292; RA 41514–9: Asp/P, vii, 87
17 RA 41514–9: Asp/P, vii, 109
18 Alnwick MSS, quoted in Asp/P, vii, 77
19 Asp/P, vii, 61
20 RA 41514–19: Asp/P, vii, 109
21 RA 41529–30: Asp/P, vii, 113
22 RA 41520: Asp/P, vii, 114
23 *Plumer Ward*, i, 336
24 Asp/P, vii, 64
25 Howick MSS, quoted in Asp/P, vii, 189
26 RA, 41572–6, 41596–9, 41609–13: Asp/P, vii, 158, vii, 182, vii, 184; Blair Adam MSS, quoted in Asp/P, vii, 139–46, 160–4
27 Asp/P, vii, 136
28 RA 36562: Asp/P, vii, 190
29 Holland *(Journal)*, ii, 289
30 Howick MSS, quoted, vii, 191
31 Holland *(Journal)*, ii, 290; Asp/P, vii, 190
32 *Glenbervie Journals*, ii, 105–6
33 Holland *(Journal)*, ii, 274–5
34 Holland *(Further Memoirs)*, 74
35 RA 41634–6: Asp/P, vii, 194

36 RA 41637–8
37 RA 41639–40
38 Asp/P, vii, 137
39 RA 41644–5: Asp/P, vii, 200
40 National Library of Wales, MS. 2791, quoted by Michael Roberts, 368
41 *Plumer Ward*, i, 377
42 Sterling, *Coke of Norfolk*, ii, 96–7, quoted by Michael Roberts, 367
43 *Farington Diary*, vi, 106
44 *Statutes at Large*, lxv, 1–14; Huish, ii, 32–4; *The Times,* 6 February 1811; *Morning Post*, 6 February 1811; Holland (*Further Memoirs*), 91; Asp/P, vii, 208; *Glenbervie Journals*, ii, 125; *Annual Register, 1811*, 15

Sources

Manuscript
Royal Archives (Windsor Castle); British Museum – Fox MSS; Holland House MSS;
Hickleton Papers; Add. MSS, 13714, 28063, 29764, 29915, 33132–3, 33629, 34453,
34992, 37414, 37847, 38242, 38564, 38716, 41857, 43727, 47560, 47570, 47579, 51520,
51457; Brighton Pavilion MSS; Hurd MSS (Hartlebury Castle); Mary Robinson MS
Memoirs and Letters (Chequers); Chatsworth MSS; Wentworth Woodhouse Muni-
ments (Sheffield); Finch MSS (Bodleian); Crawford Muniments (Balcarres); Fre-
mantle Collection (Aylesbury); Goderich Papers (Aylesbury); Earl Grey Papers
(Durham); Fitzwilliam Papers, Brooke Records and Lord Dover's papers (Delapre
Abbey); Petworth House Archives (Chichester); Ragley MSS (Warwick); Pretyman
Papers (Ipswich); Markham Papers (York); Capell Manuscripts (Hertford); Harrowby
Papers (Sandon Hall); Wellington Papers (Stratfield Saye); Farquhar Correspondence
and Hook MSS (Bucklebury); Denbigh MSS (Pailton House); Brougham MSS
(University College, London); Lord Chamberlain's Papers (Public Record Office);
Brooks's Club Archives.

Newspapers and Journals
Adam's Weekly Courant, Brighton Gazette, Brighton Herald, Daily Advertiser, The
Diary, European Magazine, Evening Mail, The Gazeteer and New Daily Advertiser,
General Advertiser, General Evening Post, Gentleman's Magazine, Lloyd's Evening Post,
London Advertiser, London Chronicle, London Evening Post, London Gazette, London
Packet, London Recorder or Sunday Gazette, Morning Chronicle and London Advertiser,
Morning Post, Morning Herald, Morning Star, Oracle, Parker's General Advertiser,
Public Advertiser, St James's Chronicle, Sun, Sussex Advertiser, The Times, True Briton,
The World

Historical Manuscript Commission Reports
The Manuscripts of the Earl of Lonsdale (13th Report, Appendix, Part VII); The
Manuscripts and Correspondence of James, 1st Earl of Charlemont (13th Report,
Appendix, Part VIII); The Manuscripts of the Earl of Carlisle (15th Report, Appendix,
Part VI); The Manuscripts of the Duke of Rutland (14th Report, Appendix, Part I);
The Manuscripts of J. B. Fortescue preserved at Dropmore (13th Report, Appendix,
Part III, 14th Report, Appendix, Part V); The Manuscripts of the Marquess of Ailes-
bury (15th Report, Part VII)

Sources

Printed

Abbot Diary: Colchester, Charles, Lord, ed., *The Diary and Correspondence of Charles Abbot, Lord Colchester* (3 vols, 1861)

AIRLIE, Mabel, Countess of, *In Whig Society* (1921)

ALBEMARLE: George Thomas, Earl of Albemarle, *Fifty Years of my Life* (2 vols, 1876)

ANGELO, Henry, [Domenico Angelo Malevolti Tremanondo], *Reminiscences of Henry Angelo with Memoirs of his Late Father and Friends* (2 vols, 1830)

ASPINALL, A., *Politics and the Press, c. 1780–1850* (Home and Van Thal, 1949)

ASPINALL *(George III Correspondence):* Aspinall, A., ed., *The Later Correspondence of George III* (5 vols, Cambridge University Press, 1962–70).

ASPINALL *(Prince's Correspondence):* Aspinall, A., ed., *The Correspondence of George, Prince of Wales, 1770–1812* (8 vols, Cassell, 1963–71).

ASPINALL *(Princess Charlotte's Letters):* Aspinall, A., ed., *Letters of the Princess Charlotte* (Home and Van Thal, 1949)

ASPINALL *(George IV Correspondence):* Aspinall, A., ed., *The Letters of King George IV, 1812–30* (3 vols, Cambridge University Press, 1938)

ASPINALL and SMITH: Aspinall, A., and Smith, E. Anthony, eds., *English Historical Documents, 1783–1832* (Eyre and Spottiswoode, 1959)

Auckland Correspondence: Bath and Wells, Bishop of, ed., *Journal and Correspondence of William, Lord Auckland* (4 vols, 1861–2)

BAKER, Herschel, *John Phillip Kemble* (Harvard University Press, 1942)

Barnard Letters: Powell, Anthony, ed., *Barnard Letters, 1778–1824* (Duckworth, 1928)

BARTLETT, C. J., *Castlereagh* (Scribner's, 1967)

BELL, Robert, *The Life of the Right Honorable George Canning* (1846)

Berry Journals: Lewis, Lady Theresa, ed., *Extracts of the Journals and Correspondence of Miss Berry* (3 vols, 1865)

BINGHAM, Madeleine, *Sheridan: The Track of a Comet* (Allen & Unwin, 1972)

BIRKENHEAD, Sheila, *Peace in Piccadilly: The Story of Albany* (Reynal and Co., 1958)

Bland Burges Letters: Hutton, James, ed., *Selections from the Letters and Correspondence of Sir James Bland Burges* (1885)

Book, or the Proceedings and Correspondence upon the Subject of the Inquiry into the Conduct of the Princess of Wales, The (Edn. printed by Richard Edwards, 1813)

BOULTON, William B., *Thomas Gainsborough: His Life, Work, Friends and Sitters*(1905)

BRAYLEY: Edward Wedlake, *Illustrations of His Majesty's Palace at Brighton: formerly the Pavilion* (1838)

BROUGHAM *(Statesmen):* Brougham, Henry, *Historical Sketches of Statesmen who Flourished in the Time of George III* (3 vols, 1845)

BROUGHAM *(Life):* Brougham, Henry, *The Life and Times of Henry Lord Brougham written by Himself* (3 vols, 1871)

Buckingham Memoirs: Buckingham and Chandos, The Duke of, *Memoirs of the Court and Cabinets of George the Third* (2 vols, 1855)

Sources

Burke Correspondence: Copeland, Thomas W., gen. ed., *The Correspondence of Edmund Burke* (Cambridge University Press, 9 vols, 1958–70)

Bury Diary: Steuart, A. Francis, ed., *The Diary of a Lady in Waiting by Lady Charlotte Bury: Being the Diary Illustrative of the times of George IV* (2 vols, 1908)

CALVERT: *An Irish Beauty of the Regency* (1911)

CAMPBELL: Campbell, Lord, *Lives of the Lord Chancellors and Keepers of the Great Seal of England* (1846)

Candid Enquiry into the Case of the Prince of Wales, A (1786)

CANNON, John, *The Fox–North Coalition* (Cambridge University Press, 1970)

CECIL, Lord David, *The Young Melbourne* (Constable, 1939)

CHENEVIX TRENCH: Chenevix Trench, Charles, *The Royal Malady* (Longmans, 1964)

CHIFFNEY: Chiffney, Samuel, *Genius Genuine* (1804)

CHILDE-PEMBERTON: Childe-Pemberton, W. S., *The Romance of Princess Amelia . . . Including Extracts from Private and Unpublished Papers* (1910)

CHRISTIE, Ian R., *Myth and Reality in Late Eighteenth Century Politics* (University of California Press, 1970)

—— *The End of North's Ministry, 1780–82* (St. Martin's Press, 1958)

CLARK, Mrs Godfrey, ed., *Gleanings from an Old Portfolio* (3 vols, 1896)

CLARKE, Mary Anne, *The Rival Princes* (2 vols, 1810)

COLERIDGE, Ernest Hartley, *The Life of Thomas Coutts, Banker* (2 vols, 1920)

CONNELL, Brian, *Portrait of a Whig Peer* (Deutsch, 1957)

COLVIN, H. M., *A Biographical Dictionary of English Architects, 1660–1840* (John Murray, 1954)

Cornwallis Correspondence: Ross, Charles, ed., *Correspondence of Charles, first Marquess Cornwallis* (3 vols, 1859)

Creevey Papers: Maxwell, Sir Herbert, ed., *The Creevey Papers: A Selection from the Correspondence and Diaries of the Late Thomas Creevey, M.P.* (1905)

CRESTON: Creston, Dormer, *The Regent and his Daughter* (Eyre and Spottiswoode, 1952)

Croker Papers: Jennings, Louis J., ed., *The Croker Papers* (3 vols, 1884)

CROLY: Croly, George, *The Personal History of His Late Majesty King George the Fourth* (2 vols, 1841)

D'Arblay Diary: Barrett, Charlotte, ed., *Diary and Letters of Madame D'Arblay* (4 vols 1876)

D'ARBLAY, Mme, *Memoirs of Dr Burney* (1832)

DERRY, John W., *The Regency Crisis and the Whigs 1788–9* (Cambridge University Press, 1963)

—— *Charles James Fox* (Batsford, 1972)

Devonshire Diary: The Diary of Georgiana, Duchess of Devonshire [printed in Walter Sichel's *Sheridan*, 399–426 (1909)]

Sources

EHRMAN, John, *The Younger Pitt* (E. P. Dutton, 1969)

Elliot Letters: Minto, the Countess of, ed., *Life and Letters of Sir Gilbert Elliot, First Earl of Minto* (3 vols, 1874)

ELWIN, Malcolm, see *Noels and Milbankes*

ERREDGE, John Ackerson, *History of Brightelmston* (1862)

Farington Diary: Grieg, James, ed., *The Farington Diary by Joseph Farington RA* (8 vols, Hutchinson, 1922–28)

FITZGERALD, Percy, *The Life of George the Fourth* (2 vols, 1881)

FOORD, Archibald S., *His Majesty's Opposition, 1714–1830* (Oxford University Press, 1964)

FORTESCUE *(George III Correspondence)*: Fortescue, Sir John, ed., *The Correspondence of King George the Third, 1760–83* (6 vols, 1927–28)

FOTHERGILL, Brian, *Sir William Hamilton* (Harcourt, Brace and World, 1969)

FOSTER, Vere, ed., *The Two Duchesses* (1898)

Fox Correspondence: Russell, Lord John, ed., *Memorials and Correspondence of Charles James Fox* (4 vols, 1853–57)

Frampton Journal: Mundy, Harriot Georgiana, ed., *The Journal of Mary Frampton* (1885)

Francis Letters: Francis, Beata and Eliza Keary, eds., *The Francis Letters by Sir Philip Francis and Other Members of the Family* (n.d.)

Francis Memoirs: Merivale, Herman, ed., *Memoirs of Sir Philip Francis* (2 vols, 1867)

FULFORD, Roger, *Samuel Whitbread, 1764–1815: A Study in Opposition* (Macmillan, 1967)

—— *George the Fourth* (Duckworth, 1935)

—— *Royal Dukes: The Father and Uncles of Queen Victoria* (Duckworth, 1933)

Fulke Greville Diaries: Bladon, F. McKno, ed., *The Diaries of Colonel the Hon. Robert Fulke Greville* (Lane, 1930)

GALT, J., *George III, His Court and Family* (1820)

GARLICK, Kenneth, *Sir Thomas Lawrence* (Routledge and Kegan Paul, 1954)

GEORGE, M. Dorothy, *Catalogue of Personal and Political Satires* (vols v–xi, British Museum 1935–54)

—— *English Political Caricature to 1792* (Oxford University Press, 1960)

—— *English Political Caricature 1793–1832* (Oxford University Press, 1960)

Georgiana: Bessborough, Earl of (ed.), *Georgiana* (John Murray, 1955)

GILLEN, Mollie, *The Prince and His Lady* (Sidgwick and Jackson, 1970)

Glenbervie Journals: Bickley, Francis, ed., *The Diaries of Sylvester Douglas (Lord Glenbervie)* (Constable, 1928)

Granville Leveson Gower Correspondence: Granville, Castalia Countess, ed., *Lord Granville Leveson Gower (First Earl Granville) Private Correspondence 1781–1821* (2 vols, 1916)

GRAY, Denis, *Spencer Percival* (Barnes & Noble, 1963)

GREENWOOD, Alice Drayton, *Lives of the Hanoverian Queens of England* (vol. ii, 1911)

Sources

Greville Memoirs: Strachey, Lytton and Fulford, Roger, eds, *The Greville Memoirs, 1814–1860,* vol. i (Macmillan, 1938)

Gronow Reminiscences: The Reminiscences and Recollections of Captain Gronow (2 vols. 1892)

HAMILTON, Edwin, *A Record of the Life and Death of HRH the Princess Charlotte* (1817)

Hamilton Letters: Anson, Elizabeth and Florence, eds, *Mary Hamilton . . . At Court and at Home . . . 1756–1816* (1925)

Harcourt Papers: Harcourt, Edward William, ed., *The Harcourt Papers* (14 vols, 1880–1905)

HAWES, Frances, *Henry Brougham* (St. Martin's Press, 1957)

Hawkins Memoirs: Hawkins, Laetitia, *Anecdotes, Biographical Sketches and Memoirs* (2 vols, 1822)

HAYTER, John, *The Herculanean and Pompeian Manuscripts.* (n. d.)

—— *A Report upon the Herculanean Manuscripts* (1811)

HAYWARD, A., *Diaries of a Lady of Quality from 1797 to 1844* (1864)

Historical Account of the Public and Domestic Life and Reign of George IV, An (1830)

History of the Life and Reign of George the Fourth, The (3 vols, 1831)

HOBHOUSE, Christopher, *Fox* (John Murray, 1934)

HOLLAND *(Journal):* Ilchester, the Earl of, ed., *Journal of Elizabeth, Lady Holland 1791–1811* (2 vols, 1908)

HOLLAND *(Memoirs):* Holland, Henry Edward, Lord, ed., Holland, Henry Richard, Lord, *Memoirs of the Whig Party During my Time* (2 vols, 1852–4)

HOLLAND *(Further Memoirs):* Stavordale, Lord, ed., Holland, Henry Richard, Lord, *Further Memoirs of the Whig Party, 1807–1821* (1905)

HORN, D. B. and Ransome, Mary, eds, *English Historical Documents, 1714–83* (Oxford University Press, 1957)

HUISH, Robert, *Memoirs of George the Fourth* (2 vols, 1831)

HUNTER, Richard, see Macalpine

ILCHESTER, Countess of (with Lord Stavordale), *The Life and Letters of Lady Sarah Lennox* (2 vols, 1901)

JEFFERYS, Nathaniel, *A Review of the Conduct of His Royal Highness, the Prince of Wales* (1806)

—— *A Letter Addressed to Mrs Fitzherbert in Answer to a Complaint that her Feelings have been Hurt by the mention of her Name in the Review of the Conduct of the Prince of Wales* (1787)

Jerningham Letters: Castle, Egerton, ed., *The Jerningham Letters: Being Excerpts from the Correspondence and Diaries of the Hon Lady Jerningham and of her Daughter Lady Bedingfield* (2 vols, 1896)

JESSE, J. H., *Memoirs of the Life and Reign of King George III* (5 vols, 1901)

315

Sources

KILVERT, Rev Francis, *Memoirs of the life and Writings of the Rt Rev Richard Hurd* (1860)

Knight Autobiography: Kaye, Sir J. W. and Hulton J., eds, *The Autobiography of Miss Cornelia Knight* (2 vols, 1861)

LANDON, H. C. Robbins, ed., *The Collected Correspondence and London Notebooks of Joseph Haydn* (Barrie and Rockliff, 1959)

LANGDALE, Hon Charles, *Memoirs of Mrs Fitzherbert* (1856)

Leeds Memoranda: Browning, Oscar, ed., *The Political Memoranda of Francis Fifth Duke of Leeds* (1884)

LESLIE, Anita, *Mrs Fitzherbert* (Scribner's, 1960)

LESLIE, Shane, *George the Fourth* (Ernest Benn, 1926)

—— *The Life and Letters of Mrs Fitzherbert* (2 vols, Burns and Oates, 1939–40)

Letter to the Prince of Wales, on a Second Application to Parliament to Discharge Debts Wantonly Contracted since May 1787, A (1795)

Letter to the House of Peers on the Present Bill, depending in Parliament, relative to the Prince of Wales debts by A Hannoverian (1795)

Lieven Letters: Quennell, Peter, ed., *The Private Letters of Princess Lieven to Prince Metternick 1820–26* (1948)

LLOYD, H. E., *George IV, Memoirs of his Life and Reign* (1830)

LOCKHART, J. G., *Memoirs of the Life of Sir Walter Scott* (1837–38)

LUTTRELL, Barbara, *The Prim Romantic: A Biography of Cornelia Knight, 1758–1837* (Chatto and Windus, 1965)

Lyttelton Correspondence: Wyndham, Hon. Mrs Hugh, ed., *Correspondence of Sarah Spencer Lady Lyttelton, 1787–1870* (1912)

MACALPINE, Ida, and Richard Hunter, *George III and the Mad Business* (Pantheon, 1970)

MACFARLANE, Charles, *Reminiscences of a Literary Life* (1917)

MACKAY, William, and W. Roberts, *John Hoppner R.A.* (1909)

Malmesbury Diaries: Malmesbury, 3rd Earl of, ed., *The Diaries and Correspondence of James Harris First Earl of Malmesbury* (4 vols, 1844)

Markham Memoir: Markham, Sir Clements, *A Memoir of Archbishop Markham, 1719–1807* (1906)

MARPLES, Morris, *Six Royal Sisters: Daughters of George III* (Michael Joseph, 1969)

MARSHALL, Dorothy, *The Rise of George Canning* (Longmans, 1938)

Memoirs of His Royal Highness the Prince of Wales (1808)

MILES, W. A., *A Letter to His Royal Highness the Prince of Wales with a Sketch of the Prospect before him* (1808)

MILLAR, Oliver, *The Tudor, Stuart and Early Georgian Pictures in the Collection of her Majesty the Queen* (New York Graphic, 1963)

—— *Later Georgian Pictures in the Collection of her Majesty the Queen* (Praeger, 1970)

Sources

MITCHELL, L. B., *Charles James Fox and The Disintegration of the Whig Party, 1782–1794* (Oxford University Press, 1970)

MOLLOY, J. Fitzgerald, ed., *Memoirs of Mrs Robinson* (1894)

MOORE *(Journals)*: Russell, Lord John, ed., *Memoirs, Journal and Correspondence of Thomas Moore* (1853)

MOORE *(Sheridan)*: Moore, Thomas, *Memoirs of the Life of the Right Honourable Richard Brinsley Sheridan* (2 vols. 1825)

MURRAY, Hon. Amelia, *Recollections of the Early Years of the Present Century* (1868)

MURRAY, Robert H., *Edmund Burke* (Oxfdrd University Press, 1931)

MUSGRAVE, Clifford, *Life in Brighton* (Faber, 1970)

—— *The Royal Pavilion: An Episode in the Romantic* (Leonard Hill, 1964)

NAMIER, Sir Lewis, *Crossroads of Power* (Hamish Hamilton, 1962)

NEW, Chester W., *The Life of Henry Brougham to 1830* (Clarendon Press, 1961)

NICHOLLS, John, *Observations on the Situation of His Royal Highness the Prince of Wales* (1795)

NIGHTINGALE, J. *Memoir of the Public and Private Life of . . . Caroline, Queen of Great Britain* (1820)

Noels and Milbankes: Elwin, Malcolm, ed., *The Noels and Milbankes*, (Macdonald 1967)

Northumberland Diaries: Greig, James, ed., *The Diaries of a Duchess: Extracts from the Diaries of the First Duchess of Northumberland, 1716–1776* (1926)

OLIVER, J. W., *The Life of William Beckford* (Oxford University Presss, 1932)

OMAN, Carola, *The Gascoyne Heiress: The Life and Diaries of Frances Mary Gascoyne Cecil* (Hodder and Stoughton, 1968)

Paget Papers: Paget, Sir Augustus B., ed., *The Pagei Papers: Diplomatic and other Correspondence of the Rt Hon Sir Arthur Paget* (2 vols, 1896)

Papendiek Journals: Delves Broughton, Mrs Vernon, ed., *Court and Private Life in the Time of Queen Charlotte; Being the Journals of Mrs Papendiek* (2 vols, 1887)

Parliamentary History of England, The

PARRY, Edward, *Queen Caroline* (Benn, 1930)

PELLEW, George, *The Life and Correspondence of the Right Honourable Henry Addington, First Viscount Sidmouth* (3 vols, 1847)

PETRIE, Sir Charles, *The Four Georges: A Revaluation* (1935)

PITT LENNOX, Lord William, *My Recollections from 1806 to 1873* (2 vols, 1874)

PLUMB, J. H., *The First Four Georges* (Batsford, 1956)

Plumer Ward: Phipps, Hon. Edmund, *Memoirs of the Political and Literary Life of Robert Plumer Ward* (1850)

Porphyria – A Royal Malady: Articles published in or commissioned by the British Medical Journal (British Medical Association, 1968)

PYNE, W. H., *The History of the Royal Residences* (1819)

317

Sources

RAE, William Fraser, *Wilkes, Sheridan, Fox: the Opposition under George the Third* (1927)

RAIKES, Thomas, *A Portion of the Journal Kept by Thomas Raikes Esq. from 1831 to 1847* (4 vols, 1856–7)

REID, Loren, *Charles James Fox: A Man for the People* (University of Missouri Press, 1969)

RICHARDSON, Joanna, *George IV: A Portrait* (Sidgwick and Jackson, 1966)

—— *The Disastrous Marriage: A Study of George IV and Caroline of Brunswick* (Jonathan Cape, 1960)

ROBERTS, Henry D., *A History of the Royal Pavilion, Brighton* (Country Life, 1939)

ROBERTS, Michael, *The Whig Party, 1807–1812* (Frank Cass, 1965)

ROBERTS, W., *Sir William Beechey, R.A.* (1901)

ROGERS *(Table-Talk)*: Bishop, Morchard, ed., *Recollections of the Table-Talk of Samuel Rogers* (Richards Press, 1952)

ROLO, P. J. V., *George Canning: Three Biographical Studies* (Macmillan, 1965)

Romilly Memoirs: Memoirs of Sir Samuel Romilly (3 vols, 1840)

ROSE, John Holland, *Life of William Pitt* (2 vols, Bell, 1924)

Rose Diaries: Harcourt, The Rev. Leveson Vernon, ed., *The Diaries and Correspondence of the Rt Hon George Rose* (2 vols, 1860)

RUSSELL, Lord John, *The Life and Times of Charles James Fox* (3 vols, 1859–66)

Shelley Diary: Edgcumbe Richard, ed., *The Diary of Frances, Lady Shelley* (2 vols., 1912–13)

SHERIDAN *(Letters)*: Price, Cecil, ed., *The Letters of Richard Brinsley Sheridan* (Clarendon Press, 1966)

SHERIDAN *(Journal)*: Le Fanu, William, ed., *Betsy Sheridan's Journal: Letters from Sheridan's Sister* (Eyre and Spottiswoode, 1960)

SICHEL, Walter, *Sheridan* (2 vols, 1909)

Slight Reminiscences of a Septuagenarian from 1802 to 1815 by Emma Sophia, Countess Brownlow (1867)

STANHOPE, Earl, *Life of the Right Honourable William Pitt* (4 vols, 1867)

Stanhope Memoirs: Memoirs of the Lady Hester Stanhope as related by herself in conversation with her physician (3 vols, 1845)

STAPLETON, A. G., *Political Life of George Canning* (2 vols, 1831)

STEEGMAN, John, *The Rule of Taste from George I to George IV* (Macmillan, 1968)

STOCKDALE, J., *The History and Proceedings of the Lords and Commons . . . with Regard to the Regency* (1789)

STOKES, Hugh, *The Devonshire House Circle* (1917)

STROUD, Dorothy, *Henry Holland* (A. S. Barnes, 1966)

STUART *(Daughters of George III)*: Stuart, Dorothy Margaret, *The Daughters of George III* (Macmillan, 1939)

STUART *(Foster)*: Stuart, Dorothy Margaret, *Dearest Bess: The Life and Times of Lady Elizabeth Foster, afterwards Duchess of Devonshire from her Unpublished Journals and Correspondence* (Methuen, 1955)

Sources

Tooke, Horne, *A Letter to a Friend on the Reported Marriage of His Royal Highness, the Prince of Wales* (1787)

Tour to York, A Circumstantial Account of His Royal Highness the Prince of Wales's visit to that City (1789)

Twiss, Horace, *The Public and Private Life of Lord Chancellor Eldon* (3 vols, 1844)

Two Words of Counsel, and one of Comfort. Addressed to His Royal Highness the Prince of Wales by an old Englishman (1795)

Vindication of the Conduct of Lady Douglas during her Intercourse with the Princess of Wales . . . etc. (1814)

Vulliamy, C. E. *Aspasia: The Life and Letters of Mary Granville, Mrs Delany, 1700–1788* (Bles, 1937)

Walpole Correspondence: Lewis, W. S., ed., *The Yale Edition of Horace Walpole's Correspondence* (Oxford University Press, 34 vols, 1937–65)

Walpole *(George III)*: Barker, G. F. Russell, ed., Walpole, Horace, *Memoirs of the Reign of King George the Third,* (4 vols, 1894)

Walpole *(Last Journals)*: Steuart, A. Francis, ed., *The Last Journals of Horace Walpole During the Reign of George III* (2 vols, 1910)

Watson, J. Steven, *The Reign of George III, 1760–1815* (Oxford University Press, 1959)

Weigall, Lady Rose, *A Brief Memoir of Princess Charlotte of Wales* (1874)

White, R. J., *The Age of George III* (Walker and Co., 1969)

Wilkins, W. H., *Mrs Fitzherbert and George IV* (2 vols, 1905)

Wilks, John, *Memoirs of Her Majesty, Queen Caroline* (1822)

Williamson, G. C., *Richard Cosway, R.A., and his Wife and Pupils* (1897)

Willis, G. M., *Ernest Augustus, Duke of Cumberland and King of Hanover* (McClelland, 1954)

Wilson, Harriette, *Memoirs of Harriette Wilson written by Herself* (4 vols, 1825)

Windham Papers: Windham, Rt Hon. William, *The Windham Papers* (2 vols, 1913)

Wraxall: Wheatley, Henry B., ed., *The Historical and Posthumous Memoirs of Sir Nathaniel William Wraxall, 1772–1784* (5 vols., 1884)

Ziegler, Philip, *Addington: A Life of Henry Addington, First Viscount Sidmouth* (John Day, 1966)

—— *King William IV* (Harper & Row, 1973)

Index

Index

148, 157–8; Lady Hester Stanhope on, 218; Lady Maria Stuart on, 147; Queen Victoria on, 160; Walpole on, 145

Carpenter, Lady Almeira (d. 1809), 114n.

Castlereagh, Robert Stewart, Viscount (1769–1822), Princess Caroline and, 221; Secretary for War, 224

Catholic emancipation, Catholic Relief Bill, 185, 188: attitude of George III to, 224; the Prince abandons support of, 227

Chambers, Sir William (1726–96), 34

Chapman, Mrs, royal nurse, 3

Charlemont, James Caulfield, 4th Viscount and 1st Earl of (1728–99), 38n.; on the Prince, 39; and the Prince's portrait, 41n.

Charlotte Augusta, Princess (1796–1817), birth of, 149; and re-election of Fox, 157; mentioned in the Prince's will, 168, 169; George III and, 189, 200, 201, 204; appearance, 201; Queen Charlotte on, 201, 202; Minto on, 202; a mimic, 202; her excitable temperament, 202–3, 204; proposals for her upbringing and education, 203, 204–5; writes to the Prince, 205, 245–6; and Edwardina Kent, 216; the Prince and, 225, 241, 242–6; her character, 242; anecdotes about, 242, 243; rules about visits to her mother, 243; her will, 244, 245; on her father's illness, 250; in the garden of Carlton House, 281

Charlotte Augusta Matilda, Princess Royal, later Queen of Württemberg (1766–1828), 258; birth, 4; and her father, 78; and the Prince, 101, 260–1; on Princess Charlotte, 242; her marriage, 261

Charlotte (Sophia), Queen (1744–1818), and the Prince, 1, 2, 3, 7, 23, 27–8, 41, 44, 70, 87–8, 98, 99, 101, 105, 112, 153, 164–5, 168, 190, 200, 228, 249, 277; her children, 4; and her husband's illness, 77, 78, 79, 97, 98, 187, 189, 193, 195, 196, 198; on her husband in his illness, 79, 85, 88; and Dr Warren, 80; manages Household at Kew, 88; and York, 88, 100; and bulletins on health of George III, 89; Elliot on, 98; at the Windsor concert, 99; Hawkesbury on, 105; the Prince writes to, 121, 148, 149, 157, 159; and Lady Jersey, 130, 142; on Princess Caroline, 134, 144, 145, 148, 151, 158; Princess Caroline on, 137;

on the Crown, 165; on Rev. Thomas Willis, 187; and the Regency question (1804), 190; bad-tempered, 193, 195; and her husband, 199; on Princess Charlotte, 201, 202, 246; and Fox, 220; and her daughters, 258–9; and a marriage between Princess Elizabeth and Duke of Orleans, 262; Princess Amelia and, 266; and the Regency Bill, 274; and Perceval, 277

Chesterfield, Philip Stanhope, 5th Earl of (1755–1815), 24

Chiffney, Samuel (1753?–1807), 109–10

Cholmondeley, 4th Earl and 1st Marquess of (1749–1827), and Mrs Elliott, 23; Princess Caroline and, 159–60; his salary, 174

Clarence, William, Duke of, later King William IV; (1765–1837), 73n., 120, 194; birth, 4; in financial difficulties, 59; and the Regency crisis, 100; and the Prince, 111, 146, 168, 177, 186, 233, 252, 274; early history, 117–18; on George III, 118; and Dorothea Jordan, 118–19, 135; his speeches in the House, 119; borrows money, 126; and Princess Caroline's wedding, 146; on his brother and his father, 161–2; the Prince's gift to, 177; and George III, 177; on the Prince and York, 182; Norfolk and, 233; and Princess Sophia, 263; and Cumberland, 269

Clarke, Mrs Mary Anne (1776–1852), 228, 269

Clermont, Countess of (c. 1734–1820), 57

Clermont, Earl of (1722–1806), 73, 143; the Prince wounds, 42; entertains the Prince, 57; greets Princess Caroline, 143

Clifford, Sophia, Lady de (c. 1743–1828), Princess Charlotte's governess, 204; and Princess Charlotte, 242; the Prince's instructions to, 243, 246

Cockerell, Sir Charles, 231

Cockerell, Samuel Pepys (1754–1827), 231

Cole, William, 211–12

Collins, Richard (1755–1831), 42

Cornwallis, Charles Cornwallis, 1st Marquis and 2nd Earl (1738–1805), on recovery of George III, 102

Cosway, Richard (c. 1742–1821), 42n.; and the Prince, 39; Prince commissions, 42

Cotes, Francis (1725?–70), 3

Coultworth, Mrs Henrietta, 3

George Augustus Frederick—*cont.*

career, 120–1, 164–7, 181–2, 197, 228, 249, 250; attitude to his military duties, 121–2; and Duchess of York, 125, 165; and Lady Jersey, 130–1, 147, 148, 149, 150, 158, 159, 170, 173 *and* n.; and Sussex, 132, 179; solution to his financial problems, 135; and Princess Caroline, 135, 143–4, 145, 147, 148, 149–50, 159, 160, 161, 162, 196, 202, 203, 205, 207, 208, 225, 226, 243; and Malmesbury, 144; at his wedding to Princess Caroline, 146–7; and the royal family, 156; makes a will, 168–9; and Clarence; 177; and Cumberland, 181, 188n., 269–70, 277–8, 278n.; and Lord Lieutenancy of Ireland, 184; and the Whigs, 184–5; and the Regency question (1804), 185–6, 204; plans for a new government, 186–7, 193; complains to Lord Chancellor, 195, 196; and Princess Charlotte, 202, 203, 204, 225, 241, 242–6; and the 'Delicate Investigation', 208, 218, 222; and the Whig party, 220, 221; and royal patronage, 221; and Grenville, 224; sensitive to public opinion, 226, 227–8; and Princess Caroline's debts, 227; his enthusiasm for *Chinoiserie*, 232; his good humour, 233–4; and his friends, 235–7; and Lady Horatia Seymour, 238–9, 240; and Minny Seymour, 239–42, 246; fond of children, 242; and Lady Hertford, 246, 247–8, 252–3, 255–7; and Nelson, 250–1, 251n.; distress over death of friends, 250–1, 254; as a guest, 253 and n., and Lady Bessborough, 255; his illegitimate children, 256n.; and his sisters, 260, 261, 262, 263, 265–6, 267–8, 274; and the Regency Bill, 273, 274–5; and formation of a new government, 275, 276; his nervousness, 276, 278–9; suspects Perceval, 277; sworn in as Regent, 280

letters:

to Princess Caroline, 151–2, 153, 158, 160; to Queen Caroline, 121, 148, 149, 157, 197; to the Lord Chancellor, 100; to Cholmondeley, 159–60; to Lady de Clifford, 243; to Bishop Fisher, 244; to Mrs Fitzherbert, 50, 171, 256; to Fox, 52; to George III, 29, 58, 181, 243; to Mary

Hamilton, 14–15; to Lady Hertford, 254; to Perceval, 279; to Miss Pigot, 256, to Sheridan, 96; to Dr Turton, 249; to York, 21, 22, 26, 27, 44, 112, 113–14, 126, 183

opinions of:

Charlotte Albert on, 9; Bedford on, 274; Mary Berry on, 249; Lady Bessborough on, 190, 248, 254–5; Bloomfield on, 253; Brummell on, 39; Burges on, 249; Burke on, 40, 104–5; Carlton House servant on, 278n.; Princess Caroline on, 144, 217–18; Charlemont on, 39; Clarence on, 161–2; Creevey on, 194–5, 220, 232; Croker on, 39; Cumberland on, 250; Duchess of Devonshire on, 25n.; Elliot on, 84; Mrs Fitzherbert on, 173, 174; Fitzwilliam on, 251–2; Fox on, 110; Freemantle on, 229, 254; Fullerton on, 84; George III on, 11, 31–2; Glenbervie on, 184n.; Grenville on, 221; Grey on, 194; Mrs Harcourt on, 186; Hare on, 112; Miss Hayman on, 201; Holdernesse on, 10; Lady Holland on, 268; Holland on, 254, 267, 274; Hurd on, 10; Edward Jerningham on, 252; Lady Jerningham on, 232–3; Keppel on, 242; Lady Susan Leveson-Gore on, 105; Lonsdale on, 253n.; McMahon on, 274; Malmesbury on, 141, 186, 187, 190; Melbourne on, 147; Moira on, 227; Nelson on, 251; Frederica Planta on, 9; Portland on, 111; the Prince on himself, 10; Mary Robinson on, 16, 18–19; St Leger on, 90–1; Lady Horatia Seymour on, 239; Betsy Sheridan on, 25n.; Sheridan on, 84, 92, 250; Lady Maria Stuart on, 147; Lord Thomond on, 233; Queen Victoria on, 160; Wellington on, 39; Weston on, 252; Wraxall on, 38, 235

the Press reports:

The Jockey Club, 108; *Morning Post*, 73; *St James's Chronicle*, 112; *The Times*, 105, 112; Whig pamphlets, 93

the Prince quoted:

on his own appearance, 10; on his own character, 10; on his father, 23, 24, 44, 190; on his mother, 99; on Clarence's speech on the slave trade, 119; on his health, 249–50; on Princess Caroline, 157,

Index

Rowlandson, Thomas (1756–1827), 84

Roxburghe, John Ker, 3rd Duke of (1740–1804), 146

Royal Marriage Act, George III instigates, 12; and the Prince and Mrs Fitzherbert, 48, 52, 53; and Prince Augustus, 120

Royal, Princess, see Charlotte Augusta Matilda, Princess Royal

Russell, Dr Richard (d. 1771), 60–1

Rutland, Charles Manners, 4th Duke of (1754–87), 25, 55

Rutland, Mary Isobella, Duchess of (1756–1831), 73, 171; and York, 123; George III and, 198

Ryder, Richard (1766–1832), 219

St Helens, Alleyne Fitzherbert, Baron (1753–1839), 134

St James's Chronicle, on Fox's speech, 95; on the Prince's clothes, 112

St James's Palace, birth of the Prince at, 1; baby prince on display at, 2; the Prince unwelcome at, 105; wedding of the Prince and Princess Caroline at, 146; Drawing-Rooms held at, 196; violent death of Sellis at, 270; Cumberland's rooms open to the public, 278n.

St Laurent, Mlle de, and Prince Edward, 116–17, 135

St Leger, Colonel Anthony (c. 1759–1821), George III disapproves of, 24; the Prince and, 29; his portrait, 41; on the Prince and Fox and Pitt, 90–1; and Duchess of Rutland, 123

St Leger, Colonel John (1756–99), on York and Princess Frederica of Prussia, 123

Salisbury, Maria Amelia, Countess of (1750–1835), 25, 57

Sandwich, John Montagu, 4th Earl of (1718–1792), 92

Santague, 168

Sayers, James (1748–1823), his caricature of Fox, 36; Gillray and, 57

Schwellenberg, Mrs E. J. (d. 1797), 3

Scott, Sir Walter (1771–1832), 207

Scott, Sir William, later Lord Stowell (1745–1836), 219, 225

Secker, Thomas, see Canterbury, Archbishop of

Sefton, Isabella, Countess of (1748–1819),

and Mrs Fitzherbert, 57, 70; Sheridan and, 235

Sellis, Joseph, 270–1, 271n.

Sellis, Mrs, on her husband, 271

Selwyn, George (1719–91), and Mrs Elliott, 23; his opinion of Buke, 96; and Maria Fagniani, 247

Seymour, George, 256

Seymour, Georgiana Augusta Frederica, 23

Seymour, Lord Henry (1746–1830), 237

Seymour, Lady Horatia (1762–1801), and Mrs Fitzherbert, 237, 238; and the Price, 238–9, 240

Seymour, Lord Hugh (1759–1801), 131; and Lady Jersey, 156; and the Prince, 237, 239

Seymour, Mary Georgiana Emma, later Mrs George Dawson-Damer, (Minny: 1798–1848) 64n.; her parents, 237; and Mrs Fitzherbert, 237, 256; the Prince's financial provision for, 239; the case for custody of, 239–41; and the Prince, 241–2; subsequent history, 142n.

Sheffield, John Baker Holroyd (1735–1821), on the Prince's conduct, 84; on Dr Francis Willis, 86

Shelburne, William Petty, Marquess of Lansdowne, Earl of (1737–1805), 186

Shelley, Lady, on Prince William of Gloucester, 254n.

Sheridan, Betsy, 83

Sheridan, Richard Brinsley (1751–1816), 91, 194; and the Prince, 39, 63, 66, 90, 92, 99, 184, 186, 193, 197, 276, 280; Gillray caricatures, 57; upholds the Prince's cause in the House, 65–6; and Mrs Fitzherbert, 66, 92; defends the Prince and Mrs Fitzherbert in the House, 69; on the Prince's conduct, 84; and the Regency crisis, 91–2, 93, 94–5; on the Prince, 130; and the Prince's financial affairs, 164; at the Pavilion, 235–6; the Prince on, 236; Grey on, 276

Short, Rev. William (c. 1760–1826), 245

Siddons, Sarah (1755–1831), 200

Sidmouth, Viscount, see Addington, Henry

Simmons, Dr Samuel Foart (1750–1813), and George III, 192, 195, 198, 272; Mrs Harcourt on, 192

Sloane, Sir Hans (1660–1753), 33

Index

Smelt, Leonard (*c.* 1719–1800), 5
Smirke, Sir Robert (1781–1867), on Carlton House, 35
Smith, Letitia, *later* Lady Lade, *q.v.*, 22
Smith, William (*c.*1730–1819), 16
Smith, Rear-Admiral Sir William Sidney (1764–1840), and the Douglases, 207–8; and the 'Delicate Investigation', 209–10, 211, 212, 213; and Edwardina Kent, 216
Smythe, Sir John, 47
Smythe, John, 54, 63n.
Smythe, Mary Anne, 63n.
Smythe, Walter, 47
Smythe, Walter (1757–1822), 55
Sophia, Princess (1777–1848), 4n., 261; her brothers' favourite, 263; her illegitimate child, 263; and General Garth, 263, 264; and Kent, 264; and the Prince, 264, 265; Princess Amelia and, 267
Sophia Matilda, Princess (1773–1844), 114n.
Southampton, Charles Fitzroy, 1st Baron (1737–97), 45, 46; and the Prince's attempted suicide, 48; Mrs Fitzherbert and, 49; Pitt and, 66
Spencer, Major-General Sir Brent (*c.* 1760–1828), 262
Spencer, Lady Charlotte (1769–1802), 146
Spencer, George John Spencer, 2nd Earl (1758–1834), 177; the Prince and, 186; and the 'Delicate Investigation', 208; in 'Ministry of all the Talents', 220
Spencer, Lady Sarah, 218
Stafford, Marchioness of, on the Prince, 248; the Prince's hostess, 250, 251
Stafford-Jerningham, Hon. Edward, 63n
Stanhope, Lady Hester Lucy (1776–1839), on Princess Caroline, 145, 218
Stikeman, Thomas, and the 'Delicate Investigation', 212–13; and William Austin, 214
Stormont, Lord, *later* 2nd Earl of Mansfield (1727–96), 91
Stourton, Lord, 49, 63n.
Stubbs, George (1724–1806), 42n.; his portrait of the Prince, 42
Sussex, Augustus Frederick, Duke of (1773–1843), 4n.; homesick, 119–20; his marriage, 120, 131, 135, 179–80; and the Prince, 179, 274; and his father, 199
Sydney, Thomas Townshend, 1st Viscount

(1733–1800), on acrimony over Regency crisis, 96

Tarleton, Colonel Banastre, *later cr.* Baronet (1754–1833), 20n.
Taylor, Major Herbert, *later* Colonel Sir Herbert Taylor (1775–1839), 264 and n.
Taylor, Thomas, 124–5
Temple, Richard Plantagenet Temple Nugent Brydges Chandos Grenville, Earl (1797–1861), 276
Temple, Richard Temple Nugent Brydges Grenville, Earl, *later* 1st Duke of Buckingham and Chandos (1776–1839) advises the Prince, 228; hopes for office for his son, 276
Thackeray, William Makepeace (1811–63), 247
Thanet, Sackville Tufton, 9th Earl of (1767–1825), 280
Thomond, William O'Brien, 2nd Marquess of (1765–1846), on the Prince, 233
Thrale, Henry (*c.* 1728–81), 61
Thrale, Mrs Hester Lynch, *later* Mrs Piozzi (1741–1821), 61
Thurlow, Edward, 1st Baron (1731–1806), and Dr Francis Willis, 86; Pitt and, 91; and the Whigs, 91, 95; on George III's recovery and the Regency Bill, 97–8; and the Prince's debts, 127; and the Prince, 160, 193, 236; on the Prince, 163, 193; and the 'Delicate Investigation', 208, 218–19; his dress, 236; Creevey on, 236–7; on Sir John Lade, 237; and the Minny Seymour case, 239
Tierney, George (1761–1830), advises Prince, 228; a new Whig government, 276
Times, The, 122; and health of George III, 85; and the Regency crisis, 91; and George III, 103; on the Prince, 105, 112; influences public opinion of the Prince, 111; and Princess Caroline, 155; on Mrs Fitzherbert's 'public breakfast', 172n.; and the Prince, 182
Tooke, John Horne (1736–1812), 'Reported Marriage to the Prince of Wales', 64
Tories, and Catholic Relief Bill, 185; possible coalition with Whigs, 191, 193; Malmesbury on Addington's ministry, 192; resignation of Addington, 193; and the

336

Index

74 75 76 77 10 9 8 7 6 5 4 3 2 1